MW00834690

Resisting Backsliding

In the past two decades, democratically elected executives across the world have used their popularity to push for legislation that, over time, destroys systems of checks and balances, hinders free and fair elections, and undermines political rights and civil liberties. Using and abusing institutions and institutional reform, some executives have transformed their countries' democracies into competitive authoritarian regimes. Others, however, have failed to erode democracy. What explains these different outcomes? *Resisting Backsliding* answers this question. With a focus on the cases of Hugo Chávez in Venezuela and Alvaro Uribe in Colombia, the book shows that the strategies and goals of the opposition are key to understanding why some executives successfully erode democracy and others do not. By highlighting the role of the opposition, this book emphasizes the importance of agency for understanding democratic backsliding and shows that even weak oppositions can defeat strong potential autocrats.

LAURA GAMBOA is an assistant professor at the University of Utah. Her research focuses on regime change, institutions, and voting behavior in Latin America.

Resisting Backsliding

Opposition Strategies against the Erosion of Democracy

LAURA GAMBOA
University of Utah

CAMBRIDGE
UNIVERSITY PRESS

CAMBRIDGE
UNIVERSITY PRESS

Shaftesbury Road, Cambridge CB2 8EA, United Kingdom

One Liberty Plaza, 20th Floor, New York, NY 10006, USA

477 Williamstown Road, Port Melbourne, VIC 3207, Australia

314–321, 3rd Floor, Plot 3, Splendor Forum, Jasola District Centre, New Delhi – 110025, India

103 Penang Road, #05–06/07, Visioncrest Commercial, Singapore 238467

Cambridge University Press is part of Cambridge University Press & Assessment, a department of the University of Cambridge.

We share the University's mission to contribute to society through the pursuit of education, learning and research at the highest international levels of excellence.

www.cambridge.org
Information on this title: www.cambridge.org/9781009164061

DOI: 10.1017/9781009164085

© Laura Gamboa 2022

This publication is in copyright. Subject to statutory exception and to the provisions of relevant collective licensing agreements, no reproduction of any part may take place without the written permission of Cambridge University Press & Assessment.

First published 2022

A catalogue record for this publication is available from the British Library.

Library of Congress Cataloging-in-Publication Data
NAMES: Gamboa, Laura, 1983– author.
TITLE: Resisting backsliding : opposition strategies against the erosion of democracy / Laura Gamboa.
DESCRIPTION: Cambridge ; New York, NY : Cambridge University Press, 2022. | Includes bibliographical references.
IDENTIFIERS: LCCN 2022025807 (print) | LCCN 2022025808 (ebook) | ISBN 9781009164061 (hardback) | ISBN 9781009164078 (paperback) | ISBN 9781009164085 (epub)
SUBJECTS: LCSH: Democracy–Case studies. | Democracy–Venezuela. | Democracy–Colombia. | Venezuela–Politics and government. | Colombia–Politics and government. | BISAC: POLITICAL SCIENCE / General
CLASSIFICATION: LCC JC423 .G187 2022 (print) | LCC JC423 (ebook) | DDC 321.8–dc23/eng/20220729
LC record available at https://lccn.loc.gov/2022025807
LC ebook record available at https://lccn.loc.gov/2022025808

ISBN 978-1-009-16406-1 Hardback
ISBN 978-1-009-16407-8 Paperback

Cambridge University Press & Assessment has no responsibility for the persistence or accuracy of URLs for external or third-party internet websites referred to in this publication and does not guarantee that any content on such websites is, or will remain, accurate or appropriate.

To my parents and Dan, for their unabating unconditional support

Contents

Figures

Tables

Acknowledgments

This book started brewing on February 26, 2010, the day the Constitutional Court struck down Alvaro Uribe's second reelection referendum. Born and raised in a country ravaged by violence, where institutions and political elites are often dismissed as weak and corrupt and we are taught that we are "a nation despite of ourselves," it was rare for me to feel as proud of Colombia as I felt that day. Unlike our neighbors, we had been able to stop a populist authoritarian leader from entrenching in power. As years went by, and I observed Venezuela become more authoritarian, I wondered, why wasn't this wealthier, less violent, more stable and overall, more democratic country able to do the same?

Finding an answer to that question was a multiyear, collective endeavor. This book would have not been possible without the help and support of colleagues, friends, and family, to whom I am forever indebted.

At Notre Dame, I found creative, generous, kind mentors who were invaluable to this project. My dissertation advisor, Scott Mainwaring, is an outstanding scholar and an amazing human being. Always available, he generously read multiple drafts of this manuscript at every stage of the process, providing not only thoughtful and insightful feedback but also much-needed encouragement throughout the long and winding path of getting a PhD and publishing a book. His support and everlasting enthusiasm for my project were crucial to bring it to fruition. I hope I'll be able to be that kind of mentor to my students one day.

I am also indebted to David Nickerson. David was and still is a stolid source of support. Not only did he spend countless hours helping me think through the argument, methods, and evidence of this book, but he has gone above and beyond opening every door at his disposal to help me build my career. His enthusiasm and unwavering belief in the quality of my work have been essential to get me here.

I am very grateful to Michael Coppedge as well. Michael is an endless source of ideas and enthusiasm for knowledge. His heartfelt concern about issues like democracy and his ability to think out of the box to analyze them will never cease to amaze me. Michael's very honest, kind, and thoughtful feedback impelled me to build strong arguments and look for creative evidence to support my claims. I was very lucky to have him in my committee.

This book would have not seen the light of day had not I had fantastic friends all throughout grad school. Ezequiel González-Ocantos was always available to bounce ideas, read drafts, and provide strategic advice. His generosity and enthusiastic endorsement were crucial to push this project through the finish line. I do not have enough words to express my gratitude. Sandra Botero has been an outstanding friend and advocate. Generous and sharp, her advice and support have been key to navigate most stages of my academic career, including the book-writing process. I have been very lucky to have a woman like her in my camp. I am also indebted to Juan Albarracín, Rodrigo Castro-Cornejo, Chonghyun Choi, Omar Coronel, Víctor Hernández-Huertas, Tahir Kilavuz, Riitta Koivumaeki, Ana Petrova, Ji Hye Shin, and Lucía Tiscornia, who brainstormed, listened to, and read different parts of this project, providing crucial feedback. All of them, alongside Madeline Ahmed Cronin, Manuela Fernández, Xavi Lanao, Esteban Manteca, Cameron O'Bannon, Javier Osorio, Nara Pavão, Santiago Quintero, and Greg Schufeldt, lent their support at various points in time and more generally made grad school an unforgettable experience.

The information and insights I gathered while doing fieldwork in Colombia and Venezuela are the heart of this manuscript. I am forever indebted to the dozens of politicians, justices, clerks, activists, journalists, and academics who agreed to talk to me, particularly in Venezuela, where *guarimbas*, transportation stoppages, water and energy shortages, as well as state repression made this all the more difficult.

In Colombia, I am especially thankful to Congreso Visible, which provided me with key congressional data, Alejandra Tarazona, who helped me understand the world of judicial review and opened up the doors of the Constitutional Court for me, and the Universidad de los Andes, which provided me with an academic house the semester I was there. In Venezuela, I am indebted to Alexandra Panzarelli, Edwin Luzardo, and María Virginia Murguey who worked tirelessly to help me find interviews. Alexandra, in particular, was a great ally and a good friend while I was living there. I would also like to thank the people who – at the time – worked at *El Nacional's* archive and the *Departamento de Información Legislativa* for their help and guidance, as well as Mariana Ríos, for assisting my research.

I arrived to Caracas on February 2014, in the middle of what would become three months of nonstop protests. The friends that I made during the six months that I lived there were essential to navigate what could kindly be described as a "heated political environment." Valentina Macía Socías,

Illiana Muñoz, Isabella Picón, Félix Ríos, Mercedes Rojas, Mauricio Salazar, and Yana Stainova were amazing travel companions and good friends. I would have missed a lot about Venezuela without them.

I am also grateful for the generous feedback I received in workshops and conferences. Candelaria Garay, Frances Hagopian, Steven Levistky, and Scott Mainwaring read the whole manuscript and provided detailed comments during a book workshop held at the Harvard Kennedy School. Their comments, suggestions, and brainstorming were invaluable to sharpen and update the theory, rethink key concepts, and overall make of this a much better book. Caitlin Andrews-Lee, Ana Arjona, Steffen Blings, Omar Coronel, Kristin McKie, Aníbal Pérez-Liñán, Kenneth Roberts, Raúl Sánchez-Uribarri, Andreas Schedler, Guillermo Trejo, and Kurt Weyland read parts of the document at different steps of the process, providing generous and timely feedback that shaped the project. I am also thankful to the anonymous reviewers who read the manuscript and provided extensive and thoughtful comments. Their insights and criticisms were invaluable to improve the book.

Notre Dame, the University of Utah, and Utah State University have been fantastic academic houses. Notre Dame's Political Science Department, Institute for Scholarship in the Liberal Arts, and Kellogg Institute for International Studies provided funding essential to get this project off the ground. Utah State University and the University of Utah contributed funds that helped me refine the manuscript. At all these institutions, I have found not only outstanding colleagues and staff, who provided timely advice and assistance, but also bright hardworking students, whose work and questions made of this a much better manuscript. I am particularly grateful to Melanie del Pozo Peña, Chantelle Gossner, Paulina Rivera-Soto, Tyler Thomas, and Kaleb Webb for excellent work as research assistants.

At Cambridge University Press, I would like to thank Sara Doskow for inviting me to submit my manuscript and making sure the review and approval process was fast and smooth, and Rachel Blaifeder for her help, flexibility, and responsiveness throughout the production process. I could not have had better editors.

Lastly, I would have never been able to write this book without the support of my family. Back in Colombia, my parents have been an unconditional source of inspiration, encouragement, and strength. They fueled my passion for politics and taught me the importance of tolerance and compromise. The values they instilled in me shine through this project. In the United States, Dan has been a wonderful partner and ally, my rock for the past five years. His love and unfaltering support carried me through the ups and downs of the publishing process and pushed me through the finish line. He and the furry family we have built together are my world.

I

Introduction

In the past two decades, several democracies have slipped into democratic recession. Faced with economic or security crises, democratically elected executives in Latin America, the Middle East, Eastern Europe, and Africa have used their popularity to push for legislation – particularly constitutional amendments – that, over time, destroys systems of checks and balances, hinders free and fair elections, and erodes political rights and civil liberties. Across the world, these heads of government have found ways to subvert democratic norms while simultaneously maintaining a democratic façade. Using and abusing elections and institutional reform, they are turning new and old democracies alike into competitive authoritarian regimes.

Throughout the second half of the twentieth century, Venezuela was one of the most stable and prosperous democracies in Latin America. It had regular elections, strong institutions, and more wealth than any of its regional counterparts. Unlike other countries in the region, it did not succumb to right-wing dictatorships or protracted guerrilla warfare. Venezuela had forty years of democracy when Hugo Chávez was elected in 1998. Once in power, Chávez introduced constitutional amendments that strengthened his hold over congress, courts, and oversight agencies, and extended his time in office. He used that power to distort the electoral playing field to such an extent that it became almost impossible for the opposition to defeat him. In twenty years, Venezuela went from being one of the most promising democracies in the continent to one of its most egregious authoritarian regimes.

Not all countries, however, have suffered this fate. In Colombia, Alvaro Uribe tried to erode democracy but failed. In line with the Chavista playbook, between 2002 and 2010, Uribe introduced constitutional amendments to undermine the independence of the legislature and the courts, enhance the powers of the executive, and extend his time in office. Uribe was popular, populistic, polarizing, and willing to undermine democratic institutions to achieve his preferred policies. His government harassed journalists and members of the opposition and the courts, and worked in tandem with illegal armed actors to systematically intimidate those who criticized his administration. War-ridden, Colombia's democracy had not been as stable as Venezuela's, yet Uribe was not able to impair democratic institutions. Despite his attempts to undermine checks and balances and thwart the fairness of elections, Colombia's constitutional order remained fairly strong. Uribe was unable to reelect himself for a third term and stepped down, giving way to a new democratically elected president.

Venezuela and Colombia are not the only countries where executives with hegemonic aspirations sought to entrench their rule. Between 1978 and 2019, Latin America has seen the rise of at least twenty-five leaders willing to undermine democratic institutions in order to fulfill their policy agenda. Fourteen of them – Carlos Menem (1989–99) in Argentina, Alberto Fujimori (1990–2000) in Peru, Jorge Serrano Elías (1991–3) in Guatemala, Evo Morales (2006–19) in Bolivia, León Febres (1984–8) and Rafael Correa (2007–17) in Ecuador, Arnoldo Alemán (1997–2002) and Daniel Ortega (2007–present) in Nicaragua, Roberto Suazo (1982–6), Juan Manuel Zelaya (2006–9), and Juan Orlando Hernández (2014–22) in Honduras, Nayib Bukele (2019–present) in El Salvador, Chávez and Uribe – tried to change or circumvent their nation's constitution in order to remove checks on their presidency and hold on to power. However, only six of them – Fujimori, Chávez, Morales, Correa, Ortega, and Hernández – successfully transformed their countries' democracies into competitive authoritarian regimes. The other seven did not.

Why do some potential autocrats[1] successfully erode democracy while others fail? This is the central question of this book, and one I will explore by comparing the dynamics of erosion in Colombia and Venezuela. Unlike traditional democratic breakdowns (e.g., military or civilian coups) the erosion of democracy happens over time. It takes years for an executive with hegemonic aspirations to succeed in eroding democracy. In the discussion that follows, I conceptualize this phenomenon in two stages. The first focuses on the factors that increase the likelihood of electing these hyper-ambitious leaders. The second focuses on the circumstances that, once in power, help or hinder these executives' success in their attempts to erode democracy.

Weakly institutionalized party systems, weak states in crisis and – to a lesser extent – weak economic performance are critical to understanding where and when we are likely to see executives willing to undermine democratic institutions in order to advance policy goals. These factors, however, cannot fully explain why some of these leaders are successful in their attempts to erode democracy while others are not. In order to better understand this puzzle, *Opposition at the Margins* brings attention to the opposition, an often

---

[1] I use executives/presidents with hegemonic aspirations interchangeably with potential autocrats.

overlooked actor. Because the erosion of democracy happens sequentially, those who oppose executives with hegemonic aspirations have ample opportunities to respond. Their goals and strategies, I argue, are crucial to account for the success or failure of potential autocrats.

Some exceptions notwithstanding (Gamboa 2017; Cleary and Öztürk 2020; McCoy and Somer 2021;), when analyzing the erosion of democracy, the spotlight often falls on the executive: the circumstances that brought her to power and the institutional context in which she started her term, her access to resources, her popularity, and/or her domestic or international support (see, e.g., Mazzuca 2013a; Svolik 2015a; Haggard 2016a; Handlin 2017a; Corrales 2018a; Weyland and Madrid 2019a; Weyland 2020). These accounts often obscure the role of those out of power. They either assume that once these would-be autocrats are in office, there is little that can be done against their hegemonic aspirations, or maintain that only weak potential autocrats fail, and do so because of their own shortcomings or mistakes. Without disregarding the balance of power between the government and the opposition during the processes of democratic erosion and how this context may shape the choices available to those fighting the potential autocrat, *Opposition at the Margins* complements existing accounts by emphasizing the importance of opposition agency. As I will show, using the right combination of goals and tactics, even weak oppositions have opportunities to defeat strong incumbents. The decisions they make are as important as the resources they possess.

1.1 THE ARGUMENT IN BRIEF

I define the erosion of democracy as a type of regime transition from democracy to autocracy that happens over time. Like classic democratic breakdowns (i.e., civilian or military coups), democratic erosion entails a regime change. In this type of democratic backsliding, incumbents introduce decrees, legislation, or constitutional amendments that enhance their powers and increase their time in office. Individually, these reforms strengthen some of the executive's powers but fail to fully capture state institutions or provide budgetary powers large enough that would seriously unbalance the electoral playing field. Over time, however, these alterations accumulate to a point in which not only do they hinder horizontal accountability (O'Donnell 1994, 2007, 49–78) but also skew the electoral playing field by thwarting electoral accountability (O'Donnell 2007, 49–75). These alterations increase the executive's hold over courts, congress, and oversight agencies and allow her to extend her time in office. This enables the head of state not only to run for two or more terms (in presidential systems) but, more importantly, to manipulate the electoral process to such an extent that it becomes extremely difficult for the opposition to defeat her. A democracy that has undergone erosion, therefore, is no longer a democracy, but a competitive authoritarian regime (Levitsky and Way 2010, 5–16).

Contrary to classic breakdowns, the erosion of democracy happens gradually. In civilian or military coups, authoritarian leaders, once in office, quickly dismiss elections, ban opposition parties, and/or close state institutions. Executives with hegemonic aspirations however, want to keep a democratic façade (Schedler 2013). Although they could close congress and the courts, in the post–Cold War environment these tactics are likely to trigger an adverse response from the international community and/or jeopardize domestic support (Lührmann and Lindberg 2018). Accordingly, potential autocrats instead chose to introduce constitutional amendments or legislation that expand their hold over congress, courts, and oversight agencies slowly. It takes years before they can successfully skew the electoral playing field to such an extent that it becomes impossible to defeat them.

In other words, the rise of an executive with hegemonic aspirations and the breakdown of democracy do not happen simultaneously. Therefore, I study these events independently. I conceptualize the erosion of democracy in two stages. The first focuses on the likelihood that a country elects a potential autocrat. Following existing literature, I argue that countries that have weak states with governance problems (Mainwaring 2012a; Diamond 2015a; Handlin 2017a), weakly institutionalized party systems (Carreras 2012a; Mainwaring 2018a), and poor economic performance (Svolik 2015a; Haggard 2016a) are more likely to see the rise of these leaders. These characteristics cannot entirely explain why some of these executives successfully erode democracy while others fail, however. To understand this puzzle, the outcome of the second stage, I focus on the role of the opposition. Because democratic erosion happens over time, even after a leader with hegemonic aspirations assumes office, the opposition has institutional and noninstitutional resources it can use against the incumbent. How it uses these resources, and what it employs them for, is critical to understand why some executives can more easily erode democracy than others.

The degree of toleration for a government's actions domestically and abroad is contingent upon the nature of the opposition's challenge (Gartner and Regan 1996). Because executives with hegemonic aspirations come to power in democracy, opposition strategies and goals deemed unacceptable in democratic politics are risky gambles. While these strategies could potentially stop autocrats in the short term, they increase the government's incentives to repress (i.e., violate freedoms of speech, assembly, or association, legally or verbally harass opponents, or violate integrity rights [Davenport 2007]) and decrease the costs of doing so. Such opposition tactics and goals enable the incumbent to paint the opposition as "radical" or "undemocratic," endow her with "legitimate" reasons to remove opposition leaders from office, prosecute or jail them, and enhance the incumbent's ability to rally citizens around the flag and push for more aggressive antidemocratic reforms.

Extrainstitutional strategies with radical goals – that is, tactics that use noninstitutional repertories like coups, protests, boycotts, or strikes to remove the president before the end of her constitutional term – fit these criteria. They convey a rejection of the established institutional mechanisms for redress and create a zero-sum game (McAdam 1999, 57–8). This combination of strategies and goals presents an existential threat to the incumbent – boosting the appeal of repression – and will likely be seen as unwarranted domestically and abroad – curbing the costs to repress. If successful, this combination of strategies and goals can halt the process of democratic erosion, but at the cost of breaking democracy altogether, further polarizing society, or martyrizing the potential autocrat. However, if failed, this combination of strategies and goals will likely jeopardize the opposition's legitimacy inside and outside the country, providing the executive with more leeway to remove opposition leaders from office, and prosecute or jail them, as well as galvanize enough support to push for more aggressive antidemocratic reforms that, weakened, the opposition will be ill equipped to stop.

Strategies and goals that are considered part of "normal" democratic politics, on the other hand, are a safer gamble. While unlikely to bring the process of democratic erosion to an immediate halt, they increase the costs and reduce the incentives to repress. They protect the opposition's legitimacy, hindering the executive's ability to credibly label it as "undemocratic" or "radical," reducing the incumbent's capacity to harass or repress the opposition while keeping a democratic façade and taming her ability to rally around the flag in support for more aggressive antidemocratic reforms.

Institutional strategies with moderate goals – that is, tactics that use institutions like elections, congress, or courts to stop or modify antidemocratic reforms – fall in this category. This combination of strategies and goals convey an implicit acceptance of the proper channels of conflict resolution in a democracy and are less threatening for the ruling elite (McAdam 1999, 57–8), thus increasing the costs and decreasing the incentives to repress. Using electioneering, litigation, legislative tactics, or lobbying to modify specific reforms not only represents a low threat to the executive but also fails to provide her with "legitimate" reasons to attack the opposition or support a push for more aggressive reforms. These tactics are overall less costly to the opposition. If successful, they allow the opposition to buy time, keep some presence in the legislature, and be better equipped to repeal more radical antidemocratic reforms further down the road. If failed, the erosion of democracy may continue but the opposition lives to fight another day.

Following this logic, *moderate extrainstitutional strategies* – that is, strategies that use noninstitutional repertoires to stop or modify antidemocratic reforms – and *radical institutional strategies* – that is, tactics that use institutions to remove the president before the end of her constitutional term – fall somewhere in between. Extrainstitutional strategies with moderate goals decrease the incentives for repression but also the costs of doing so. Although potentially effective to exert pressure on the incumbent and call attention to her abuses, these tactics can easily turn illegal or violent, in which case they could provide the head of government with "legitimate" reasons to crack down on the opposition. Institutional strategies with radical goals increase the incentives for repression but also the costs of doing so. Although they can successfully remove an executive from office while protecting the opposition's legitimacy, they can also threaten the incumbent's existence and thus – if failed – risk a more aggressive response.

Accordingly, oppositions that resort to *radical extrainstitutional strategies* and, depending on the circumstances, *radical institutional* or *moderate extrainstitutional* strategies, run a high risk of curtailing their ability to prevent the erosion of democracy. Likely to fail (Baykan, Gürsoy, and Ostiguy 2021), these tactics can undermine their legitimacy and resources while also increasing the incumbent's incentives and support to advance more aggressive antidemocratic reforms that a weakened opposition will be less suited to stop. On the contrary, oppositions that resort to *moderate institutional strategies* alongside some types of *moderate extrainstitutional* or *radical institutional strategies* have a good shot of enhancing their ability to prevent democratic erosion. Although moderate in their achievements, these tactics can safeguard the opposition's legitimacy and resources, protect courts and oversight agencies, and hinder aggressive antidemocratic reforms.[2]

The argument outlined earlier draws from approaches that highlight agency and international factors in processes of regime change. Some scholars suggest that transitions from and to democracy are elite-driven (Linz 1978; O'Donnell and Schmitter 1986; Berman 1998; Capoccia 2007a; Mainwaring and Pérez-Liñán 2013). They argue that democratic breakdowns are the outcome of elites' strategic choices in response to crises. Like these theories, I emphasize the importance of actors and their decisions. Unlike these theories – and in line with more recent work on democratic backsliding and polarization (Gamboa 2017; Levitsky and Ziblatt 2018a; McCoy and Somer 2019, 2021; Cleary and Öztürk 2020) – I pay attention to elites' choices even after an executive with hegemonic aspirations has attained power.

Elite decisions, of course, do not happen in a vacuum. International factors are also essential to understand transitions from and to democracy (Brinks and Coppedge 2006; Levitsky and Way 2010; Bunce and Wolchik 2011; Mainwaring and Pérez-Liñán 2013; Schenoni and Mainwaring 2019). International factors shape the balance of power between regime coalitions and constrain what is deemed acceptable or unacceptable in pursuit of political change. My theory highlights the importance of international and domestic audiences in shaping the executive's and the opposition's strategic choices. Contingent on the assumption that these audiences have a normative preference for democracy that motivates authoritarian leaders to keep a democratic

---

[2] Some parts of this argument were originally published in *Comparative Politics* (Gamboa 2017). They are reprinted here with their permission.

façade, I argue that some goals and strategies are more useful than others at preventing the erosion of democracy.

1.2 THE IMPORTANCE OF UNDERSTANDING THE EROSION OF DEMOCRACY

My argument has three relevant implications for the study of democratic politics. First, this book offers an updated and broader understanding of democratic breakdowns. Following the trend of scholars who have theorized democratic backsliding in recent years (Bermeo 2016a; Dresden and Howard 2016a; Cameron 2018; Waldner and Lust 2018a), I distinguish democratic erosion from declines in the quality of democracy and civilian/military coups. I analyze it as a type of democratic breakdown that happens sequentially, as a process rather than a one-shot game.

This approach distinguishes the rise of an authoritarian leader from her ability to undermine democracy. Conventional theories to the study of democratic breakdowns have mostly focused on the factors that bring to power leaders with a normative preference for dictatorship or a very weak preference for democracy. With classic democratic breakdowns in mind, they assume that once these leaders are in office, there is little that can be done to prevent a democratic reversal and, as a result, they fail to consider what happens afterward.

Common approaches to regime change fall in this group. Low economic development (Przeworski et al. 2000; Svolik 2008), economic performance (Svolik 2015a; Haggard 2016a), governance problems (Fortin 2011; Mainwaring 2012a; Andersen et al. 2014; Diamond 2015a; Handlin 2017a), and weak institutions (Carreras 2012a; Pérez-Liñán and Mainwaring 2013; Mainwaring 2018a; Ginsburg and Huq 2019a; Weyland and Madrid 2019a; Weyland 2020), they claim, increase the likelihood of democratic breakdown. Economic and security difficulties lead to legitimacy crises that undermine popular support for democracy and unsettle democratic institutions. Feeble institutions, in turn, make electoral politics unpredictable, increasing the probability that leaders willing to circumvent democracy attain power.

As Chapter 3 will show, these theories are good at explaining why executives with hegemonic aspirations are elected in the first place, but they are less satisfactory when it comes to explaining why some of these leaders successfully erode democracy while others fail. Economic recessions and weak states with governance problems can shake an executive's hold on power. Once this incumbent has been replaced by the potential autocrat, these variables should decrease her support and her ability to erode democracy, not the other way around. In other words, they should not necessarily overdetermine the concentration of power in the hands of the new president. By conceptualizing the erosion of democracy as a process, not only do I move away from accounts that see regime backsliding as inevitable once a hyper-ambitious leader comes to power, but I also specify the effect that structural, institutional, and state-centered variables have on democratic erosion.

Second, analyzing the erosion of democracy as a process allows me to highlight the importance of the opposition's tactics and goals after an executive with hegemonic ambitions has attained power. Few scholars have analyzed the role of the opposition in processes of democratic backsliding (for exceptions, see Gamboa 2017; Abi-Hassan 2019a; Cleary and Öztürk 2020; McCoy and Somer 2021). Recent studies of democratic erosion have mostly emphasized the role of the executive and/or the structural or institutional landscape these leaders face. These scholars argue that the erosion of democracy is the outcome of the incumbent's ex ante popularity (Levitsky and Loxton 2013a; Corrales 2018a; Weyland and Madrid 2019a), institutional strength (Batory 2016a; Stoner-Weiss 2010), strategic choices (Carlos de la Torre and Lemos 2016; Balderacchi 2017a; Handlin 2017a, 2018), resources (Hidalgo 2009; Hawkins 2010a; Mazzuca 2013a), ideology (Weyland 2013), domestic and/or international support (Carlos de la Torre 2013; Corrales 2015), and/or the strength of the institutions she is trying to co-opt (Weyland 2020). Few of them look at the opposition, and when they do, they think of its choices as heavily constrained by feeble institutions and/or resource asymmetries.

The balance of power between the government and the opposition at the outset of erosion or the institutional setting it plays out in does not overdetermine the outcome. Variables such as economic growth, mineral resources, weak institutions, and popularity cannot fully distinguish between successful and failed cases of erosion. Indeed, Hugo Chávez had access to limitless oil revenues that helped him enhance his powers and extend his time in office, but neither Daniel Ortega nor Juan Orlando Hernández, who also succeeded in eroding democracy, had a similar advantage. The Colombian economy during Alvaro Uribe's government did much better than Ecuador's during Rafael Correa's administration, yet the latter eroded democracy, while the former did not. Rafael Correa came to power in the midst of unstable institutions that helped him erode democracy; Chávez, however, did not. The average popularity of Correa was high, but so was Uribe's. In fact, it was higher than Hernández's, Chávez's, or Evo Morales's. Similarly, political polarization was higher in Colombia during Alvaro Uribe's government than in Honduras during Juan Orlando Hernandez's government. Yet the former failed to erode democracy while the latter did not.

This is true if we look more closely at the two cases analyzed in this book. It is often tempting to succumb to the fallacy of retrospective determinism, whereby we judge an institutional framework or an opposition relatively weak because of its ultimate demise or failure to prevent the erosion of democracy and relatively strong because of its ultimate resilience or success in protecting democratic governance. To avoid this problem, Chapters 4 and 5 provide detailed accounts of the balance of power between government and opposition in both of my cases and the institutional landscape in which they deployed their strategies. I show that at the beginning of his government, the opposition to

Chávez was not only stronger than the opposition to Uribe but also capable of selecting among a wide set of institutional and extrainstitutional strategies. Instead of focusing on the executive and/or the vulnerability of the institutions she takes over, I join scholars that argue we ought to recognize the agency of the opposition as well (Lindberg 2009; Bunce and Wolchik 2011; Gamboa 2017; McCoy and Somer 2019; Cleary and Öztürk 2020; Jiménez 2021; Ong 2021). The resources available to the head of government, as well as her ability to use them, I posit, can be curbed or enhanced by the opposition's strategic choices. Whereas moderate institutional strategies alongside some types of moderate extrainstitutional or radical institutional strategies can help the opposition protect the resources it has (while frustrating the government's attempts to co-opt them), radical extrainstitutional strategies alongside some types of moderate extrainstitutional or radical institutional strategies, can hinder the opposition's ability to do the same. Consequently, the first set of strategies and goals can hamper the incumbent's ability to increase her leverage vis-à-vis those who oppose her. The second set can enhance it.

This latter point is crucial. The third wave of democracy ended most military and single-party dictatorships. Between 1974 and 1999, eighty-five countries democratized (Geddes 1999), and classic coups d'état, executive coups and election-day frauds declined (Bermeo 2016a). Unfortunately, however, this democratic awakening was not durable. Not only did some regimes fail to fully democratize (Brownlee 2007; Levitsky and Way 2010; Schedler 2013a), but, even more concerning, new and old democracies began experiencing democratic setbacks. According to Freedom House's 2021 report, since 2005, the number of countries with democratic declines has outweighed the number of countries with democratic gains every year (Repucci and Slipowitz 2021).

The erosion of democracy has become an increasingly common type of democratic reversal. It has proven to be pervasive and hard to prevent. The cases of democratic erosion have increased since the 1990s. Initially circumscribed to nations of the Global South in Africa and Latin America, democratic backsliding has spread to economically more developed and/or "poster boy" democracies like Poland and Hungary. Today, even fully consolidated democracies, like the United States, have seen threats of backsliding via executive overreach (Levitsky and Ziblatt 2018a; Roberts 2019).

Few of the mechanisms established to protect and advance democracy across the world have succeeded in constraining executives with hegemonic ambitions. These incumbents have found ways to subvert democratic norms without breaching international democratic standards. The international community (standard-bearer of democratization during the 1980s and 1990s in the West) has few means of sanctioning them (Meyerrose 2020). By studying how these leaders succeed (or fail) in their attempts to erode democracy, I provide insights not only on what countries need to do to prevent potential autocrats from coming to power but, more importantly, on what the opposition and the international community can do to improve their chances of stopping the processes of democratic erosion.

1.3 RESEARCH DESIGN

There are many ways in which scholarship can benefit from using a mixed methods approach (Seawright and Gerring 2008; Tarrow 2010; Goertz 2017). In this case, I use quantitative and qualitative analytic techniques in order to answer two different types of questions. The first – what variables increase the likelihood of electing executives with hegemonic aspirations? – focuses on the average effect that a variable, or set of variables, has on a given outcome. I wish to know under what conditions countries elect potential autocrats and to what extent these and other related variables influence the autocrat's ability to erode democracy, not the causal path by which they come to power. Therefore, quantitative multivariate analysis is appropriate to answer this type of question.

In Chapter 3, I use descriptive and analytic quantitative techniques to assess the average effect of economic development and growth, perceptions of the economy, state capacity, state performance, trust in institutions, and party system institutionalization on the probability that a country will see the rise of a potential autocrat. I identify presidents with hegemonic aspirations using an updated version of Mainwaring and Pérez-Liñán's (2013) regime preferences database and an original dataset of constitutional amendments introduced by democratically elected Latin American presidents between 1978 and 2019. Unlike existing datasets on institutional reform (e.g., Comparative Constitutions Project, Latin American Constitutional Change Database), my dataset records attempts to amend the constitution regardless of whether they were successful or not. This allows me to distinguish between presidents who do not try to erode democracy, presidents who try to erode democracy and fail, and presidents who try to erode democracy and succeed. I measure the independent variables using existing databases such as the World Bank's for economic development and growth, mineral exports, and state performance; Hanson and Sigman's (2021) for state capacity; Latinobarómetro (1995–2017) for perceptions of the economy and trust in institutions; Mainwaring's (2018) for electoral volatility; Helmke's (2017) and Elkins and Ginsburg's (2021) for institutional strength; the Executive Approval Project (2019) for president approval ratings; and Varieties of Democracy (2021) for political polarization.

In the first stage, I identify twenty-five cases of presidents with hegemonic aspirations in Latin America (for details, see Table 3.1). Two of them – Fujimori (1990–2000) and Jorge Serrano Elías (1991–3) – launched coups. Twelve introduced reforms or legislation that circumvented or changed the constitution in order to enhance their powers and extend their time in office. Five of them successfully eroded democracy, six failed, and one is too early in the process to determine success or failure.

The second question – why, once elected, some potential autocrats successfully erode democracy while others fail? – is concerned with a very specific event. I do not wish to understand the average effect of a variable or set of variables in a president's ability to erode democracy, but rather trace the set of interrelated causes, the process by which she transforms, or fails to transform, a democracy into a competitive authoritarian regime. Accordingly, qualitative methods are more appropriate to answer this question (Goertz and Mahoney 2012). In Chapters 4 and 5, I use comparative historical analysis (Mahoney 2003; Mahoney and Thelen 2015) to assess the conditions that enable some presidents with hegemonic aspirations, but not others, to increase their powers and extend their time in office beyond a second term. The leverage of comparative historical analysis derives from within-case analysis (George and Bennett 2005; Bennett 2010; Bennett and Checkel 2015). Consequently, I use process tracing to evaluate the causal mechanisms that connect the opposition's strategic choices and goals with the executive's ability to erode democracy in a case of successful erosion (Hugo Chávez in Venezuela) and a case of failed erosion (Alvaro Uribe in Colombia). These cases allow me to analyze the effects of opposition strategic choices and goals on the incumbent's ability to undermine democracy at different points in time. I use detailed case knowledge to outline the government's and the opposition's resources, describe the strategic choices available, and connect the ones the opposition chose to its ability to protect (or fail to) and utilize (or not) these resources when facing more radical power grabs.

1.3.1 Case Selection

I chose to study Venezuela and Colombia using a qualitative *set theory* logic (Goertz and Mahoney 2012; Goertz 2017) and a most similar systems design (Gerring 2008; Seawright and Gerring 2008). The qualitative set theory logic for case selection prioritizes causal mechanisms (Goertz 2017). It dictates that we should select cases that allow us to assess both the causal mechanisms and the *constraint causal mechanisms*. That is, the mechanisms by which the outcome happens ($Y=1$) whenever that causal condition is present ($X=1$), and the mechanisms that prevent the outcome from happening ($Y=0$) whenever that condition is absent ($X=0$) (Goertz 2017). Table 1.1 shows how the eleven cases of presidents with hegemonic aspirations who tried to erode democracy distributed across the main independent and dependent variables.

   Out of these eleven cases, eight align with my argument. The opposition used mostly radical extrainstitutional strategies against Hugo Chávez (Venezuela, 1999–2013), Evo Morales (Bolivia, 2006–19), and Rafael Correa (Ecuador, 2007–17) – though opposition strategies in Ecuador are harder to categorize[3] – enabling these presidents to erode democracy; the opposition avoided radical

---

[3] After the Supreme Electoral Tribunal (TSE) approved a plebiscite to convene a constitutional assembly, the opposition legislative majority decided to remove TSE's head judge Jorge Acosta, and impeach the four justices that had sided with the president (Basabe Serrano and Polga Hecimovich 2013). Such a move was unconstitutional (Machado 2008), but not exactly extra-institutional or radical. It, however, allowed the government to use that as an excuse to remove from congress all the fifty-seven deputies who had voted in favor of impeachment.

TABLE 1.1. *Case selection*

		OPPOSITION RESPONSE (X)	
		Moderate Institutional (X=0)	Radical Extrainstitutional (X=1)
DEMOCRATIC EROSION (Y)	Erosion (Y=1)	A Ortega Hernández	B Chávez Morales *Correa*
	Failed Erosion (Y=0)	C Suazo Febres Menem *Alemán* Uribe	D Zelaya

Note: Opposition strategies for these cases (in italics) are harder to categorize.

extrainstitutional strategies and used mostly moderate institutional strategies against León Febres (Ecuador, 1984–8), Carlos Menem (Argentina, 1989–99), Roberto Suazo (1982–6), Arnoldo Alemán (Nicaragua, 1997–2002), and Alvaro Uribe (Colombia, 2002–10), hindering their ability to erode democracy. Daniel Ortega (Nicaragua, 2007–present), Juan Orlando Hernández (2014–22), and José Manuel Zelaya (2006–9) deviate from the theory. Their cases, however, do not invalidate the argument, but help refine it and establish scope conditions.

I select my cases from Cells B and C of Table 1.1. Following the selection logic outlined earlier, I chose: (a) a case from the cell in which neither extra-institutional strategies nor democratic erosion are present (X=0 and Y=0) and (b) a case in which radical extrainstitutional strategies and democratic erosion are present (X=1 and Y=1). I then use a most-similar systems design to select the case of Alvaro Uribe and Hugo Chávez within these two cells. Venezuela and Colombia are similar in many ways. They democratized at the same time, had similar, very stable, two-party systems for most of the post-WWII era, and had traditional parties that declined roughly at the same time, in the 1990s. Both Hugo Chávez and Alvaro Uribe came to power in the midst of crises, and they were both very popular, populistic, polarizing, and willing to circumvent democracy. These similarities along theoretically relevant variables (i.e., those normally associated in previous work with the rise of potential autocrats and threats to democratic stability) make these cases comparable in the context of this book.

That being said, these cases are by no means identical; no two cases in comparative politics are ever an exact match. Crucially, Venezuela, unlike Colombia, owns very large oil reserves. Extraordinary oil revenues accrued during the commodity boom of the 2000s certainly helped Chávez erode democracy by allowing him to increase his military and civilian support. Uribe did not have those kinds of resources, but process tracing allows me to take this alternative explanation into account and show that Uribe's comparative deprivation did not hinder his ability to secure the endorsements he needed to pursue a hegemonic project. The Colombian president was, and still is, beloved by the military, and his approval ratings were actually higher than Chávez's throughout his government. Moreover, Chávez did not gain automatic control over these resources when he attained power in 1999. As I show in Chapter 4 and in line with my theory, an opposition misstep enabled him to gain full control over the petroleum company four years into his first term.

There are also other differences between the cases, but far from undermining comparability, such differences make the comparison interesting and productive. First, Colombia had a fifty-year-long armed conflict that Venezuela did not have. However, the Colombian armed conflict biases the case against my theory. In general, civil strife should decrease the likelihood that democracy survives. In the case of Colombia, the armed conflict provided a clear focal point for the president to seek support for his hegemonic project in a classic "rally around the flag" fashion. This might explain, for example, why Uribe was always more popular than Chávez. Second, the power of the Venezuelan and Colombian oppositions vis-à-vis the government at the onset of the process of erosion was different. The opposition to Hugo Chávez started off stronger than the opposition to Uribe. It had significant influence over the petroleum company, the armed forces, and the major media outlets, one-third of the seats in congress (post-2000), some support inside courts and oversight agencies, and the ability to mobilize millions of supporters to the streets. On the contrary, when Uribe came to power, the opposition had no access to any outstanding resource, no influence over the armed forces or major media outlets, one-third of the seats in congress, some support inside courts and oversight agencies, and the ability to mobilize some – not quite as many – supporters to the streets. Still, and despite these differences, Uribe was not able to erode democracy, and Chávez was.

Beyond the differences outlined earlier, the other two important issues to consider are whether Uribe and Chávez were equally determined to erode democracy and the strength of institutions they faced. It is possible that, from the outset, Chávez was simply more willing to undermine democratic institutions than Uribe was. Unfortunately, it is impossible to know for sure. Our perception of an executive's willingness to undermine democratic institutions is imperfect and often tainted by the fallacy of retrospective determinism. Looking backwards in 2021 – as Venezuela's regime crisis deepens – it is easier to perceive Chávez as more willing to undermine democratic institutions than

Uribe (or other unsuccessful potential autocrats). It is also impossible to disentangle Chávez's drive to undermine democracy from the opposition he faced. As I show throughout *Opposition at the Margins*, Chávez resorted to highly polarizing tactics that, unlike in Colombia, were met with similarly polarizing moves from the opposition. Had the opposition exercised more restraint, it is possible – even if not certain – that Chávez might not have resorted to more aggressive antidemocratic reforms. Finally, even if Chávez's authoritarian tendencies were stronger than Uribe's, he did not narrow all the choices available to the opposition when he got to power in 1999 or even in the years immediately after. Although increasingly constrained as the process of erosion moved forward, the Venezuelan opposition faced several viable paths up until 2006, many of which did not involve radicalization. In Chapter 4, I carefully reconstruct these alternatives. I show that it was ultimately the opposition's choice of radical extrainstitutional strategies that provided Chávez the cover he needed to destroy Venezuela's democracy without having to show his true authoritarian colors until 2007 or 2008.

Something similar happens with institutional strength. It is possible that, from the outset, democratic institutions in Venezuela were just weaker than democratic institutions in Colombia, making it easier for Chávez to co-opt them as well as curtailing the opposition's ability to use them. In Chapters 4 and 5, I discuss these countries' distinct forms of institutional weakness in detail. In general, however, it is not clear that institutions in Colombia were any more or less vulnerable than Venezuela's. Between Venezuela's transition to democracy and the election of Hugo Chávez, the country had replaced its constitution once and amended it twice. Between Colombia's transition to democracy and Alvaro Uribe's rise to power, this country had also replaced its constitution once, but amended it seventeen times. Colombia's younger constitution might have been less prone to replacement but was by no means less prone to modification.

By the same token, there is no evidence that the institutional landscape at the onset of erosion inevitably skewed the Venezuelan opposition into extrainstitutional strategies. Which institutions to use and how to rely on them is certainly shaped by the institutional context. Oppositions in Colombia and Venezuela had access to a different set of institutional resources, but they both had powerful tools they could use. As I show in Chapter 4, up until 2005, the opposition in Venezuela was fairly strong in congress and – for a while – had some leverage inside the courts and oversight agencies. As I show in Chapter 5, throughout Uribe's government, the opposition in Colombia was not particularly strong in congress but had more reliable courts to resort to. Both oppositions had the ability to use moderate institutional strategies.

1.3.2 What We Can Learn from the Cases That Do Not Fit the Theory

No theory is airtight. Suggesting a particular set of necessary or sufficient conditions does not eliminate the possibility that there might be falsifying cases:

cases in which in the absence of the necessary condition, the outcome still happens, or in the presence of a sufficient condition, the outcome does not happen. Cells A and D in Table 1.1 fall in this category. Although the opposition relied mostly on moderate institutional strategies, and avoided extrainstitutional ones, Ortega and Hernández successfully eroded democracy. And in the case of Zelaya, the opposition resorted to radical extrainstitutional strategies that successfully put an end to the president's hegemonic project (although breaking democracy altogether). These three cases help outline the scope conditions of the theory (Goertz 2017, 90–122), highlighting important assumptions underlying the argument. I will outline these conditions in more detail in Chapter 2. Later, however, I discuss the mechanisms that, absent radical extrainstitutional strategies, led to democratic erosion in Nicaragua and Honduras (2017), as well as the mechanisms that, despite the use of extrainstitutional strategies, prevented the erosion of democracy in Honduras (2009) (see Table 1.2 for more details).

1.3.2.1 Time
One of the key factors underlying my theory is time. If democracy quickly breaks down, the opposition has few opportunities to fight back. The case of Daniel Ortega in Nicaragua underscores that point. Ortega came to power in Nicaragua thanks to an alliance between the *Frente Sandinista de Liberación Nacional* (FSLN) and the *Partido Constitucionalista Liberal* (PCL) led by Arnoldo Alemán (1997–2002).[4] Together, these parties co-opted courts and oversight agencies before Ortega ran for office in 2006 (Pérez-Baltodano 2010). Although Alemán did not erode democracy himself, he helped set the stage for Ortega to do so. Unlike the oppositions in Colombia, Venezuela, Ecuador, Bolivia, or Argentina, by the time the Sandinista leader came to power, the Nicaraguan opposition had few of the resources it needed to put up a fight. He controlled all branches of power from the first day of his government. Whereas in other cases, the oppositions had several resources and strategic choices available immediately after a potential autocrat came to power; in Nicaragua, the opposition found itself without much capacity and time to react.

1.3.2.2 Audiences with a Normative Preference for Democracy
The theory assumes that executives with hegemonic aspirations want to keep a democratic façade. They fear that overtly authoritarian moves will unleash domestic and/or international backlash, and therefore wait until the opposition gives them "legitimate" reasons to advance antidemocratic reforms. This only works, of course, if the potential autocrat faces domestic or international audiences with leverage and a normative preference for democracy. That was

---

[4] Most of the antidemocratic reforms introduced by Alemán were meant to protect him from prosecution after he stepped down.

TABLE 1.2. *Cases details*

NAME	COUNTRY	PERIOD	STRATEGIES & GOALS				EROSION	THEORY	SCOPE CONDITIONS		
			Moderate Institutional	Radical Institutional	Moderate Extra Institutional	Radical Extra-Institutional			Support (Mean)	International Preference for Democracy	Time
R. Suazo	Honduras	1982-1986	✓				No	Confirms		Weak	Yes
L. Febres	Ecuador	1984-1988	✓			✓	No	Confirms	40%	Weak	Yes
C. Menem	Argentina	1989-1999	✓		✓		No	Confirms	41%	Strong	Yes
A. Uribe	Colombia	2002-2010	✓		✓		No	Confirms	65%	Strong	Yes
A. Aleman	Nicaragua	1997-2002	✓		✓		No	Confirms	39%	Strong	Yes
JM. Zelaya	Honduras	2006-2009	✓			✓	No	Confirms	45%	Strong	Yes
H. Chávez	Venezuela	1999-2013	✓	✓	✓	✓	Yes	Confirms	47%	Strong	Yes
E. Morales	Bolivia	2006-present	✓	✓	✓	✓	Yes	Confirms	51%	Strong	Yes
R. Correa	Ecuador	2007-2017	✓		✓	✓	Yes	Confirms	68%	Strong	Yes
JO. Hernández	Honduras	2014-present	✓		✓		Yes	Deviates	47%	Weak	Yes
D. Ortega	Nicaragua	2007-present	✓		✓		Yes	Deviates	57%	Strong	No

Classic Democratic Breakdowns (*Self-Coups*)

A. Fujimori	Perú	1990-2000
J. Serrano	Guatemala	1991-1993

✓ Dominant opposition strategies and goals
✓ Secondary opposition strategies and goals
Note: Highlighted are the cases for which that particular scope condition does not hold.

not the case of Juan Orlando Hernández in Honduras (2014–22). Even though the opposition used mostly institutional strategies with moderate goals to oppose him, the Honduran president was able to not only pack the court and change the constitution to extend his time in office (Landau, Dixon, and Roznai 2019) but also reelect himself in highly questionable elections and enforce the outcome despite the criticism of domestic and international organizations (Malkin 2017; Rodríguez 2019). He was able to do so, in part, thanks to the quick endorsement of the US president Donald Trump (2017–21), who showed ample disregard for democratic processes and norms domestically and abroad (Carrillo 2017; Levitsky and Ziblatt 2018a). Had Trump had a normative preference for democracy and reacted differently, Hernández might have been forced to repeat the elections following the demands of the Organization of American States (Levitsky 2018).

1.3.2.3 Support for Executives with Hegemonic Aspirations
Built into the theory is the assumption that potential autocrats have military and/or civilian support. Without it, they are less likely to try to enhance their powers and extend their time in office, and if they do so, they are more likely to fail. That is the case of Manuel Zelaya (2006–9), whose term was cut short in 2009 when overnight the army escorted him out of the country. In 2008, the Honduran president tried to push for a referendum that would have allowed him to call for a constitutional assembly and rewrite the constitution in order to enhance his powers and extend his time in office (Ruhl 2010; Weyland 2013). Defying Congress and the Supreme Court, which had decided against the project, Zelaya asked the army to go ahead with the ballot. In response, the opposition launched a coup. The move was not much different from the strategy used by the Venezuelan opposition against Hugo Chávez or Recep Tayyip Erdogan (Turkey, 2003–present) in 2002 and 2016, respectively. Unlike the Venezuelan or the Turkish incumbents who neutralized the coup attempts, the Honduran leader did not have strong military or civilian support to fight back. His approval rating at the time of the coup was 37 percent, and he did not have the organizational means to mobilize supporters to reverse the putsch. Democracy definitively broke down in Honduras in 2009, but it did not erode. The rupture in this Central American country represented a more traditional democratic breakdown.

To summarize, using an original database of institutional reforms introduced by democratically elected Latin American presidents, I am able to identify twenty-five presidents with hegemonic aspirations, eleven of whom introduced legislation or institutional reforms to undermine democratic institutions in a slow fashion. Five of them eroded democracy, six did not. Out of those eleven cases, I chose a case of successful erosion (Hugo Chávez) to evaluate the mechanisms that connect radical extrainstitutional tactics with an executive's ability to erode democracy, and a case of failed erosion (Alvaro Uribe) to assess the constraining mechanisms that connect the absence of extrainstitutional radical strategies and the use of moderate institutional and moderate extrainstitutional strategies with an incumbent's inability to erode democracy.

1.3.3 Qualitative Evidence

I collected the data to trace the dynamics of erosion in Colombia and Venezuela during twelve months of intensive fieldwork (2013–14). In the time I spent in both countries, I conducted eighty-eight interviews – fifty-two in Venezuela and thirty-six in Colombia – with politicians, journalists, congressional staffers, justices, clerks, members of advocacy groups and academics, and I did archival research in newspapers and congress (see Appendix A for more details).

In Colombia, I reviewed the weekly political magazine *Revista Semana* between 2002 and 2010. Using data from *Congreso Visible* alongside my own data on members of congress' support for the government, I also identified and reviewed the congressional debates of sixteen bills introduced by the government coalition to increase the powers of the executive and/or extend Uribe's time in office. Together, the interviews, newspaper, and archival research enabled me to analyze the danger posed by different antidemocratic bills, the strategies used by the opposition inside the legislative to stop them, and the extent to which these strategies helped curb Uribe's attempts to erode democracy.

In Venezuela, the data collection process was a bit more convoluted. On the one hand, an excellent archive publicly available in *El Nacional* allowed me to review this newspaper between 1998 and 2010 with relative ease. On the other hand, government control over the National Assembly and its archive (*Archivo Legislativo de la Asamblea Nacional*) made legislative data difficult to obtain. With the help of some officials inside the National Assembly, I was eventually able to access a list of all bills introduced between 2000 and 2010, their author, the dates of their debates, and whether they were approved or not. I used that document to build a legislative dataset and identify congressional bills introduced by the government coalition in order to increase the powers of the executive.[5]

Ideally, I would have reviewed the debates for each one of these bills. Unfortunately, I was denied access to the official transcripts. Luckily, the Legislative Information Office (*Dirección de Información Legislativa* [DIL]) – in charge of providing information to the public regarding new laws – has files of all bills approved since 2000, including their debates. In this office, I was able to review fifteen congressional antidemocratic amendments introduced and approved by the government.

---

[5] Chávez's attempts to increase his time in office happened outside the Legislative Assembly, via the 2007 and 2009 referendums and the 1999 Constitutional Assembly.

1.3.3.1 Empirical Implications

I use the evidence outlined earlier to detail the pathway between opposition strategic choices and regime outcomes. Because each case serves a different purpose, I reconstruct the causal pathway differently in Venezuela and Colombia (and design the chapters accordingly). In Venezuela, I use the data collected for three purposes. First, I resort to interviews, newspapers, and secondary sources to demonstrate that the erosion of democracy in this country was not fait accompli in 1999. I do that by describing the various institutional and noninstitutional resources the opposition had and how they were, or could have been, useful to defeat Chávez. Second, I utilize a similar set of data to demonstrate that it was, in fact, the use of radical extrainstitutional strategies that jeopardized these resources. I describe specific instances of these strategies and reveal how each one of them undermined the legitimacy of the opposition while boosting that of the president. I also illustrate how these strategies enhanced Chávez's ability to remove opposition members from state institutions, replace them with loyalists, and then use these institutions to further erode democracy. Together, the data collected provides enough evidence to show that the Venezuelan leader was able to undermine horizontal accountability without losing his democratic façade.

Third, using the legislative dataset, I show the viability of institutional and moderate extrainstitutional strategies, regardless of the context. The fact that the opposition had several seats in the National Assembly in 2000–5 but almost none in 2006–10 provides useful within-case variation to examine my argument. It allows me to compare the performance of congress with or without the members of the anti-Chavista coalition. Using descriptive statistics, I show that having members of the opposition in the legislature made a significant difference in the amount of legislation introduced and passed, as well as the overall delay of the legislative process, including pieces of legislation key to the erosion of democracy. I complement this evidence with in-depth analysis of a few pieces of legislation, where I show how the opposition used moderate institutional strategies to effectively delay processes of co-optation of courts and media outlets.

The burden of proof is slightly different in Colombia. Here I use evidence to perform a different set of tasks. First, I show that the survival of democracy was not fait accompli in 2002. For that purpose, I use interviews and newspapers to describe the threats that Uribe posed. I demonstrate that he was as populistic and polarizing, and as willing to erode democracy, as his Venezuelan counterpart. I also demonstrate that courts, congress, and oversight agencies were in real jeopardy.

Second, I connect the absence of radical extrainstitutional strategies to the persistence and enhancement of the opposition's legitimacy vis-à-vis the president's. I further tie that legitimacy to the opposition's ability to keep its presence in congress, courts, and oversight agencies. I rely on newspapers and interviews to show not only that the opposition was legitimate but that legitimacy afforded it important leverage domestically and abroad as well. Relying on within and cross-case variation, I provide evidence to suggest that, given a chance, Uribe would have taken advantage of the opposition's lack of legitimacy to undermine his opponents and remove them from office.

Finally, I outline how institutional and moderate extrainstitutional strategies helped prevent the erosion of democracy. Using congressional records, court rulings, and interviews, I show how legislative obstruction and targeted boycotts and demonstrations tamed Uribe's antidemocratic reforms. Crucially, relying on within-case variation, I demonstrate that, without active input from congress, it would have been much harder for the Constitutional Court to rule against the president in a case about the legality of his attempt to expand presidential term limits.

1.4 BOOK PLAN

This book is organized as follows. Chapter 2 outlines the theory. I start by defining the dependent variable. Doing so allows me to separate the rise of executives with hegemonic aspirations from their ability to erode democracy. I leave the theory and analysis of the first stage of democratic erosion for Chapter 3 and move to the second stage, where I describe the actors, their preferences, the strategies available to them, and their trades and payoffs. Within that framework, I outline the mechanisms by which oppositions that use radical extrainstitutional strategies betting on short term wins, end up curtailing their ability to protect democracy, the mechanisms by which oppositions that use moderate institutional strategies help prevent the erosion of democracy – even if not immediately – and the mechanisms by which oppositions that resort to radical institutional strategies and/or moderate extrainstitutional strategies can help or hinder their ability to shield democratic institutions from erosion. In this chapter, I also analyze some of the scope conditions and explore some of the potential drivers behind opposition strategic choices.

Chapter 3 focuses on the first stage of the argument. Based on the extant literature on regime and regime change, I highlight a set of variables that are essential to understanding the rise of presidents with hegemonic aspirations. Using an original dataset as well as data collected from several other sources, I show that weak states, weak party systems, and weak economic performance increase the likelihood of electing executives willing to circumvent democracy. I also show that these variables are not as useful to explain the variation between the Latin American potential autocrats who successfully eroded democracy and the ones who failed. This chapter assesses other alternative explanations as well. I show that, while favorable economic conditions and weak institutions at the onset of erosion as well as mass support and polarization during a hegemonic president's term help potential autocrats erode democracy, they do not guarantee this outcome.

Chapters 4 and 5 use comparative historical analysis to address this puzzle. They trace the dynamics of erosion in Venezuela and Colombia, respectively. Chapter 6 expands that analysis to four other cases: Evo Morales in Bolivia, Recep Tayyip Erdogan (2003–present) in Turkey, Law and Justice Party (2015–present) in Poland, and Viktor Orbán (2010–present) in Hungary. The first three cases conform to the theory. I show how opposition's radical extrainstitutional strategies jeopardized their ability to prevent the erosion of democracy in Bolivia and Turkey, and how moderate institutional and extrainstitutional strategies have helped delay the erosion of democracy in Poland. The last case, Hungary, does not conform to the theory. I use it to assess important scope conditions, in particular the importance of having time (and the institutional resources time affords) and an international community with a normative preference for democracy. Chapter 7, the conclusion, highlights the theoretical and empirical contributions of *Opposition at the Margins*.

2

Opposition Strategies against the Erosion of Democracy

In this chapter, I develop a theory that focuses on the opposition's strategic choices to fight the erosion of democracy. I define democratic erosion as a type of regime transition that happens over time, giving the opposition ample opportunity to respond, even after a leader willing to circumvent democracy has attained power. The strategies the opposition chooses and the goals it uses them for, I argue, are critical to understanding why some executives with hegemonic aspirations successfully erode democracy and others do not.

I classify opposition strategies in three groups. Extrainstitutional strategies with radical goals are the least likely to help protect democracy. Though they promise immediate payoffs, they carry a lot of risk. By retaliating outside institutions hoping to oust the executive before the end of her constitutional term, oppositions jeopardize their legitimacy domestically and abroad. Such a response not only increases the incentives and decreases the costs of repression[1] – providing the potential autocrats with more leeway to remove opposition leaders from office, prosecute them, or jail them – but also allows the autocrat to rally around the flag and push for more aggressive reforms that, weakened, the opposition will be ill-equipped to stop.

In contrast, institutional strategies with moderate goals are more likely to protect democracy. Although they have small immediate payoffs, they carry less risk. By using legislation, litigation, lobbying, and/or electioneering to fight potential autocrats, the opposition protects its legitimacy domestically and abroad. Such a response decreases the incentives and increases the costs of

---

[1] Repression is understood here comprehensively as an "application of state power that violates First-Amendment-type rights, due process in the enforcement and adjudication of law, and personal integrity or security." (Davenport 2007, 2) This includes violations of freedom of speech and assembly; violations to freedom of association; verbal or legal harassment; and violations to integrity rights.

repression. Not only does it fail to provide the incumbent with "legitimate" reasons to remove opposition leaders from office, prosecute, or jail them, but it also fails to enhance her support to push for more aggressive reforms. Accordingly, moderate institutional strategies can not only slow the pace of erosion but also increase the odds that the opposition will keep some presence in congress, courts, and oversight agencies, which in turn equip the opposition to repeal more aggressive antidemocratic reforms down the road.

Moderate extrainstitutional strategies and radical institutional strategies fall somewhere in between. Extrainstitutional strategies with moderate goals decrease the incentives for repression but also the costs of doing so. Although effective to exert pressure on incumbents and make visible their abuses, without proper preparation, these tactics have a high risk of turning illegal or violent, in which case they could provide the potential autocrat with legitimate reasons to repress and justify further power grabs. Institutional strategies with radical goals increase the incentives for repression but also the costs of doing so. While they protect the opposition's legitimacy and can be, at times, successful in removing the incumbent, they threaten the executive's existence, and thus risk a more aggressive response.

Existing approaches to explain the erosion of democracy are mostly one of two types. The first type focuses on the factors that drive potential autocrats to power. Economic crises (Haggard 2016), weak institutions (Coppedge 2005; Bejarano 2010), polarization (Haggard and Kaufman 2021), and weak states (Diamond 2015; Handlin 2017), these works argue, severely constrain the set of possible outcomes once a leader willing to circumvent democracy attains power. After a potential autocrat is in office, these accounts imply, there is little recourse.

The second set of approaches focuses on factors that help these hyperambitious leaders hold on to power once they have become heads of state. They highlight the executives' power vis-à-vis the opposition's, either in terms of their wealth (Weyland, Madrid, and Hunter 2010b; Mazzuca 2013; Weyland 2020), popularity and support (Levitsky and Loxton 2013a; Weyland 2013; Corrales 2016; Laebens 2020), institutional resources (Stoner-Weiss 2010; Batory 2016; Weyland and Madrid 2019a), strategic choices (Balderacchi 2017), or international support (Corrales 2015). This approach also considers the overall strength of the opposition the executive faces (Corrales 2018) and/or the strength of the institutions she is trying to co-opt (Weyland 2020). The implication of these arguments is that only weak authoritarian leaders in strong institutional contexts fail.

The theory I advance in this book challenges these implications. By conceptualizing the erosion of democracy as a process rather than a one-shot event, it distinguishes the factors that drive leaders with hegemonic aspirations to power from the mechanisms by which they erode democracy. Economic crises, weak states, and weak institutions might help bring leaders willing to undermine democracy to power, but they do not help them erode democracy several years afterward.

As a result of focusing on process, my approach also introduces time into the analysis of democratic backsliding, allowing me to look beyond the executive's strength. Opposition's actions can play a significant role in enhancing or undermining a potential autocrat's resources as well as in boosting or jeopardizing the institutions the executive seeks to capture. Rather than focusing on the correlation of forces between government and opposition or the strength of the institutions they are fighting over, I suggest we see the erosion of democracy through what Bunce and Wolchik (2011, 216) call the "regime defeat" lens and focus on the decisions oppositions make: their goals and strategies, and how different combinations of these elements have different consequences for regime change.

This chapter is organized as follows: Section 2.1 defines the erosion of democracy. I distinguish it both from sudden breakdowns and declines in the quality of democracy. Sections 2.2 and 2.3 develop my theory, outlining the executive's and the opposition's preferences, the strategic choices these actors make, and the mechanisms by which moderate/radical institutional strategies and moderate/radical extrainstitutional strategies can help protect or hinder democracy. In Section 2.4, I situate this theory in a broader context and highlight the importance of the opposition's strategic choices to better understand transitions from democracies to competitive authoritarian regimes.

2.1 DEMOCRATIC EROSION

Many scholars use the notion of democratic erosion to refer to slow democratic reversals, but it is unclear what kind of democratic setback should count as an erosion of democracy and what kind should not (Fish 2001; Erdmann 2011; Cameron 2018; Mounk 2018, 23–131; Waldner and Lust 2018; Ginsburg and Huq 2019, 43–6; Lührmann and Lindberg 2019). Democratic erosion has been used to describe a decline in the level and/or quality of democracy without regime change (Haggard and Kaufman 2021, 2–4) as well as to discuss transitions away from democracy into some type of hybrid or fully authoritarian regime.

While both of these phenomena are important, they are distinct from each other. To highlight their differences, I offer a nuanced definition of democratic erosion. Relying on the growing literature that theorizes this phenomenon (Schedler 1998; Erdmann 2011; Bermeo 2016; Cameron 2018; Waldner and Lust 2018; Ginsburg and Huq 2019; Lührmann and Lindberg 2019; Gerschewski 2021a, 2021b), I define the erosion of democracy as a process: a transition from democracy to autocracy that happens gradually over time.[2]

---

[2] In an insightful analysis, Gerschewski (2021a, 2021b) suggests using "erosion" to describe exogenous-driven backsliding and "decay" to describe endogenous-driven backsliding. For the sake of simplicity, however, I do not make that distinction and keep the term "erosion" for both.

Governments that[3] successfully erode democracy[4] gravely weaken formal institutions that promote horizontal accountability and guarantee free and fair elections to such an extent that they thwart electoral accountability as well. Eroded democracies, therefore, are those at the end point of the process of democratic erosion (what Haggard and Kaufman [2021, 11] call "reversion"). They have undergone formal changes to the rules of the game that are severe enough to significantly skew the electoral playing field without shutting it down. Albeit minimally competitive, a democracy that has undergone erosion, therefore, is no longer a democracy but a competitive authoritarian regime (Levitsky and Way 2010, 5–16).[5]

2.1.1 Democratic Erosion as a Type of Regime Transition

Democratic breakdowns have been traditionally conceived as a type of regime change: a transition away from democracy in which democratic institutions are overthrown by force or manipulation in such a way that makes it very difficult to reestablish them in the short term (Linz 1978, 9). Like sudden democratic breakdowns, the erosion of democracy is a type of regime change – a transition away from democracy that entails formal changes to the rules of the game that curtail the checks on the executive to such an extent that they make alternation almost impossible.

In sudden democratic breakdowns, authoritarian leaders attain power via civilian or military coups. Once in office, they often cancel elections and/or close congress, courts, and oversight agencies in order to stay in power and rule at will. When Augusto Pinochet became Chile's leader via a military coup, the military junta under his command closed congress, banned or suspended political parties, imposed media censorship, annulled all electoral registration lists, and declared a "state of siege" to give military tribunals jurisdiction over civilians (Snyder 1994). In a matter of days, Pinochet had full control of all government institutions.

Similarly, in processes of democratic erosion, executives with hegemonic aspirations, once in power, introduce institutional reforms that seek to hinder the checks on the executive and extend the leader's time in office. These reforms – what Landau (2013) calls "abusive constitutionalism" – include (a) an increase in the legislative powers of the head of government (i.e., veto, decree, exclusive introduction of legislation, budgetary powers, and proposal of referenda); (b) an increase in the nonlegislative powers of the executive (i.e.,

---

[3] Although democratic reversals can be driven by nonstate actors, I conceive democratic erosion as a government-led phenomena (Schedler 1998; Haggard and Kaufman 2021, 2–4).

[4] What Bermeo (2016) calls "executive aggrandizement" and Svolik (2015) calls "presidential takeover."

[5] To the extent to which competitive authoritarian regimes can become fully authoritarian, a democratic erosion, over time, could lead to a fully authoritarian regime.

cabinet formation, cabinet dismissal, censure, dissolution of assembly, appointment of judicial and oversight officers, and the ability to overstep judicial
review) (Shugart and Carey 1992; Metcalf 2000; Negretto 2013, 71–104);
and (c) transformations to electoral rules in order to allow reelections, increase
immediate term limits, or gerrymander electoral maps to maintain incumbent
parliamentary majorities.

By itself, each of these alterations is insufficient to transform a democracy
into a competitive authoritarian regime (i.e., fully erode democracy). Together,
over time, however, these modifications build on each other and slowly hinder
horizontal accountability, skewing the electoral playing field to such an extent
that, eventually, they thwart electoral accountability as well. These reforms
help the executive keep and strengthen, sometimes, artificial majorities in
congress; pack the courts or render them inoperable; and/or overturn the
decisions of institutions that provide horizontal accountability. Accumulated
over time, they effectively eliminate the checks on the head of government, who
is then able to manipulate elections through electoral laws, campaign finance,
and media access, to such an extent that it becomes extremely difficult for the
opposition to defeat her or prevent her from extending her time in office beyond
a second term (Levitsky and Way 2010, 5–16).

Turkish former prime minister and current president Recep Tayyip
Erdogan's (2003–present) first set of constitutional amendments between
2007 and 2010, for example, increased his hold over important institutional
vetoes and lengthened his time in office, but did not immediately enhance his
control over courts and oversight agencies or allow him to run the country
indefinitely (Turam 2012; Özbudun 2015). Building on these, however, later
reforms increased Erdogan's control over the judiciary (Özbudun 2014) and
transformed Turkey's parliamentary system into a presidential one, allowing
the potential autocrat to further subordinate the courts, curtail the legislature,
write presidential decrees with force of law, and declare a state of emergency with
few constraints left to oppose him. Building on previous changes, these new
modifications unchecked his power and allowed him to manipulate electoral
rules to such an extent that he became almost impossible to defeat electorally.

The Turkish case shows how fully eroded democracies are no longer democracies – not even "delegative democracies" – but competitive authoritarian
regimes. Unlike fully eroded democracies, delegative democracies are "not alien
to the democratic tradition" (O'Donnell 1994, 60). Executives in these delegative democracies often hamper institutions that provide horizontal accountability (i.e., courts, congress, and oversight agencies), but the damage they inflict is
not enough to hinder electoral accountability[6] as well. Despite these changes,

---

[6] Electoral accountability is part of what Guillermo O'Donnell (2007, 50–51) names "vertical
accountability." Although often used as synonyms, vertical accountability includes both "soci-
etal" and "electoral" accountability. To avoid confusion, I use "electoral accountability" instead
of "vertical accountability."

these leaders still compete in somewhat clean elections in which the opposition has a somewhat decent chance to succeed.

Poland since 2015 is a good example of a country undergoing a process of democratic erosion without fully eroding. Although its democracy has deteriorated, the regime has not turned competitive authoritarian yet. The ruling Law and Justice (PiS) party has introduced legislation to curtail the powers of the courts, control public media outlets, allow for broader surveillance measures, and increase its hold over electoral authorities (Sadurski 2018). These changes have decreased democracy in Poland considerably, but they have not significantly curtailed the opposition's ability to defeat the ruling party yet. Up until 2020,[7] the opposition still had a third of the seats in the legislature and important financial resources; the ability to mobilize millions of Poles to the streets; access to privately owned media outlets; influence over political and nonpolitical elites; and strong links with the EU political establishment (Przybylski 2018). Whereas PiS is strong, those who oppose it have used these resources to slow down and even stop some of the incumbent power grabs.

Contrary to what happened in Poland, in eroded democracies like Turkey, the head of government hindered democratic institutions to such an extent that it is almost impossible to restore them in the short term. The institutional changes Erdogan's government enacted over time affected not only the checks on the executive (horizontal accountability) but also the opposition's ability to compete for power in free and fair elections (electoral accountability).

A complete erosion of democracy is also different from "democratic backsliding," which is understood as "a deterioration of qualities associated with democratic governance" without regime change (Waldner and Lust 2018, 95); "democratic decline" which is a process by which democratic regimes experience a loss of democratic quality that can end in some kind of diminished democratic regime, a hybrid regime, a fully authoritarian regime (Erdmann 2011); or autocratization, which refers to "substantial de-facto declines of core institutional requirements for electoral democracy" (Lührmann and Lindberg 2019, 1096). Democratic backsliding, declines of democracy, or autocratizations do not require a regime transition. Advanced democracies, like Portugal or Germany, have seen democracy decline (Coppedge et al. 2021) but are still considered stable democracies. The quality of democracy in these countries might have decreased, but they have not experienced a regime change, nor are there consistent signs that these nations will experience one. Similarly, Venezuela has seen autocratization since 2010; the decline, however, has come after the country turned authoritarian in 2007–8. These changes have deepened Venezuela's authoritarianism but have not caused regime change. The country was considered authoritarian then and is still considered authoritarian today.

---

[7] In 2019, the opposition coalition won a simple majority in the Senate.

On the contrary, a full erosion, as understood in this theory, always entails a regime change. A country faces a *process of erosion* when there is evidence that it is transitioning from a democracy to a semi-authoritarian regime, and a *full erosion of democracy* in those cases in which this process has pushed the regime outside the democratic camp into the authoritarian camp, turning the government into a competitive authoritarian regime.

2.1.2 Erosion as a Process

Both sudden democratic breakdowns and democratic erosions are regime transitions. However, they are different in the amount of time they take to push regimes outside the democratic camp into the authoritarian camp after a potential autocrat has attained power.[8] Sudden democratic breakdowns are one-shot games. Authoritarian leaders in this type of democratic reversals come to power via military or civilian coups. Once in office, they quickly suspend the constitution, dismiss elections, ban opposition parties, and/or close democratic institutions (i.e., congress, courts, and oversight agencies), leaving the opposition very little time to respond. Egypt in 2013 is an example of this. The military arrested the sitting president, Mohamed Morsi, and suspended the constitution. They did not formally close congress or take over the courts, but they imprisoned most of the top members of the Muslim Brotherhood, the president's party, only days after seizing power (Masoud 2014). Although this breakdown was the outcome of a longstanding crisis, after the coup, the opposition had almost no opportunity to respond.

Unlike these classic democratic breakdowns, democratic erosions happen over time. During the 1980s and 1990s, governments, intergovernmental organizations, and citizens in the West developed a normative preference for democracy. Afraid of domestic or international sanctions, executives with hegemonic aspirations have incentives to maintain a democratic façade (Kuntz and Thompson 2009). They would rather avoid overt attacks against democratic institutions and enhance their powers and increase their time in office incrementally using institutional reforms instead.

During the third wave of democracy between the 1970s and 1990s – when a significant number of countries in Europe, Latin America, Asia, and Africa transitioned to democracy – governments and intergovernmental organizations in the western world, like the European Union, the United States, and the Organization of American States (OAS), developed a normative preference for democracy (Pevehouse 2002; Bunce and Wolchik 2011, 278–306; Mainwaring and Pérez-Liñán 2013, 205–41). Whereas between the 1950s and 1980s, the United States and European countries condoned and, in some

---

[8] Both classic democratic breakdowns and democratic erosion have lengthy processes of democratic decline before executives with hegemonic aspirations attain power.

cases, even supported, coups such as Brazil's (1964), Uruguay's (1973), Chile's (1973), or Argentina's (1976), in the past three decades, explicit attempts to overthrow democratic governments by force have been frowned upon. Since the late 1980s, the European Union, Western regional organizations, and the United States (except 2017–21)[9] have valued democracy in and of itself. These actors have been, for the most part,[10] committed to defending democratic regimes regardless of the government's ideology (Schenoni and Mainwaring 2019).

For example, in 2009, when the army arrested and exiled Honduras's democratically elected president, Manuel Zelaya, clearly violating democratic rules, the OAS suspended Honduras, most nations withdrew their ambassadors from the country, and the European Union, the United States, and the World Bank suspended all economic assistance, causing the Honduran economy to collapse (Ruhl 2010). The fact that the army had taken a sitting president into custody and sent him to a different country was an unambiguous attack against democracy. In line with Arceneaux's and Pion-Berlin's (2007) argument, this lack of ambiguity made it easy for NGOs, transnational organizations, and foreign governments to build enough consensus to push for sanctions against the coup plotters.

Domestic actors have developed a similar distaste for authoritarianism since the third wave of democracy. Whereas in the mid-twentieth century, political elites and important segments of the population accepted coups under some circumstances, by the 1980s that was no longer the case. Despite distrust for some democratic institutions, Latin Americans have – at least in principle (Carlin and Singer 2011) – since preferred democracy over other types of government (Lagos 2001): 79 percent believe that there is no reason to close or govern without congress, and 81 percent believe the same about the courts (LAPOP 2004–14). A good example of this shift can be seen in the attempted coup in Paraguay in 1997. When General Lino César Oviedo threatened to overthrow Juan Carlos Wasmosy's government (1993–7), thousands of Paraguayans took to the streets to oppose the military insubordination. Their pressure to protect democracy, as well as international pressure, forced Oviedo to resign and allowed Wasmosy to stay in office (Valenzuela 1997). Given this climate, executives who wish to diminish the checks on the executive and

---

[9] The rise of Donald Trump (2017–21) to the presidency (temporarily) changed that. Not only did he openly endorse leaders with dubious democratic credentials such as Vladimir Putin and Rodrigo Duterte (Philippines, 2016–present) (*The Economist* 2017) but also his administration cut back the United States's role in democracy promotion efforts (Rogin 2017; Hill 2018).

[10] Although countries in the West certainly increased their normative preference for democracy, this preference has not always trumped their economic and strategic interests. There are regions in the world in which, although they publicly condemn the authoritarian practices of a country, they are unwilling to sever their alliances, or cut the economic support that helps these leaders.

extend their stay in office in order to achieve their policy goals have more often chosen to do so incrementally via institutional reforms (Bermeo 2016).

The shift from sudden breakdown to gradual erosion is exemplified by Daniel Ortega (2007–present) in Nicaragua. In the past, Ortega showed complete disregard for democratic institutions. After overthrowing Somoza's dictatorship using guerrilla warfare, he built an overtly Marxist authoritarian regime. Today, Ortega still has very little regard for democracy, but rather than dismantling democratic institutions by force, he resorted to constitutional amendments. Before he was reelected, he signed a pact in 2000 with the former president, Arnoldo Alemán (1997–2002), that allowed him to pack the Supreme Electoral Council (CES) and paved the way for his electoral victory in 2006 (Ortega Hegg 2007). Once in office, the president introduced a series of constitutional amendments that increased his control over congress, courts, and oversight agencies, permitting him to stay in power and rule at will (Pérez-Baltodano 2010). Individually, none of these reforms represented a blatant attack against democracy; none of them crossed an obvious threshold. This made it hard to mobilize people against the authoritarian changes inside the country, and difficult for NGOs, foreign governments, and transnational organizations to build the consensus required to push for sanctions against the regime.

In contrast, more recent openly antidemocratic behavior has generated widespread disapproval. In 2018, Ortega violently suppressed social protests. In response, the country saw massive mobilizations against him.[11] These were widely endorsed by other countries in the region, which mobilized to demand free and fair elections in light of the government's nonstop violent repression.[12] This time, the line between prodemocratic action and outright "sovereignty violation" was clear. Ortega could not credibly frame foreign interventions as a dangerous illegitimate interference in domestic politics to shift the blame to foreign powers (Schlipphak and Treib 2017) or rally the public in his favor.

Several scholars have studied the processes that lead to the breakdown of democracy. Economic and security crises, semi-loyal and disloyal oppositions, loss of efficacy, effectiveness, and legitimacy (Linz 1978) as well as intricate interactions between government and opposition elites (Capoccia 2007a; Mainwaring and Pérez-Liñán 2013) have preceded the rise of antidemocratic leaders in the past and still do today. Sudden democratic breakdowns and erosions of democracy are similar in that respect. Where they differ is on the aftermath. In sudden breakdowns, once the authoritarian civilian or military leader comes to power, it is too late to save democracy. She immediately dismisses the constitution, closes or fully occupies congress and the courts,

---

[11] Ones that the state repressed even further killing more than 200, according to the Inter-American Commission of Human Rights (2018).

[12] OAS Permanent Council Resolution 1108 (2172/18), *La situación en Nicaragua*, CP/RES. 1108 (2172/18), July 18, 2018.

and persecutes opposition members. In democratic erosions, on the contrary, institutions remain available for the opposition even after a leader with hegemonic aspirations has been elected to office. These executives slowly modify courts and congress without immediately co-opting them or shutting them down. While institutional availability decreases with each power grab, it takes years before the incumbent can successfully skew the electoral playing field to such an extent that it is impossible to defeat them.

2.2 THE EXECUTIVE AND THE OPPOSITION

Defining the erosion of democracy as a type of regime breakdown that happens over time highlights the importance of the role of the opposition. Because they happen over time, unlike sudden breakdowns, democratic erosions provide the opposition an opportunity to respond. Even after the authoritarian leader is in office, the opposition still has some institutional (e.g., significant presence in congress, courts, and/or oversight agencies) and noninstitutional resources (e.g., control over media outlets and ability to mobilize) it can use against the incumbent. How the opposition uses these resources is an important factor in understanding the erosion or survival of democracy. Hegemonic executives' ability to successfully introduce institutional reforms to dismantle checks and balances and stay in power can be shaped not only by their degree of civilian and/or military support but also by the opposition's response to their initial attempts to erode democracy.

2.2.1 The Executive

I assume that executives and opposition leaders are office seekers with policy interests: They wish to attain office in order to pursue policy goals. Potential autocrats lack a normative preference for democracy: They are willing to undermine democratic institutions in order to achieve their preferred policies. Furthermore, these incumbents often come to power against seated elites and in contexts of crisis (i.e., low governance, low economic development, or violence) in which they face very weak governmental arrangements that offer leverage for disruption (Skowronek 1993, 1–33). Not only are they *willing* to introduce antidemocratic reforms in order to attain policy goals, but they also come to power in a context that *empowers* them to do so.

For these early antidemocratic reforms to have a greater chance to succeed, it is important for executives with hegemonic aspirations to have military or organized civilian support. High-ranking officers willing to go beyond their stipulated duty and/or civilian leaders willing and able to mobilize large groups of people can help insulate these executives from forced removals and strengthen their position vis-à-vis the opposition. They can also help pressure members of congress or mobilize people to vote in favor of the reforms.

Executives who lack civilian or military support will be less likely to try to reform the constitution or more likely to fail if they try to do so.

In Honduras, for instance, when Manuel Zelaya (2006–9) tried to push an illegal referendum that would increase his powers and allow him to extend his time in office, the army deposed him. Unlike what happened in Venezuela or Turkey, where Chávez and Erdogan were able to mobilize their supporters to reverse the 2002 and 2016 coups, in Honduras, Zelaya was unable to deploy people to turn around the putsch. Because he did not have organized civilian or military support, Zelaya's attempts to erode democracy backfired. Although democracy in Honduras broke down, it did not erode. The rupture in 2009 was akin to the sudden breakdowns in Chile (1973) or Brazil (1964), not the democratic backsliding that happened in Venezuela, Hungary, or Bolivia in the 2000s.

Executives with hegemonic aspirations who have civilian or military support can use different strategies to reduce the checks on their office and stay in power. Initially, they could close congress. However, as mentioned earlier, sanctions and rewards from domestic and international audiences increase the incentives to keep a democratic façade. Potential autocrats would rather avoid major blows to democratic institutions that could trigger a negative response. They prefer to introduce institutional reforms sequentially either via congress using constitutionally sanctioned procedures or via elections and the courts, using extraconstitutional procedures.[13]

The initial reforms might hinder horizontal accountability, but they are not serious or extensive enough to thwart electoral accountability as well. They might decrease some of the checks on the executives and allow them to extend their time in office but will likely fail to politicize state institutions or provide budgetary powers large enough that they would seriously unbalance the playing field.[14]

In Argentina, Carlos Menem (1989–99) tried to undermine democracy. During his government, he introduced constitutional amendments that allowed him to stack the Supreme Court with loyalists and run for a second term. Despite the fact that these reforms left the president somewhat unchecked, turning Argentina into a "delegative democracy" (O'Donnell 1994), they did not skew the electoral playing field. Menem had a strong coalition in congress, controlled the Supreme Court, and was able to run for a second term, but he was not able to deploy state institutions, uneven media, or resource access to such an extent that the elections would be unfair. In fact, during the 1990s, "the fairness of elections was unquestioned, basic civil and political rights were

---

[13] Unwritten procedures. They are not illegal (as in prohibited by the law), but they are not contemplated by the law either.

[14] Levitsky and Way code a playing field as uneven if (1) state institutions are widely politicized and deployed by the incumbent, (2) there is uneven media access, or (3) there is uneven resource access (Levitsky and Way 2010, 368).

broadly and consistently protected, and press freedom was extensive" (Levitsky 2000, 58). Moreover, Fernando de la Rúa, who opposed Menem's candidacy, won the presidential elections in 1999.

Later reforms introduced by these hyper-ambitious leaders, however, pose more serious threats to democracy. Building on previous changes, they enhance the executive's ability to enlarge her majority in congress, fully undermine courts and congress, engage in extensive court packing, and further extend her tenure in office, all while crowding the opposition out. Consequently, these reforms allow the potential autocrat to politicize and deploy state institutions that deal with electoral rules and media access and give her extensive budgetary powers. Provided the incumbent keeps her civilian and/or military support, if these reforms pass, she will not only be able to run for a third (or more) term but also – in an unfair election – will very likely win.

Like Menem, between 1999 and 2004, Venezuelan president, Hugo Chávez, introduced a series of amendments that increased the powers of the presidency and extended his time in office. Up until 2004, however, the Venezuelan president did not have full control over the parliament, nor had he been able to completely purge state institutions of opposition members. The second set of reforms, approved between 2004 and 2009, changed that. Compounded with previous amendments, these reforms allowed Chávez and, more recently, Nicolás Maduro (2013–present) to control congress, courts, and oversight agencies; curtail the independence of the press; gerrymander electoral districts; and run for indefinite reelections. The national elections in 2005 and 2006 were for the most part free and fair (European Union Election Observation Mission 2006); those in 2008 onwards were not. In these contests, the government has used state institutions to harass opposition candidates, state-owned petroleum company revenues to buy support, and state-owned media outlets to advertise government candidates while preventing opposition candidates from doing the same (Corrales 2015; Alarcón, Álvarez, and Hidalgo 2016).

2.2.2 The Opposition

The opposition, composed of office seekers with policy interests as well, wants to stop the potential autocrat's reforms. It can have radical or moderate goals. Radical goals embody a fundamental challenge to the existing political structure, while moderate goals call only for "piecemeal" reform (McAdam 1999, 57). In the case of democratic erosions, oppositions are fighting executives who, despite their hegemonic aspirations, were democratically elected and have not yet finished their constitutional term. In this context, I conceive of radical goals as those that aim to oust the incumbent. Akin to the disloyal goals outlined by Juan Linz, they seek to deny legitimacy to participants in the political process who "have the right to rule thanks to the support they received from the electorate" (1978, 30), while they still enjoy democratic legitimacy. Moderate goals are those that seek to thwart the executive's project, fighting against

TABLE 2.1. *Strategies and goals*

		Goals	
		Moderate	Radical
Strategies	Institutional	Electioneering Legislating Lobbying Litigation	Recall Referendum Presidential Impeachment
	Extrainstitutional		Coups Guerrilla Warfare
		Protests, Boycotts, Strikes	

specific reforms, but not delegitimize her presidency or prevent her from completing her term.

In order to achieve these goals, the opposition can use different strategies. Because erosion happens over time, even after the executive introduces the first set of amendments, the opposition has institutional options left. Consequently, it can resort to either institutional or extrainstitutional strategies to oppose the government. The former relies on conventional political channels: courts, congress, or elections (Stephan and Chenoweth 2008). The latter eschews these institutional channels and fights the government outside courts, congress, or elections using legal or illegal, violent or nonviolent repertoires of contention such as protests, coups, guerrilla warfare, boycotts, or strikes (Table 2.1) (McAdam and Tarrow 2000).[15]

To be sure, the opposition is rarely a unified actor. Different factions can use different strategies and have different goals. However, not all opposition groups are equally visible. Some opposition factions have more legitimacy among their followers than others. These factions represent a more credible threat to the government than more peripheral and less popular opposition groups.

During the transition to democracy from Francisco Franco's dictatorship in Spain, for instance, the opposition was divided into two groups: a moderate partisan opposition willing to use institutional strategies (*Partido Socialista Obrero Español – PSOE*), and a radical opposition – the armed wing of the Basque separatist movement (*Euskadi Ta Askatasuna – ETA*) – willing to use violence against the government. Although ETA represented a threat to the incumbents, the group's ideas and methods were unpopular even among those who opposed Franco. It was very unlikely that the armed group would govern once Spain became democratic. The Franquistas were willing to transition to

---

[15] Institutional strategies, by definition, are always nonviolent and (borderline) legal.

democracy despite ETA's existence because they were confident that the opposition group that could eventually attain power and effectively influence government was PSOE, which would implement more moderate policies and respect the agreements signed during the transition (Bermeo 1997).

Similarly, in cases of democratic erosion, opposition factions vary in how much they threaten the incumbent. In Bolivia, the radical extrainstitutional tactics of the governors in the lowlands against Evo Morales (2006–19) eventually carried more weight than the moderate institutional strategies of the opposition senators in the capital. Had Evo Morales lost power, it would have been this more radical group that would have likely led the government. Similarly, in Colombia, the legal partisan opposition was a more credible representative of the "anti-Uribistas" than the guerrilla groups in the countryside. Had Uribe stepped down, the guerrilla would have had a minimal influence over the government. As long as these groups are distinct from each other, executives with hegemonic aspirations will tend to react to the ones that present a more credible threat.

2.3 STRATEGIES AND GOALS

Potential autocrats have legitimacy constraints. They want to keep a democratic façade. Openly authoritarian practices not only risk an adverse response from the international community but could also generate rejection within these leaders' constituencies and endanger their support (Kuntz and Thompson 2009). In Serbia, for instance, in 1998, the authoritarian leader Slobodan Miloševic introduced a series of laws that severely curtailed civil rights and liberties as well as the independence of local governments and launched a series of violent attacks against opponents and "weak supporters." The legislation, the attacks, and the increasing evidence that Milosevic had stolen the 1998 elections undercut the Serbian president's support. These actions violated accepted constitutional and political practices, which alienated citizens as well as members of security forces, who felt uneasy with what they were asked to do (Bunce and Wolchik 2011, 97–100).

Because they are restricted by these legitimacy constraints, executives' ability to remove opposition leaders from office, prosecute or jail them and/or push for more aggressive antidemocratic reforms is constrained by the nature of the opposition's challenge: the goals they have and the strategy they choose to achieve them. Strategies and goals deemed as unwarranted in democratic politics increase the incentives and decrease the costs of repression and large-scale institutional reform (Gartner and Regan 1996; Cleary and Öztürk 2020). To the extent that the government enjoys democratic legitimacy, these tactics allow the head of government to paint the opposition as "radical" and "undemocratic." Not only do they provide the executive with "legitimate" reasons to remove opposition leaders from office and prosecute or jail them but also enable her to rally around the flag to push for more aggressive antidemocratic reforms.

On the contrary, strategies and goals that are considered part of normal democratic politics increase the costs and reduce the incentives of repression and large-scale institutional reform. These tactics and goals protect the opposition's legitimacy, hindering the executive's ability to credibly label it as "undemocratic" or "radical." They limit the executive's capacity to remove opposition members from office, prosecute or jail them *while* maintaining a democratic façade.[16]

Following this logic, strategies that embrace radical goals represent a larger challenge than strategies that espouse moderate goals. Radical goals create a zero-sum game that is more threatening to the ruling elite. They increase the incentives to repress and crowd out the opposition via institutional reform. Strategies that advance moderate goals, on the contrary, seek to change pieces of the executive's project, but do not attempt to block the entire agenda at once or push her out of office before the end of her constitutional term. They are, therefore, less threatening for the ruling elite. Not only do they reduce the stakes of the situation, allowing some space to negotiate, but they also endanger only those groups whose interests are related to the opposition's specific claim (McAdam 1999, 58). Accordingly, moderate goals decrease the incentives to repress or even push for more aggressive antidemocratic reforms.

The opposition to Uribe's 2003 referendum in Colombia exemplifies the outcome of moderate goals. In this case, the opposition boycotted a referendum that would have increased Uribe's powers while reducing that of congress and the courts. Even though the Uribistas disliked the electoral boycott, they did not feel existentially threatened by it. The failed referendum hampered Uribe's security agenda and his ability to have a pocket legislature but did not finish him or his policies. On the contrary, in 2005, the Venezuelan opposition boycotted the congressional elections, in order to delegitimize the sitting government and push Chávez to resign. Unlike their Colombian counterparts, the Venezuelan opposition's boycott posed an existential threat to the government and created a zero-sum situation. Had the opposition succeeded in delegitimizing Chávez, the Venezuelan president would have had to step down.

In addition to goals, the strategies adopted by the opposition influence the executive's costs to repress or implement large-scale antidemocratic reforms. Institutional strategies represent a smaller challenge than extrainstitutional strategies. Tactics that use elections, congress, or the courts "implicitly convey an acceptance of the established, or 'proper,' channels of conflict resolution"

---

[16] It is possible that an executive with hegemonic aspirations represses the opposition even if she does not have "legitimate" reasons to do so. This move, however, is costly and could end with her losing her democratic façade. To what extent that is sufficient deterrent or not, as I explore in Chapter 6, depends largely on the normative preference for democracy and leverage of domestic and international audiences.

(McAdam 1999, 57). They are seen as unambiguously legitimate tactics in democratic politics. They increase not only the costs to repress but also the ability to justify more aggressive antidemocratic reforms. In contrast, extrainstitutional strategies convey a rejection of the established mechanisms for seeking redress. Although oftentimes legitimate tactics in democratic politics, these strategies are more ambiguous and run the risk of turning violent or illegal. They can, therefore, be more easily portrayed by the head of government as unwarranted, decreasing the costs to repress and enhancing her ability to justify more aggressive antidemocratic reforms.

For example, because it was an institutional strategy, even though it sought to oust the president, the recall referendum in Venezuela (2004) took place in relative peace. Recall referendums are a tool available in the Venezuelan constitution. It was hard for Chávez to paint it as an "undemocratic" maneuver. Using repression against the opposition in retaliation would have been seen as unwarranted domestically and abroad. This tactic contrasts with the extrainstitutional strategy involving the national indefinite strike that the opposition used a year earlier. Although strikes are legal, indefinite strikes that seek to oust a democratically elected president are not part of regular democratic politics. It was therefore easier for Chávez to paint the perpetrators as "reactionary" and "undemocratic," and use it as an excuse to purge state institutions and prosecute and jail opponents.

2.3.1 Combining Strategies and Goals

Previous work has grouped opposition tactics by giving priority to either goals (Cleary and Öztürk 2020) or strategies (Gamboa 2017). I propose a more nuanced account of how these work in tandem. I group strategies and goals into three groups according to their impact on the opposition's ability to protect democracy (see Table 2.2). As I outlined in the first chapter, *moderate institutional strategies* are the most likely to help protect democracy from a potential autocrat. Although they have small immediate payoffs, they safeguard the opposition and can slow down the pace of erosion, increasing the costs and

TABLE 2.2. *Strategies and goals with costs and incentives to crowd out the opposition*

		Goals	
		Moderate	Radical
STRATEGIES	Institutional	↓ Incentives ↑ Costs	↑ Incentives ↑ Costs
	Extrainstitutional	↓ Incentives ↓ Costs	↑ Incentives ↓ Costs

decreasing the incentives to repress or introduce more aggressive antidemocratic reforms. In contrast, *radical extrainstitutional strategies* are the least likely to help protect democracy from a potential autocrat. Significant immediate payoffs notwithstanding, they put in danger the opposition's democratic credentials and facilitate more aggressive antidemocratic reforms. These tactics not only decrease the costs of repression while increasing incentives to do so, but they can also be used to justify more aggressive antidemocratic reforms. *Moderate extrainstitutional strategies* and *radical institutional strategies* fall somewhere in between. Depending on the context and the repertories used, they can help or jeopardize the opposition's ability to protect democracy.

2.3.1.1 Moderate Institutional Strategies
Activities such as electioneering, legislation, and litigation have small short-term payoffs but carry little risk. Although the changes they produce are small and incremental (i.e., stopping or delaying individual attempts to erode democracy), this combination of tactics and goals decreases the incentives and increases the costs to crowd out the opposition. It helps protect the opposition's legitimacy domestically and abroad, denying the potential autocrat "legitimate reasons" to remove opposition leaders from office or rally around the flag to push for more aggressive antidemocratic reforms. If these tactics succeed, the opposition will slow the erosion of democracy and increase its chances to keep enough presence in congress, courts, and oversight agencies in order to protect the very institutional resources the government of a potential autocrat is trying to seize. If these tactics fail and the erosion of democracy continues unhindered, they still protect the opposition, whose members survive to fight another day.

During Uribe's government in Colombia, for example, the legal opposition kept its distance from guerrillas and fought the government using mostly institutional strategies with moderate goals. As a result, they never lost the high ground. Accordingly, Uribe's attempts to frame his opponents as dangerous and illegitimate failed. Even though he resorted to illegal wiretapping and evidence-manufacturing, he was never able to defame the opposition and credibly paint them as terrorists. Moreover, the government's tactics eventually became public and cost Uribe some support.

Though some opposition factions may become frustrated with the slow and incremental – sometimes nonlinear – pace of success, institutional strategies with moderate goals can be effective to oppose executives with hegemonic aspirations. Unless completely controlled by the government, elections, courts, and legislatures are competitive arenas. Even if they have few seats, these bodies will often provide spaces for the opposition to supervise, challenge, debilitate, and, in some cases, defeat incumbents (Levitsky and Way 2010, 3–23; Bunce and Wolchik 2011, 20, 35–50).

In democracies, even heads of government with extensive powers are limited on what they can achieve via executive decrees, without breaching their democratic façade. As long as the opposition keeps some presence in the legislature, it has the ability to delay, modify and, under very specific circumstances, even stop government projects. It can also tame and slow down reforms that would debilitate courts and oversight agencies and increasingly uncheck the executive, protecting its ability to use the judiciary or the electoral arena to fight the incumbent's power grabs.

It is often assumed that small oppositions cannot do much in congress. As a minority, they seldom have the numbers they need to pass legislation (Morgenstern, Negri, and Pérez-Liñán 2008). However, recent analyses have shown the importance of legislative procedure and the tools it provides to obstruct the legislative process (Hiroi and Renno 2014; Botero and Gamboa 2021). Obstruction, scholars argue, lengthens the deliberative process, which does not sit well with the government of a potential autocrat. Some legislatures require certain bills to be fully debated by the end of one legislative term. In this case, delays in a bill's transit put the legislation at risk. Longer debates also allow for better public scrutiny and increase the probability that the bill will be modified by friends and foes, thus reducing the benefits the government will accrue from it (Döring 1995; Hiroi and Renno 2014).

Accordingly, even if too small to swiftly sink the executive's reforms, oppositions facing potential autocrats have institutional alternatives left. As long as they keep their seats in the legislature, they can use rules of procedure to lengthen the deliberative process and increase public scrutiny, opening up spaces to modify, and even stop, antidemocratic reforms. Although each act of moderate institutional obstruction is minimal, as long as the incumbent has domestic and international legitimacy concerns, these acts could accumulate to delay undemocratic reforms and protect institutional resources – such as courts and oversight agencies (including electoral authorities) that could protect against aggressive reforms down the road.

Contingent on the tools available, even small opposition coalitions can, therefore, use legislative procedure to slow down the executive's agenda, reduce the scope of some of the bills, and generate procedural mistakes. These strategies can help tone down the potential autocrat's project, increase public scrutiny, and increase the pressure to strike down a given reform, or provide elements that can be used during judicial review to rule against the bill. In doing so, these tactics can help stop or slow down legislative projects that would otherwise allow the incumbent to enhance his powers and extend his stay in office indefinitely. Even if individual bills pass, this type of obstruction can delay the executive's agenda enough to protect state institutions or at least protect some pockets of opposition support within these institutions.

2.3.1.2 *Moderate Extrainstitutional Strategies*

Under certain circumstances, legal and nonviolent, extrainstitutional strategies that pursue moderate goals can be very effective in protecting democracy. These tactics decrease the incentives to repress or advance antidemocratic reforms. Not only can they heighten the visibility of the executive's abuse of power and the opposition's public support, but, during elections, they can also help mobilize voters and pressure electoral authorities to stick to the true result (Bunce and Wolchik 2011, 85–113; Trejo 2014). Outside elections, moderate extrainstitutional strategies can also demonstrate public support for democratic institutions, when the public might otherwise be pressured to favor a popular executive.

In Colombia, the Constitutional Court stood up to Alvaro Uribe. During the time in which it was examining the reform that would have allowed the president to run for a second immediate reelection, the opposition organized campaigns of public support. These demonstrations reassured justices, helping them rule against an extremely popular executive.[17] In contrast, in Venezuela, the Supreme Court failed to stop Hugo Chávez. It reviewed and approved the decree that allowed the potential autocrat to call for a constitutional assembly, as well as the powers this body assumed. Though powerful at the time, the high court lacked the legitimacy to single-handedly oppose the new, very popular, president. Without the opposition rallying to support it, the justices did not have the strength to rule against the government.

These examples illustrate how moderate extrainstitutional tactics can help prevent the erosion of democracy. This combination of strategies and goals, however, also runs the risk of doing more harm than good. Unless they are carefully planned and well organized, moderate extrainstitutional strategies are at danger of turning or tolerating violence (Chenoweth 2020). Civil resistance that fails to eschew violent fringes can still decrease the incentives to remove opposition leaders from key institutions or push for more aggressive antidemocratic reforms, but will likely decrease the costs to do so as well. Extrainstitutional strategies with moderate goals that tolerate even marginal violence are likely to be framed in ways that paint them as undemocratic and unwarranted (Wasow 2020), undermining the opposition's legitimacy domestically and abroad. For instance, after Donald Trump (2017–21) came to power in the United States, white supremacists organized several rallies. In 2017, thousands of people came out to protest one of these rallies in Berkeley. During the demonstration, a small subset of the protesters violently attacked the white supremacists. The act did not increase support for the opposition. On the contrary, several people in the anti-white supremacist demonstration were arrested and, although the protest was mostly peaceful, the attacks allowed Trump's government and its supporters to paint the opposition as generally unlawful and violent.

2.3.1.3 *Radical Institutional Strategies*

Like moderate extrainstitutional strategies, radical institutional strategies can either help or hinder the opposition's ability to protect democracy. On the one

---

[17] Author's interview with Constitutional Court justice, Bogotá, January 20, 2014.

hand, these tactics use established channels of conflict resolution, increasing the cost to repress as well as the ability to justify more aggressive antidemocratic reforms. Information asymmetries notwithstanding,[18] if successful, these tactics have the ability to remove the potential autocrat from power with little or no harm to the opposition's democratic credentials. On the other hand, radical institutional strategies pose an existential threat to the executive and thus increase the incentives to repress or advance more aggressive antidemocratic reforms. In this sense, radical institutional strategies are risky gambles. If they succeed – which is hard when facing a potential autocrat with the ability to mobilize citizens and a nontrivial control of seats in the legislature (Pérez-Liñán 2007, 14–39) – they can halt the erosion of democracy without damaging the opposition's democratic credentials. If they fail, however, they can create a dangerous zero-sum game by increasing the stakes of the situation and escalating the rivalry between government and opposition to a point in which the cornered executive might feel compelled and even justified to push for more aggressive antidemocratic reforms.

In Bolivia, for example, the opposition called for a recall referendum against Evo Morales. Even though the referendum threatened the potential autocrat's rule, it took place in relative peace. Although it failed to remove the president, it did not hinder the opposition's legitimacy, kept its resources intact, and strengthened opposition prefects who had been recalled (Uggla 2009). On the contrary, in 2008, the opposition to the Turkish prime minister Recep Tayyip Erdogan's party overreacted to legislation that sought to lift a headscarf ban by asking the Constitutional Court to outlaw AKP. The court did not close AKP but cut its financial assistance.[19] Facing a grave threat, Erdogan introduced institutional reforms that enhanced his hold over the judiciary.

2.3.1.4 *Radical Extrainstitutional Strategies*

Extrainstitutional strategies with radical goals are the least likely to help protect democracy. They can have immediate payoffs, but they carry high risks. This combination of strategies and goals poses a major challenge to the government. Not only do the tactics convey a rejection of the established mechanisms for redress but, because the objective is to oust the executive, these strategies also create a zero-sum game that unites the government and leaves little space to negotiate.

Consequently, radical extrainstitutional strategies increase the incentives and reduce the costs to repress or advance more aggressive antidemocratic reforms (Gartner and Regan 1996; McAdam 1999, 57–8). When hegemonic presidents make their first attempts to increase their powers and extend their

---

[18] Information asymmetries make it hard to assess whether the impeachment is an appropriate consequence to a given behavior or not (Helmke 2020, 99–102).

[19] "Turkey's court decides not to close AKP, urges unity and compromise." *Hürriyet*, June 30, 2008.

time in office, democracy – even if diminished – is still in place. These leaders still enjoy the democratic legitimacy afforded to them by electoral victories. The use of an extrainstitutional strategy that seeks to oust them before the end of their constitutional term can be seen as unwarranted inside and outside the country, and, thus, decrease the opposition's international and domestic legitimacy, increase the tolerance for repression, and risk whatever institutional and noninstitutional resources the opposition has left.

Radical extrainstitutional strategies are, in this sense, a very dangerous gamble. If the opposition successfully removes the executive using contentious repertories – although it rarely does (Baykan, Gürsoy, and Ostiguy 2021) – it can bring the process of erosion to a halt, but at the cost of breaking democracy altogether, further polarizing society, and/or martyrizing the potential autocrat who can use the public's outrage to stage a comeback. If the opposition fails to remove the executive using extrainstitutional strategies, regardless of whether or not the tactics were violent, this approach will prove costly, as potential autocrats will be ready and able to capitalize on the opposition's "mistakes" using the move to identify possible adversaries inside the government; leveraging the opposition diminished domestic or international democratic credentials to remove opposition leaders from office, prosecute them, and jail them without losing her democratic façade; and using the event to rally around the flag and gather enough support to push for more aggressive antidemocratic reforms that without presence in the legislature, courts, or oversight agencies, the opposition will be ill-equipped to stop.

In Bolivia, for example, regional leaders in the southeast of the country refused to recognize Morales's leadership and used strikes, protests, and government building takeovers to force the president to grant them autonomy and full control over their resources, with the intention of effectively defunding the central government. Morales did not back down and mobilized his supporters. Eventually, gunmen affiliated with the opposition prefects attacked a progovernment protest and killed thirteen people.

The massacre was criticized both domestically and abroad. Moreover, Morales used it as an excuse to deploy the army, impose a state of siege, and arrest the prefect of the region where the massacre had taken place. In the end, this extrainstitutional strategy with radical goals "ended the possibility that the opposition could present itself as the victim in the fight for democracy, and allowed the government to regain control over the political situation" (Uggla 2009, 258). If it had not been for the massacre, the government would have had a harder time taking over the gas-producing regions and removing regional authorities that were an obstacle to Morales's project without sacrificing its democratic façade. Had the opposition used moderate institutional or even moderate extrainstitutional strategies, it could have delayed Morales's process of executive aggrandizement or forced the government to give up some of its democratic legitimacy. Moreover, it could have opened up a new set of opportunities that might have given Bolivia a better chance to avoid an erosion of democracy.

2.3.2 Choosing Strategies and Goals

The rise of executives with hegemonic aspirations represents a very serious threat to democracy. Once a potential autocrat attains office, oppositions are forced to operate in the midst of high levels of uncertainty and chose from a constrained set of alternatives. These difficulties notwithstanding, neither the rise of a potential autocrat nor her initial attempts to undermine democracy, overdetermine the opposition's choice of tactics and goals.

In a democracy, using radical extrainstitutional strategies to oust the executive is costly and risky. If they fail, opposition leaders who oppose outside institutions in order to overthrow the government are likely to end up exiled or jailed. Normally, the opposition would rather fight via elections, congress, or the courts and use legal nonviolent protests, strikes, or boycotts only to oppose individual bills. Polarizing populist incumbents with a clear disregard for democratic institutions, however, increase the opposition's incentives to choose extrainstitutional strategies in order to pressure the executive to leave office before the end of her constitutional term (Corrales 2011; Balderacchi 2017a).

Institutions constrain the set of possible outcomes; they lengthen actors' time horizons and stabilize agents' expectations (North 1990). If the rules of the game are set, political elites know what they are playing for and what to expect if they lose. They can plan accordingly and design long-term strategies. However, if the opposition is facing a potential autocrat, the political battle is over the rules of the game themselves, and everything is up for grabs (Schedler 2013b, 115–17). There is no constraint to the set of possible outcomes. In such an uncertain high stakes situation, the opposition has reason to expect anything and fear for its political survival. Political leaders cannot know what they are fighting for or what will happen if they lose. Consequently, they have shorter time horizons and more incentives to oppose outside of congress, courts, or elections in hopes to remove the executive from office.

Venezuela is a good example of this transformation. For decades, traditional elites in this country competed for power using democratic rules. For forty years, they respected electoral outcomes, and not once did traditional parties try to use extrainstitutional strategies to oust a president before the end of her constitutional term.[20] In 2002, however, civil society organizations, unions, business associations, and media owners launched a coup d'état against the sitting president, Hugo Chávez. The coup was the opposition's response to forty-nine presidential decrees, debated in secret and enacted at the last minute. Opposition leaders often claim the coup was the product of the anxiety in

---

[20] In 1962, the Venezuelan Communist Party (PCV) and the Revolutionary Left Movement (MIR), in alliance with the guerrilla group *Fuerzas Armadas de Liberación Nacional*, launched two failed coups against Rómulo Betancur's government, and in 1992, Chávez led a coup against Carlos Andrés Pérez. However, none of these groups/individuals were part the traditional elite.

response to these decrees, as well as the uncertainty about what Chávez could do afterward (Nelson 2009).

Having said that, neither this uncertainty nor the initial power grabs potential autocrats engage in are sufficient to produce a radical extrainstitutional response. Oppositions have incentives to avoid radical extrainstitutional strategies and, at first, many do (Cleary and Öztürk 2020). Actors have regime as well as policy preferences (Mainwaring and Pérez-Liñán 2013). Oppositions with a high normative preference for democracy will be unlikely to try to unseat a democratically elected head of government from the streets, even if she shows disregard for democracy. Actors also weigh their tactics and objectives based on perceived cost and probability of success (Cunningham 2013). Even if they face a very aggressive potential autocrat, oppositions can avoid radical extrainstitutional strategies if they perceive these to be costly and unlikely to succeed.

To the extent that potential autocrats are democratically elected, oppositions also have the ability to choose tactics and goals. Unless the hegemonic executive engages in sudden democratic breakdowns like self-coups, the opposition starts with a diminished but non-insignificant set of institutional and noninstitutional resources it can resort to. Although these are bound to narrow if and when democracy erodes, in the early stages the opposition has the ability to pursue a variety of strategies and goals. For example, despite Viktor Orbán's (2010–present) increasing, aggressive, and successful attempts to erode democracy, the Hungarian opposition has not resorted to radical extrainstitutional strategies. While the speed of erosion in the country made institutional strategies short-lived and the opposition has been increasingly forced to use contentious tactics to fight the incumbent, mobilization in the country has been used to protest reforms that increase the executive's hold over state institutions or hinder freedom of expression, not to remove Orbán or his party from power. Similarly, having access to significant institutional resources did not define opposition strategies in Bolivia. Notwithstanding control of the Senate, a faction of those opposing Morales chose to fight the incumbent using extrainstitutional strategies instead.

This does not mean that opposition strategic choices and goals are entirely independent from other factors. Who leads the opposition, what kind of experience they have opposing sitting executives, the type and perception of their resources, and how much they stand to lose can influence the type of strategies and goals oppositions use against the would-be autocrats. Oppositions composed of politicians who know how to work with institutions might be more inclined to choose institutional strategies over extrainstitutional strategies than oppositions led by social movements or civil society leaders. Similarly, oppositions composed by groups used to having a significant number of seats in congress and sitting heads of government might be more likely to have radical goals than oppositions who are used to being the minority in congress and have never been able to elect an executive. The latter may value institutional resources regardless of policy gains, and thus might be less prone to sacrifice them trying to oust the incumbent in hopes of quickly regaining power.

The extent to which a potential autocrat threatens an elite's privileges might also affect the opposition's calculus (Levitsky and Loxton 2013). Notwithstanding being dangerous for democracy, leaders like Uribe and Orbán are not threatening the very existence of an established social, religious, or economic elite. Their agendas target sectors of the population that are already vulnerable. It might be, therefore, easier for opposition groups in these countries to hold moderate goals. The opposite could be true for leaders like Chávez, or Erdogan, whose agendas threatened the privileges that buttressed established elites, creating a sense of urgency that could have led these groups to feel they had to oust the executive before the end of his constitutional term.

The resources and the perception of resources available could shape oppositions' choice of goals and strategies as well. The theory outlined in this chapter assumes that the opposition has resources to fight back. The type and quality of these resources, however, vary from case to case and over time. Oppositions operating in parliamentary systems, for example, might face more constraints using legislative resources than oppositions operating in presidential systems where there is a chance of divided government (Nalepa, Vanberg, and Chiopris 2018). In Turkey, for example, the opposition started off relying heavily in the judiciary to control Erdogan. In Bolivia, in contrast, the less radical faction of the opposition relied heavily on the Senate. Similarly, oppositions in weak institutional contexts (i.e., where institutions can be easily changed or ignored), for example, might favor extrainstitutional strategies over institutional ones. By the time Fidesz and PiS came to power, Hungary and Poland were consolidated democracies with strong ties to the West. The institutional resources available to oppositions in these countries were fairly strong. On the contrary, when Daniel Ortega regained power in 2007, Nicaragua was still a developing democracy with a convoluted history of underdevelopment, corruption, and violence. The institutional resources available to the opposition in the Central American country were fairly weak. This difference in institutional strength could have curtailed Nicaragua's opposition's ability to choose moderate or radical institutional strategies vis-à-vis moderate or radical extrainstitutional strategies. Similarly, by the time Hugo Chávez came to power – even after the 1999 constitution – the opposition had access to congress, courts, and oversight agencies. Four years later, successful incumbent power grabs had changed that. The set of strategies (though, not goals) available in 2002 were therefore different from the set of strategies available in 2004.

The perception of resources available also matters when selecting a strategy. Lack of perceived institutional strength might increase the likelihood of choosing extrainstitutional strategies, regardless of the ability to use them. In 2002, the Venezuelan opposition had almost half of the seats in congress, enough power to legislate or veto legislation. Yet the perception was that they did not have enough institutional resources to fight Chávez's power grabs. Led by social movements and civil society leaders, the opposition chose mostly extra-institutional strategies instead.

Regardless of why some oppositions decide to use some strategies and goals and not others, the fact remains that, notwithstanding some constraints, in most cases of democratic erosion, elites fighting the potential autocrat have an opportunity to choose tactics and goals. As I show below, the Venezuelan opposition could have chosen to fight Chávez using moderate institutional or moderate extrainstitutional strategies. The same is true for oppositions in Bolivia and Turkey. Similarly, the opposition in Colombia had the option to fight Uribe using radical extrainstitutional strategies. The same is true for oppositions in Hungary and Poland.

2.4 SCOPE CONDITIONS

The theory outlined earlier is contingent on five factors. First, my universe of cases is composed of democracies. Once a country is authoritarian (competitive or not), a different logic applies. For instance, in 2017, the Venezuelan opposition led a series of protests demanding Nicolás Maduro's resignation. Such a move did not hurt its legitimacy. Maduro came to power after Venezuela had become a competitive authoritarian regime. Since then, he has deepened authoritarianism in the country. Maduro is not a democratic or democratically elected president. The opposition's use of street protests to remove him is, therefore, deemed inside and outside the country as an appropriate measure to fight the dictatorship.

The second factor is the existence of a potential autocrat. The use of extra-institutional strategies, such as demonstrations, strikes, or boycotts, to remove the incumbent before the end of her constitutional term is not exclusive to democracies at risk of erosion. Executives that are not looking to enhance their powers or extend their time in office might face oppositions that use these tactics. In such cases, these strategies will delegitimize the opposition as well. However, because the head of government is not looking to "crowd out" those who oppose her, she will not take advantage of the opposition's behavior to enhance her powers.

Between 2002 and 2005 in Bolivia, for instance, a series of protests triggered by the construction of a gas pipeline proposed by President Sánchez de Losada quickly turned into a protest that called for the president's and vice president's resignation. Although the opposition used extrainstitutional strategies to oust the executive, neither Sánchez de Losada nor his vice president, Carlos Mesa, were ready, willing, or able, to capitalize on the opposition's strategic choice in order to enlarge their powers. Similarly, Alvaro Uribe staged a series of protests to undermine Juan Manuel Santos's (2010–18) presidency. The protesters overtly called on the Colombian president to resign. Santos, however, did not have hegemonic aspirations. He had no interest in capitalizing on these protests in order to enhance his hold over state institutions or extend his time in office.

Consequently, although the Uribista opposition lost some legitimacy, it was not crowded out.

Third, as mentioned earlier, to be successful in eroding democracy, a potential autocrat needs to have civilian and/or military support. As shown by the Honduran coup referenced earlier, without high-ranking officers and/or civilian leaders willing and able to mobilize large groups of people in support of the incumbent, the executive will be more vulnerable to forced removals. In this case, radical extrainstitutional strategies might work to the opposition's advantage and force the potential autocrat to step down.

The fourth factor is time. If democracy breaks down in a quick manner, the opposition has little opportunity to fight back. As mentioned earlier, in classic democratic breakdowns like Chile's in 1973 or Egypt's in 2013, the opposition was quickly deprived of institutional or extrainstitutional resources to fight back. Although not equally extreme, the same could be said for the breakdown of democracy in Perú, where, in 1992, Alberto Fujimori (1990–2000) decided to close congress and the courts, immediately depriving the opposition of any resource it might have left. Although cases like Peru are usually thought of as democratic erosions – it took Fujimori two years to gain full control over state institutions and undermine free and fair elections – they stand apart from cases like Venezuela, Bolivia, or Turkey, where the erosion of democracy took six, four, and ten years, respectively.

The last scope condition is the existence of domestic and/or international audiences with leverage and a normative preference for democracy. When these are absent, executives with hegemonic aspirations have more leverage to overtly threaten democratic institutions. In other words, if an executive does not fear domestic or international sanctions for implementing clearly antidemocratic practices, she does not need to keep a democratic façade. In that scenario, she does not need to wait for the opposition to use radical extrainstitutional strategies in order to crack down and advance antidemocratic reforms.

Russia is a good example of that. This country, where Vladimir Putin (2000–present) eroded democracy, is relatively independent from both the European Union and the United States (Levitsky and Way 2010, 186–201; Stoner-Weiss 2010) and has a population that overwhelmingly believes in a weaker version of democracy (i.e., it is all right for the leader to have a "strong hand" as long as he is popularly elected) (Hale 2011). Accordingly, unlike most hegemonic leaders in Latin America, Vladimir Putin was able to erode democracy more steadily. He did not need the opposition to give him "legitimate" reasons to remove its leaders from office, prosecute, or jail them because he faced international and domestic communities that were less likely to push back when he did.

2.5 CONCLUSION

The theory described in this chapter highlights the role of the opposition as central to the erosion of democracy. Because the erosion of democracy is a process, the opposition has ample opportunities to respond. It has institutional and noninstitutional resources, even after a potential autocrat has attained power, and can use these resources to prevent her from turning a democracy into a competitive authoritarian regime. How the opposition uses these resources, and what it uses them for, is critical to understand why some executives with hegemonic aspirations successfully erode democracy and others do not.

Both potential autocrats and those who oppose them are office seekers with policy interests. Potential autocrats want to enhance their powers and extend their time in office to push their policy agenda. To do so, they could close congress and the courts. But because they want to keep a democratic façade, they use constitutional amendments instead.

The opposition wants to oppose the executive's reforms. To do so, they could use institutional or extrainstitutional strategies with radical or moderate goals. Moderate institutional strategies are best suited to protect democracy. Although they have small immediate payoffs, these tactics help maintain the legitimacy of the opposition domestically and abroad. They increase the costs to repress and decrease the incentives to pursue aggressive antidemocratic reforms, making it harder for the government to crowd out the opposition and protecting the very institutions the potential autocrat is trying to seize. Although, as we will see in Chapter 6, these strategies are not airtight; at the very least, they buy the opposition time. They open up the set of possible outcomes, increasing the likelihood of preventing the erosion of democracy.

In contrast, extrainstitutional strategies with radical goals are the least helpful to protect democracy. Although they can have larger immediate payoffs, these tactics can threaten the opposition's legitimacy domestically and abroad. This approach decreases the costs of repression and increases the incentives to crowd out the opposition, jeopardizing the institutional resources the government is trying to seize. In other words, while the potential autocrat might try to undermine democracy regardless of the opposition's behavior, these tactics make it more attractive, easy, and virtually costless.

Even if weak, oppositions facing a process of democratic erosion haven an opportunity to protect democracy. As Chapters 4 and 5 will show, the ability to use these strategies is not completely determined by the overall distribution of power between government and opposition. In fact, the opposition in Colombia was relatively weak. Despite having few institutional and noninstitutional resources, however, it was able to prevent a popular president like Alvaro Uribe from eroding democracy using institutional strategies and nonviolent legal extrainstitutional strategies with moderate goals. On the contrary, the opposition in Venezuela was fairly strong. Although it had a very good set of institutional and noninstitutional resources, it was not able to prevent the erosion of democracy. It opted for extrainstitutional strategies in hopes of ousting Hugo Chávez before the end of his constitutional term and lost the institutional resources it sought to protect.

For this theory to work, however, the erosion of democracy needs to happen over time with domestic and international audiences with leverage and a normative preference for democracy. As I will show in Chapter 6, the absence of domestic and international audiences with a normative preference for democracy limits the executive's incentives to keep a democratic façade. It decreases the costs of cracking down on the opposition or pushing antidemocratic reforms, allowing the executive to undermine democratic institutions regardless of whether the opposition "legitimizes" such behavior or not.

3

Electing Leaders with Hegemonic Aspirations

This chapter focuses on the first stage of the erosion of democracy. In it, I assess the factors that increase the likelihood of having an executive with hegemonic aspirations and the extent to which these factors explain whether this head of government successfully erodes democracy or not.

Following existing theories of democratic backsliding, I focus on four variables commonly known to increase a country's vulnerability to potential autocrats: low economic development, economic crises, weakly institutionalized party systems, and weak states with governance problems. Using an updated (2019) version of Mainwaring and Pérez-Liñán's (2013) regime and policy preferences dataset alongside an original database of constitutional amendments introduced by all democratically elected presidents in Latin America between 1978 and 2016, I evaluate the effect of these factors both on the likelihood of having a president with hegemonic aspirations and the likelihood that she successfully erodes democracy. Descriptive and analytic quantitative analyses show that, although there is some relationship between these variables and electing a potential autocrat, this correlation wanes when we assess their effect on democratic erosion. In other words, while helpful to explain why some countries see the rise of would-be autocrats, these factors are less useful in explaining the variation among Latin American leaders who succeed in eroding democracy and those who fail.

In what follows, I provide an overview of structural, state-centered, institutional, and behavioral theories that have been used to explain democratic reversals. I hypothesize that low economic development, economic crises, weak states with governance problems, and inchoate party systems increase the likelihood of electing presidents who try to erode democracy. I also define and operationalize the dependent variable. I conceptualize executives with hegemonic aspirations as heads of state without an intrinsic preference for democracy. Although they pay lip service to democratic governance, they exhibit authoritarian behavior and/or enact policies that seek to enhance their powers and extend their time in office. I follow this definition and operationalization with the description of the data and the analysis. I assess the impact of the central independent variables on the likelihood of electing leaders with hegemonic aspirations, as well as their effect on the probability they successfully erode democracy.

3.1 THE RISE OF PRESIDENTS WITH HEGEMONIC ASPIRATIONS

The rise of a potential autocrat is, and should be, a rare event. Although voters vary on their risk propensity (Morgenstern and Zechmeister 2001; Berinsky and Lewis 2007) and regime preferences (Booth and Seligson 2009, 38–65; Kiewiet de Jonge 2013; Rhodes-Purdy 2017, 31–55), it is reasonable to assume that, in general, most voters are risk averse (Bartels 1986, 198) and have – in the abstract (Carlin and Singer 2011) – a normative preference for democracy. Under normal circumstances, they will likely choose known politicians who have proven to respect democracy, over unknown politicians who might, or might not, respect the country's democratic regime.

Under less "normal circumstances," however, this behavior might not hold. Context affects the weight citizens give to different considerations when casting their vote (Lupu, Oliveros, and Schiumerini 2019, 1–27). Structural, institutional, and state-centered arguments suggest that lower levels of economic development and economic downturns (Przeworski et al. 2000; Maeda 2010; Svolik 2015b), weak institutions (Mainwaring and Scully 1995; Fish 2005, 193–245; Carreras 2012a; Weyland and Madrid 2019a), and weak states with governability problems (Mainwaring 2012a; Diamond 2015a; Handlin 2017a) increase the likelihood of a democratic breakdown. These factors create legitimacy crises that weaken regime arrangements, increasing the likelihood that voters will choose antisystemic mavericks or outsiders who are willing to break horizontal and, eventually, electoral accountability in order to achieve their policy goals.

3.1.1 Economic Development and Growth

Higher levels of economic development decrease the likelihood of democratic breakdowns. Authors like Przeworski et al. (2000, 78–137) and Svolik (2008, 2015b) have found that, in general, democracies are more resilient as the level of economic development increases. Both consolidated and unconsolidated democracies are less likely to experience a democratic breakdown at higher levels of per capita GDP (Svolik 2008, 2015b; Przeworski et al. 2000, 78–137).

The same is true for economic performance. Overall, higher levels of economic growth increase the probability that democracy survives. Recessions, however, have a different effect on consolidated and unconsolidated democracies. The former are likely to outlast economic crises; the latter are not. A drop in GDP growth from 4.5 percent to 0.1 percent increases the risk of a democratic breakdown by 20 percent in transitional democracies but has no effect in consolidated democracies (Svolik 2015b, 725).

The influence of economic factors on regime change is not limited to military or civilian coups. Democracies with lower levels of GDP per capita and economic growth are more likely to erode (Svolik 2015b). Indeed, countries at lower levels of economic development, and in particular those that experience an economic recession, are vulnerable to the erosion of democracy.

Economic performance shapes voting behavior in Latin America (Gélineau and Singer 2015) and elsewhere. Economic downturns lead to legitimacy crises that unsettle democratic institutions (Linz 1978). People who feel negatively toward the economy are less likely to trust politicians, parliaments, or parties (Norris and Inglehart 2019, 143) and more likely to support leaders campaigning on antiestablishment appeals (Norris and Inglehart 2019, 286). Although these grievances need not correlate with the objective state of the economy, economic downturns are likely to enhance these feelings (Singer 2011; Carlin, Love, and Martínez-Gallardo 2015; Zechmeister and Zizumbo-Colunga 2013), increasing the likelihood that a country will have a president with hegemonic aspirations.

During crises, insecure voters are more likely to put regime preferences aside (Levitsky 2000). They will vote for politicians who promise to solve the crisis even if there are signs that might suggest these leaders do not have a strong preference for democracy. Hugo Chávez and Lucio Gutiérrez (Ecuador, 2003–5), for example, were elected, after leading coups d'état against democratically elected governments; Daniel Ortega (Nicaragua, 2007–present) was elected after heading a revolutionary, undemocratic regime between 1979 and 1990; and Alvaro Uribe was elected despite promoting and publicly supporting self-defense armies that were involved in human rights abuses and had strong ties with paramilitary groups (Dugas 2003).

With this in mind, we should expect, first, countries with lower levels of economic development to be more likely to have executives with hegemonic aspirations than countries with higher levels of economic development (Hypothesis 1) and, second, countries with lower levels of economic growth to be more likely to elect executives with hegemonic aspirations than countries with higher levels of economic growth (Hypothesis 2). We should also expect countries in which citizens express negative feelings toward the economy – regardless of its objective state – to be more likely to elect executives with hegemonic aspirations than countries where citizens have a more favorable opinion of the economy (Hypothesis 3).

3.1.2 State Capacity and Governability

A similar argument can be made for state strength. Ineffective states are more likely to undergo legitimacy crises that bring authoritarian leaders to power (Linz 1978, 14–49). Weak states are unable to effectively implement policy goals (Sikkink 1991; Hanson and Sigman 2021). They lack the extractive, coercive, and/or bureaucratic capacity to raise revenue, protect their citizens, and develop their policies. This deficiency hinders their ability to deliver benefits and services to the people (Møller and Skaaning 2011; Savoia and Sen 2015), which hurts the legitimacy of the regime, leading to state crises (Handlin 2017a, 38–44). In democracies, citizens agree on the procedures to build a "government that can make legitimate claims on their obedience" (Linz and Stepan 1996, 27). If a significant group of people does not accept that claim and questions the legitimacy of the state and its institutions, democracy can break (Linz and Stepan 1996, 27).

In other words, democracies in countries with weak states in crisis are less likely to survive (Diamond 2008; Fortin 2011; Mainwaring 2012a; Cornell and Lapuente 2014; Handlin 2017a). Robust democracies exist in tandem with solid states. Building democratic regimes in countries where the state is unable to provide basic services, collect taxes, and/or curb corruption and crime is a daunting task. In these countries, democracy is less likely to fulfill its promise and more likely to lose legitimacy, and thus increase the probability of electing a head of government who is indifferent toward democracy. Even accounting for economic downturns, state crises are key to understanding the rise of presidents like Hugo Chávez in Venezuela, Alberto Fujimori (1990–2000) in Perú (Seawright 2012), or Evo Morales (2006–19) in Bolivia (Pachano 2006; Mayorga 2011; Handlin 2017a).

A government's inability to adequately provide essential goods and services creates a crisis of democratic representation (Mainwaring 2006; Morgan 2011, 49–54). In such crises, voters question the representativeness of elected officials, opening the doors for outsiders and incentivizing politicians to promote anti-systemic radical agendas. Traditional political elites perceived to be hopelessly corrupt and/or unrepresentative of their constituencies will fuel negative emotions among the electorate. Political anger and/or anxiety, in turn, will decrease voters' risk-aversion, increasing the likelihood that citizens will eschew voting habits and choose an unknown politician instead of a more traditional, better known, candidate (Seawright 2012, 5–21).

Outsiders, by themselves, need not be detrimental to democracy. However, in crises of democratic representation, voters not only reject traditional politicians but also the mechanisms of democratic representation themselves (Mainwaring, Bejarano and Pizarro Leóngomez 2006). They are more willing to support leaders with radical agendas regardless of their regime preferences. States in crisis fail to fulfill the promise of democracy. In scenarios of weak government performance and low trust in democratic institutions (i.e., state crises), voters are less likely to care about the regime, and more inclined to support a leader who promises to deliver, even if he has to bend democratic rules to do so. This situation allows antiestablishment politicians to successfully compete outside traditional cleavages (e.g., left–right); pitting themselves against traditional political elites along the antisystemic/systemic cleavage in which they have the comparative advantage of being new or "refurbished" (Carreras 2012a; Mainwaring and Pérez-Liñán 2013; Handlin 2017a, 29; Mainwaring 2018a; Ginsburg and Huq 2019a; Weyland and Madrid 2019a).

With this in mind, we should expect countries with low state capacity to be more likely to have executives with hegemonic aspirations than countries with higher levels of state capacity (Hypothesis 4). In particular, and in line with Handlin's (2017a, 38–44) argument, we should observe countries with lower levels of government performance and trust in institutions (i.e., state crises) to be more likely to elect executives with hegemonic aspirations than countries with higher levels of government performance or trust in institutions (Hypotheses 4a and 4b).

3.1.3 Party System Institutionalization

Institutions shape elites' behavior. They reduce uncertainty and provide incentives to cooperate with democratic rules (North 1990; Przeworski and Maravall 2003). More specifically, institutionalized parties and party systems have important consequences for democratic stability (Bernhard et al. 2015). They structure political competition, make electoral politics more predictable, and legitimize democracy (Mainwaring and Scully 1995; Carreras 2012a; Mainwaring 2018a).

On the contrary, inchoate party systems often fail to structure political competition, to make electoral politics predictable or legitimize democracy. In weakly institutionalized party systems, parties are less likely to control candidate selection, and party affiliation is less likely to structure voting patterns. In these environments, outsiders, mavericks, or amateurs – often personalistic antisystemic candidates who question the legitimacy of democratic institutions – are not only more likely to run for office but also more likely to win (Coppedge 2005; Mainwaring, Bejarano, and Pizarro Leongómez 2006; Morgan 2011; Seawright 2012; Mainwaring 2018a).

In institutionalized party systems, parties are very important vehicles to attain office. They have strong roots in society, and people have strong party attachments that structure how they vote. Party leaders control nominations because they have a hold on resources – such as recognizable labels, logistic, and/or economic support – that are essential for winning elected office (Aldrich 1995). These leaders are reluctant to endorse personalistic antisystemic candidates because they do not know if they will abide by the party rules. On the other hand, in weakly institutionalized party systems, party leaders have less control over nominations because they do not command the resources candidates need to win.[1] These parties often have weak roots in society, fewer people

---

[1] Either the party has a weak label and/or the candidate has access to economic and/or logistic resources outside the organization.

have strong party attachments, and parties fail to structure how they vote (Lupu, Oliveros, and Schiumerini 2019, 1–27). In the absence of strong partisanship, people are more likely to change who they vote for (Greene 2011). As a result, it is easier for personalistic antisystemic candidates to run for office as outsiders, amateurs, or mavericks, and they are more likely to win.

Although not every maverick, outsider, or amateur is a potential autocrat, in Latin America, these are not entirely unrelated. Of approximately sixteen leaders who won the presidency as amateurs, mavericks, or outsiders between 1978 and 2019, eight were presidents with hegemonic aspirations. Of those, five tried to undermine democracy once they became presidents. Accordingly, we should expect countries with lower levels of party system institutionalization to be more likely to have presidents with hegemonic aspirations (Hypothesis 5).

3.2 OPERATIONALIZING PRESIDENTS WITH HEGEMONIC ASPIRATIONS

Following Mainwaring and Pérez-Liñán (2013, 29–33), I assume that political elites have regime and policy preferences. Executives with hegemonic aspirations are office seekers with policy interests and no normative preference for democracy. Although they do not value dictatorship intrinsically, they are reluctant to accept policy sacrifices in order to preserve democracy. In other words, these potential autocrats do not try to erode democracy for the sake of it but are willing to do so it if that advances their policy agenda.

3.2.1 Identifying Executives with Hegemonic Aspirations

In this chapter,[2] I operationalize executives with hegemonic aspirations as democratically elected presidents who show no preference for democracy. In order to qualify as one of these potential autocrats, a head of government must be a democratically elected executive who shows no preference for democracy either before or after she attains office.

3.2.1.1 *Defining the Universe of Cases*
The first two conditions delimit the universe of cases. Leaders need not become heads of government or be democratically elected to show little or no preference for democracy. Actors with little or no preference for democracy who fail to attain power and/or come to office undemocratically are, however, unlikely to expose a country to the erosion of democracy. Although capable of attacking democracy from the sidelines and potentially decreasing its quality, they will likely lack the

---

[2] Based on the definition outlined in the previous paragraph, an executive with hegemonic aspirations can be a president or a prime minister; however, the focus of this chapter is Latin America, and all the governments analyzed here are presidential regimes. Consequently, I narrow my operationalization of the concept to presidents.

power to skew the playing field to such an extent that it becomes impossible to defeat the incumbent. Democracies in which leaders with no normative preference for democracy fail to attain power remain democratic because they were never at risk of eroding. They can increase our understanding of what makes democracy (fail to) thrive but cannot aid our understanding of what helps or hinders the ability of an executive to erode it (Ginsburg and Huq 2018).

Similarly, if a president willing to undermine democracy is not democratically elected – or part of a democratic succession in cases in which the head of government is impeached or resigns before the end of her constitutional term – the regime is no longer democratic. This particular leader can show no preference for democracy before or after she becomes president and deepen levels of authoritarianism, but cannot fuel a gradual transition from democracy to autocracy, and thus cannot erode democracy.

3.2.1.2 *Defining Willingness to Erode Democracy*

The third condition refers specifically to an actor's willingness to erode democracy. Measuring that willingness is complex. Focusing on a leader's expressed support for democracy can be deceiving. Most presidential candidates avoid running on overtly authoritarian platforms, regardless of their regime preferences. They pay lip service to democracy, even if they care little about it. A narrow focus on executives' expressed regime preferences would therefore lead to false negatives. We would be at risk of qualifying some leaders as being unquestioningly supportive of democracy, when in fact they are not.

Focusing more openly on a leader's more tacit support (or lack thereof) for democracy could address this problem. Levitsky and Ziblatt (2018a, 21–4) developed a set of behavioral standards and indicators to identify authoritarian behavior even when a politician appears to praise democracy. According to these scholars, candidates whose comments or behaviors suggest rejection of the democratic rules of the game, denial of legitimacy to opponents, tolerance of violence, or willingness to curtail the civil liberties of those who oppose them, can be qualified as being antidemocratic.

These standards, and the indicators proposed by the authors to assess them (Levitsky and Ziblatt 2018a, 23–4), are conceptually sound but impractical within the scope of this book. Speeches, and mostly media pieces,[3] are likely to contain information to indicate whether or not a leader fits the authors' criteria. Unfortunately, there is no easy way to survey all these documents from 1978 to 2019 across eighteen Latin American countries. Although most media outlets in the region have websites that are easy to search, many of them do not have news archives, and those that do rarely have them going back to 1978.

I address this problem identifying a leader's willingness to erode democracy using their regime preferences instead. According to Mainwaring and Pérez-

---

[3] Official discourses are, for the most part, carefully crafted and devoid of language that could undermine a president's democratic credentials.

Liñán (2013, 80), actors have regime preferences. They have a normative preference for democracy when they prefer a democratic regime intrinsically, regardless of policy outcomes, and a normative preference for dictatorship when they embrace a nondemocratic regime in principle, independent of policy outcomes. While actors who have a normative preference for democracy cannot have a normative preference for dictatorship (or vice versa), the absence of a normative preference for democracy does not mean a normative preference for dictatorship (or vice versa). Executives with hegemonic aspirations fall into that camp. They do not have a normative preference for dictatorship, but they do not have a normative preference for democracy either. Their support for democracy is contingent on policy outcomes. They will endorse democratic institutions when they help them achieve their policy goals and undermine them when they do not.

Identifying executives with hegemonic aspirations using regime preferences rather than the criteria outlined by Levitsky and Ziblatt (2018a, 20–24) balances conceptual and empirical needs. Mainwaring and Pérez-Liñán (2013) infer "absence of a normative preference for democracy" whenever an actor (a) expresses indifference or ambivalence toward democracy, (b) expresses hostility toward democratic institutions, (c) questions the validity of democratic procedures if the results are unfavorable, (d) claims to the be sole representative of the people, (e) questions the legitimacy of or dismisses peaceful opponents as enemies of the people, (f) introduces programs of partisan indoctrination, or (g) once in government, manipulates institutional rules to their advantage. Although slightly less detailed than Levitsky and Ziblatt's, these criteria not only tap into the same underlying concept but also have readily available data to measure the dependent variable: a dataset of the regime and policy preferences of Latin American actors between 1945 and 2010, as well as the information used to code them.[4]

3.2.1.3 Measuring Willingness to Erode Democracy

I assume that presidents come to office with a set of regime and policy preferences.[5] If a leader has a strong preference for democracy, she will not try to undermine democratic institutions when these obstruct her policy agenda. The fact that she does suggests she did not have a strong preference for democracy to begin with.

Ideally, we should observe this a priori lack of a normative preference for democracy both before and after a leader becomes head of government. In practice, however, that kind of consistency is hard to observe, and an exclusive focus on an executive's preference for democracy before or after she attains

---

[4] For Mainwaring and Pérez-Liñán's (2013) online appendix, see http://kellogg.nd.edu/democra cies-materials.shtml.

[5] Some scholars disagree with this assumption. Sahar Abi-Hassan (2019b), for example, argues that Chávez's radicalization was the outcome of the opposition's uncompromising attitude.

office could lead to false negatives. As mentioned earlier, politicians running for office in free and fair elections have strong incentives to maintain a democratic façade. They will likely avoid slippages that could potentially hinder their ability to present themselves as democratic candidates until they win the election. Focusing exclusively on their behavior and/or interventions before they attain office could lead us to wrongly classify a given leader as having a strong preference for democracy when in fact she does not. For example, when campaigning, Juan Manuel Zelaya (Honduras, 2006–9) toed the party line, giving little indication that he lacked a normative preference for democracy.[6] Classifying him as nonhegemonic would have been, however, wrong. Once in office, Zelaya tried to undermine democratic institutions in order to achieve a set of policy outcomes. He introduced a referendum to change the constitution in order to decrease the checks on the executive and extend his time in office.

The opposite mistake can happen as well. The behavior of some leaders, once they become president, might suggest a strong preference for democracy, not because they are unwilling to undermine democracy in order to achieve policy goals but because circumstances prevent them from attempting to hinder democratic institutions in order to achieve their desired outcomes. For example, Ollanta Humala (2011–16) came to power in Perú with dubious democratic credentials (Levitsky 2011). During his 2006 presidential bid, he aligned himself with known potential autocrats like Hugo Chávez, threatened to repudiate elections and destabilize the government if one of his opponents won the election, and – following the rule book of other potential autocrats in the region – called for a constitutional assembly (McClintock 2006; Carlos de la Torre 2017). Although his 2011 campaign was more moderate, by the time he became president, it was unclear whether he was going to govern democratically or not (Tanaka 2011). Once in office, these doubts disappeared. The available evidence suggests that, as president, Humala had a strong, if inconsistent, preference for democracy. It is possible, but unlikely, that the Peruvian president changed his regime preferences once he attained the presidency. It is more likely, however, that the conditions of his government hindered his ability to undermine democratic institutions. Coding him based only on his government behavior, we would wrongly classify him as a nonhegemonic, when chances are, he was.

In order to avoid these problems, I evaluate whether a president qualifies as a president with hegemonic aspirations or not based on their observed regime preferences before *or* after they become presidents. This choice is admittedly imperfect. While it reduces the likelihood of having false negatives, it increases the probability of classifying a president as hegemonic when in fact she was not. In practice, however, that risk is relatively low. Sixteen (64 percent) of the

---

[6] Mainwaring and Pérez Liñán code the Liberal Party as having a strong normative preference for democracy since 1994.

twenty-five presidents identified as having hegemonic aspirations in this book show lack of a preference for democracy both before and after they attain office. Of the remaining nine, one showed lack of a preference for democracy before he attained office but an inconsistent preference for democracy after he became president. The other eight showed absence of a preference for democracy once they attained power but showed inconsistent or even strong support for democracy (0.5 or 1) before they became presidents. The different scores are in Table 3.1.

3.3 DATA AND METHODS

To assess the hypotheses outlined earlier, I built a dataset with information about democratically elected Latin American presidents between 1978 and 2019.[7] The unit of analysis is country-president.[8] The dependent variable assesses whether these presidents show absence of a normative preference for democracy or not. I constructed this variable using Mainwaring and Pérez-Liñán's (2013) dataset in conjunction with original data collected using expert surveys and primary and secondary sources. The independent variables measure levels of economic development, economic growth, state capacity, and party system institutionalization. They also measure the percentage of fuel exports, ethnic fractionalization, authoritarian legacies, and age of democracy that these countries had on each president's election year. I built these variables using information from the World Bank, Hanson and Sigman (2021), Mainwaring (2018b), Carreras (2012a), Latinobarometer (1995–2018), and V-Dem (2021).

3.3.1 Dependent Variable

As previously mentioned, the database for the dependent variable includes eighteen Latin American countries.[9] All the countries in the sample enter as democracies either in 1978 or after their transition to democracy with their first democratically elected president. Altogether, the sample has 134 presidents, divided into clusters of seven presidents in average. I constructed the dependent variable with a combination of existing and new data. I measured preferences

---

[7] I exclude President Alberto Fernández (Argentina, 2019–present) from the analysis because his government starts on December 2019, and most data is only available up until 2019.

[8] In this chapter, I analyze the factors that bring presidents with hegemonic aspirations to power, not the ones that allow them to stay in office after their first term. Accordingly, I count presidents who ran for one or more immediate terms as a single observation, and presidents who ran for two or more nonconsecutive terms as two or more observations.

[9] I exclude Cuba and Haiti from all the analyses. Cuba has been a stable authoritarian regime since before 1978. Haiti has had very short and convoluted democratic periods. Its highest V-Dem electoral democracy index is 0.43, and Freedom House has deemed it an electoral democracy only twice: between 1994–99 and 2006–09.

TABLE 3.1. *Presidents with hegemonic aspirations*

NAME	COUNTRY	PERIOD	OUTSIDER	PREF. DEMOCRACY (DURING TERM)		PREF. DEMOCRACY (BEFORE TERM)
				M-PL Database	Expert Survey	
Carlos Menem	Argentina	1989–99		1	1	0.5
Hernan Siles Zuazo	Bolivia	1982–5		0	0	0
Evo Morales	Bolivia	2006–19		0	1	0
Fernando Collor de M.	Brazil	1990–2	Outsider	0	0	0
Jair Bolsonaro	Brazil	2019–present		0	0	0
Álvaro Uribe	Colombia	2002–10	Maverik	0.5	1	0.5
Joaquín Balaguer	D. Republic	1986–96		0	0	0
Leon Febres	Ecuador	1984–88		0	0	0
Abdala Bucaram	Ecuador	1996–7		0	0	0
Lucio Gutiérrez	Ecuador	2003–5	Outsider	0	0	0
Rafael Correa	Ecuador	2007–17	Outsider	0	1	0.5
Nayib Bukele	El Salvador	2019–present	Maverik	0	0	1
Jorge Serrano E.	Guatemala	1991–3	Maverik	0	0	0
Alfonso A. Portillo	Guatemala	2000–4		0	0	0
Roberto Suazo	Honduras	1982–6		0	0	0.5
Jose Azcona del H.	Honduras	1986–90		0	0	0

Jose M. Zelaya	Honduras	2006–9		0	0	1
Juan O. Hernández	Honduras	2014–present		0	0	0.5
Arnoldo Alemán	Nicaragua	1997–2002		0	0	0
Daniel Ortega	Nicaragua	2007–present		0	1	0
Alan García	Perú	1985–90		0	0	1
Alberto Fujimori	Perú	1990–2000	Outsider	0	1	0
Ollanta Humala	Perú	2011–16	Maverik	1	0	0
Raúl Cubas	Paraguay	1998–9		0	0	0
Hugo Chávez	Venezuela	1999–2013	Outsider	0	1	0

Notes: The scores for preference for democracy during the president's term in the M-PL column are my own coding using data from Mainwaring and Pérez-Liñán, as well as primary and secondary sources. All data for Bolsonaro, Bukele, and Hérnandez is my own. The cells marked in gray signal instances in which the indicators suggest a weak preference for democracy.

for democracy using Mainwaring and Pérez-Liñán's (2013) dataset and an original database on presidents' attempts to introduce institutional reforms in order to increase their powers and/or extend their time in office. Other details of the dataset are available in Appendices B and C.

3.3.1.1 Identifying Presidents with Hegemonic Aspirations in Government

Mainwaring and Pérez-Liñán (2013) score actors'[10] regime preferences for democracy as strong (1), inconsistent (0.5), or absent (0). I qualified presidents who scored zero in this measurement as executives with hegemonic aspirations. Twenty-two democratically elected presidents fit this criterion (see Table 3.1).

I used expert surveys combined with primary and secondary sources to complement and update Mainwaring and Pérez-Liñán's dataset. Of all the criteria outlined by these authors to identify absence of a normative preference for democracy, a president's willingness to manipulate institutional norms in order to gain political advantage is, perhaps, the clearest of all. Not only is it factual (i.e., whether a president introduces a reform to enhance her powers or not is not on the eyes of the beholder) but also relatively easy to document. The survey contained questions assessing whether an executive had introduced reforms that enhanced the powers of the executive (vis-à-vis courts and/or congress) and/or increased the president's time in office (see details in Appendix C).

Out of 134 presidents in the sample, seven introduced one or more amendments in order to strengthen the powers of the executive *and* lengthen their time in office beyond a *second* term. Five had already been classified as presidents with hegemonic aspirations in Mainwaring and Pérez-Liñán's dataset. The other two, Carlos Menem and Alvaro Uribe, were originally classified as having a strong (1) and an inconsistent (0.5) preference for democracy, respectively (see Table 3.1).

Alone, neither increasing the powers of the executive nor increasing a president's time in office indicate a leader readiness to erode democracy. Strong executives are not, per se, dangerous for democracy, and there are times at which these reforms might improve a democratic regime. We cannot say that a president who introduces a constitutional amendment to increase her time in office beyond one term has hegemonic aspirations either. An immediate reelection can have positive consequences for democracy. It can increase accountability and responsiveness, help incumbents construct and sustain legislative

---

[10] For the most part, government preferences match the presidents. I only changed the scores for Marco Vinicio Cerezo (from 0 to 0.5), Luis Angel González Macchi (from 0 to 1), and Julio César Turbay (Colombia, 1978–82) (from 1 to 0.5). Cerezo and González Macchi were originally scored based on their parties. The coder reports suggest, however, these presidents' regime preferences were different from the ones of the organizations they represented. Turbay appears as having strong preference for democracy in the dataset, but the coder report scores it as having an inconsistent preference for democracy. I agree with the coder's score.

coalitions, and lengthen time horizons when planning and executing policies (Carey 2003; Penfold, Corrales, and Hernández 2014).

Menem and Uribe, however, went past that. Not only did they try to uncheck the executive[11] but also sought to stay in office beyond a second term. Their actions signaled a lack of concern with horizontal accountability and a disregard for vertical accountability. They make clear that neither president was worried about governing unchecked or perpetuating himself in office. Accordingly, I classify them as presidents with hegemonic aspirations.

3.3.1.2 *Identifying Executives with Hegemonic Aspirations before They Become Presidents*

As mentioned earlier, measuring presidents' authoritarian tendencies based solely on what they do once they attain office can result in a biased sample. Therefore, I measured their preference for democracy before they attained office as well. Whenever possible, I used Mainwaring and Pérez-Liñán's (2013) coding. For all other presidents, I used information obtained either on Mainwaring and Pérez-Liñán's coder reports and/or primary and secondary sources.

Presidents who scored zero in their pre-government normative preference for democracy were qualified as presidents with hegemonic aspirations. Sixteen out of the twenty-four presidents classified as potential autocrats based on their normative preference for democracy while in government showed absence of a normative preference for democracy before they attained power as well. The new measurement added only one president to the list: Ollanta Humala (Perú, 2011–16).

All in all, I identify twenty-five presidents with hegemonic aspirations (coded as 1 in a dichotomous "hegemonic" variable). These presidents showed, either before or after being elected, willingness to undermine democratic institutions. Of those, fourteen introduced legislation or constitutional amendments to enhance their powers, uncheck the presidency, and/or extend their time in office.[12] The other eleven did not.

3.3.2 Independent Variables

I have seven independent variables to assess the rise of potential autocrats: economic development, economic crises, perception of the economy, party system institutionalization, state capacity, state performance, and trust in institutions. I measure economic development using GDP per capita with midyear

---

[11] Carlos Menem tried to decrease legislative and nonlegislative checks on the executive and tried to pack the Supreme Court (Helmke 2003; Gervasoni 2018, 15). Studies of subnational politics in Argentina also suggest Menem had exhibit authoritarian behavior during his time as governor of La Rioja province (Gervasoni 2018, 43–66).

[12] Menem, Morales, Uribe, Febres, Correa, Suazo, Zelaya, Hernández, Alemán, Ortega, Bukele, Chávez and Serrano and Fujimori who launched self-coups.

population and constant 2010 (US$) in the year of the election.[13] I measure economic crises using the annual percentage GDP per capita growth in the year of the election. The data for these indicators comes from the World Bank. It is available for all presidents.

I measure economic perceptions using Latinobarómetro survey data, which asks respondents to describe their country's economic situation on a scale from 1 to 5. I use the election-year average to make a preliminary assessment of the impact that mean economic perceptions have on the likelihood of electing a potential autocrat. Unfortunately, this variable is only available for sixty-four presidents (see more details in Appendix B).

3.3.2.1 Party System Institutionalization

An institutionalized party system is one in which parties interact in regularly stable ways, generating expectations of stable future interactions. It has stable membership, and the main parties continue to be key contenders election after election; stable results in intraparty competition; and parties with stable ideological positions, across several election cycles (Mainwaring, Bizzarro, and Petrova 2018). In order to assess the effect of party system institutionalization (PSI) on the likelihood of electing presidents with hegemonic aspirations, I operationalize PSI using lower house electoral volatility for the congressional election immediately before the presidential election. Even though it only measures one core characteristic of PSI, volatility is a relevant indicator of party system institutionalization, and, at least for Latin America, correlates with measures of stable membership and ideological stability (Mainwaring, Bizarro, and Petrova 2018).[14] In the absence of publicly available scores of party membership or ideological positions that go back in time to 1978, electoral volatility is the best measure available to gauge the stability of patterns of electoral competition in the region. I include lower house electoral volatility for all but thirteen presidents: Three of them came to power as a result of a democratic succession but were not popularly elected, nine were elected after a long period without elections, and one has no data available online.

3.3.2.2 State Capacity and Crisis

State capacity is a contested concept. Scholars have not found a precise definition of it (Hendrix 2010; Soifer 2012; Cingolani 2013; Savoia and Sen 2015; Hanson and Sigman 2021), and measuring it is further complicated by the lack of appropriate data. Following the advice of Soifer (2012) and Hanson and Sigman (2021), I use a minimal definition of state capacity: a state's ability to implement policy goals effectively. I measure it using Hanson and Sigman's (2021) index, which is based on three core dimensions of state capacity:

---

[13] I use the natural logarithm for the regressions.
[14] I thank Scott Mainwaring for making the data available.

extractive capacity (tax revenues), coercive capacity (military expenditures, military personnel, and state's presence in the territory), and administrative capacity (bureaucratic quality, administrative efficiency, implementation of government decisions, and confidence in civil service). These authors use Bayesian latent variable analysis with twenty-one indicators of these core dimensions in order to combine them into a single indicator (-2.31 to 2.96).

Although Hanson and Sigman's State Capacity covers relevant dimensions of the concept and is the only one that goes as far back as 1978, it has important shortcomings. First, it only has data up to 2015. Second, it does not provide information about a state's perceived ability to provide goods and services to its citizens.

In order to make up for these deficiencies, I perform descriptive analyses using two other indicators: state performance and trust in institutions. Following Handlin's (2017a, 271–5) operationalization of state crisis, I measure state performance using the Worldwide Governance Indicators and trust using Latinobarómetro (1995–2018) questions regarding confidence in institutions (see details in Appendix B). These indicators are limited. The data used to build them is only available starting in the mid-1990s. Accordingly, we can only measure performance and trust during election years for sixty-seven and sixty-four presidents, respectively. Notwithstanding these limitations, these variables illustrate the importance of national perceived and objective governability in the likelihood of electing executives with hegemonic aspirations.

3.3.3 Alternative Explanations

In addition to the main independent variables, I include controls for mineral exports, ethnic fractionalization, age of democracy, and whether a country had a military dictatorship or not. Scholars have argued that mineral wealth hinders democracy (Ross 2001; Brownlee, Masoud, and Reynolds 2013; Mazzuca 2013a; Weyland 2020) because it alleviates social pressures for accountability, strengthens the state coercive apparatus, and depresses democratizing social and cultural changes (Ross 2001). Although irrelevant for military or civilian coups, fuel exports have a significant negative impact on the likelihood of experiencing a presidential takeover (Svolik 2015b). In order to control for the impact of mineral wealth, I include the country's mean fuel exports (as a percentage of merchandise exports) as measured by the World Bank.

Scholars have also argued that consolidated democracies are less prone to breakdowns (Svolik 2008). Countries like Costa Rica – that have been democratic for several decades – are more likely to have democratic institutions that carry regime legacies (Pérez-Liñán and Mainwaring 2013) and are therefore less vulnerable to the crises that might bring potential autocrats to power. Democratic consolidation is often measured in terms of how long democracy has survived. Longstanding democracies, scholars argue, are more likely to consolidate and become resistant to common causes of democratic breakdowns like economic recessions or having authoritarian neighbors. In order to control for the longevity of democracy, I use the natural logarithm of the number of years since the last transition to democracy for each election year.

The literature has also suggested that a country's type of authoritarian regime before it transitioned to democracy can impact a democracy's ability to survive. Scholars have long argued that a military authoritarian past can affect the survival of democracy (Cheibub 2007), but the scope or mechanisms of this effect are unclear. Some argue that the effect is differential. Svolik (2008) shows that having a military authoritarian past has a negative effect on democratic consolidation but has no impact on democratic survival among consolidated democracies. He also shows that military legacies have different effects across different types of breakdowns. While they increase the risk of traditional breakdowns, they decrease the risk of incumbent takeovers (Svolik 2015b). Others argue the effect is null. Sing (2010), for instance, shows that, accounting for legislative effectiveness and the United States's foreign policy, the effect of military legacies on democratic breakdowns in Latin America disappears. In order to control for the effect of a military past, I include a variable that scores one if the authoritarian regime before transition was military and zero otherwise.

Scholars have also posited that, under particular circumstances, ethnic diversity could hinder democracy (Alesina et al. 2003; Jensen and Skaaning 2012). Although this effect has been put into question (Fish and Brooks 2004; Coppedge 2012, 292–3), presidents with hegemonic aspirations, like Morales, for instance, have used inclusive ethnic appeals together with classical populist strategies in order to win elections (Madrid 2008). Countries with large indigenous populations that have been traditionally ignored by political elites could be more vulnerable to presidents with hegemonic aspirations than more ethnically homogeneous countries in the region. I control for ethnic diversity using the ethnic fractionalization index compiled by Alesina et al. (2003) and reproduced in Carreras's (2012a) dataset.

3.3.4 Methods

Due to the characteristics of the dataset (i.e., unbalanced panel of eighteen clusters, each with seven observations on average), I use both descriptive and regression analysis to assess the impact of my main independent variables on the likelihood of electing a president with hegemonic aspirations. These approaches complement each other. I use Lowess (weighted local regression) as the first step to individually assess the relationship between low economic development, perception of the economy, economic crises, party system institutionalization and state capacity, state performance, trust in institutions, and having a president with hegemonic aspirations. Lowess is a nonparametric strategy to fit smooth curves to empirical data. Unlike other techniques, which make several assumptions about the structure and the nature of the data, the

Lowess estimation strategy fits the curve based on the data. It allows it to speak for itself (Jacoby 2000). With a small N and a dichotomous variable, Lowess curves are a great way to provide clear depictions of how each of the independent variables relates to the dependent variable.

Unfortunately, it is hard to use Lowess for multivariate analysis. In order to assess the joint effect of most of the independent variables and control for alternative explanations, I run a series of panels with fixed and random effects models using all variables available since 1978. Because the presidents are clustered in countries, we cannot assume that the observations are independent or that the errors are not correlated with each other. In order to account for the correlation of two observations within a given cluster, I run a linear probability model (LPM) with fixed effects (FE). This model gives each country a different intercept, increasing the explained variance. Unfortunately, FE models are only useful to assess variation within clusters. Any variable that is constant, or nearly constant, within countries, either drops out or is poorly estimated. In order to include oil exports, ethnic fractionalization, and military past in the model, I also run a LPM and a logistic regression with random and fixed effects. These models allow me to look for variance across countries in important variables.

Together, the Lowess curves and the LPM with fixed and random effects provide evidence that weakly institutionalized party systems and low state capacity increase the likelihood of electing presidents with hegemonic aspirations. They also suggest that low economic development and weak economic performance, while individually influential, have a lesser role in bringing these potential autocrats to power once we take into account other factors.[15] This evidence, however, should be read with caution. Although the coefficients do not change much across different models, their significance levels vary quite a bit. This is probably due to the size of the data and the small variation in the DV.[16]

3.4 ANALYSIS

All economic variables have a negative relationship with the likelihood of electing a potential autocrat in Latin America, though they vary in strength. As Figure 3.1 shows, twenty-one (84 percent) presidents with hegemonic aspirations – represented in the *y*-axis –came to power in countries that had an election-year GDP per capita below the Latin American mean ($5,559).

---

[15] Figures D8 and D9 in the Appendix show partial regression plots for each of the main variables using the random and the fixed effects LPM.

[16] Out of 112 cases used in the analysis – due to missing data, the analysis drops 22 presidents (including 3 potential autocrats). Most of them belong to different clusters. Argentina, Brazil, Colombia, Dominican Republic, Paraguay, and Venezuela have one. Bolivia, Guatemala, Honduras, Nicaragua, and Perú have two; Ecuador has four.

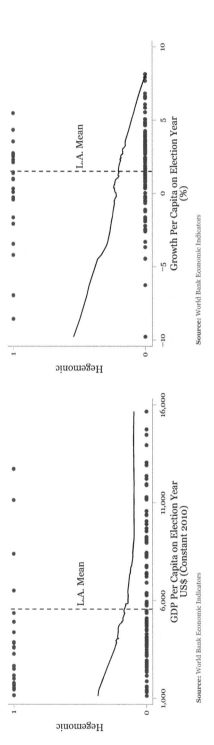

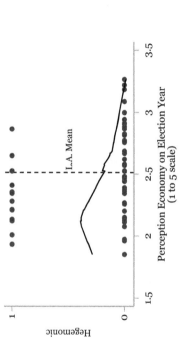

FIGURE 3.1. Lowess presidents with hegemonic aspirations and the economy

Overall, countries that elect potential autocrats have an average election-year GDP per capita 34 percent lower than countries that do not elect hegemonic presidents, a difference that reaches traditional thresholds of statistical significance ($p<0.01$).[17] This does not mean that all, or even most, countries with low economic development elect potential autocrats. Rather, what the data suggests is that in a region where the majority of the countries have below-average economic development, very few presidents with hegemonic aspirations will rise in countries with high GDP per capita. Out of the eighty (61 percent) presidents who came to power with an election-year GDP per capita below the Latin American mean, twenty-one (26 percent) had hegemonic aspirations. In comparison, out of the fifty-one (39 percent) presidents who came to power with a GDP per capita above the Latin American mean, four (8 percent) had hegemonic aspirations.

Evidence of a negative relationship between the rise of presidents with hegemonic aspirations and economic growth is slightly more complicated. Potential autocrats have an election-year economic growth per capita 82 percent lower than their nonhegemonic counterparts ($p<0.03$).[18] However, the number of hegemonic presidents elected above and below Latin America's average economic growth is not very different. Contrary to what happens with economic development, sixty-nine Latin American presidents (53 percent) came to power in countries with above-average (1.5 percent) election-year per capita economic growth. Of those, 13 percent (nine) had hegemonic ambitions. In comparison, sixty-two (47 percent) presidents in the sample came to power in countries with below-average election-year per capita economic growth. Of those, 26 percent (sixteen) had hegemonic ambitions. The vast difference in mean growth per capita between hegemonic and nonhegemonic presidents seems to be driven largely by Menem (–8.5 percent) and Fujimori (–7 percent) who came to power with very low levels of economic growth.[19]

Citizens' perceptions of the economy seem to influence the likelihood of electing a president with hegemonic aspirations. The average election-year perception of the economy for potential autocrats is 10 percent lower than the average election-year perception of the economy for their nonhegemonic counterparts ($p<0.015$).[20] As shown in Figure 3.1, ten of the thirteen potential autocrats for which there is data available (77 percent) came to power in countries and years where the perception of the economy was below the Latin American mean (2.51).

Like what happens with economic development, however, this does not mean that countries with negative perceptions of the economy will surely elect

---

[17] See Figure D1 and Table D1 in the Appendix.
[18] See Figure D2 and Table D2 in the Appendix.
[19] Appendix D, includes a partial regression plot that supports this assertion (Figure D8).
[20] See Figure D3 and Table D3 in the Appendix.

presidents with hegemonic aspirations. Rather, what the available data suggests is that in a region where a slight majority of the presidents come to power in countries where citizens have below-average perceptions of their nations' economies, countries with positive perceptions of the economy will rarely see presidents with hegemonic aspirations. Out of the sixty-four presidents for which we have data, thirty-three (52 percent) came to power with below-average election-year perceptions of the economy. Of those, ten (30 percent) had hegemonic ambitions. In contrast, thirty-one (48 percent) presidents came to power with above-average election-year perceptions of the economy. Of those, three (10 percent) had hegemonic ambitions.

All state capacity and governance indicators have a negative relationship with the rise of potential autocrats as well. As shown in Figure 3.2, countries with high state capacity at the time of the election rarely elect presidents with hegemonic aspirations. Out of the twenty-three hegemonic presidents in the sample with data available for this variable, only four (17 percent) came to power with election-year state capacity scores above the Latin American mean (0.33).

Although these numbers do not imply that low levels of state capacity will often drive leaders with hegemonic aspirations to power – out of the seventy presidents elected with below-average election-year state capacity, fifty-one (73 percent) did not threaten democracy – it does suggest that having a very weak state will reduce its defenses against the rise of potential autocrats. As shown in Figure 3.2, not only is the proportion of potential autocrats among presidents elected with below-average levels of state capacity (27 percent) comparatively high vis-à-vis the proportion of potential autocrats among presidents elected with above-average levels of state capacity (7 percent) but countries with hegemonic presidents tend to have comparatively weaker states as well. Mean election-year state capacity for potential autocrats is 84.5 percent lower than mean election-year state capacity for their nonhegemonic counterparts ($p<0.002$).[21]

The relationship between state strength and the rise of presidents with hegemonic aspirations is further confirmed when we analyze state performance. As shown in Figure 3.2, all potential autocrats, for which there is data on this indicator (14), came to office with levels of state performance below the Latin American average (−0.28). Their average state performance (−0.69) is 74 percent lower than the average state performance of their nonhegemonic counterparts (−0.18) ($p<0.004$).[22]

Like what happens with state capacity, although countries with low levels of state performance are not always doomed to elect executives with hegemonic aspirations, they are more likely to do so than countries with low levels of

[21] See Figure D4 and Table D4 in the Appendix.
[22] See Figure D5 and Table D5 in the Appendix.

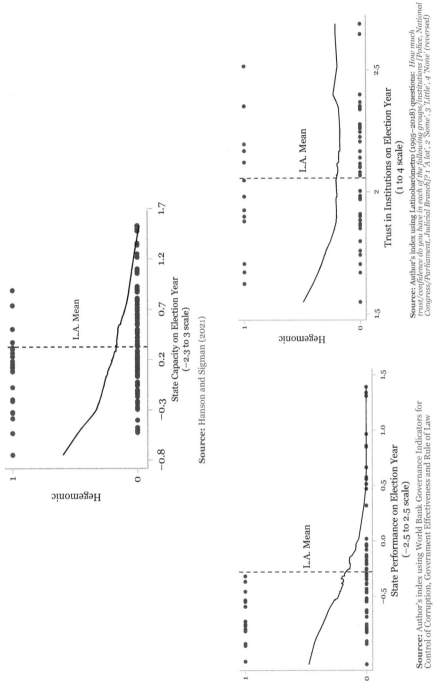

FIGURE 3.2. Lowess election of presidents with hegemonic aspirations and governance

Source: Hanson and Sigman (2021)

Source: Author's index using World Bank Governance Indicators for Control of Corruption, Government Effectiveness and Rule of Law

Source: Author's index using Latinobarómetro (1995–2018) questions: *How much trust/confidence do you have in each of the following groups/institutions [Police, National Congress/Parliament, Judicial Branch]? 1 'A lot', 2 'Some', 3 'Little', 4 'None' (reversed)*

economic development, economic growth, or negative perception of the economy. A majority of Latin American presidents, forty-four (64 percent), for whom there is data available, came to power in countries with below-average levels of state performance. Fourteen (32 percent) of them were presidents with hegemonic aspirations. On the contrary, a minority of Latin American presidents, twenty-five (36 percent), came to power in countries with above-average levels of state performance. None of them tried to erode democracy.

Unlike these variables, the relationship between trust in institutions and the rise of potential autocrats is very weak. Although eight of the thirteen potential autocrats, for which there is data available, were elected in countries where confidence in institutions was below the Latin American average (2.06), the average election-year trust in institutions among potential autocrats (2) is only marginally lower (3 percent) than the overall election-year trust in institutions among nonpotential autocrats (2.07), and the difference is not statistically significant.[23] Out of the thirty-two presidents who came to power in countries with below-average trust in institutions, eight (25 percent) were potential autocrats. The latter, however, had almost identical levels of confidence on institutions (1.84) vis-à-vis their nonhegemonic counterparts (1.86).

Different from what happens with trust in institutions, the relationship between party system institutionalization and hegemonic presidents is fairly strong. Countries that have high electoral volatility are more likely to see the rise of a president with hegemonic aspirations. As shown in Figure 3.3, sixteen (67 percent) out of the twenty-four potential autocrats, for which there is data, came to power in countries with lower house electoral volatility levels above the Latin American average (26). The average electoral volatility in the countries in which they became presidents (34) is 40.5 percent higher than the average electoral volatility of the countries in which their nonhegemonic counterparts attained office (24) ($p<0.004$).[24]

Out of fifty-two presidents in countries with above-average electoral volatility, sixteen (31 percent) showed a low normative preference for democracy, suggesting that the relationship between party system institutionalization and the rise of executives with hegemonic aspirations is stronger than the relationship between the latter and any of the economic variables. Not only is the proportion of potential autocrats at above-average levels of electoral volatility relatively high (67 percent) but also the average level of electoral volatility for these sixteen hyper-ambitious leaders (43.6) is 12.5 percent higher than the average electoral volatility of their nonhegemonic counterparts (38.8).

While it is useful to describe these basic relationships, Lowess graphs are not equally useful in assessing multivariate relationships or control for other variables. Table 3.2 shows the results of four different models that assess the

[23] See Figure D6 and Table D6 in the Appendix.
[24] See Figure D7 and Table D7 in the Appendix.

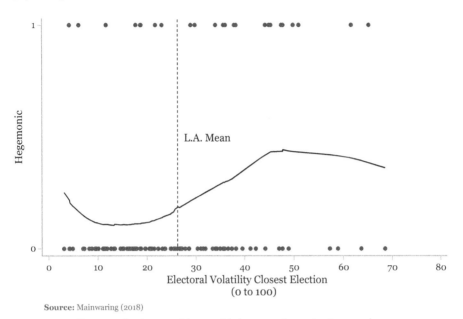

Source: Mainwaring (2018)

FIGURE 3.3. Lowess election presidents with hegemonic aspirations and party system institutionalization

relationship of the main variables,[25] controlling for the alternative explanations specified above. Models 1 and 2 analyze the relationship using LPM with fixed and random effects. Models 3 and 4 analyze the same relationship using logistic regression with fixed and random effects.

The results provide little support for Hypotheses 1 and 2. While individually important, once we account for other variables, GDP per capita and GDP per capita growth have a negative but statistically insignificant impact on the likelihood of electing a president with hegemonic aspirations.[26] The results, however, support Hypotheses 3 and 4. The effect of state capacity is fairly clear. The coefficient is negative and significant at the 90 percent level of confidence ($p<0.021$, $p<0.027$, $p<1.2$, $p<0.07$) in all but one model, but inconsistent across Models 1 and 2. According to Model 1, one standard deviation increase in state capacity decreases the likelihood of electing a potential autocrat by 16 percent; but according to Model 2, one standard deviation increase in state capacity reduces the likelihood of electing a president with hegemonic aspirations only by 8 percent. The effect of lower house volatility is evident -the coefficient is positive and significant across all models ($p<0.026$, $p<0.055$, $p<0.007$, $p<0.011$, $p<0.013$, $p<0.028$, $p<0.019$, $p<0.046$)- but inconsistent

[25] GDP per capita and state capacity are highly correlated ($r = 0.75$). In order to avoid multicollinearity, I run models with each of these variables separately.
[26] Partial regression plots in the appendix support this conclusion.

TABLE 3.2. *Likelihood of electing presidents with hegemonic aspirations*

Variable	Model 1 (FE)		Model 2 (RE)		Model 3 (Logit FE)		Model 4 (Logit RE)	
	Capacity	GDP PC	Capacity	GDP PC	Capacity	GDP PC	Capacity	GDP PC
Economic Development		-0.185 (0.232)		-0.093 (0.059)		-2.192 (2.010)		-0.662 (0.435)
Economic Growth	-0.014 (0.013)	-0.019 (0.013)	-0.016 (0.012)	-0.019 (0.012)	-0.128 (0.134)	-0.167 (0.114)	-0.104 (0.093)	-0.140 (0.086)
LH Electoral Volatility (0–1)	0.873** (0.324)	0.689* (0.324)	0.718** (0.272)	0.545* (0.261)	5.491* (2.212)	4.530* (2.057)	4.439* (1.885)	3.497* (1.752)
State Capacity	-0.328+ (0.176)		-0.163+ (0.088)		-2.209 (1.426)		-1.438+ (0.786)	
Democracy Age	0.039 (0.053)	0.022 (0.058)	-0.004 (0.045)	-0.003 (0.044)	0.290 (0.432)	0.295 (0.387)	0.001 (0.322)	0.008 (0.294)
Mean Fuel Exports			0.000 (0.002)	0.001 (0.002)			0.009 (0.015)	0.014 (0.015)
Ethnic Fractionalization			-0.008 (0.228)	0.016 (0.227)			-0.242 (1.635)	-0.299 (1.606)

	(1)	(2)	(3)	(4)	(5)	(6)
Military Past	0.016 (0.159)	0.100 (0.088)	0.099 (0.087)		0.895 (0.827)	0.929 (0.803)
Constant	1.546 (1.860)	0.032 (0.170)	0.778 (0.511)		−2.947* (1.274)	2.408 (3.806)
r_2	0.127	0.071				
Bic	95.362	115.440	67.093	79.477	131.343	145.830
N	112	121	78	89	112	121

Note: Standard Errors in Parentheses $+p<0.1$, $*p<0.05$, $**p<0.01$, $***p<0.001$

in Models 1 and 2 as well. Higher levels of lower house electoral volatility increase the probability of electing a potential autocrat. All else equal, a one-point increase in electoral volatility increases the probability of electing a hegemonic president by 69 or 87 points in Model 1 and 54 or 72 points in Model 2. In other words, one standard deviation increase in electoral volatility enhances the likelihood of electing potential autocrats by 10 or 13 percent (Model 1) or by 8 or 11 percent (Model 2).

Together, the Lowess graphs and the models suggest that countries with low state capacity and weakly institutionalized party systems are more likely to see the rise of president with hegemonic aspirations. Although there is a negative relationship between economic development and growth and the election of a potential autocrat, the effect of these variables seems overall less important. Notwithstanding hard to analyze side by side with other variables, the Lowess graphs also suggest that the effect of state capacity is likely related to state performance. In the next section, I assess the extent to which these variables increase the odds that, once elected, hegemonic presidents will successfully erode democracy.

3.5 THE RISE OF PRESIDENTS WITH HEGEMONIC ASPIRATIONS AND THE EROSION OF DEMOCRACY

Most mass-based, structural, institutional, and state-centered theories of democratic erosion have focused on the factors that increase the likelihood that an authoritarian leader attains power. As shown earlier, in general, leaders with hegemonic aspirations rise to power in countries with poor economic, institutional, and governance conditions. However, how poor, how inchoate, or how weak a state is when these leaders attain office can influence the president's ability to erode democracy as well. In this section, I study the effect of state capacity and performance, trust on institutions, and party system institutionalization, and institutional weakness in the erosion of democracy. Using descriptive analytic techniques, I show that most of these variables have little influence on a president's ability to erode democracy. Coming to power in countries with weak economic performance, negative perceptions of the economy, weak states in crisis, inchoate party systems or weak institutions, though at times helpful to undermine democratic institutions, is neither necessary nor sufficient to guarantee the erosion of democracy.

3.5.1 Development, Growth, Capacity, and Institutions in the Erosion of Democracy

Economic downturns, negative perceptions of the economy, and weak states with governability problems weaken sitting presidents. Unless these issues persist, once a potential autocrat is in office, the economic or state-related factors that helped her get elected should not increase her ability to consolidate power. Accordingly, we should not expect economic crises, negative perceptions of the economy, or weak or underperforming states to affect the likelihood that a potential autocrat successfully erodes democracy during an election year.

The story of institutional factors, however, is different. Weak and distrusted institutions on election day can not only help potential autocrats come to power but could also facilitate their efforts to erode democracy (Mayka 2016; Ginsburg and Huq 2018; Weyland and Madrid 2019a; Weyland 2020). While feeble institutions can be easier to destroy, this relationship need not be deterministic. Countries like Guatemala and Perú show that democracy can survive even in the presence of weakly institutionalized party systems (Tanaka and Meléndez 2014) and overall institutional weakness.

3.5.2 Operationalizing the Erosion of Democracy

In Chapter 2, I defined the erosion of democracy as a type of regime transition that happens over time. An eroded regime is, therefore, no longer a democracy but a competitive authoritarian regime. Not only has it lost its horizontal accountability, but it has very diminished vertical accountability as well. In other words, an eroded democracy has undergone formal changes to the rules of the game that are serious enough to make it almost impossible to defeat the incumbent.

Operationalizing this definition is not straightforward (Handlin 2017c; Cameron 2018). Levitsky and Way (2010, 365–8) have a well-developed set of conditions to assess competitive authoritarianism. In their view, a regime is competitive authoritarian if there is evidence of violation of civil liberties or unfair elections, including those that are fought in an uneven playing field. However, most democracies have some degree of unfairness in their elections. A strict understanding of these indicators would easily lead us to classify all but a few countries as competitive authoritarian regimes. For example, there is ample evidence of partisan gerrymandering in the United States (Edwards et al. 2017), a clear example of an uneven playing field. Yet most would consider the United States to be democratic. Notwithstanding being faulty, its elections still meet the minimum standards to be qualified as reasonably free and fair.

In order to address this inherent vagueness, I used three different indicators to assess if and when a democracy had eroded. First, I coded the cases myself. I coded as erosion any case in which the president successfully changed the constitution in order to enhance her powers *and* stay in office beyond a second term. Alone, neither increasing the powers of the executive nor increasing a president's time in office indicate an eroded democracy. Together, however, they provide a very strong signal that the president has undermined the evenness of the playing field in order to stay in office.

While this indicator can only be used in presidential regimes, I believe it is particularly important. In presidential systems like the ones throughout Latin America, enhancing the powers of the president *alongside* successfully reforming the constitution to allow for two or more immediate reelections is a powerful indicator of a significant decline in vertical accountability. Unlike parliamentary democracies, in presidential systems, term limits are essential to the possibility of turnover (i.e., the ability of opposition parties to win). In Latin America, limits to presidents' reelection were a cornerstone of their transitions to democracy. Except Dominican Republic, all countries in the region started their democratic period with prohibitions regarding immediate reelections (Penfold, Corrales, and Hernández 2014). The ability of Latin American presidents to override these prohibitions in order to stay in office beyond a second term is, therefore, a strong signal of backsliding.

Following Handlin's (2017c) suggestion, I triangulate my coding using two other indicators built using the National Elections Across Democracy and Autocracy dataset (NELDA 4.0) (Hyde and Marinov 2015) and V-Dem indices. The former provides information about the characteristics of every national election between 1946 and 2015.[27] It codes incumbent abuses in a dichotomous manner. I use questions regarding media bias, harassment, bans on the opposition, election boycotts, and concerns regarding the freedom and fairness of elections.[28] If scored one in any of these indicators, I classified the regime as eroded, unless the election was during or right after a transition to democracy.

V-Dem, the second dataset, has expert-coded questions on the freedom and fairness of elections, intentional irregularities in elections, autonomy of the election management body, opposition harassment by the government, media censorship and bias, and barriers to forming parties – all of which are highly correlated. I conduct factor analysis on these questions to build a competitive authoritarianism index. I dichotomize the index as one, if the score was above the mean or zero otherwise.

I coded countries with at least two of the three indices as successfully eroded (Table 3.3). These are Ecuador under Correa, Honduras under Hernández, Nicaragua under Ortega, Perú under Fujimori, and Venezuela under Chávez. I made two changes to this list. First, I removed Alberto Fujimori. Although there is no question that the potential autocrat transformed Perú's democracy into a competitive authoritarian regime, he did not accomplish this through gradual institutional reforms. Instead, he launched a self-coup in 1992, which – alongside Jorge Serrano (Guatemala, 1991–3) – makes this a case of classic democratic breakdown, rather than erosion.

---

[27] There are only thirteen democratically elected presidents since 2015, and only two of them – Jair Bolsonaro (2019–present) and Nayib Bukele (2019–present) – are hegemonic.

[28] For a list of questions included, see Table B.3.

TABLE 3.3. *Successful and failed erosion of democracy in Latin America*

Name	Country	Period	Erosion AUTHOR	Erosion NELDA	Erosion VDEM	Final score
Carlos Menem	Argentina	1989–99	0	0	0	
Hernan Siles Zuazo	Bolivia	1982–5	0	1	0	
Evo Morales	Bolivia	2006–19	1	0	0	*Erosion*
Fernando Collor de Mello	Brazil	1990–2	0	0	0	
Jair Bolsonaro	Brazil	2019–present	0	NA	0	
Alvaro Uribe	Colombia	2002–10	0	1	0	
Joaquin Balaguer	Dominican Republic	1986–96	0	1	0	
Leon Febres	Ecuador	1984–8	0	1	0	
Abdala Bucaram	Ecuador	1996–7	0	0	0	
Lucio Gutiérrez	Ecuador	2003–5	0	0	0	
Rafael Correa	Ecuador	2007–17	1	1	0	Erosion
Jorge Serrano Elías[a]	Guatemala	1991–3	0	1	0	
Alfonso Antonio Portillo	Guatemala	2000–4	0	0	0	
Roberto Suazo	Honduras	1982–6	0	0	0	
Jose Azcona del Hoyo	Honduras	1986–90	0	0	0	
Jose Manuel Zelaya	Honduras	2006–9	0	0	0	

(*continued*)

TABLE 3.3. (continued)

Name	Country	Period	Erosion			Final score
			AUTHOR	NELDA	VDEM	
Juan Orlando Hernández	Honduras	2014–22	1	1	1	Erosion
Arnoldo Alemán	Nicaragua	1997–2	0	0	0	
Daniel Ortega	Nicaragua	2007–present	1	1	1	Erosion
Alan García	Perú	1985–90	0	0	0	
Alberto Fujimori[a]	Perú	1990–2000	1	1	1	Breakdown
Ollanta Humala	Perú	2011–16	0	0	0	
Raul Cubas	Paraguay	1998–9	0	0	0	
Nayib Bukele	El Salvador	2019–present	0	NA	0	
Hugo Chávez	Venezuela	1999–2013	1	1	1	Erosion

[a] These presidents classify as having hegemonic aspirations but their attempts to undermine democracy are closer to traditional democratic breakdowns than they are to democratic erosions. Accordingly, I exclude them from the analyses in Section 3.5.3.

Second, I added Evo Morales. Although neither NELDA nor V-Dem qualify elections to be unfair or unfree in Bolivia, as early as 2017 it was clear Morales was not willing to step down. In 2017, he used his control over the Constitutional Court to outright ignore the results of a referendum that would have blocked him from running for a fourth term. The elections for such a referendum might have been minimally free and fair, but the fact that the president was able to ignore the outcome signaled the damage done to vertical accountability in the country. Regime change in Bolivia would be further confirmed by the 2019 presidential elections. Although it is unclear whether there was fraud and to what extent it might have significantly changed the outcome of the election (Idrobo, Kronick, and Rodríguez 2020b), the electoral contest had significant irregularities, including manipulation of electoral laws, Morales's flagrant use of state resources to campaign and the uneven access to media outlets (EU Election Expert Mission 2019).

3.5.3 Analysis

None of the variables that help bring presidents with hegemonic aspirations to power seem to predetermine the erosion of democracy. As shown in Figure 3.4, neither lower levels of economic development or growth nor poor perceptions of the economy on election year have an overwhelming impact on the erosion of democracy. As shown below, cases of erosion and survival are distributed somewhat evenly across different levels of these variables.

Three out of the five successful cases of erosion – Morales's ($1,700), Hernández's ($2,001), and Ortega's ($1,448) – had election-year GDP per capita levels below the hegemonic mean ($3,922), but so did twelve out of the sixteen cases of unsuccessful erosion. Similarly, three out of the five successful hegemonic presidents – Juan Orlando Hernández (2.12), Daniel Ortega (2.21), and Hugo Chávez (2.28) – came to power in a country with perceptions of the economy below the presidents with hegemonic aspirations' mean (2.3), but so did three out of the seven unsuccessful hegemonic presidents, for which we have data available. Moreover, of all the cases of erosion, only Hugo Chávez and Juan Orlando Hernández came to power with levels of growth per capita below the Latin American mean, and the president with the worst level of GDP per capita growth, Carlos Menem (−8.54 percent), failed to erode democracy.

State capacity on election day does not predetermine the erosion of democracy either. As Figure 3.5 shows, cases of erosion and nonerosion are equally distributed across different levels of state capacity.[29] No successful president with hegemonic aspirations came to power with election-year state capacity levels below the potential autocrats' (0.06) and Correa (0.50) had election-year

---

[29] This can be partly explained by the lack of variance in state capacity on election year among presidents with hegemonic aspirations. While the overall scale goes from −2.31 to 2.96 (in the world) and −1.35 to 1.55 in Latin America, the values for this subgroup go from −0.75 to 0.89.

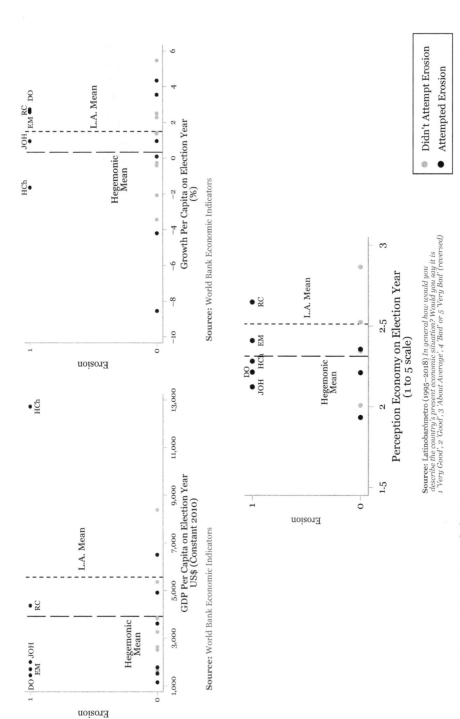

FIGURE 3.4. Democratic erosion and election-year economy

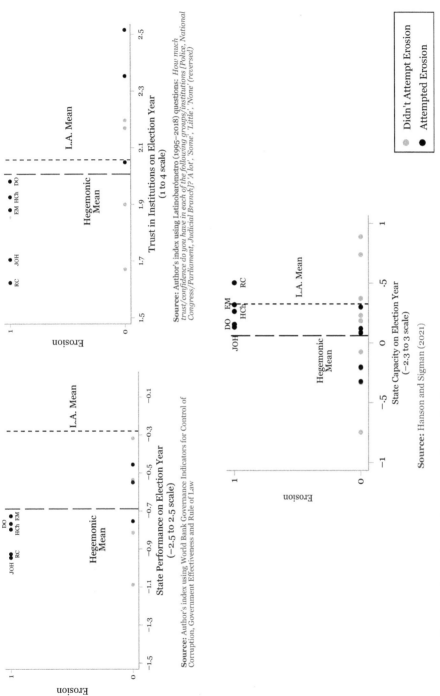

FIGURE 3.5. Democratic erosion and state capacity on election year

state capacity levels above the Latin American mean (0.33) when he became president.

The relationship between erosion performance and trust in institutions is stronger, although not entirely determinant. All five cases of successful erosion happened in countries with election-year state performance and trust in institution levels below the hegemonic presidents' mean (-0.69 and 2) and the Latin American mean (-0.28 and 2.06). On the other hand, all the cases of failed erosion happened in countries with state performance levels below the Latin American mean, and three of them were in countries with state performance levels below the hegemonic presidents' mean.

Similarly, of the thirteen presidents with hegemonic aspirations for which we have data, all five potential autocrats who successfully eroded democracy came to power in countries where trust in institutions was below the potential autocrats' and the Latin American mean. Only three out of the seven presidents who did not attempt or failed to erode democracy came to power under similar circumstances. Of these, one (Uribe) came to power with election-year trust in institutions above the hegemonic presidents' mean.

The aforementioned evidence suggests that low levels of state performance and trust in institutions ease the path to democratic erosion, but do not guarantee it. Not only does election-year performance and institutional trust among hegemonic presidents not vary much,[30] but there are cases of presidents like Lucio Gutiérrez, who, despite coming to power in countries with very low trust in institution and a very weak state performance, did not erode democracy.

Not surprisingly, something similar happens with party system institutionalization. As shown in Figure 3.6, all leaders with hegemonic aspirations who successfully eroded democracy came to power when lower house (LH) electoral volatility was above the Latin American (26) mean, and three of them came to power with LH electoral volatility above the hegemonic presidents' mean (34). In contrast, potential autocrats who failed or did not try to erode democracy are distributed evenly across different levels of LH electoral volatility. Eight came to power in countries with LH volatility above the hegemonic presidents' mean; the other seven became presidents in countries with LH volatility levels below the hegemonic mean.

In general, higher levels of party system institutionalization seem to increase the likelihood that a president with hegemonic aspirations will erode democracy, but do not necessarily guarantee it. Similar to what happens with trust in institutions, coming to office in inchoate party systems facilitates the erosion of democracy but does not assure it. It can explain Morales's (65.14), Chávez's

---

[30] Performance among presidents with hegemonic aspirations ranges from -1.09 to -0.32 with a mean of -0.69 and a standard deviation of 0.23. Trust in institutions among presidents with hegemonic aspirations ranges from 1.62 to 2.51 – in a 1–4 scale – with a mean of 2 and a standard deviation of 0.26.

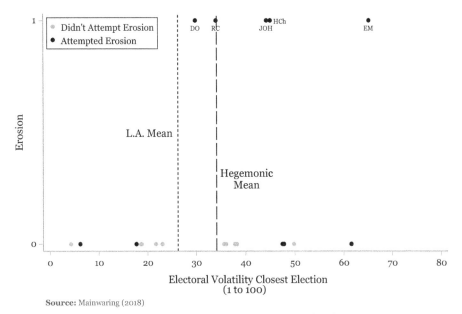

Source: Mainwaring (2018)

FIGURE 3.6. Democratic erosion and electoral volatility in the closest election

(44.95), or Hernández's (44.19) ability to erode democracy, but it cannot explain Alemán's (61.52), García's (49.8), Uribe's (47.75), or Febres's (47.44) inability to do the same.

Weakly institutionalized party systems are, however, just one particular form of institutional weakness. Beyond political parties, there are other forms of institutional feebleness that could determine a potential autocrat's ability to erode democracy as soon as she attains power. Weyland (2020) suggests that unstable or easy-to-modify institutions are a necessary condition for the erosion of democracy. In order to assess this relationship, I use Helmke's (2017) Inter-Branch Crises in Latin America (ICLA) dataset and Elkins and Ginsburg's (2021) Chronology of Constitutional Events. The first one provides a count of interbranch crises between 1985 and 2008; the second offers a count of constitutional changes between 1811 and 2019.

In order to avoid conflating democratic erosion (i.e., reforms enacted by potential autocrats to enhance their powers or extend their tenure) with the institutional instability they find when they attain power, I calculate the average of interbranch crises and constitutional changes[31] from the moment the country transitions to democracy (or the year we have data available) to the year the potential autocrat starts her term. Though circumscribed to one type of institutional weakness – the ability to change a norm or threaten an institution in

---

[31] Including amendments and replacements.

order to avoid compliance[32] – the preelection frequency of interbranch conflicts and constitutional changes should provide a preliminary assessment of the effect that institutional strength has on the erosion of democracy (Figure 3.7).

While helpful, neither interbranch crises nor constitutional changes seem to be necessary or sufficient to erode democracy. Successful and unsuccessful potential autocrats are similarly distributed across both variables. Certainly, presidents like Rafael Correa – who came to power in a country with a history of eighteen interbranch crises since 1985 – or Juan Orlando Hernández – who came to power in a country with 21 constitutional changes since 1982 – benefited from very weak institutions. Likewise, leaders like Menem – who came to power in a country with one interbranch crisis since 1985 and no history of constitutional changes since 1983 – had a harder time eroding democracy. However, institutional instability cannot explain the success of presidents like Hugo Chávez – whose country had experienced two interbranch crises before he came to power and barely three constitutional changes since it transitioned to democracy in the 1950s – or the failure of presidents like Alvaro Uribe – who came to power in a country that had experienced three interbranch crises before he came to power and fifteen constitutional changes since the 1970s.

This evidence suggests that although some of the conditions under which potential autocrats come to power aid or enhance their ability to erode democracy, they do not overdetermine this outcome. Low economic development or poor economic performance could explain why Ortega or Chávez undermined democracy, but it cannot explain why Alemán or Menem did not. Similarly, negative perceptions of the economy can explain why Hernández, Ortega, and Chávez and eroded democracy but cannot explain why Uribe did not. Likewise, governance indicators could explain why Morales, Chávez, Correa, and Ortega eroded democracy but cannot explain why Gutiérrez or Humala did not, and weak institutions can explain why Correa or Hernández eroded democracy but have less power explaining why Uribe or Menem did not (Figure 3.8).

This conclusion holds true even if we account for the combined effect of these variables (see Figure 3.8). An index averaging the standardized versions of these factors[33] shows that four of the five successful autocrats had generally low – below the hegemonic leaders' mean (–0.43) – levels of economic

---

[32] In their coedited volume, Brinks, Levitsky, and Murillo define weak institutions as those that set nontrivial goals and achieve them and identify two types of institutional weakness: noncompliance and instability (2020, 8–24). Constitutional changes and interbranch crises speak to the latter, but do not say much about the former.

[33] Doing multivariate analysis with twenty-one observations is impossible. In order to get some idea of whether these variables, together, had an impact on a president's ability to erode democracy, I built an index by standardizing all the relevant variables and averaging these standardized values for each president. The index goes from –1.46 to 1.52, has a mean of –0.04, and a standard deviation of 0.56. Among presidents with hegemonic aspirations, the index goes from –1.46 to 0.36 has a mean of –0.43, and a standard deviation of 0.42.

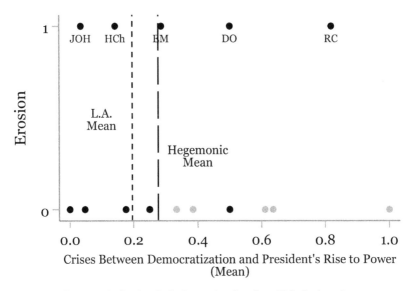

Source: Author's calculations using data from Helmke (2017)

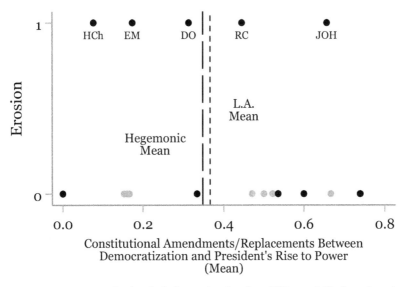

Source: Author's calculations using data from Elkins and Ginsburg (2021)

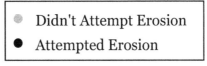

FIGURE 3.7. Democratic erosion and institutional weakness

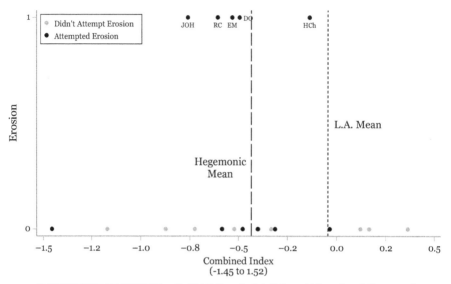

FIGURE 3.8. Democratic erosion and combined index of election and preelection variables

development and growth, perceptions of the economy, state capacity, performance, trust in institutions, party system institutionalization, interbranch crises, and constitutional changes.[34] It also shows that seven of the sixteen unsuccessful potential autocrats also had generally low (below the hegemonic leaders' mean) levels of these same factors.

3.5.4 Other Potential Causes for the Erosion of Democracy

Structural variables are not static, of course. State capacity, party system institutionalization, economic development, and economic growth can change over time. These changes could explain the variation between successful and failed cases of democratic erosion. Other macro variables, unrelated to the state of the country when these presidents came to power, could be at fault as well. An incumbent's popularity and a country's polarization, for instance, have been blamed for potential autocrats' success. Below I assess the overall impact of each of these variables.

---

[34] I invert the indicators for lower house volatility, Interbranch Crises, and Constitutional Changes to match the direction of the other variables.

3.5.4.1 *Economic Factors*

Economic development and growth, in particular if it comes from gas or oil revenues, could help presidents with hegemonic aspirations erode democracy. It can provide the presidents with resources to distribute patronage and/or fulfill campaign promises. Increased support could, in turn, help the executive increase his hold over state institutions and extend his time in office.[35]

Svolik (2015), for instance, shows that fuel exports increase the likelihood of "presidential takeovers," and Mazzuca (2013) argues that "rentier populism" – the exploitation of a single government-owned natural resource like oil in Venezuela or gas in Bolivia – has helped consolidate left-wing "radical hegemonies" in Latin America. There is no doubt that hegemonic presidents like Hugo Chávez, Evo Morales, and Rafael Correa have used the revenues of mineral resources to fuel their projects via patronage (Hidalgo 2009; Hawkins 2010a, 195–230; Weyland, Madrid, and Hunter 2010; Weyland, Madrid, and Hunter 2010a; Mazzuca 2013a; Weyland 2013; Weyland 2020).

I evaluate the impact of mineral wealth, economic development, and economic growth using data from the World Bank. I measure the first variable using the average of fuel exports as percentage of GDP during the president's term. I measure the second and third variables using average GDP per capita growth and average GDP per capita ($2010) during the president's term.[36]

The evidence pertaining to fuel exports is weak. As shown in Figure 3.9, out of the eight potential autocrats who relied heavily on mineral exports during their terms (i.e., more than 25 percent of their GDP per capita came from mineral exports), three – Chávez (87 percent), Correa (57 percent), and Morales (48 percent) – successfully eroded democracy; the other five did not. Similarly, out of the thirteen hegemonic presidents who did not rely heavily on mineral exports, two – Hernández (0.22 percent) and Ortega (0.63 percent) – successfully eroded democracy; the other eleven did not.[37]

Economic growth and economic development paint an inconclusive story. As shown in Figure 3.9, all successful presidents with hegemonic aspirations experienced above-average economic performance. Economic growth clearly helps erode democracy. It does not, however, guarantee it. Out of the twelve

---

[35] The effect of state capacity on the erosion of democracy after a president with hegemonic aspirations attains power is hard to assess. Once a hegemonic president is in office, these variables conflate with the dependent variable. After all, by consolidating power, hegemonic presidents are, by definition, strengthening the state and diminishing the variation in vote shares.

[36] I do not assess the impact of perceptions of the economy in this section because they are endogenous to the process of erosion. Perceptions of the economy rely, to a certain extent, on citizens' ability to gather formal or informal information on the state of the economy. A potential autocrat's ability to censor the media and/or distribute patronage at will necessarily affect that perception. Citizens' perception of the state of the economy could be then an outcome, not a cause of the erosion of democracy.

[37] For details on presidents' scores on this and other indicators, see Table D9 in the Appendix.

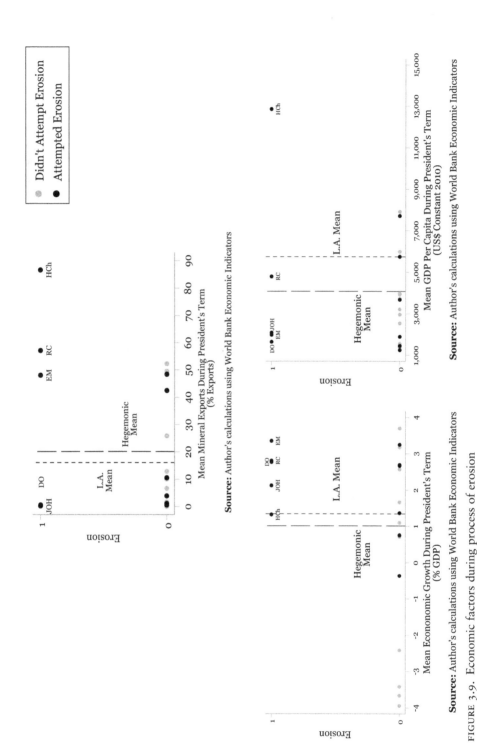

FIGURE 3.9. Economic factors during process of erosion

presidents with hegemonic aspirations with economic growth above the Latin American mean (1.34 percent), eight did not erode democracy. Sizable economic growth during their governments seems to have aided Morales (3.35 percent) and Correa (2.80 percent) erode democracy but did not help Gutiérrez (3.7 percent) or Uribe (3.24 percent).

The connection between the economy and success or failure in eroding democracy is more complicated when we look at GDP per capita. Except for Chávez ($12,857), all presidents with hegemonic aspirations who successfully eroded democracy had an average government GDP per capita below the Latin American mean ($5,741), and all but Correa ($4,787) had an average GDP per capita below the hegemonic presidents' mean. In other words, whereas presidents with hegemonic aspirations who successfully eroded democracy certainly had access to large amounts of money, and these were particularly easy to use for Chávez, Morales, and Correa, who had state-owned oil and gas companies, it is not clear that these presidents always had more funds available than their nonsuccessful hegemonic counterparts, or that these funds impacted their ability to erode democracy.

3.5.4.2 *President Approval*

Besides the economy, two other variables are commonly blamed for the erosion of democracy: the president's popularity and polarization. As mentioned in earlier chapters, popular support is related to a president's ability to protect herself from forced removals and push for antidemocratic reforms. Many of the presidents discussed in this book were charismatic. They appealed to their supporters to fight against their oppositions and/or push the executive's initiatives. At the very least, presidents with hegemonic aspirations need popular support to win the elections that allow them to stay in office (Velasco Guachalla et al. 2021).

Using data from the Executives Approval Project (Carlin et al. 2019), I assess the effect of presidents' popularity on their ability to erode democracy. The EAP data combines survey marginals of presidential popularity into a single monthly or quarterly series. The series goes as far back as 1978 for Costa Rica and Ecuador. It starts in the 1980s in Guatemala, Honduras, Perú, Uruguay, and Venezuela and, in the 1990s, in all other countries (except the Dominican Republic, which has data starting in 2000). The dataset has data for up to and including 2019.

Presidential approval ratings in Latin America suggest that popularity helps but is far from sufficient to guarantee success in eroding democracy. Half of the eighteen presidents with hegemonic aspirations, for which there is data available, had above-average approval ratings (>44 percent). Five of them (all successful potential autocrats in the sample) eroded democracy. The other four – including presidents like Uribe with the four highest approval rating in the region and the second highest among leaders with hegemonic aspirations (65 percent) – did not (Figure 3.10).

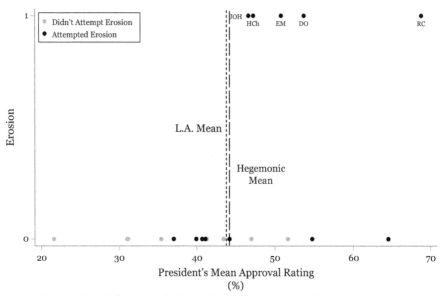

Source: Author's calculations using data from the Executive Approval Project 2.0 (Carlin et al. 2019)

FIGURE 3.10. President approval during process of erosion

3.5.4.3 *Polarization*

Recent scholarship has focused on polarization to explain the erosion of democracy (Handlin 2018; McCoy, Rahman, and Somer 2018; Nalepa, Vanberg, and Chiopris 2018; Somer and McCoy 2018; Graham and Svolik 2020). Presidents with hegemonic aspirations, these scholars argue, are polarizing political entrepreneurs who use antisystemic rhetoric to divide the political arena and society in two. Political polarization, they posit, creates "Us" versus "Them" dynamics, turning politics in a zero-sum game, in which the victory of a team (Us) is perceived as an absolute loss for the other team (Them), and vice versa. In this context, citizens and elites are more likely to support a president with hegemonic aspirations, either because they are uncertain about his level of authoritarianism (Nalepa, Vanberg, and Chiopris 2018) or because they do not care as long as their team wins (McCoy, Rahman, and Somer 2018; Graham and Svolik 2020).

Unfortunately, the kind of survey data needed to accurately assess this proposition is not available for Latin America between 1978 and 2019.[38] In

---

[38] One of the mechanisms to measure polarization is questions of antipartisanship. These questions are, however, relatively new and thus very few surveys in Latin America include them.

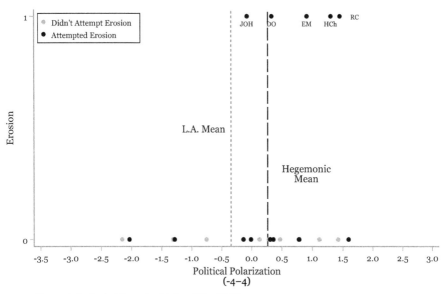

Source: Author's calculations using data from V-Dem (2021)

FIGURE 3.11. Political polarization during process of erosion

order to circumvent this problem, I use V-Dem's (2021) "Political Polarization"[39] indicator that uses country experts to assess the extent to which society is polarized. The original variable is standardized and ranges from −3.7 to 4.1 (in the world) – least polarized to most polarized – and from −3.3 to 3.5 in Latin America.

The data in Figure 3.11 suggests that polarization is important but insufficient to erode. In general, most presidents with hegemonic aspirations hinder tolerance. Mean political polarization for potential autocrats (0.26) is significantly higher than polarization among their nonhegemonic counterparts (−0.48) ($p > 0.06$). Overall, regardless of whether they succeed or fail in their attempts to undermine democracy, presidents with hegemonic aspirations seem to resort to polarization as part of their toolkit strategy.

However, not all polarizing political entrepreneurs succeed. Out of the five presidents who successfully eroded democracy, one – Hernández (−0.078) – had levels of political polarization below the hegemonic mean (0.26). Moreover, despite being expert polarizers, eleven of the sixteen presidents with hegemonic aspirations in the sample with above-average levels of political

---

[39] Question: *Is society polarized into antagonistic political camps?*

polarization – including leaders with very high levels of political polarization like Collor de Mello (1.42), Balaguer (1.11), and Uribe (0.79) – did not try or tried and failed to erode democracy.

In other words, there does not seem to be a condition that, ex ante guaranteed the erosion of democracy in Venezuela (Chávez), Bolivia (Morales), Ecuador (Correa), Honduras (Hernández), and Nicaragua (Ortega), and the survival of democracy elsewhere. Even if we take fuel exports, economic development and growth, popularity, and political tolerance together, they are not sufficient for the erosion of democracy. An index averaging the standardized versions of these factors[40] shows that out of the presidents who successfully eroded democracy, four – Ortega (0.03), Morales (0.56), Correa (1.15), and Chávez (1.35) – had high levels (above the hegemonic presidents' mean [0.014]) of economic development and growth, mineral revenues, popularity, and polarization. The same index also shows, however, that, out of the sixteen hegemonic presidents who did not try or failed to erode democracy, six had high levels (above the potential autocrats' mean) of economic development and growth, mineral revenues, popularity, and political intolerance.

This holds true even if we add institutional weakness at the time the president attains power to the mix. The leverage that economic development and growth, mineral resources, popularity, and polarization give to a potential autocrat can certainly increase in the midst of feeble institutions (Weyland 2020). I account for this possibility with a second index[41] that combines the aforementioned variables with interbranch crises and constitutional changes. All but one (Ortega [-0.03]) of the successful autocrats have above-average (0.027) levels of this second index. Weak institutions seem to boost the advantages that the other variables provide.

They are not, however, sufficient to explain the erosion of democracy. Five of the sixteen unsuccessful potential autocrats – Collor de Mello, Zelaya, Bucaram, Febres, Gutiérrez, and Uribe –also had above-average levels of economic performance, mineral wealth, popularity, polarization, and weak institutions. The Colombian ex-president has, in fact, the second highest index (0.84) of the whole group, suggesting that while these variables certainly help potential autocrats erode democracy, they do not overdetermine this outcome (Figure 3.12).

---

[40] I standardized all relevant variables and averaged them for all presidents in the sample. The resulting index goes from −1.18 to 1.35, has a mean of −0.002, and a standard deviation of 0.45. Among presidents with hegemonic aspirations, the index goes from −0.98 to 1.35, has a mean of 0.014, and a standard deviation of 0.61.

[41] I standardized all relevant variables and averaged them for all presidents in the sample. The resulting index goes from −1.18 to 0.95, has a mean of −0.011, and a standard deviation of 0.43. Among presidents with hegemonic aspirations, the index goes from −0.98 to 0.95, has a mean of −0.027, and a standard deviation of 0.54.

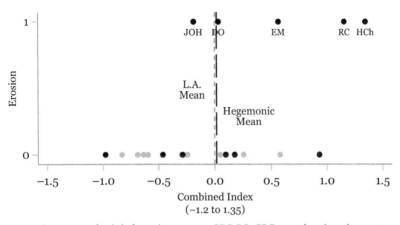

Source Author's index using average GDP PC, GDP growth, mineral exports, president approval and political polarization during the president's term. All variables are standarized.

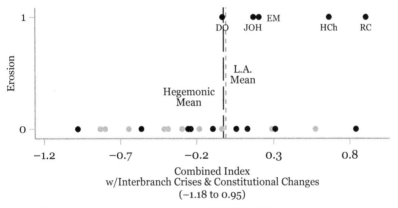

Source Author's index using average GDP PC, GDP growth, mineral exports, president approval and political polarization during the president's term. As well as mean interbranch crises and constitutional reforms before the president came to power. All variables are standarized

⬤ Didn't Attempt Erosion
● Attempted Erosion

FIGURE 3.12. Democratic erosion and combined index of variables during process of erosion

3.6 CONCLUSION

Scholars have argued that the erosion of democracy is the outcome of structural, institutional, and/or state-centered factors that drive presidents with hegemonic aspirations to power. As shown earlier, low state capacity and weakly institutionalized party systems – and to a lesser degree economic performance – are very helpful to explain the rise of presidents with hegemonic aspirations but are less helpful explaining why, once in power, some of them successfully erode democracy while others fail. Countries that experience economic downturns, with weak states and inchoate party systems, are more likely to elect presidents who try to enhance their powers and extend their time in office beyond a second term. Once these leaders are presidents, however, the factors that brought them to power – even the institutional strength they found when they attained office – do not seem to have a consistent effect on the likelihood that they erode democracy.

Of course, institutionalization, state capacity, and, in particular, economic development are not frozen in time. They could, and often do, change after a potential autocrat attains power, and as part of the process of democratic erosion, these factors certainly help explain why some of these leaders successfully erode democracy while others fail. An overview of economic development and growth after presidents with hegemonic aspirations are elected suggests, however, that access to large amounts of resources is neither necessary nor sufficient for the erosion of democracy.

The same is true for popularity and polarization. A president's popular support and his ability to polarize are often deemed as characteristics that can single-handedly make or break the erosion of democracy. The evidence presented earlier, however, suggests that neither of these variables are determinant factors. Although most hegemonic presidents are fairly popular and expert polarizers, and this is particularly salient for those who succeed in eroding democracy, these characteristics do not explain away the erosion of democracy. Presidents with very high approval ratings who promote polarization have failed to erode democracy, while presidents with lower approval ratings who foster less polarization have successfully transformed their countries' democracy into competitive authoritarian regimes.

Although it is clear that access to resources, popularity, and polarization are important assets for potential autocrats – especially in the contexts of weak institutions – they do not ex ante determine the fate of countries that see the rise of executives with hegemonic aspirations. This is, in part, because none of these factors work in a vacuum; actors other than the president have an influence on these variables as well. The erosion of democracy is, ultimately, a process. We need to analyze the mechanisms behind it, in particular, the role of the opposition. As mentioned earlier, during a process of democratic erosion, the opposition has ample opportunities to respond. As I will show in the following chapters, the strategies it uses and the goals it uses them for are critical not only to better understand why some potential autocrats are able to erode democracy while others are not but also how important variables like popularity, polarization, trust in institutions, and access to resources play into these dynamics.

In the chapters that follow, I use comparative historical analysis to trace the dynamics of erosion in Venezuela and Colombia. I show the mechanisms by which the opposition's extrainstitutional strategies with radical goals failed to prevent Chávez from eroding democracy in Venezuela, as well as the mechanisms by which the opposition's institutional and extrainstitutional strategies with moderate goals successfully avoided the erosion of democracy in Colombia.

4

"Chávez Vete Ya": The Erosion of Democracy in Venezuela

Up until the 1990s, Venezuela was one of the longest-running and most stable uninterrupted liberal democracies in Latin America. Today, it is an authoritarian regime. In nineteen years, Hugo Chávez and his successor, Nicolás Maduro, managed to destroy the system of checks and balances, end free and fair elections, and terminate political rights and civil liberties. The government has delayed and canceled elections, circumvented the authority of the elected legislature, imprisoned political opponents without trial, used lethal force against protesters, and banned opposition parties. How is it that Venezuela, historically one of the most robust democracies in the region, turned into the second most authoritarian country in Latin America?

Venezuela's regime change is an archetypal case of democratic erosion. Democracy in the country did not break down in one day. Hugo Chávez came to power via a free and fair election in 1999. It took him six years to undermine horizontal accountability and another three to erode electoral accountability. Throughout that process, the Venezuelan opposition had several institutional and noninstitutional resources at its disposal. Between 1999 and 2005, the opposition had a meaningful presence in congress, courts, oversight agencies, the state-owned petroleum company (PDVSA), and the military; it controlled important media outlets, and it could mobilize millions of Venezuelans to the streets. Many of these resources were useful to obstruct Chávez's project. As I will show below, had the opposition avoided radical extrainstitutional strategies and relied solely on moderate/radical institutional or moderate extrainstitutional strategies, it would have had a better chance to protect these resources, and delay the erosion of democracy. With time, perhaps, it could have even stopped Venezuela's regression into a competitive authoritarian regime.

The opposition, however, chose mostly extrainstitutional strategies to oust the president. A coup d'état in 2002, an indefinite strike in 2002–3, and an electoral boycott in 2005 diminished the opposition's ability to present itself as protector of democracy, legitimized Chávez's government and his polarizing discourse, and enabled him to remove opposition members from congress, courts, oversight agencies, the military, and PDVSA. In doing so, the opposition lost internal and external legitimacy, which gave Chávez "legitimate reasons" to repress, and cost it the very institutions it wanted to protect. The absence of opposition or independent individuals in these institutions hindered the opposition's ability to fight against more aggressive antidemocratic reforms after 2005, allowing the government to turn the country into a competitive authoritarian regime.

There are two common explanations for the erosion of democracy in Venezuela. The first one assumes democratic erosion is the outcome of long-standing structural and institutional characteristics, and thus almost inevitable once Chávez came to power (Coppedge 2005; Brewer-Carías 2010; Morgan 2011; Seawright 2012). The second one assumes the erosion of democracy was the outcome of Chávez's exceptional access to resources, strategic choices, and/ or institutional strength (Hidalgo 2009; Corrales 2011; Corrales and Penfold-Becerra 2015). Both of these explanations portray the opposition as helpless. The evidence displayed in this chapter shows that was not the case. The opposition started off with a variety of strategies it could pursue. Not only did it have institutional and noninstitutional resources well into Chávez's first term, but for several years it was actually stronger than the executive. As politically skilled as the Venezuelan president was – and as wrenching as the opposition choices were (Martínez Meucci 2012) – it is improbable that he could have overpowered the opposition while keeping his democratic credentials, if the latter had not slowly given away some of these resources using extrainstitutional radical strategies. As this chapter shows, had the opposition not resorted to these tactics, it would have been very difficult for the potential autocrat to fully purge the military and PDVSA or take over the National Assembly – all of which were key to Chávez's successful erosion of democracy – without engaging in overtly authoritarian moves that could have endangered his presidency.

In what follows, I trace the process of democratic erosion in Venezuela. I start with Chávez's first "power grabs," the 1999 Constitution and the 2000 Enabling Law. I show that, although aggressive, these power grabs did not fully erode democracy, and in 2001, the opposition still had plenty of institutional and noninstitutional resources left. I then move to the three radical extrainstitutional opposition strategies that these power grabs engendered – the coup, the indefinite strike, and the electoral boycott – and their consequences. At the time, the opposition had enough resources to implement institutional strategies or extrainstitutional strategies with moderate goals, but because it chose the "insurrectional" route instead, it gradually lost these resources, as well as the institutions it wanted to protect, reducing its capacity to fight more aggressive power grabs at each step. In the final section, I discuss the 2004 recall referendum and the legislative performance of opposition parties between 2000 and 2005. I show that, similar to what happened in Colombia, these institutional strategies strengthened the opposition, kept its legitimacy, and slowed down Chávez's reforms. The evidence displayed in this section suggests that if the opposition had avoided radical extrainstitutional strategies and used moderate institutional or even radical institutional and/or moderate extrainstitutional strategies instead, it would have been better able to protect its presence in congress, courts, and oversight agencies. This could have slowed down the process of democratic erosion, and, therefore, provide the opposition with more time and opportunities to curtail the president's ability to turn Venezuela into a competitive authoritarian regime.

4.1 THE "SLOW DEATH OF DEMOCRACY" IN VENEZUELA

In 1998, Hugo Chávez won office in the middle of crisis. State performance and confidence in institutions scored 4.01 and 3.77 out of 10 that year. The fall of petroleum oil prices in the 1970s, combined with the Latin American debt crisis in the 1980s, created an atmosphere of crisis that Venezuelan political parties and politicians failed to manage. The situation triggered a legitimacy crisis that weakened Venezuela's democratic institutions in the 1990s (Morgan 2011; Seawright 2012) and paved the way for the populist outsider who tapped into these legitimate grievances in his bid for the presidency.

It took Chávez nine years to completely erode democracy. Between 1999 and 2006, he hindered horizontal accountability through institutional reforms that established his full control over the National Assembly (AN) (2005–15), the Supreme Court (TSJ) (2004), oversight agencies (2005), the armed forces (2002), and the PDVSA (2003). Once the checks on the presidency were gone, the government began to undermine electoral accountability as well.[1] Starting in 2007, it denied broadcast licenses to opposition media outlets (2007), banned some opposition candidates from running for office (2008), used legislation to circumvent resources and responsibilities away from opposition-elected officials (2008), illegally put forward a second referendum that allowed Chávez to run for a third term (2009), used gerrymandering to secure an artificial majority of seats in the National Assembly (2010), used the army and oversight agencies to harass opposition candidates, and severely limited the opposition's access to campaign resources.

In 2006, elections in Venezuela – while increasingly irregular – were still somewhat fair (European Union Election Observation Mission 2006). By 2008, that was no longer the case. Although most elections after 2008 (up until 2015) were technically competitive, it was nearly impossible to defeat the Chavista

---

[1] This does not mean that Chávez did not try to hinder electoral accountability before 2006. The 2004 and 2006 elections had several irregularities. These violations, however, were not extensive enough to severely skew the electoral playing field.

government in these contests. After 2006, Venezuela had very little horizontal or electoral accountability. Nine years after Chávez came to office, the most stable and uninterrupted democracy in Latin America had been eroded and transformed into a competitive authoritarian regime.

4.1.1 The 1999 Constitutional Assembly

Immediately after being sworn into office, Hugo Chávez called for a constitutional assembly (ANC). At the time, the Venezuelan constitution could only be reformed by congress. During the 1990s, however, the legislature had been unable to pass a comprehensive constitutional reform (Brewer Carías 2008). In the midst of a grave economic and political crisis, Venezuelans began calling for a new constitution. During the campaign, Chávez promised to give them just that.

Chávez's victory in the 1998 presidential elections made it clear that a constitutional assembly was imminent. Trying to get ahead, many political leaders asked the newly elected congress – where opposition parties like Democratic Action (AD), Copei, and other smaller organizations had won a plurality of the seats – to reform the constitution in order to allow and, more importantly, regulate the ability to use a referendum to call for a constitutional assembly. The legislature, however, was unable to reach an agreement to do so (Brewer Carías 2008, 150–1).

Accordingly, in February 1999, Chávez issued a presidential decree, in which he called for a referendum asking citizens not only to decide whether they wanted to call for a constitutional assembly or not but also if they would allow the president to decide the mechanism to elect the representatives to it.[2] Even though the 1961 Constitution permitted only nonbinding referendums, the Supreme Court – delegitimized by media outlets and the public – chose not to rule against the popular incumbent and approved Chávez's decree word for word, giving the referendum a green light. Procedurally, Venezuela's Supreme Court's decision was very similar to the one made by Colombia's Supreme Court before the 1990 Constitutional Assembly. Although questionable from an institutional point of view, as shown by the Colombian case,[3] the decision in and of itself did not doom democracy in Venezuela.

Venezuelans approved the referendum in April 1999. Because the court's ruling allowed the government to design the mechanism to select the delegates for the ANC, Chávez was able to put forward electoral rules that significantly enhanced his coalition's chances to win.[4] As a consequence, the opposition only

---

[2] Decreto No. 3, Gaceta Oficial No. 36.634 of February 2, 1999.

[3] The 1991 Constitution is overall regarded as very democratic, more so than the 1886 Constitution that preceded it.

[4] One-hundred and four representatives were elected in twenty-four regional districts (according to population percentage), twenty-four representatives were elected in a national district, and three

obtained 5 percent of the ANC seats (6 out of 131). Fully controlled by the Chavista coalition, it took the constitutional assembly less than six months to come up with a new constitution. Venezuelans approved the draft in December of that same year.

Although the ANC and 1999 Constitution enhanced participation and inclusion for formerly marginalized urban and rural sectors (García-Guadilla 2018), it also concentrated power in three important ways. First, a few days after their first meeting, the ANC declared itself an "original constituent power" (*poder constitucional originario*). It closed congress and began legislating instead,[5] intervened in the judiciary, and suspended the regional elections that were supposed to take place in the fall of 1999. Second, the new constitution enhanced some of the powers of the president and increased his time in office. It reduced the size of congress and made it unicameral,[6] lengthened the presidential term one year and allowed for one immediate reelection, and gave the president full autonomy over military promotions. Third, the ANC named a mostly Chavista "legislative commission" that dismissed judges and oversight agents, named replacements, and legislated for six months with little restraint (Brewer-Carías 2000).

Despite dramatically transforming the system, the 1999 Constitution did not erode democracy. Institutional engineering is a complicated endeavor. It takes a type of foresight that most politicians, in particular those with little experience in politics, do not have. Accordingly, the new constitution did not give full control over state institutions to the president. Notwithstanding its small presence, the opposition had some minimal leverage in the new constitutional design. According to Ricardo Combellas[7] and Antonio Digiampaolo,[8] former members of the ANC, except for a couple of areas – namely, the appointment of military officers and the presidential term – Chávez had not thought through the new institutional framework.[9] Consequently, the 1999 Constitution kept a good part of the 1961 Constitution intact (Brewer Carías 2008, 149–298),

---

representatives were elected in a special indigenous district. For the regional district, voters could vote for as many candidates as there were seats available. In the national district, people could vote for up to ten candidates. Candidates could nominate themselves, could be nominated by a party, or could be nominated by a civil society group. The multiple ballot structure has strong majoritarian tendencies. If a party wins a simple majority in each district, it can win all the seats. Chávez went to each region to support his candidates and supported two different sets of candidates in the East (10) and the West (10). In the end, he got 103 of the 104 regional district seats, and 20 of the 24 national district seats.

[5] Such a practice was not unheard of. In 1990, the Colombian ANC did the same.

[6] It eliminated the Senate, where the opposition had a strong representation (Corrales 2011).

[7] Author's interview, Caracas, March 28, 2014. This and all translations from Spanish are the author's.

[8] Author's interview, Caracas, June 19, 2014.

[9] The mind behind the project was Luis Miquilena, a leftist politician and one of Chávez's main advisers, who split from Chavismo two years afterward.

allowed national recall referendums, and, at least on paper, strengthened bodies such as the judicial branch (Sanchez Urribarri 2011). Furthermore, neither the new constitution nor the laws of the "legislative commission" approved tampered with important entities such as PDVSA, increased the state's hold over media outlets, hindered civil liberties, or completely co-opted oversight agencies (Petkoff 2011). In the "mega-elections" (*megaelecciones*) of 2000 – called by Chávez to reelect the president, congress, and regional authorities – the CNE even sanctioned the president for using public resources to campaign.[10]

4.1.2 From the "Mega-Elections" to the Enabling Law (2000–2)

Despite being democratic and participatory in many ways, the Constitution of 1999 was an important power grab but not a definitive one. Although the mega-elections in 2000 were favorable to the president – who managed to count his first presidential term starting that year, not 1999 – the opposition won a little over a third (59 out of 165) of the congressional seats,[11] as well as eight governorships and several important mayorships.

According to Angel Medina, longtime member of AD, deputy for Justice First (PJ), and a former head of the Judicial Counsel Office in Congress, having a presence in the National Assembly (AN) then, even if useless to pass legislation or stop most reforms, was essential to slow down what would have been a faster process otherwise.[12] In "the first Assembly, there were spaces to use delaying tactics and to debate."[13] Even though the newly elected AN courts (TSJ) and oversight agencies (state attorney, comptroller, and ombudsman) were mostly favorable to the government, due to the sizable presence of the opposition in congress, the appointees to these offices had to be mostly "negotiated" names (Petkoff 2011, 33).

The second power grab happened three months after the mega-elections when the National Assembly approved a one-year Enabling Law (*Ley Habilitante*). This law permitted Chávez to rule by decree for one year in areas related to financial and socioeconomic matters, infrastructure, transportation and services, citizen and legal security, science and technology, and state organization and operation.[14] The president, however, did not use his powers of decree right away. In the utmost secrecy, he waited until a year later to

---

[10] Interview with Eugenio Martínez, political journalist in *El Universal*, Caracas, March 21, 2014; Gioconda Soto. "Invitan al cuerpo diplomático a verificar limpieza." *El Nacional*, May 11, 2000.
[11] *Acción Democrática* (AD) won thirty-three seats, Copei and *Proyecto Venezuela* (PRVZL) six seats each, Primero Justicia (PJ) five seats, *La Causa R* (LCR), *Un Nuevo Tiempo* (UNT) 3, and *Lo Alcanzado por Yacury* (LAPY) three seats each, and *Convergencia* one seat.
[12] Author's interview, Caracas, March 4, 2014.
[13] Author's interview, Caracas, March 27, 2014.
[14] Gaceta Oficial No. 37.077, November 14, 2000.

disclose the presidential decrees. In the meantime, he polarized the situation (Corrales 2011). He hardened his discourse (Martínez Meucci 2012, 42–3) and attacked the Venezuelan Workers Unions (CTV), dismissing the existing authorities – whom he saw as part of the establishment – and trying to elect pro-government leaders by popular vote.[15]

The government announced forty-nine presidential decrees in November 2001, one day before the expiration of the Enabling Law. The decrees made important changes to government, land usage, and the oil industry. They stated that lands would be rated according to their usage, and poorly or non-used lands would be expropriated (Medina and López Maya 2003, 20–5). They also gave the state a leading role in market research, price setting, and administration of oil resources, and put the executive in charge of the exploration, extraction, transportation, and storage of petroleum (Medina and López Maya 2003, 25–33).

Although the decrees did not make major changes in property rights[16] or seriously increase the state's control over institutions, they generated strong opposition among business leaders, landowners, PDVSA managers, and upper- and middle-class sectors (Medina and López Maya 2003, 41). The types of reforms these bills enacted, but, more importantly, the brusque manner and the polarized atmosphere in which they came about, created a sense of uncertainty among the opposition. People were afraid of what Chávez would do afterward.

Although not as significant as the 1999 Constitution, the forty-nine decrees authorized by the Enabling Law were a power grab. They threatened property rights and changed important regulations of the oil industry, which, until then, had been thought to be apolitical. Moreover, these reforms were done in a manner that was confrontational – enacted in one night and disregarding calls for moderation and negotiation (Martínez-Meucci 2012, 58). The reaction they sparked had more to do with the ways the decrees came about than with the changes they made.[17] Although some opposition members claim that Chávez used the Enabling Law to increase his hold over the state,[18] the decrees did not change horizontal institutions such as courts, congress, or oversight agencies.

---

[15] Although they had representatives from Copei, *Unidad Democrática Renovadora* (UDR) and *Marcha al Socialismo* (MAS) in their leadership, traditionally, the CTV had been mostly affiliated to AD (Coppedge 1994). Chávez tried to co-opt the union in December 2000 with a referendum that called for the renovation of all union leaders. When his candidates lost the referendum and opposition leaders, like Carlos Ortega, remained in control of the CTV, he refused to recognize the new authorities.

[16] Between 1960 and 1999, the government had redistributed two million hectares of privately owned land, an average of 51,000 a year; between 1999 and 2003, the government redistributed 2,609 ha of privately owned land, an average of 652 a year (Alegrett 2003).

[17] Author's interview with Miguel Angel Martínez Meucci, Professor at the Universidad Simón Bolívar, Caracas, April 25, 2014.

[18] Author's interview with constitutional law professor, Caracas, April 25, 2014.

Moreover, their implementation faced a lot of obstruction inside PDVSA, and they failed to transform land ownership to the extent Chávez would have liked.

4.2 EXTRAINSTITUTIONAL STRATEGIES WITH RADICAL GOALS

Despite the new constitution and the Enabling Law, three years into Chávez's government, the opposition still had institutional resources left (see Figure 5.2). Composed of unions, business associations, media owners, civil society organization, and politicians associated with the political and economic elites who had governed Venezuela in the past, the opposition had effective control over PDVSA, where the board of directors and most of the managers opposed Chávez; sympathizers inside the military; a meaningful presence in congress; and some support in courts and oversight agencies. The opposition leverage in these institutions had even increased since 2000 because of Chávez's reluctance to negotiate his 2001 decrees. His reluctance, combined with his increasingly polarizing discourse, had splintered and weakened the Chavista coalition, and strengthened the opposition in congress, the TSJ, and the CNE (Martínez Meucci 2012, 64–5).[19] The departure of Luis Miquilena[20] from Chávez's government in December 2001 increased the opposition coalition in the AN from fifty-nine seats to sixty-nine out of 165[21] and threatened to flip the CNE and the TSJ, where "Chavistas-Miquilenistas" controlled several seats (Sanchez Urribarri 2011).

The opposition, however, did not take full advantage of these resources. Unlike what happened in Colombia, where individual politicians survived the gradual deinstitutionalization of the traditional parties (Albarracín, Gamboa, and Mainwaring 2018a; Gamboa 2020a), in Venezuela, the party system collapse meant that people no longer trusted parties, politicians, or politics.[22] In 1998, 41 percent of Venezuelans expressed feeling distrust for politics, 4 percent more than the rest of Latin America (Latinobarometer 1998). Discredited, party leaders and politicians were silenced, and leaving unions, business associations, media owners, and other civil society organizations at the heart of the remaining opposition.

Thinking they could finish Chávez's presidency before the end of his constitutional term, these leaders chose highly risky but potentially immediately successful radical extrainstitutional strategies – a coup (2002), a strike (2003), and an electoral boycott (2005) – to fight the government. It was not,

---

[19] Interview with Ernesto Alvarenga, former member of the AN for the MVR, Caracas, July 18, 2014.
[20] Miquilena was a longstanding left-wing politician, cofounder of the Movement Fifth Republic (Chávez's political party). During the first years of Chávez's government, he served as president of the ANC and the National Legislative Commission.
[21] "La Asamblea Nacional En El Filo de La Navaja." 2002. *VenEconomía* 19(8).
[22] Author interviews with political science professor at CENDES, Caracas, March 6, 2014; Eduardo Fernández, former leader of Copei, Caracas, July 27, 2004; and Ramón Guillermo Aveledo, former secretary of the Mesa de Unidad Democrática, Caracas, August 4, 2014.

however, the only alternative at their disposal. Suggesting the availability of other alternatives, most members of opposition parties such as PJ, AD, Copei, and some factions of Movement Towards Socialism (MAS) and Proyect Venezuela (PV) with representation in congress thought this course of action would hurt more than it would help, as early as March 2001, Julio Borges, the National Assembly deputy for Primero Justicia at the time, said in an interview to *El Universal*, that "visceral anti-Chavismo is the greatest favor done to the President . . . What we have to look for is to be the alternative to Chávez, which means having your own speech, your own ideas and proposing them to let people be guided by our principles and solutions."[23]

This opinion was echoed by other interviewees, like Teodoro Petkoff, an opposition politician, journalist, and founder of the newspaper *Tal Cual*, who said to me that "Chávez, who was already worn out by 2002, would have continued to wear himself out." "Had the opposition fought back democratically," Petkoff continued, "he wouldn't have won his [2006] reelection."[24] These and other moderate opposition members, however, did not have the power or the legitimacy they needed to lead the opposition out of the "insurrectional" path. As posited by Eduardo Fernández, longstanding member and former leader of Copei:

[Politicians] were conspicuous by their absence ... First, was the demonization of politics ... We got to a point in which it was hard for somebody who was devoted to politics, like myself, to find spaces in the media to call for a broad policy in order to build new majorities ... And then was the radicalism. The same media outlets that had helped President Chávez attain power, once they realized that the president was "left-handed" [leftist], offered their spaces for a more radical policy that, as I said, consolidated the regime... There were no spaces, for those who proposed more reasonable policies to express themselves.[25]

As these moderate politicians predicted, the extrainstitutional strategies, in order to oust Chávez, backfired. They empowered Chávez to "brand" the opposition as "radical" and "undemocratic" inside and outside the country, provided him with "legitimate" reasons to prosecute, jail, and remove opposition leaders from elected and nonelected offices, and allowed him to gather enough support to push for more aggressive reforms that, out of office, the opposition was unable to stop. Between 1999 and 2006, Chávez was able to do irreparable harm to democracy without losing his democratic façade.

4.2.1 The Coup

As mentioned earlier, the forty-nine presidential decrees of November 2001 enraged middle- and upper-class sectors, who, under the leadership of

[23] Interview to Julio Borges in Ernesto Villegas Pojak. "Oposición visceral favorece a Chávez." *El Universal*, March 11, 2001.
[24] Author's interview, July 28, 2014.   [25] Author's interview, Caracas, July 27, 2014.

Fedecámaras (the national business association), the CTV, and private media outlets (*El Nacional*, *El Universal*, *Venevisión*, *Globovisión*, and *RCTV*), organized frequent mobilizations that lasted up until 2002. Initially, the protesters asked the government to revise and reverse some of the decrees (Medina and López Maya 2003, 40–4). When Chávez refused, they started to call for the president's resignation instead. What up until then had been an extrainstitutional strategy with *moderate goals* morphed into an extrainstitutional strategy with *radical goals*.

In response to the popular mobilization, Chávez hardened his discourse. Like in the game of chicken, government and opposition escalated their behavior waiting to see who drove off the road first (Magdaleno 2014). In February 2002, high-ranking members of the armed forces, such as Admiral Carlos Molina, Aviation Colonel Pedro Vicente Soto, and the National Guard Captain Pedro Flores Rivero, asked for Chávez's resignation.[26] Chávez obviously refused, and knowing it would fan the flames, he responded in kind by replacing PDVSA's board of directors later that month. As Chávez would declare later, "The thing about PDVSA was necessary ... because when I grabbed the whistle in a 'Aló Presidente' and started firing people, I was provoking the crisis; when I named Gastón Parra Luzardo and the new board we were provoking the crisis."[27]

As Chávez expected, his move hit a sensitive cord in Venezuela's society: "[t]hey [the opposition] answered and we had the conflict."[28] PDVSA was proudly conceived to be apolitical and meritocratic, and Chávez's advances were seen as attempts to politicize it. A large number of managers and workers opposed the new board. The opposition called for a general strike against the appointment. As the conflict unfolded, Chávez's resignation became the opposition's endgame. In an interview with *El Nacional* in March, Humberto Calderón Berti, a politician from Copei, declared, "A new PDVSA board will fix nothing, if Chávez remains president of Venezuela."[29] And a month later, Pedro Carmona, president of Fedecámaras, also said, "If there is no change, we will have to proceed through other ways, and consider other mechanisms that could even pose the possibility of a transition or an alternative to this government."[30]

The PDVSA stalemate worsened when the new board fired three managers who had supported the opposition strike. As the president's approval rating

---

[26] Fernández, Antonio. "Un País Democrático No Puede Esperar Solución Desde El Cuartel." *El Nacional*, February 25, 2002.
[27] Chávez Frías, Hugo. "Cadena Nacional Desde La Asamblea Nacional: Presentación de Cuentas a La AN." Caracas, January 15, 2004, 12.
[28] Chávez Frías, Hugo. "Cadena Nacional Desde La Asamblea Nacional: Presentación de Cuentas a La AN." Caracas, January 15, 2004, 12.
[29] Hernández, Katiuska. "Calderón Berti: Será Inevitable Un Paro En La Industria." *El Nacional*, March 6, 2002.
[30] Hernández, Katiuska. "Fedecámaras: Apoyo Total." *El Nacional*, April 8, 2002.

plummeted – from 61 percent in July 2001 to 35 percent by February 2002 (Datanálisis 2013) – the CTV and *Fedecámaras*, with the support of Venezuela's largest media outlets, scheduled the strike for April 9, followed by a massive street demonstration two days afterward. The protest, initially scheduled to finish at the PDVSA headquarters, continued to Miraflores,[31] calling not only for the reversal of these layoffs and the presidential decrees but, mostly, also for the end of Chávez's presidency under the rallying cry: "Chávez go away, now!"

As protesters were moving toward the presidential palace, where Chávez's supporters were waiting for them, anonymous shooters[32] began to fire on the crowd. The protesters, however, kept moving, and Chávez called the army to the streets. The military commanders refused to obey the president's order and asked for his resignation instead.

Up until April 12, the opposition had the upper hand. They had successfully removed Chávez from office, and now they needed to find a transitional government. Ignoring the calls of politicians on both sides of the aisle – some of whom were even offering to rally Chavista and non-Chavista votes inside the National Assembly in support for the interim government[33] – the coup leaders refused to follow the constitutional line of succession. Instead, Pedro Carmona swore himself in as president, named a new cabinet, abolished the 1999 Constitution, closed congress and the courts, dismissed regional authorities, and started a prosecution against Chavista officers.[34] It became clear that Chávez's dismissal was not aimed to preserve democratic institutions, but rather eradicate Chavismo from the political arena. Upset with this turn of events, and with Chavista supporters mobilizing in support of the president, the military withdrew their support of the de facto government. Some sectors of the armed forces who had not participated in the coup released Chávez from prison and brought him back on April 13.

Even today, it is hard to tell whether the coup was planned or not. Some analysts believe it was (Medina and López Maya 2003; Martínez Meucci 2012); others believe it was the unfortunate outcome of government allies firing on the protesters (Nelson 2009). Some people in Venezuela even claim that it

---

[31] There is some disagreement as to whether this was planned or not. Some scholars and political leaders – including opposition leaders – suggest this was planned (Medina and López Maya 2003). Other sectors, including some of the leaders of the demonstration, suggest this emerged naturally from the crowd, and there was nothing they could do about it (author's interview business leader, Bogotá, April 12, 2014).

[32] After the coup, both sides blamed each other for the shooting. There were victims from both sides, and the government shut down the investigation. There is not enough evidence to lean toward either version of the events (Medina and López Maya 2003; Nelson 2009).

[33] Author's interview with Ernesto Alvarenga (Caracas, July 8, 2014) and Teodoro Petkoff (Caracas, July 28, 2014).

[34] Author's interview with former politician affiliated to Copei, Caracas, August 10, 2014.

was not a coup, but a "power vacuum" instead.[35] Regardless of what we call it, the coup was a radical extrainstitutional strategy. It is clear from the events of April 2002 that the opposition wanted to oust the president before the end of his constitutional term and was willing go outside institutions to do so.

4.2.1.1 The Aftermath

Losing the coup gamble had disastrous consequences for the opposition. It hurt the opposition's support and democratic credentials. It gave Chávez a "legitimate" excuse to remove opposition members from office and the armed forces without losing his democratic façade. Domestically, the coup increased Chávez's level of support. According to surveys conducted by Datanálisis, whereas in February 2002, 35 percent of the Venezuelans approved of the president's performance and 58 percent disapproved of it, by June of that same year those numbers had changed to 45 percent approval and 55 percent disapproval. Although Venezuelans did not see institutions as an essential part of a democracy – 50 percent believed democracy could function without congress – they disapproved of overtly authoritarian moves. Fifty percent disagreed with the idea of closing congress and abolishing parliament, and 54 percent stated it was not "ok" for a government to disregard congress or other institutions in order to deal with a difficult situation (Latinobarometer 2001).

This event diminished the opposition's legitimacy as well. Immediately after the coup, the OEA invoked the Inter-American Democratic Charter and condemned the "alteration of the constitutional regime" (McCoy and Diez 2011, 10). Even the United States, which opposed Chávez's government and would have liked to see his opponents in government, backpedaled its support to the interim government and agreed that the opposition's actions were undemocratic (McCoy and Diez 2011, 10).

Moreover, like what happened in Turkey in 2016, the coup allowed the government to remove opposition members from key institutions. First, it made it easier to identify and purge disloyal elements inside the military. According to Eugenio Martínez, a political journalist at *El Universal*, "The coup gave Chávez the legitimacy, the reasons, and the information. Because, if it hadn't been for the coup, many people who opposed Chávez would have stayed in the government."[36]

Using the coup as an excuse, the government dismissed and pressed charges against high-ranking officers. Generals Efraín Vásquez and Pedro Pereira and Admirals Héctor Ramírez and Daniel Comisso were charged with rebellion. Although the Supreme Court eventually acquitted them in August 2002,[37] they were forced out of the army, and many of them had to flee the country shortly

---

[35] Author's interview with a Professor of Constitutional Law, April 25, 2014.
[36] Interview with Eugenio Martínez, journalist at *El Universal*, Caracas, March 21, 2014.
[37] It ruled that there had not been a coup but a "power vacuum," and, therefore, the military could not be charged with rebellion.

afterward. Later, other high-ranking members of the military, such as General Manuel Rosendo, were dismissed as well. Overall, between April and September 2002, a total of 200 officers were fired, forced to retire, or demoted.[38]

The coup also gave Chávez "legitimate" reasons to harass and prosecute opposition leaders, regardless of their participation in the putsch. Pedro Carmona was sentenced to house arrest while awaiting trial. He escaped and sought asylum in Colombia, where he lives now.[39] Henrique Capriles, Baruta's local mayor for the opposition party Primero Justicia, also faced charges. Even though he did not participate in the coup, the government accused him of instigating disturbances in the Cuban embassy between the 11th and the 13th of April. Capriles was jailed in 2004 and finally acquitted in 2006.

Finally, the coup allowed the president to intervene in the Metropolitan Police (PM). Shortly after being reinstated, Chávez blamed the shootings on the PM. The government prosecuted and jailed eight members of this body,[40] and seized most of their weapons and gear. Except for the army, the Metropolitan Police was the largest armed group in the country. Under the command of Alfredo Peña, the metropolitan mayor who notwithstanding initially supportive of Chávez had become increasingly vocal against his government, this body policed five municipalities of the Caracas metropolitan area (Libertador, Chacao, Baruta, Hatillo, and Sucre). It controlled crime, worked with the communities, and handled street protests. The coup gave Chávez the perfect excuse to incapacitate and eventually control this body (Nelson 2009, 267).[41]

In other words, the coup hurt the opposition in many ways, especially its support inside the armed forces. In line with the theory outlined in Chapter 2, it hindered the opposition's legitimacy and support and increased the president's, allowing Chávez to legitimately remove opposition members from key institutions. While there was certainly a chance that the coup had successfully removed Chávez and halted the erosion of democracy, using this radical extra-institutional strategy was very risky. The odds of successfully and sustainably removing Chávez from office before the end of his constitutional term were mild. Not only did Chávez have substantial organized civilian support he could

---

[38] Mayorca, Javier Ignacio. "Se Profundizó La Crisis de Liderazgo En La Fuerza Armada." *El Nacional*, September 11, 2002.

[39] Although Carlos Ortega remained initially untouched, the government brought charges against him in 2003 due to his participation in the PDVSA strike. He fled the country in March of that year.

[40] Deputies Henry Vivas and Lázaro Forero, security secretary Iván Simonovis, and functionaries Eramso Bolívar, Julio Ramón Rodríguez, and Luis Enrique Molina were sentenced to thirty years in prison; the first corporal Arube Salazar was sentenced to seventeen years; and the police functionary Marcos Hurtado was sentenced to sixteen years.

[41] In 2004, the Chavista mayor Juan Barreto politicized the PM; and in 2008, Chávez used a rule of decree to absorb it as part of the executive branch.

effectively mobilize against the coup (Ellner 2004) but it is unclear that – at that point – the international community would have supported such an abrasive form of democratic breakdown (Arceneaux and Pion-Berlin 2007). Moreover, a successful coup would have broken Venezuela's democracy anyway, while turning Chávez into a martyr. Even if the country had a quick return to democracy, the consequences of the radical extrainstitutional strategy would have forced the opposition to choose between allowing Chávez to compete and win elections (again) or ban him from running for office hindering Venezuela's transition to democracy.

4.2.2 The Strike

Although it backfired, the coup did not deplete the opposition's pockets of support. After the events of April 2002, the opposition still had plenty of resources left. It controlled PDVSA, and due to defections before and during the coup, it had a larger coalition in congress,[42] the TSJ, and the CNE.[43] After the coup, half of the TSJ justices were favorable to the opposition, CNE board members had a simple majority, and eighty-five members inside the National Assembly were ready to vote against the president.[44]

Right after the coup, both government and opposition declared that they wanted to negotiate. The putsch had rattled the international community, and neither government nor opposition wanted to be seen as intransigent (Martínez Meucci 2012, 79–87). In reality, however, both sides saw advantages in keeping polarization alive (Corrales 2011). On the one hand, Chávez thought it could further his control over state institutions. On the other hand, the opposition believed it could oust the president without having to negotiate. Although some of the more moderate opposition leaders wanted to de-escalate the conflict, they were weak within the opposition forces, and their calls were utterly ignored.[45]

Consequently, even though the Organization of American States (OAS) and the Carter Center started working on the foundations for a government–opposition negotiation on June, both sides kept a radical discourse and further escalated their actions. As the government moved forward sanctioning, dismissing, and pressing charges against institutional, political, civilian, or military leaders it deemed responsible for the coup, the opposition moved their

---

[42] According to Ernesto Alvarenga, at some point, opposition members of congress alongside Chavista defectors had the numbers to elect the president of the National Assembly. Author's interview Caracas, July 8, 2014.

[43] As mentioned earlier, some defections happened before the coup; others, however, happened as a consequence of Chávez asking the army to repress the protest in the streets.

[44] "La Asamblea Nacional En El Filo de La Navaja." 2002. *VenEconomía* 19(8).

[45] Author's interviews with Teodoro Petkoff, Caracas, July 28, 2014; Américo Martín, Caracas, March 20, 2014; Ernesto Alvarenga, Caracas, July 8, 2014; Julio Borges, Caracas, July 23, 2014; and Armando Briquet, Skype, September 2, 2014.

followers to the streets, hoping that enough pressure would force Chávez to resign (López Maya 2007, 156–76). These calls were further endorsed by several active and retired officers of the armed forces, who gathered in the Altamira Square (*Plaza de Altamira*) of Caracas between October and December to encourage people to "rebel" against the government (López Maya 2007, 165). These officers' actions worked to the president's advantage. The OAS publicly condemned the "sit in" (Martínez Meucci 2012, 111), and the government forced the active members of the armed forces who participated to retire.

Despite this escalation, the OAS and the Carter Center finally convinced government and opposition – now under an umbrella organization called Democratic Coordinating Unit (CD)[46] – to negotiate in November 2002. The agreement, however, did not reduce the tension. Both sides had agreed to negotiate in order to keep their legitimacy – appear conciliatory and "reasonable" – but their endgame remained the same.[47]

Consequently, both the government and the opposition kept an ambivalent attitude toward the negotiation table (Martínez Meucci 2012). On the one hand, the president continuously did things that were perceived as hostile by the opposition. On November 17, the National Guard intervened in the headquarters of the Metropolitan Police, which had been, until then, under the command of the Caracas mayor Alfredo Peña, who had opposed Chávez since April 2002. On the other hand, the opposition kept the street mobilizations alive. It believed that it should keep pressuring the government "from all possible sides." For them, the table was not meant to come to an agreement, but rather it was "meant to serve as a space in which to negotiate the terms of his [Chávez's] 'surrender'" (McCoy and Diez 2011, 73).

Early in November, the opposition collected signatures to schedule a "consultative referendum," asking Venezuelans if they wanted Chávez to resign immediately. At the negotiating table, the CD threatened a general strike if the government failed to schedule the referendum (Martínez Meucci 2012, 120). Even though the CNE slated the referendum for February 2003,[48] media owners, business leaders, and union leaders went through with their threat. Feeling that the measure was going to give oxygen to the president, they called for a general strike on December 2, confident that such a move was going to "kill the government" right away (Martínez Meucci 2012, 121).

Originally, the strike was supposed to last a couple of weeks – a moderate extrainstitutional strategy in support of the referendum initiative. However, strengthened by the support of the Petroleum People (*Gente del Petróleo*) (a

---

[46] The Democratic Coordinating Unit had representatives from political parties and civil society associations. Unfortunately, it was too broad and had too many voices in it. It never held de facto power, and leaders outside the CD often went rogue.
[47] Interview with member of the negotiation team, Puerto Rico, June 27, 2015.
[48] Decision that the government fought tooth and nail.

quasi-union composed by middle and top PDVSA managers), its leaders turned it into an "indefinite strike" with the intent of pushing Chávez to resign (López Maya 2007, 176) – a radical extrainstitutional strategy. According to Américo Martín, opposition representative in the Carter Center–OAS led negotiation:

...It [the opposition] felt strong with the people in the streets. And it hoped that, if it continued with the demonstrations, these would translate in the government's fall ... And all those who at some point, from their experience, asked that it ceased to do what it was doing ... were criticized. I, myself, called. I said: *No, no, the strike cannot be indefinite. I have never seen an indefinite strike, other than to oust the government.*[49]

Up until 2003, no president had survived a PDVSA strike. Initially, the radical extrainstitutional strategy put the government up against the wall. Between December 2002 and January 2003, the national GDP dropped by 4.5 billion dollars (Banco Central de Venezuela 2013), the national production of goods and services partially collapsed, people were laid off, and small business owners went broke (López Maya 2007, 192–3). There was a moment in which even Chavista followers thought it was a matter of time before the president had to resign.[50] However, slowly but steadily, the government regained control over the situation. It used the armed forces that – after the coup – it now controlled to get PDVSA up and running again and successfully overcame food shortages with the help of neighbor countries such as Brazil (Martínez Meucci 2012, 139). By mid-January, it was evident that the opposition was losing control of the strike, and by February, when activities were "officially" reinitiated, the strike had practically faded away.

4.2.2.1 The Aftermath

The strike did not have the outcome its leaders expected. On the contrary, as Américo Martín suggests, "The indefinite strike was condemned to failure..., but they wanted to keep it, and they kept it, and they kept it, and they kept it, and that weakened the opposition and strengthened the government."[51] Like the coup, this radical extrainstitutional strategy also hurt the opposition's support and allowed Chávez to remove opposition members from a key institution – PDVSA – without losing his democratic credentials. The strike diminished the opposition's support inside the country, hindered the opposition's ability to negotiate a favorable agreement at the OAS and Carter Center negotiation table, and gave the government a perfect window to remove opposition members from PDVSA and replace them with loyalists.

As mentioned earlier, the strike seriously hurt the Venezuelan economy. Venezuela holds the largest oil reserves in the world. According to the World Bank, in 2003, petroleum exports made up 82 percent of the country's GDP.

---

[49] Author's interview, Caracas, March 20, 2014.
[50] Interview with Chavista follower, Bogotá, April 12, 2014.
[51] Author's interview, Caracas, March 20, 2014.

Due to the halt in oil production, the country's GDP dropped by 17.6 percent (Corrales and Penfold-Becerra 2011),[52] midsize and small businesses went broke, and the employment rate suffered a 5 percent decrease in those months (López Maya 2007, 193). Citizens, however, did not blame the government for the economic downturn. Rather, by mid-January, public opinion surveys suggested that 76 percent of people thought the strike had not fulfilled its objective, 64 percent believed the strike hurt citizens more than it hurt the government, and 52 percent believed there were more effective ways to protest (López Maya 2007, 192). Right after the strike, many Venezuelans who had self-identified as members of, or sympathizers with, the opposition moved into the undecided ("neither–nor") column. According to Datanálisis, before the strike, a little more than 35 percent of Venezuelans supported the opposition; later that year, that number dropped to a little less than 30 percent. By the same token, before the strike, a little more than 35 percent of Venezuelans self-identified as "neither government nor opposition supporters." Later that year, that number increased to approximately 45 percent.

Internationally, the strike did not hurt the opposition's legitimacy as much as the coup did. Contrary to what the Venezuelan government wanted, the OAS did not admonish the opposition but called for a peaceful and electoral resolution to the crisis instead (Martínez Meucci 2012, 128). The strike, however, did not generate the support the opposition was expecting either. The international community did not side with the opposition. Supported by most Latin American countries, the OAS and the Carter Center refused to endorse the strikers' push for Chávez's early resignation and favored mechanisms to call for early elections instead (McCoy and Diez 2011, 76–82).

Unfortunately, by February, that was not an option anymore. The indefinite strike hindered the opposition's ability to get a favorable agreement at the Carter Center–OAS negotiating table. As the strike grew weaker, the opposition lost leverage. Before December, the opposition had showed it had enough strength in the streets to push for early presidential elections. By late January, however, the call for early elections seemed unrealistic, and what became feasible was a recall referendum instead. This referendum, nonetheless, was never the opposition's top choice. It could only be requested after Chávez had completed half of his term, which meant that, even in favorable circumstances, it would only take place after August 2003. The fact that the opposition had to settle for a recall referendum was not the outcome of an ineffective mediation strategy, as Martínez Meucci (2012) argues, but rather the result of squandering their leverage at the negotiation table. The recall referendum not only was a mechanism already available in the 1999 Constitution[53] but also the only

---

[52] The Central Bank reports a decrease of 2,284,964 thousand Bolivares (VEB) between the GDP in the third trimester of 2002 and the GDP in the first trimester of 2003, a GDP drop of 23 percent.
[53] Author's interview with member of the international negotiation team, Puerto Rico, May 27, 2015.

proposition the government had been willing to consider two months prior (Martínez Meucci 2012, 142).

Perhaps the most serious consequence of the strike was that it provided an opportunity for the government to impose full control over PDVSA. The strike provided Chávez with information and "good" reasons to get rid of approximately 18,000 PDVSA managers and employees (60 percent of the staff) who were fired for ceasing to work and replaced with Chavista loyalists (Corrales and Penfold-Becerra 2011, 78). PDVSA, which until then had been controlled by the opposition, was lost to the government after the indefinite strike. In short order, the executive transformed the company into an instrument to fulfill its project (López Maya 2007, 193).

Chávez's ability to gain direct control over the petroleum company was a pivotal moment in the erosion of democracy in Venezuela. During the oil boom, between 2000 and 2010, PDVSA received approximately $209 billion dollars in oil revenues (approximately 32 percent of the country's GDP).[54] Had the government not taken control over the company, Chávez might not have been able to use these revenues for building domestic and international support. After 2003, Chávez dismantled the company's oversight system[55] in order to divert more of its revenues to fund social, agricultural, and infrastructure projects domestically and abroad. Most notably, control over PDVSA after the strike allowed Chávez to set aside a fund (*Fondo para el Desarrollo Económico y Social del País – Fondespa*) directly run by PDVSA's president and cabinet member that allowed the government to distribute funds locally and internationally without reporting to the Central Bank or the National Assembly (Corrales and Penfold-Becerra 2011, 79–80).

Locally, the government leveraged its control over oil revenues to bankroll *Fondespa,* a fund created to pay for the poverty alleviation program's Missions (*Misiones*). The Missions designed to offer housing, health services, subsidized food, and education to poor communities, were created in 2003 in order to increase Chávez's support, which they largely achieved. Although these programs improved basic social indicators, the money was distributed using clientelistic criteria. Between 2003 and 2008, PDVSA spent more than $23 billion dollars on these social programs (Corrales and Penfold-Becerra 2011, 83). On the eve of the recall referendum and the local elections in 2004, the government invested close to 4 percent of the country's GDP into the Missions (Corrales and Penfold-Becerra 2011), and on the eve of the presidential elections, in 2006, that figure had risen to 6 percent (Daguerre 2011). The electoral outcome of the Missions was clear. Not only did they increase Chàvez's popularity in

[54] *PODE 2009–2010: Petróleo y Otros Datos Estadísticos.* Ministerio del Poder Popular de Petróleo y Minería (September 14, 2015).

[55] Before 2004, PDVSA was under the supervision of the Ministry of Oil, the Central Bank, an internal comptroller, and the Securities Exchange Commission of the United States (Corrales and Penfold-Becerra 2011, 79–80).

time for the recall referendum (Corrales and Penfold-Becerra 2011; McCoy and Diez 2011; Martínez Meucci 2012) but also his overall popular support. Whereas in 2000, 3,757,773 people (59 percent of valid votes) voted for Chávez; in 2006, after two years of Missions, twice as many people did the same. That year, Chávez obtained 7,309,080 votes (63 percent of valid votes). Although the opposition also increased its overall support in this period, this increase was not nearly as significant as the government's. In fact, between 2000 and 2006, the opposition saw a small decrease in its vote share. In 2000, Francisco Arias got 2,359,459 votes (38 percent of valid votes), while in 2006, Manuel Rosales got 4,292,466 votes (37 percent of valid votes).

Internationally, Fondespa was set up to pay for investments, aid, and subsidies to a large number of countries in South America and the Caribbean. According to Corrales and Penfold-Becerra (Corrales and Penfold-Becerra 2015, 105), in 2008, Venezuela was the third largest South–South foreign aid contributor among the non-OECD countries. These contributions helped Chávez buy international support. This support guaranteed allies inside international organizations, as well as silence in the face of his increasingly authoritarian moves.

In sum, the strike allowed Chávez to take over the state-owned petroleum company and have discretionary control over the vast resources of the oil boom. As suggested by a government negotiation delegate in a conversation with Francisco Diez, a mediator of the OAS–Carter Center negotiation table, Chávez was able to buy domestic and international support:

we are very happy with this strike. Now we have a revolution! Finally! Until now everything had been *pico* [kisses], but now we managed to control PDVSA and put it to the service of the people. That is truly revolutionary! And that has made people support us with everything again. We are taking little trucks to the shantytowns with a video that shows how all the PDVSA money never reached the people, and how that is going to change from now on. The opposition does not understand anything. (Cited in Martínez Meucci 2012, 122)

It is hard to know for sure whether Chávez would have been able to take over PDVSA without the strike. Without the "excuse" of the strike, the government could probably have fired some people inside the company and perhaps, in time, taken control of the board of directors anyway (Corrales and Penfold-Becerra 2011, 77), but as I have suggested, time is a crucial resource for oppositions working to slow or halt the erosion of democracy. The strike, however, facilitated a faster turnover. It handed Chávez a historic opportunity to infiltrate the petroleum company. Without it, the government would never have been able to find and fire as many opposition members as it did without losing its democratic façade.[56] Taking over the company would have taken

---

[56] Author's interview with Eugenio Martínez, political journalist at *El Universal*, Caracas, March 21, 2014.

more time, delaying Chávez's access to the oil windfall, and thus hindering his ability to use oil revenues in order to buy support in the 2004, 2005, and 2006 electoral contests.

4.2.3 The Electoral Boycott

Despite being severely weakened by 2003, the opposition was still not entirely powerless. It still had some institutional and noninstitutional resources it could use against the executive. It controlled most of the media, half of the judiciary (ten of twenty members in the TSJ and most of the Electoral and Administrative Rooms), part of the National Electoral Council (CNE), and had a majority coalition in the National Assembly. As I will show later in this chapter, the opposition was able to use these positions effectively to denounce and obstruct important government initiatives and rule against the president in serious matters (Sanchez Urribarri 2011). Even though Chávez's power and legitimacy had increased as a consequence of the coup and the indefinite strike, the opposition's presence in these institutions still proved able to prevent, or at least tame, his project.[57]

Starting in 2001, the Supreme Tribunal of Justice and CNE sided with the opposition several times. In November 2001, the government asked the CNE, and later the TSJ, to nullify the elections of the national union association (CTV), which had not gone its way. Both the CNE and the TSJ refused to do so. In July 2002, the TSJ chose not to charge the military personnel who had participated in the April putsch and ruled that there had not been a coup but a "power vacuum" instead. In October 2002, the TSJ ruled in favor of the opposition's challenge to the government's intervention in the Metropolitan Police. A month afterward, it disregarded the government's petition to nullify the CNE's decision to schedule an opposition "consultative referendum" that asked people if they wanted Chávez to resign. Even though not all of the decisions of courts and oversight agencies benefited the opposition,[58] these rulings suggest that these institutions were not yet entirely co-opted by the government.

As of March 2003, the opposition still had some resources to fight the president. Now everything depended upon the Carter Center–OAS led negotiation, where the opposition was trying to speed up an agreement to hold a recall referendum, which the government, strengthened by the failed strike, had no interest in doing. In 2002, the opposition was not strong enough to push Chávez out of office but was strong enough to negotiate.[59] Before December 2002, when the opposition privileged the insurrectional strategy and dismissed

---

[57] Author's interview with a board member of First Justice, Caracas, April 29, 2014.
[58] In a second ruling, the TSJ decided against the "consultative referendum" eight days before it took place.
[59] Author's interview with member of negotiation team, Puerto Rico, May 27, 2015.

the referendum as an alternative, pressure from the streets, low petroleum prices, and Chávez's weak support might have been enough to facilitate a speedy referendum. In March 2003, however, none of these factors existed anymore. The coup and the strike hindered the opposition's ability to use mass mobilization and protest to push for a better agreement and thwarted its capacity to supervise the use of PDVSA resources. With petroleum prices on the rise and little restraint, Chávez was able to buy support.

The referendum eventually reached the ballot box, but it arrived too late. Even though the agreement was signed in May 2003, the elections did not take place until August 2004. Chávez used all sorts of legal strategies to postpone the vote. As part of the OAS–Carter Center agreement, the government and the opposition named a new CNE board.[60] Although the new body ended up with two rectors linked to the government, two linked to the opposition, and a third "neutral," the institution turned out to be slightly biased in favor of the government.[61] The new electoral officers, together with the Constitutional Chamber inside the TSJ, allowed the president to delay the referendum: not only did it invalidate signatures the opposition initially collected in February 2003 and required the opposition to collect them again but also requested that approximately a million signatories verify the validity of their signatures as well. By the time the referendum took place, petroleum prices were rising, and Chávez's popularity was picking up. Consequently, the opposition lost.

The defeat demoralized the opposition.[62] Although the election results were certified by the OAS[63] and the Carter Center,[64] the radical sector of the

---

[60] During the negotiation, the government requested to replace the CNE. The CNE had authorized the opposition's consultative referendum in 2002, and Chávez thought this was a sign that the organization was biased against him.

[61] The AN was in charge of electing the directors, but gridlock moved the issue into the courts. On August 2003, the TSJ appointed new rectors: two from the opposition, two from the government, and a third "neutral" one to preside. According to McCoy and Diez (2011, 111–13), initially, the TSJ chose Eleazar Días Rangel, who had been approved both by the government and the CD. He was the chief editor of the newspaper (*Ultimas Noticias*), who despite being Chavista had shown independent judgment several times. Before the election became public, however, media outlets unilaterally aired very critical reports about Días Rangel, forcing him to decline the appointment. Left without a "consensus" candidate, the TSJ chose Francisco Carrasquero instead. Carrasquero, closely linked with the Chavista president of the TSJ, was unknown; therefore, neither side had a problem with him. According to Teodoro Petkoff, even though Días Rangel was Chavista, he also had an independent mind; chances are he would have been fairer than Carrasquero ever was (Author's interview, Caracas, June 28, 2014).

[62] Author's interview with Edwin Luzardo from Alianza Bravo Pueblo, Caracas, March 2014.

[63] "Results of the Presidential Recall Referendum Held in Venezuela on August 15, 2004." CP/ RES. Organization of American States. Accessed July 11, 2020. http://www.oas.org/council/ resolutions/res869.asp.

[64] Carter Center. "Observing the Venezuela Presidential Recall Referendum: Comprehensive Report." Carter Center, February 2005. http://www.cartercenter.org/documents/2020.pdf.

opposition cried fraud.[65] They claimed that the upcoming elections were not going to be fair and suggested boycotting them in hopes to deny legitimacy to the CNE, the results of the 2004 referendum, and ultimately the government,[66] suggesting even the possibility of capitalizing the low turnout in order to launch Article 350 of the constitution,[67] calling to "disown any regime, legislation, or authority that violates democratic values, principles and guarantees."[68] Poll data at the time suggested the opposition could have won about thirty seats in the parliamentary elections of 2005,[69] but the radical sector, led by media outlets,[70] created an atmosphere that pushed candidates and voters to abstain.

4.2.3.1 *The Aftermath*

This extrainstitutional strategy with radical goals backfired as well. Most of my interviewees agreed it was one of the worst mistakes the opposition could have made. It did not increase the incentives or the costs to prosecute or jail the opposition members, but significantly decrease the costs of removing them from the legislature. The government was able to get a 100 percent Chavista assembly without engaging in a costly purge that would have likely hurt its democratic legitimacy. Despite the very low turnout, the international community sanctioned the elections. Reports from the European Union (European Union Election Observation Mission 2006) and the OAS (Organization of American States 2006) declared that, notwithstanding some irregularities, the election

[65] Notwithstanding there is little evidence of fraud, some sectors of the opposition still claim that the results did not match the popular will (author's interviews with members of electoral NGO, Caracas, July 29, 2014, and Caracas, August 3, 2014). Supported by statistical analyses (Hausmann and Rigobon 2011), they argue that the machines were, in fact, tampered with, and the government changed enough votes to win. The evidence in support of these claims is, however, underwhelming. Some analysis use opposition polling data to compare results (Prado and Sansó 2011); others look for anomalies in the distribution of votes between computerized voting centers and manual voting centers, assuming that both of these were equal in everything but vote choice (Taylor 2005; Febres Cordero and Márquez 2006; Pericchi and Torres 2011); other compare data from the 1998 and 2002 presidential elections versus the 2004 referendum, without taking into account the change in government and opposition coalitions, or even that Chávez's support might have changed in those years (Jiménez 2011).

[66] Lugo, Hernán. "Convocan para el 4-D 'toque de queda electoral.'" *El Nacional*, November 30, 2005.

[67] Torrealba, Kairine. "Parlamento Teñido de Rojo." *El Nacional*, December 29, 2005.

[68] Not all opposition politicians declared the same motives to abstain. The boycott happened in a snowball process that started with radical factions advocating to boycott the election in an effort to delegitimize the election and the government, but ended with less radical factions, withdrawing their candidates with more moderate requests. Reyes, Ascensión. "Adecos Se Retiran de Elecciones y Piden La Renuncia Del CNE." *El Nacional*, November 29, 2005; Reyes, Ascensión, and Jorge Maneiro. "Se Retiró Primero Justicia." *El Nacional*, December 1, 2005; Reyes, Ascensión, Lesbia Pinto, and Dámasco Jiménez. "Se Fracturó La Unidad de La Oposición." *El Nacional*, November 30, 2005.

[69] Authors interview with board member of Primero Justicia, April 29, 2014.

[70] After the coup and the strike, the opposition had lost all other visible leaders.

was democratic. They even admonished the opposition for abstaining from participating.

More seriously, the new parliament sped up the government's efforts to co-opt other institutions. As I will show later, between 2006 and 2010, the National Assembly sanctioned twice the number of laws it sanctioned between 2000 and 2005 and did so almost three times as fast as it did before. In its second period, the AN also replaced the CNE rectors and TSJ justices, getting rid of whatever opposition members they had left. It also introduced legislation to further change the AN's rules of procedure in order to avoid opposition obstruction in the future,[71] altering several laws to further the Chavista project. In 2007, the government called for a referendum that would have seriously tightened the control of the executive over state institutions. Although the opposition was able to gather enough support to defeat the initiative, the government used the 100 percent Chavista National Assembly and his control over the TSJ and CNE to illegally launch a second referendum in 2009 that got a majority of the votes and allowed the president to run for immediate reelection indefinitely, effectively eroding democracy.

4.3 INSTITUTIONAL STRATEGIES WITH MODERATE AND RADICAL GOALS

So far, I have used process tracing to outline the causal mechanisms by which extrainstitutional strategies with radical goals led to the erosion of democracy in Venezuela. Leveraging within-case variation, in the next sections, I briefly discuss two of the instances in which the Venezuelan opposition used institutional strategies and introduce some of the causal mechanisms by which these tactics could have hindered Chávez's ability to erode democracy.

Using an original parliamentary database, built with data collected at the Legislative Archive of the National Assembly, and archival research, in this section I show that within Venezuela, institutional strategies that used elections and congress between 2000 and 2005 not only protected the opposition's legitimacy domestically and abroad but also strengthened the anti-Chavista coalition and were able to slow down the government's institutional reforms. While using institutional or moderate extrainstitutional strategies in Venezuela was not without risk (Martínez Meucci 2012), the gamble was a safer one. As the evidence presented below suggests, when successful, these tactics in fact slowed down the erosion of democracy; and when failed, they allowed Chávez to continue undermining democracy unhindered but protected the opposition's

---

[71] In December 2010, they introduced a massive reform of the AN's rules of procedure. The file of the debate (Exp. 970) only has the cover page, suggesting this bill passed without any debate. This reform changed important rules. For instance, the president of parliament was no longer required to yield the floor to deputies who wanted to talk (Gaceta Oficial Sesión Extraordinaria No. 6014, December 23, 2010).

resources and legitimacy. Had the anti-Chavista coalition stuck to institutional strategies or extrainstitutional strategies with moderate goals and foregone extrainstitutional strategies with radical goals, they might have been more likely to curb, and even stop, Chávez's erosion of democracy.

In Chapter 5, where I discuss the case of Alvaro Uribe in Colombia, I provide a more detailed explanation of the mechanisms by which moderate institutional strategies, alongside nonviolent legal moderate extrainstitutional strategies, help prevent the erosion of democracy. The purpose of this section is to show (a) that these strategies were available to the opposition in Venezuela, and (b) that their outcomes are not case dependent. Opposition institutional strategies have similar outcomes regardless of whether they dealt with Hugo Chávez or Alvaro Uribe.

4.3.1 Moderate Institutional Strategies: The Opposition Inside the AN (2000–5)

As mentioned, between 2000 and 2005, the opposition had a sizable representation in the AN and was able to use it in order to slow down Chávez's consolidation of power and efforts to erode democracy. In what follows, I compare the 2000–5 legislative term, in which the opposition had seats in the AN, against the 2006–10 term, in which the opposition had no seats in the AN. Although the government had a legislative majority in both terms, the evidence suggests not only that it was able to introduce and approve more bills between 2006 and 2010 but also that it was able to do so faster than it did before.

From 2000 to 2010, the AN debated 967 bills: 412 between 2000 and 2005, and 555 between 2006 and 2010. The opposition introduced fifty-five of those bills and approved fifteen; the government[72] introduced 804 of those bills and approved 669.[73] As shown in Figure 4.1, of the government bills, 31 percent were introduced between 2000 and 2005, while 69 percent were introduced between 2006 and 2010. Out of the 669 government-authored bills, 28 percent were approved between 2000 and 2005, and 72 percent were approved between 2006 and 2010. In other words, whereas between 2000 and 2005 the government had a bill approval rate of 75 percent, between 2006 and 2010 this rate spiked to 87 percent.

The government was also able to approve bills faster between 2006 and 2010 than it was between 2000 and 2005. If we measure the

---

[72] Introduced by the president, the vice president, a cabinet member, members of the government coalition in congress, or Chavista citizen groups.

[73] There are 108 bills without a clear author. Most of them (ninety-seven) were coauthored by the government and opposition deputies; eleven of them do not have clear information about who introduced them.

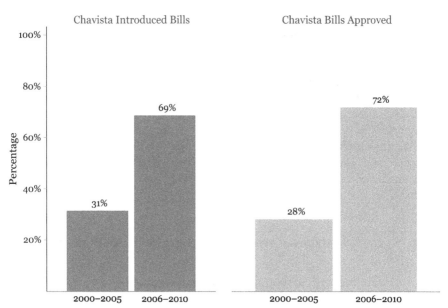

FIGURE 4.1. Percentage of government bills introduced and approved, 2000–5 and 2006–10

time – in days – between a bill's introduction and the first time it was sanctioned,[74] the government bills introduced between 2000 and 2005 took an average of 217 days to go through congress, while bills introduced between 2006 and 2010 took thirty-six days, 83 percent fewer days (Figure 4.2).

This is also true for bills that regulate courts and oversight agencies, usually called Organic Laws (*Ley Orgánica*). Between 2000 and 2010, the AN debated 140 organic laws (or reforms to organic laws) and approved 81. The government introduced eighty-six of the 140 organic laws – 40 percent between 2000 and 2005, 60 percent between 2006 and 2010 – and approved fifty-two; 25 percent between 2000 and 2005, and 75 percent between 2006 and 2010. Whereas in the first legislative period, it took the government an average of 785 days to push an organic law through congress; in the second legislative period, it took an average of only 157 days, one-fifth as much.

This pattern remains when we compare similar bills across legislative periods. In January 2003, the government introduced the Organic Law of the Supreme Tribunal of Justice (LOTSJ), in order to increase the number of justices and break the government–opposition tie inside the TSJ in its favor. It took 490 days to approve this bill. In December 2009, the government

---

[74] Some of these bills were sanctioned two and three times. Most of the time, this means that they were vetoed by the president. In that case, the delay cannot be attributed to the opposition but rather to the government.

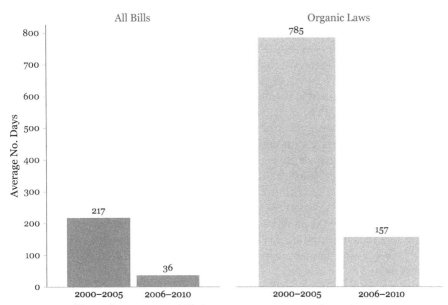

FIGURE 4.2. Time of government bills in congress, 2000–5 and 2006–10

reintroduced the LOTSJ. This time, however, without the opposition, it took the National Assembly 159 days to approve it. Similarly, in January 2003, the government introduced the Law of Social Responsibility on Radio and Television (*Ley de Responsabilidad Social en la Radio y en la Televisión, LRS, or simply, "Ley Resorte"*) in order to increase the government's control over media outlets. It took the AN 679 days to approve this bill. In August 2005 and December 2010, the government introduced two reforms to the LSR bill. It took the AN ninety days to approve the first one and only eleven to approve the second one.

If we look into the debates over some of these laws, it is clear that the opposition was using parliamentary procedure to obstruct the bill, and that by doing so it was able to significantly slow down the president's reform. When debating the LOTSJ, for instance, the opposition was able to delay the bill for a year. The piece of legislation was introduced in January 2003. Although there is no information about the debates inside the parliamentary commissions, the plenary debate of this bill did not take place until August 28, 2003, and it was not approved until May 18 of the next year.

As previously mentioned, the LOTSJ was meant to help the government co-opt the Supreme Tribunal of Justice. The "power vacuum" ruling in 2002 made evident that Chávez did not have full control over this high court, and was thus vulnerable to rulings he could not influence. The LOTSJ was supposed to change that by increasing the number of justices in the TSJ, allowing the AN to elect the new justices by simple majority, and increasing the AN's powers to dismiss justices. In the heat of the battle between government and opposition, and with the recall referendum approaching, the government did not want to take chances and pressed its coalition in the AN to approve the bill fast.

The opposition, however, employed a skillful use of parliamentary procedure.[75] Most bills in Venezuela need two debates. The first debate went fairly quickly. The government was able to approve the entire project in a single session on January 28, 2003. The second debate, on the contrary, was very slow. It took the AN twelve sessions – most of them twenty-four hours long – to approve the bill. During those twelve sessions, the opposition (1) registered as many speakers as they could (between twenty and thirty);[76] (2) asked to verify the quorum using roll call voting every hour, as allowed by the AN rules; (3) made different motions that not only interrupted the flow of the debate but also had to be voted on before they were dismissed; (4) asked to verify each voting procedure using roll call voting twice; (5) put between two and six bill amendments up for a vote; and (6) recorded approximately twelve dissenting votes for every decision made.

As Juan José Caldera, congressmen for the opposition, told *El Nacional* on November 2003:

> Since Chavismo introduced this bill on January 6, it has been a year, and although Chávez has said this is the year of the revolutionary offensive, this bill has not been able to leave the Parliament. The opposition has some credit there ... The line that the opposition holds is making impossible the approval of this law[77]

These tactics proved to be viable. The opposition was not able to stop the bill, but it delayed it enough so that most of the decisions about the recall referendum happened before the new Chavista-leaning TSJ was sworn into office.[78] Had the opposition kept its seats in congress the next period, they might have been able to delay more consequential bills as well. Although the delays could have not guaranteed the survival of democracy in Venezuela, they would have opened up the set of possible outcomes, perhaps allowing the opposition to be better able to contest the 2006 elections.

4.3.2 Radical Institutional Strategy: The Referendum

The recall referendum that took place in August 2004 is a prime example of an institutional strategy with radical goals. It used elections in order to oust the

---

[75] Some of these procedural "tools" had already been curtailed with a reform to the AN's regulation (Gaceta Oficial No.37.706 of June 6, 2003).

[76] In the first session, on August 28, they registered a little over seventy speakers; later on, however, they were not able to do that anymore. On September 25, 2003 (*VenEconomía*, October 2003), the government coalition modified the AN's regulation, allowing any member of congress to end the debate once 25 percent of the deputies present had talked.

[77] Casas, Cenovia. "Aumento de Magistrados de La Sala Electoral Compromete El Revocatorio." *El Nacional*, November 1, 2003.

[78] Gaceta Oficial 37.942, May 20, 2004.

president before the end of his constitutional term. Although the recall referendum was not very successful in delaying Chávez's project and thus seen by some as a form of "appeasement" (Martínez Meucci 2012), unlike the coup and the strike, it did not delegitimize the opposition, nor did it enable the government to remove opposition members from key institutions. Rather, the recall referendum strengthened the opposition's electoral capabilities and even slightly tarnished Chávez's "democratic" image abroad.

The recall referendum was a long and tortuous process for the opposition. The latter collected the first set of signatures on February 2003 but had to collect them all over again in November under rules agreed upon with the government in the OAS–Carter Center led negotiation. After reviewing the new set of signatures, the newly elected CNE decided that all the signatures that had the same handwriting on the basic data (i.e., name, address, ID, etc.) had to be "repaired." The "repairs" (*reparos*) meant that the signatures had to be reviewed, and the signatories had to verify they had actually signed. The opposition had to mobilize approximately a million people to verify signatures between February and May 2004. The process was highly irregular. The government published the list of signers (Tascon List – *Lista Tascón*), leaving them vulnerable to reprisals, and the CNE allowed citizens who had signed the petition to recant.

Notwithstanding these roadblocks, the opposition was able to collect enough signatures, and the referendum was scheduled for August 2004. Unfortunately, as mentioned, the referendum failed, which led many to believe it was just a "series of concessions that were useless because, from the beginning, those making the decisions did not understand the nature and the dimensions of the problem they were facing" (Martínez Meucci 2012, 20).

While it is true that under different circumstances – some of them avoidable by the opposition – the referendum could have had a different outcome, not everything that came out of it was negative. During the referendum, the opposition began to learn how to contest elections under Chávez. Súmate[79] – an electoral NGO – used the 2004 elections to develop and diffuse strategies that sought to overcome irregularities. Chances are that, had the opposition participated in the 2005 election, they might have been able win several seats in congress.

More importantly, unlike the extrainstitutional strategies with radical goals the opposition had used before, the referendum did not help Chávez to

---

[79] The role of Súmate is hard to assess. They were in charge of most of the opposition strategy during the 2004 recall referendum. Not only were they responsible for every decision made about the recall referendum but also they organized and mobilized voters to sign the petition, revise their signatures, and go to the polls. They also provided oversight mechanisms in order to count votes. Although they claim they were in favor of participating in the 2005 elections, some opposition members believe they were the ones who infused fear about the 2005 elections, eventually supporting the decision to abstain.

legitimately remove opposition leaders from congress, courts, oversight agencies, or other key institutions. During the referendum, the government indicted Henrique Capriles, but it used his alleged participation in the coup as an excuse. It also indicted some Súmate members for accepting NED funds, but this was also done using the coup as an excuse.[80]

This, of course, does not mean that the government did not retaliate. Unlike moderate institutional strategies, the referendum created a zero-sum game that increased the incentives to repress. The government made public the list of signatories: the Tascón List and *Maisanta* database. These lists identified the signatories of the petition to recall the president, as well as the signatories of the government-led parallel petition to recall opposition deputies. There were many complaints that people who appeared in these lists were denied public services and even fired from their jobs. Most of the complaints came from people who signed against the president, although there are a few complaints from Chavista signers as well (Hawkins 2010c). Hsieh et al. (2009) have shown that petition signers suffered a 5 percent drop in earnings and a 1.3 percent drop in employment rates in 2005. Consistent with my theory, however, this behavior was condemned by the international community (Carter Center 2005; European Union Election Observation Mission 2006), which eventually forced the government to take down the list from the web, and publicly admonished those who used it.[81]

While the referendum did not have the outcome the opposition expected, it also did not have all the negative consequences of the radical extrainstitutional strategies employed by the opposition such as the coup, the strike, and the boycott. Even if he wanted to, Chávez was not able to use the referendum as an excuse to take over media outlets, fire public office holders, or remove opposition leaders from the AN, the TSJ, or the CNE. The fact that the opposition was playing by the rules protected them and hindered the president's ability to use the referendum as yet another argument to increase his hold over the state.

4.4 CONCLUSION

This chapter traced the dynamics of the erosion of democracy in Venezuela. It outlined the mechanisms by which radical extrainstitutional strategies helped Hugo Chávez augment his powers and extend his time in office. The narrative shows that, because the president was democratically elected, these tactics decreased the Venezuelan opposition's legitimacy while increasing the legitimacy of the incumbent. In doing so, these tactics gave the government a window of opportunity to remove opposition leaders from important institutions and

---

[80] Some of Súmate's founders, like Maria Corina Machado, allegedly signed the "Carmona Decree" (*Decreto Carmona*) in support of the transitional government during the coup.

[81] Da Corte and María Lilibeth. "Chávez exigió enterrar 'La famosa lista del diputado Luis Tascón." *El Universal*, April 16, 2005.

prosecute or jail them. After seven years, without institutional resources, the opposition was unable to prevent Chávez from completing his hold over state institutions.

The erosion of democracy in Venezuela was far from certain in 1999. Between 2000 and 2005, many, including some his supporters, believed that Chávez was not going to last.[82] In line with the theory outlined in Chapter 2, I detailed how the opposition not only had enough institutional and noninstitutional resources to fight the government but also that in using extrainstitutional strategies with the hope to oust Chávez, it squandered them all. Had the opposition resorted to institutional strategies or extrainstitutional strategies with moderate goals, it might have been able to stop Chávez sooner, or at least slow him down enough to have a better shot at fighting more serious reforms down the road.[83] As I will show with more detail in the next chapter where I analyze the case of Alvaro Uribe, institutional strategies or extrainstitutional strategies with moderate goals uphold the opposition's legitimacy domestically and abroad, reducing the incentives and increasing the costs to repress. They allow the opposition to stay in office and use their position to delay, modify, and even stop more radical reforms.

Starting in 2006, the Venezuelan opposition changed tactics and goals. Led by old and new politicians, it abandoned the idea of ousting Chávez, organized, and opted to use institutional strategies and moderate extrainstitutional strategies instead. Venezuela, however, was no longer democratic in the years after 2006. With the government in control of congress, courts, and oversight agencies, the opposition had few strategic choices left. The anti-Chavistas had some victories. Despite Manuel Rosales, the opposition candidate, winning only 30 percent of the vote in 2006, the opposition defeated a government's referendum the next year; in 2008, it won a number of important local offices; and in 2010, it won one-third of the National Assembly's seats – all through more moderate strategies. These victories allowed the opposition to create a new "office record," enhance its electoral constituency, give visibility to its leaders, and build an electoral programmatic discourse. They served as a platform to prepare the 2012 and 2013 presidential elections and helped the opposition win the 2015 parliamentary elections with two-thirds of the seats.[84]

The anti-Chavista coalition also improved its standing internationally. Despite the government's international coalition, what Javier Corrales (2015) calls an "alliance for tolerance" and the deafening silence of the international community up until 2016, the new goals and strategies facilitated and improved

---

[82] Author's interview with Chavista supporter, Bogotá, May 12, 2014.

[83] Interview with Venezuelan academic, Caracas, March 20, 2014; Eugenio Martínez, *El Universal* journalist, March 21, 2014; and Julio Borges, leader of Primero Justicia, Caracas, July 23, 2014; Teodoro Petkoff, Caracas, July 28, 2014.

[84] The CNE and the TSJ refused to swear into office three deputies. In the end, the opposition was only able to keep a simple majority (109 of 167).

the opposition's chances of obtaining international economic and diplomatic support.[85] Funding from democracy promotion agencies in the United States and Europe helped pay for the latest political campaigns.

The fact that the government controlled the AN (except 2015–20), the CNE, and the TSJ by 2006 severely limited these later opposition victories. After 2006, the elections have been highly unfair. The government controls (increasingly more) resources, media outlets, and state institutions, and it has become increasingly hard to defeat it. Moreover, whenever the anti-Chavista coalition has managed to win elections, the government has used congress, courts, and oversight agencies to circumvent and reduce the local politicians' access to resources, severely curtail the opposition's ability to legislate or participate in a meaningful way in the National Assembly, or simply ignore its authority. After the opposition won a qualified majority in the AN in 2016, the government used the TSJ to prevent newly elected opposition congress members from taking office, bypass the AN in order to legislate, cancel a lawful recall referendum, postpone regional elections, and elect a constitutional assembly with the ability to change the rules of the game at will.

Since 2016 the Venezuelan government has increasingly resorted to repression. As of 2017, Venezuela can no longer be classified as a competitive authoritarian regime. Even though it has held elections, they are not even minimally competitive. This country is, after Cuba, the most authoritarian in the region. Facing a humanitarian crisis of unprecedented proportions, Maduro's grip on power depends almost entirely on a corrupt group of military officials who feed off state resources while the government shields them from prosecution.

---

[85] Interview with former secretary of the Mesa de Unidad Democrática Ramón Aveledo, Caracas, August 14, 2014.

5

Preventing the Erosion of Democracy in Colombia

In the previous chapter, I showed how the Venezuelan opposition's strategic choices helped Hugo Chávez erode democracy. In this chapter, I develop the other part of my argument by highlighting the role of the Colombian opposition in preventing democratic erosion. Between 2002 and 2010, Alvaro Uribe tried to erode democracy in Colombia. Like Hugo Chávez (1999–2013) in Venezuela, he introduced several reforms that sought to reduce the checks on the executive and extend his time in office beyond a second term. He was polarizing, and willing to push as far as he could to increase the powers of the presidency and stay in office beyond a second term. His government harassed opposition members, journalists, and members of the courts and worked in tandem with illegal armed actors to systemically undermine those who criticized the president. Contrary to Chávez, however, Uribe was not able to turn Colombia's democracy into a competitive authoritarian regime. Despite his attempts to undermine the independence of the courts and the fairness of elections, Colombia's constitutional order remained fairly strong, and Uribe had to step down after his second term.

Unlike the Venezuelan opposition, the anti-Uribista coalition was not particularly strong. Composed by a loose coalition of left and centrist politicians, unions, and human rights NGOs, it had some presence in congress, some friendly newspapers and online media outlets, and some ability to mobilize people to the streets. In contrast with the anti-Chavistas, however, the opposition in Colombia had little or no access to TV or radio outlets and no support inside the armed forces, and its mobilizations against the government were not as massive or visible as those organized by its Venezuelan counterpart. The courts in Colombia – which played a critical role in stopping the presidential reforms that would have eroded democracy – were independent of the executive when Uribe became president. However, by the time Chávez came to power, so were the Venezuelan courts. Between

2002 and 2010, there was no guarantee that the judiciary in Colombia would remain independent and strong long enough to stop Uribe's second reelection reform.

Despite its comparative weakness, the opposition in Colombia was able to prevent the erosion of democracy. Following the theory outlined earlier in the book, in this chapter, I leverage within- and cross-case variation to show that by avoiding extrainstitutional strategies with radical goals and using institutional strategies and extrainstitutional strategies with moderate goals to fight the president, the opposition preserved its legitimacy domestically and abroad. The anti-Uribista coalition kept a good distance from the guerrillas, publicly criticized its violent acts, and never took to the streets in hopes to push Uribe to resign. Its reluctance to use radical extrainstitutional strategies (or validate those who used them) allowed the opposition to maintain and enlarge its coalition, keep and moderately increase its popular support, and present itself as a credible democratic representative of the non-Uribista minority, both domestically and abroad.

Notwithstanding the government's attempts to paint those who opposed it as "terrorists" or "FARC allies," the opposition kept the "moral high ground." It avoided giving the president "legitimate" reasons to remove opposition members from key state institutions, prosecute them, or jail them, which allowed them to use institutional strategies in combination with moderate extrainstitutional strategies to protect courts and oversight agencies and slow down Uribe's antidemocratic reforms. Despite being a minority, the legislative anti-Uribista coalition was able to extend the transit of Uribe's constitutional amendments through congress and denounce or manufacture procedural irregularities. The delays opened up windows to soften otherwise radical reforms and increased public scrutiny. Procedural irregularities facilitated judicial review by providing arguments to rule against some of these constitutional amendments. Aided by street demonstrations and an electoral boycott against specific reforms, these strategies helped slow down the process by which Uribe meant to weaken other branches of government and helped the Constitutional Court stop the president's second reelection reform.

For many, the survival of democracy in Colombia was a foregone conclusion. Existing scholarship credits Uribe's failure to erode democracy to either his limited willingness to undermine democratic institutions (Dugas 2003) or the strength of Colombia's institutions, in particular the Constitutional Court (Weyland 2013; Mayka 2016; Ginsburg and Huq 2018). In this chapter, I interrogate both of these points. The evidence displayed shows that Uribe was capable of eroding democracy and willing to do so. Had he had it his way, he would have curtailed the powers of the Constitutional Court. The latter survived and was able to effectively stop the president's antidemocratic reforms, thanks to the opposition's aid in congress, which would have been impossible had anti-Uribista politicians and activists given into or supported radical extrainstitutional strategies.

In what follows, I illustrate the mechanisms by which institutional and extrainstitutional strategies with moderate goals helped the opposition protect democracy in Colombia. In Section 5.1, I outline the characteristics of Colombia's government and opposition between 2002 and 2010. I show that Alvaro Uribe came to power in a context similar to Hugo Chávez and that he was similarly willing to and capable of eroding democracy. I also show that the anti-Uribista coalition was not nearly as strong as the anti-Chavista one.

In Section 5.2, I focus on the consequences of avoiding extrainstitutional strategies with radical goals. I demonstrate how the absence of these tactics allowed the opposition to keep its legitimacy domestically and abroad. This behavior helped opposition members keep and increase their coalition inside and outside congress and lobby the international community against Uribe's programs and reforms. If the opposition had not avoided extrainstitutional strategies with radical goals, it would have been easier for Uribe to create artificial majorities in congress and undermine or co-opt courts and oversight agencies, making it difficult for the opposition to use these institutions to fight later reforms that would have affected democracy more adversely.

In Section 5.2.2, I focus on the mechanisms by which moderate institutional strategies (i.e., legislative obstruction and the manufacture or report of procedural irregularities) and moderate extrainstitutional strategies (i.e., electoral boycott and peaceful demonstrations) prevented the erosion of democracy. I illustrate how members of congress used legislative procedure to delay the transit of Uribe's reforms through congress and create/denounce procedural irregularities. The delays allowed Uribistas and non-Uribistas to modify the constitutional amendments before they left congress and increased public scrutiny to mount an effective, often moderate extrainstitutional, campaign against them. The procedural irregularities provided the Constitutional Court with critical legal resources that enabled the institution to rule against some of these reforms. Without them, it would have been much harder and very costly for the court to stop Uribe's constitutional amendments. Section 5.2.3 underscores this point. Using the first reelection reform as an example, I illustrate how the effective use of procedural irregularities helped to protect Colombia from the erosion of democracy.

5.1 ALVARO URIBE: A PRESIDENT WITH HEGEMONIC ASPIRATIONS

Like Chávez, Alvaro Uribe came to power in the midst of a state crisis. In 2002, state performance and confidence in institutions scored 4.68 and 4.14 out of 10. During the 1990s, the violence stemming out of Colombia's forty-year-old armed conflict skyrocketed, and by the turn of the century, the state had lost control of an important part of the national territory (Echandía Castilla and Bechara Gómez 2006). Between 1990 and 2002, terrorist attacks increased

950 percent,[1] massacres 156 percent,[2] civilian casualties during armed confrontations 263 percent,[3] and kidnappings 195 percent[4] (Centro de Nacional de Memoria Historica). By the time Uribe came to power, people blamed the FARC for the increasing violence.[5] The public believed that the guerrillas had taken advantage of the government during Andrés Pastrana's (1998–2002) peace process (Dugas 2003; López de la Roche 2014, 46) and negotiating with them was not a viable alternative for the time being.[6]

The failure of Pastrana's peace talks not only discredited the FARC; it also discredited all those who had ever supported a negotiated alternative to end the armed conflict (Gutiérrez Sanín 2007). Throughout the 1990s, Colombia's party system – once a very stable two-party system – had become increasingly fragmented and volatile (Pizarro Leongómez 2006). The Liberal and Conservative parties had barely been able to maintain their legislative majorities. The disgraceful end of the negotiations with the FARC in 2002 was the straw that broke the camel's back. Afterward, the traditional parties were perceived as equally incompetent. They could not present themselves as credible alternatives, which triggered a legitimacy crisis that paved the way for Alvaro Uribe to attain power as an outsider (Albarracín, Gamboa, and Mainwaring 2018).

Before he ran for president, Uribe was a member of the Liberal Party (PL). He had been Medellín's mayor (1982–3) and a city's council member (1984–6). He had also been Antioquia's governor (1995–7) and a senator for the PL (1986–94). Early in 2000, he tried to run in the PL primaries, but later that year, he withdrew his nomination and ran in 2002 with an anti-partisan movement (*Movimiento Primero Colombia*) instead. His personalistic "iron-fist" and "anti-politics" (*anti-politiquería*) platform turned out to be very attractive. He won the presidential election against the traditional parties with 53 percent of the votes, 21 percent more than his closest contender Horacio Serpa (PL). He was the first candidate to win presidential elections outside the traditional parties, and the only one to do so without going into a runoff since this rule was adopted in 1991.

Uribe's performance as Antioquia's governor between 1995 and 1997 was controversial due to his promotion of the civilian self-defense forces (CONVIVIR). In theory, these groups were supposed to help provide security in areas where state security forces had little presence. In practice, however,

---

[1] From 2 in 1989 to 21 in 2002.   [2] From 58 in 1990 to 149 in 2002.
[3] From 60 in 1990 to 218 in 2002.   [4] From 1,122 in 1990 to 3,306 in 2002.
[5] Although the FARC was responsible for a portion of these crimes, so were other guerrillas as well as paramilitary groups.
[6] Right before the 2002 elections, 59 percent of the people thought that the government should try to defeat FARC. A year later, however, that number had dropped to 52 percent. In 2004, only 35 percent of the people thought the government should keep trying to defeat FARC, while 60 percent thought it should negotiate with them (Gallup 2006).

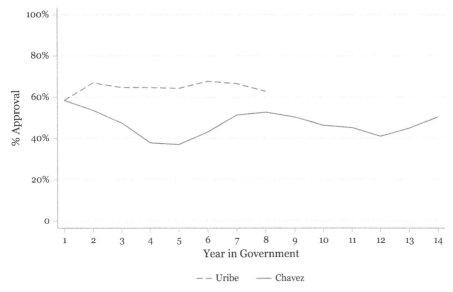

Source: Executive Approval Project 2.0 (Carlin et.al. 2019)

FIGURE 5.1. Alvaro Uribe and Hugo Chávez's approval

several of these groups built or developed strong ties with paramilitary groups and perpetrated, or helped others perpetrate, human rights abuses such as torture, extrajudicial killings, and massacres (Dugas 2003). Despite this background, Uribe's popularity in 2002 was unparalleled. His approval rating was 50 percent when he came to office, rose as high as 80 percent during his second term, and never dropped below 60 percent.[7] As seen in Figure 5.1, Chávez's popularity was not as consistent or high as Uribe's. He started his presidency with a job approval rating of 55 percent but slid to the low 30s shortly afterward (2002) and never went back to what it was in 1999. Chávez's average approval rating between 1999 and 2012 was 42 percent;[8] Uribe's was 69 percent between 2002 and 2010.

Despite having a different ideology, Uribe's style was as personalistic and polarizing as Hugo Chávez (Ortiz Ayala and García Sánchez 2014). Even though there is some debate as to whether he was a populist or not,[9] Uribe

---

[7] For details, see Figure E1 in the Appendix.   [8] For details, see Figure E2 in the Appendix.

[9] The debate stems, largely, from the debate on what is and what is not populism. For Kurt Weyland (2017), for example, Uribe (like Carlos Menem and Alan García [1985–90]) can be qualified as "predominantly yet not fully populist" because "his two-term presidency rested on unorganized mass support for his personalistic leadership, but he had a background in and counting connections to Colombia's traditional parties" (68). On the contrary, for example, according to the Global Populism Database (Hawkins et al. 2019), the former Colombian president is not a populist, because his speeches do not conform to the ideational definition of

used populist rhetoric and tactics like berating *all* politicians and bureaucrats as deceiving, cheap (*politiqueros*), and corrupt.[10] He also worked to establish an unmediated relationship with the people. Like the Venezuelan president,[11] the Colombian leader addressed the nation on TV on a regular basis. Every other Saturday he went to a different town and conducted his famous community councils (*Consejos Comunitarios*). These were televised twelve-hour long town hall meetings, in which a group of people in a given community would gather to communicate their troubles and concerns directly to the president. Although seemingly innocuous, these town hall meetings presented the president as the embodiment of the state. Uribe listened to people's private and public problems, and then, live, ordered regional authorities and cabinet members in the room – the "despised" politicians and bureaucrats – to immediately address them, regardless of whether the issue was access to clean water or a person's inability to get credit from a private bank (Cristina de la Torre 2005).

Uribe was very polarizing in other ways as well. He, and important members of his government, depicted those who criticized him – human rights NGOs and community leaders, politicians, judges, and journalists – as enemies of the state. They regularly called them "antipatriotic" and "terrorists," and accused them of aligning with foreign countries – Cuba and Venezuela – against their own (González 2013).[12] According to a member of a human rights NGO and advocacy group, Uribe "legitimized disrespect as valid political behavior. He legitimized stigmatization."[13]

Maintained in large part by his popularity, Uribe's coalition in congress was fairly strong (Milanese 2011). It included the Conservative Party, Radical Change (CR),[14] several smaller parties,[15] and members of the Liberal Party. These groups controlled 62 percent of the seats in the Senate and 65 percent of the seats in the lower house between 2002 and 2006, and 70 percent of the seats in the Senate and 54 percent of the seats in the lower house between 2006 and 2010.[16] Although some studies cast doubts on the idea that Uribe's coalition was "steamrolling" (Carroll and Pachón 2016), his popularity and refusal to

---

populism, identified by a discourse "dividing the political world into two camps: the good, identified with the virtuous will of the common people; and the evil, embodied in a conspiring elite" (Hawkins and Castanho Silva 2019, 28).

[10] His campaign manifesto, for instance, accused politicians and bureaucrats, in general, of lying to people with a "social discourse" they cannot fulfill because they have stolen the money via corruption and clientelism (Uribe 2002).

[11] Chávez addressed the nation every week in his show *Aló Presidente*.

[12] "La Ira Presidencial." *Revista Semana*, September 15, 2003. "Todopoderoso." *Revista Semana*, March 24, 2008.

[13] Author's interview, Bogotá, January 13, 2014.

[14] Cambio Radical changed its allegiance when the Uribista coalition introduced the reelection referendum in 2008.

[15] *Alas-Equipo Colombia, Apertura Liberal, Convergencia Ciudadana,* and *Colombia Democrática*, among others.

[16] My own calculations based on original coding.

affiliate with a political party, combined with legislators' need for state resources in order to feed regional clienteles and institutional changes after 2003,[17] helped Uribe keep his congressional coalition in line (Milanese 2011). Between 2002 and 2006, his government approved 62 percent of the bills it introduced; between 2006 and 2010, it approved 50 percent (Carroll and Pachón 2016).

Uribe also had the unconditional support of the armed forces. Traditionally, the military has been subordinated to and supportive of the president. Since the beginning of the National Front (*Frente Nacional*) – the sixteen-year period during which the Liberal and Conservative parties divided power equally, alternating presidents and dividing legislative bodies by half – the armed forces' obedience to the executive has been a given. Moreover, Uribe was particularly popular among the military. They liked his "iron-fist" stance against the guerrillas and the fact that he always stood behind the institution. In the words of a former member of the armed forces, "Uribe was the first president who dignified the members of the armed forces … He had zero tolerance [with violence and] assumed responsibility for the armed forces if anything went wrong. He was committed. If it hadn't been for him, there are things that we could not have done."[18]

Throughout his government, Uribe also had the endorsement of important media outlets. *El Tiempo*, Colombia's largest newspaper, had close ties with government officials. The family of Francisco and Juan Manuel Santos (vice president and minister of defense, respectively) owned this media outlet until 2007. The Spanish editorial company (*Grupo Planeta*) who bought it also kept a pro-government editorial line (López de la Roche 2014, 62–3). Along with *RCN* and *Caracol* – the two largest television broadcasting companies in the country – this important newspaper either failed to discuss political issues that could damage the government or had an openly pro-government editorial line. In October 2009, for instance, Claudia López – an activist critical of the government – wrote an op-ed criticizing how *El Tiempo* had covered some of the president's administration scandals: namely, corruption in the adjudication of agricultural subsidies and the armed forces' extrajudicial killings. Her column was canceled as a result of her essay (López de la Roche 2014, 357–64).

Despite this bias, the media in Colombia was not entirely pro-Uribe. First, none of the newspapers or TV broadcasting companies was completely co-opted. *El Tiempo*, for instance, had several op-eds written by people who opposed the government. Second, there were important media outlets that remained critical of the government such as *CM&*, *Noticias UNO*, *Revista Semana*, and *Cambio* magazine (López de la Roche 2014, 62–5, 76–8, 80–3).

---

[17] In particular, the Coalitions Law (*Ley de Bancadas*) in 2005, which forced members of a given party to vote with their party.

[18] Author's interview, Bogotá, December 9, 2013.

Uribe tried to pressure journalists in these outlets to silence their criticisms,[19] but, for the most part, he was unsuccessful.

The Colombian president was as willing as Hugo Chávez to increase his powers and extend his time in office beyond a second term in order to achieve his policy goals. Between 2002 and 2006, the Uribistas introduced several constitutional reforms that sought to reduce the checks on the executive and prolong Uribe's time in office. The government or its coalition in congress authored 75 percent of all the constitutional amendments (i.e., referendums and legislative acts) introduced during Uribe's first term.[20] Ten percent of these bills sought to uncheck the president and/or lengthen his time in office.[21] These amendments included a referendum to make congress unicameral; impeach the recently elected congressmen and call for new legislative elections;[22] a bill that curtailed the Constitutional Court's power of judicial review;[23] a reform that made permanent some presidential decree powers that would normally have time limits;[24] a bill that made it more difficult for congress to censure cabinet members;[25] a bill that sought to eliminate the National TV Commission (CNTV), the agency in charge of regulating the state's intervention on TV outlets;[26] and several bills that allowed Uribe to run for a second term.[27]

Between 2006 and 2010, Uribistas introduced more constitutional reforms that sought to uncheck the executive and extend Uribe's time in office. The government, or its coalition in congress, authored 75 percent of all the constitutional amendments introduced during Uribe's second term.[28] Eleven percent of these bills sought to reduce the checks on the president or extend his time in office beyond a second term. These reforms included a bill to curtail the Constitutional Court's power of judicial review;[29] two bills to change the appointment of justices and, in particular, restructure the Supreme Council of

---

[19] Author's interview with Rodrigo Pardo, subdirector of *El Tiempo* and director of *Cambio* magazine, during Uribe's presidency.

[20] Chávez's coalition authored 40 percent of all the constitutional amendments (i.e., organic laws) between 2000 and 2005. I did not have access to the bills' content, so it is hard to say how many of these sought to increase the powers of the executive and/or extend Chávez's time in office.

[21] There were also bills, not constitutional amendments that helped his project, like Law 974 of 2005 ("Coalitions Law"), which forced party members to vote with their party. Given that there were 3,955 bills introduced during Uribe's government, however, I decided to code only constitutional reforms.

[22] Gaceta del Congreso 323 de 2002.   [23] Gaceta del Congreso 458 de 2002.

[24] Gaceta del Congreso 174 de 2003.   [25] Gaceta del Congreso 528 de 2003.

[26] Gaceta del Congreso 344 de 2003.

[27] Gaceta del Congreso 344 of 2003, Gaceta del Congreso 341 of 2003, and Gaceta del Congreso 102 de 2004.

[28] With almost full control of the AN, Chávez's coalition authored 100 percent of all the constitutional amendments between 2005 and 2010.

[29] Gaceta del Congreso 412 of 2006.

the Judiciary[30] (CSdJ);[31] one bill to limit the Supreme Court's (CSJ) ability to investigate and judge the president;[32] two bills to decrease the power of congress to censure the president or his cabinet members;[33] three bills to change the appointment process of the National Registrar, Inspector General, General Comptroller, and Ombudsman from candidates selected by the courts, to candidates selected from politicized bodies like the National Electoral Commission (CNE)[34] or public contests;[35] one reform to eliminate the National TV Commission;[36] and a referendum that would have allowed Uribe to run for a third term.[37]

Besides the aforementioned bills, the Uribista coalition introduced other constitutional amendments that did not exactly try to increase the president's legislative or nonlegislative powers or extend his time in office but would have helped Uribe erode democracy. Between 2002 and 2010, the government coalition introduced eighteen bills that would have allowed the immediate reelection of mayors and governors. Like what happened in Venezuela in 2009, these bills attempted to rally regional support for the president's first and second reelection reforms. Like the Chavistas, the Uribista coalition also introduced a bill that would have allowed the armed forces, broadly favorable to the president, to vote. This amendment would have increased the number of Uribista voters and, more seriously, enabled the government to break the military long-standing nondeliberative tradition and politicize the armed forces.

Finally, the president's coalition in congress also introduced four bills that made it harder to try allied members of congress, expanding their ability to appeal rulings against them. These bills were introduced in the context of the *parapolítica* criminal investigations, mostly against Uribista members of the upper and lower house charged of working together with paramilitary groups in order to win their seats in 2002 and 2006. In 2010, eight out of ten politicians under investigation for this crime belonged to the government

---

[30] The CSJ is the head of the administrative and disciplinary jurisdiction in Colombia. It is composed of the Administrative and the Disciplinary Chamber. Whereas the Disciplinary Chamber justices are chosen by the Senate from lists built by the president, the Administrative Chamber justices are chosen by the Constitutional Court, the Supreme Court, and the State Department. The government's constitutional amendments sought to change the nomination process of the Administrative Chamber in hopes to fully control the CSdJ (Revelo 2009). This institution is in charge of building lists of appointees to the Supreme Court and the Council of State, administer the judicial branch resources, and administer and supervise the performance of lower courts. It is essential for the judiciary independence. Co-opting it would have given Uribe effective means to control other courts, as well as interfere in justices' appointments.

[31] Gaceta del Congreso 343 of 2007 and Gaceta del Congreso 495 of 2008.

[32] Gaceta del Congreso 600 de 2008.

[33] Gaceta del Congreso 116 of 2008 and Gaceta del Congreso 558 de 2008.

[34] Gaceta del Congreso 107 de 2008.

[35] Gaceta del Congreso 558 de 2008, Gaceta del Congreso 552 de 2008, Gaceta del Congreso 644 de 2008, and Gaceta del Congreso 654 de 2008.

[36] Gaceta del Congreso 210 de 2009.   [37] Gaceta del Congreso 623 de 2008.

legislative coalition (López 2010, 51). The parapolítica trials threatened the Uribista majorities in congress. Constitutionally, the Supreme Court was in charge of judging members of congress in a single instance. The amendments curtailed the Supreme Court's powers, allowing members of congress to appeal their sentence and remain in the legislature, protecting the Uribista majorities in congress.

5.1.1 The Opposition to Alvaro Uribe

The opposition to Alvaro Uribe was a loose coalition composed by the Alternative Democratic Pole (PDA),[38] the few members of the Liberal Party who refused to join the Uribista coalition (*liberales oficialistas*), unions, and human rights NGOs. Although the FARC also opposed the government, they had been largely discredited by their behavior during Pastrana's peace process. Despite remaining visible in national politics, they represented and were accepted by only a very small group of anti-Uribistas, and, therefore, they did not represent a legitimate threat in the struggle for national political control.

The opposition coalition was neither automatic nor natural. The left has been traditionally weak in Colombia (Wills Otero 2014). It was not until after the 2002 elections – when a radical right-wing politician became president – that they were able to join different movements and parties, with views all over the left and center-left of the ideological spectrum, in a single organization: the PDA, which only became an official party in 2005.

The Liberal Party had trouble organizing as well. When Uribe came to power, many inside the PL thought the organization should appoint him party leader and join forces with the Conservative Party (CP) to support his government. However, the PL had important members, like Piedad Córdoba and Horacio Serpa, who had strong ideological and political objections against Uribe. They won over the Liberal–Uribista coalition[39] and refused to join forces with the administration. Not without turmoil, eventually, those who wanted to follow Uribe left the party to join the newly formed U Party (PdU), named after the president.

Between 2002 and 2010, the PL and the PDA were reluctant allies. Led by former jurists like Carlos Gaviria (PDA), long-standing politicians like César Gaviria (PL), and former guerrilla (M-19) members like Antonio Navarro and Gustavo Petro (PDA), the different anti-Uribista factions agreed about the need to oppose the president's security agenda and institutional reforms and to do so legally without resorting to radical extrainstitutional strategies, but they failed

---

[38] A coalition built from the leftist movements *Polo Democrático Independiente*, *Alternativa Democrática*, ANAPO, and *Vía Alterna*, among others.
[39] Members of the Liberal Party who had supported Uribe's presidential campaign.

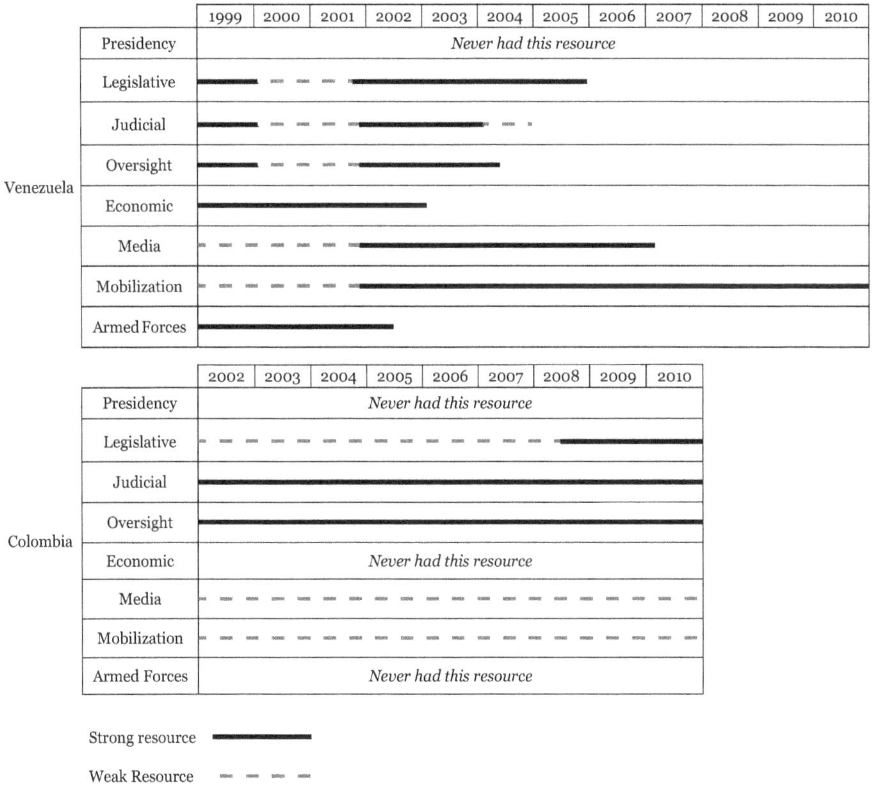

	1999	2000	2001	2002	2003	2004	2005	2006	2007	2008	2009	2010
Presidency					*Never had this resource*							
Legislative												
Judicial												
Oversight												
Economic												
Media												
Mobilization												
Armed Forces												

Venezuela

	2002	2003	2004	2005	2006	2007	2008	2009	2010
Presidency				*Never had this resource*					
Legislative									
Judicial									
Oversight									
Economic				*Never had this resource*					
Media									
Mobilization									
Armed Forces				*Never had this resource*					

Colombia

Strong resource ━━━━

Weak Resource ▬ ▬ ▬ ▬

FIGURE 5.2. Opposition resources over time

to coalesce on other topics (e.g., economic policy). Moreover, the PL and the PDA wanted to stay separate and distinguish themselves to strengthen their brand. For instance, they failed to reach an agreement to present a single candidate against Uribe in 2006.

The anti-Uribista coalition was not nearly as strong as the opposition Chávez faced when he came to power in 1999 (see Figure 5.2). First, between 2002 and 2006, the opposition coalition had only 21 percent of the seats in the Senate and 29 percent of the seats in the lower house, and between 2006 and 2010, it had only 28 percent of the seats in the Senate and 23 percent of the seats in the lower house. This number increased slightly after 2008 when some members of Cambio Radical changed sides and joined the anti-Uribista coalition. This shift, however, was neither as big or as timely as the shift in Venezuela's National Assembly between 2001 and 2002, when the opposition was able to increase its seat share from 34 percent to 48 percent due to defections in the Chavista coalition.

Second, the Colombian opposition did not have the endorsement of the mainstream media or the armed forces. As opposed to the anti-Chavista coalition, which controlled the largest media outlets in Venezuela until 2007, the anti-Uribista coalition had few channels to put their word out. Aside from very small partisan magazines and newspapers like *Semanario la Voz* and some of the more independent media outlets (i.e., *CM&*, *Noticias Uno*, *Revista Semana*, etc.), most of the media favored Uribe. The opposition in Colombia did not have the support of the armed forces either. Whereas in Venezuela important factions inside the military sided with the opposition, in Colombia the non-intervening nature of the armed forces, as well as the impressive support Uribe had inside the institution, made it highly unlikely that the military would have ever sided with the opposition against the government.

To the extent that they were independent, the anti-Uribista coalition had support inside courts and oversight agencies when Uribe came to power. However, so did its Venezuelan counterparts when Chávez became president. Throughout the 1990s, the Venezuelan courts underwent institutional changes that strengthened them and made them more independent from other branches of power. Although still weaker than the Colombian high courts (see Figure 5.3), by the end of the decade, the Supreme Court was an important political actor in Venezuela. It heard cases on important policy matters like market reform and tried cases against sitting and former presidents (Carlos Andrés Pérez, 1974–9 and 1989–93, and Jaime Lusinchi, 1984–9). In 1998 (Chávez's election year), high courts' independence in Venezuela scored as high as the Latin American average and the judiciary represented a significant constraint to the executive (Figure 5.4).

High courts' relevance did not end in 1999. At least on paper, the new constitution strengthened the courts. It created a Constitutional Chamber inside the Supreme Tribunal of Justice with broad review powers, reformed the appointment of justices – adding to the process public contests and an appointments as well as a citizens' and a congressional committee – and put the TSJ in charge of the administration of the judicial branch (Sanchez Urribarri 2011). The Supreme Tribunal of Justice designed by the charter was stronger than it had ever been before. Even though in practice the high court was weaker than the constitution suggested, up until 2004, the TSJ ruled against the government in important matters. Still, Hugo Chávez managed to co-opt Venezuela's high courts, and, since then, they have almost never ruled against the government.

Similar to what happened in Venezuela in 1999, when Uribe came to power in 2002, there was no guarantee that Colombia's strong and independent judiciary could survive his government (García and Revelo 2009). Since the 1991 Constitution, the Colombian high courts, and in particular the Constitutional Court, have been remarkably independent activist tribunals, but they are not immune from the executive (Rodríguez-Raga 2011). Like any other court, they lack the power of the sword or the purse, which makes them vulnerable to other branches of power. Like Chávez, Uribe tried to reform

— — Colombia   ———— Venezuela

Judicial Constraints on Executive

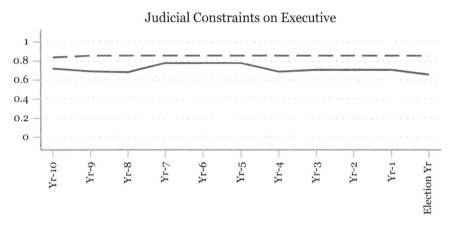

Years Before Election

Source: V-Dem (2021) Judicial Constraints on the Executive Index (0–1 scale from low constraints to high constraints)

High Court Independence

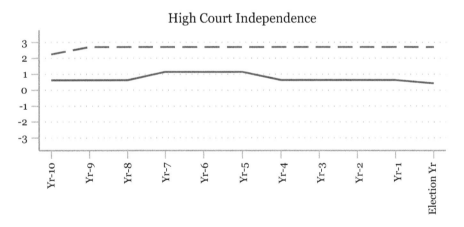

Years Before Election

Source: V-Dem (2021) High court independence (-3–3 scale from low to high court independence)

FIGURE 5.3. Courts in Colombia and Venezuela before Uribe and Chávez

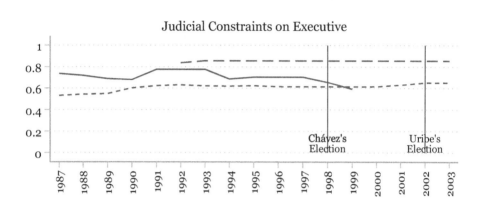

Source: V-Dem (2021) Judicial Constraints on the Executive Index (0 to 1 scale from low constraints to high constraints)

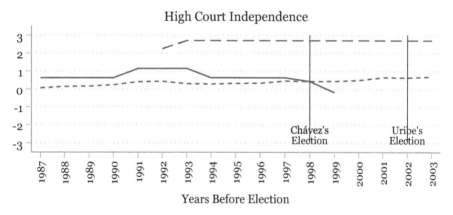

Source: V-Dem (2021) High court independence (-3 to 3 scale from low to high court independence)

FIGURE 5.4. Courts in Colombia and Venezuela vis-à-vis Latin America before Uribe and Chávez

the courts, pit them against each other,[40] and co-opt them. Unlike Chávez, however, the Colombian president failed. His reforms had strong objections

---

[40] Colombia's Constitutional Court and Supreme Court have a long-standing debate surrounding *tutelas* (a type of lawsuit meant to protect fundamental rights) against judicial rulings. The CSJ argues that there should not be tutelas against judicial rulings, and whatever decision it makes stands. The CC argues in favor of tutelas against judicial rulings, which gives it the last word over any decision made by other courts, including the CSJ (see Botero Marino and Jaramillo 2006; Quinche Ramírez 2010).

inside congress that failed to debate them,[41] his attacks against CSJ justices were never proven to be true,[42] and eight years in power gave Uribe enough time to influence the appointment of some members of high courts,[43] but not all of them. Whereas the Venezuelan opposition's ability to use the courts to check the president decreased and eventually disappeared, in Colombia it did not change.

The Supreme and, in particular, the Constitutional Court played a central role in stopping Uribe's antidemocratic reforms, but this was not a given in 2002. Key to the survival of these courts was the ability of their justices to keep their legitimacy and the institutions' intact. This ability, however, was closely related to the opposition's reluctance to use extrainstitutional strategies with radical goals, as well as their ability to use institutional strategies and extra-institutional strategies with moderate goals.

The CC had strong popular support in Colombia, but Uribe always had more. According to data from the Americas Baromenter, between 2004 and 2009 the average trust in the Constitutional Court was 2.7 out of 5, while the average trust in the executive was 3.4. Every year, the president scored 0.5–0.8 points higher in this measure than the high tribunal (LAPOP 2004–9). Aware of that, the court assessed the context in which it ruled by trying to predict the executive's reaction to its decision, as well as the costs associated with the president's response (Rubiano 2009a; Rodríguez-Raga 2011). As I will show in the next section, the opposition's strategic choices helped tame the president's reaction and lower the costs of the court's response. First, by refusing to engage in or support radical extrainstitutional strategies, the opposition remained a legitimate opponent to the government. It avoided the president's polarization game, giving the CC enough room to rule against the executive. Second, by actively using institutional strategies, the opposition provided the

---

[41] There is little empirical evidence that can explain why congress failed to debate these bills. An underlying consensus among scholars is that the lack of debate evidences the legitimacy of the courts (Rodríguez-Raga 2011; Rubiano 2009a). This, however, is hard to prove since the meetings in which these decisions were made were private, and there is no record of what was discussed there (Author's interview with Rafael Pardo, former congressman for Cambio Radical, Bogotá, May 15, 2014).

[42] The president accused auxiliary justice Iván Velázquez (*Magistrado Auxiliar*), in charge of the parapolítica investigations, of threatening a former paramilitary member (alias "Tasmania") if he did not declare against the president. It was later proven that Tasmania's testimony was staged. "El montaje." *Revista Semana*, June 21, 2008.

[43] The nine members of the CC are chosen by the Senate from nominees sent by the President, the CSJ, and the CSdJ, each of whom offered three nominees. The nomination was originally designed such that not all presidents had the opportunity to choose CC justices, and those who did could only send nominees in the third year of their four-year term. The first immediate reelection changed that. Not only was Uribe able to nominate three justices who would eventually rule important reforms like the second immediate reelection, but he was able to indirectly intervene in the Senate's selection of the other nominees to guarantee a more favorable court (Rubiano 2009a).

CC with less controversial legal arguments they could use to rule against Uribe's "power-grabbing" reforms. Third, by complementing their moderate institutional strategies with moderate extrainstitutional strategies, the opposition reassured justices inside the court of their legitimacy and public support.

5.2 MODERATE INSTITUTIONAL AND EXTRAINSTITUTIONAL STRATEGIES

Despite the overall weakness of the opposition, unlike what happened in Venezuela, Uribe was not able to erode democracy. The constitutional amendment that enabled the president to run for a second immediate term, and Uribe's reelection itself,[44] allowed him to influence[45] the election of three out of nine members of the Constitutional Court, four out of six members of the National Television Commission, seven out of nine members in the CNE, and five out of seven members of the Central Bank.[46] He was also able to appoint a co-partisan Inspector General and Ombudsman. Nevertheless, Uribe was not able to push beyond that. Out of the twenty-four constitutional amendments that Uribe's coalition introduced, only five became law, and two of those were rejected by the CC (including the bill that would have allowed him to run for a third term).

The correlation of forces between government and opposition would have suggested a different outcome. If we assume, as most of the literature does, that only weak authoritarian leaders fail, the popularity and support that Uribe had and the relative weakness of the opposition that faced him should have led to the erosion of democracy in Colombia. In order to understand why this country's democracy survived, we need to focus less on the correlation of forces between government and opposition and pay more attention to the decisions the latter made.

---

[44] The appointment of justices and oversight agents, as well as the number of years they serve, were designed such that the sitting president would not have been in power enough time to oversee the appointment of all justices and oversight agents and, if chosen during his term, they would not have been able to serve more than two years under that administration. The reelection changed that. Uribe was able to oversee the appointment of all the justices in the Constitutional and Supreme Court, the State Council (CdE), and the Supreme Council of the Judiciary as well as all the members of the National TV Commission and the Central Bank. He was also able to participate in the appointment of one Inspector General and one Ombudsman who served up to six years with him as sitting president.

[45] By designing groups of nominees in which only the government's preferred nominee fulfilled the requirements to be appointed (*ternas de uno*), by designing groups of nominees in which all of the people proposed were equally Uribista, and – in those cases in which the president did not have the power to propose nominees – by pressuring congress to either reject all of the nominees put forward or choose the one that favored the government the most.

[46] Although it was aligned with the government, only one of the seven members of the Central Bank voted unconditionally with the president (Rubiano 2009b).

In contrast to the Venezuelan opposition, the anti-Uribista coalition avoided radical extrainstitutional strategies and used institutional strategies and extrainstitutional strategies with moderate goals to fight Uribe's attempts to increase his powers and extend his time in office. It refused to play into the government's polarizing discourse both by effectively distancing itself from the FARC by avoiding public comments or actions that could have been seen as legitimizing the guerrillas and by declining to use street protests to push the president to resign.

The absence of radical extrainstitutional strategies protected the opposition's legitimacy abroad. Unlike those who opposed Chávez, Colombian opposition politicians, unions, and NGOs were never accused of being undemocratic, illegal, or radical by foreign governments or international organizations. Their actions were never seen as unwarranted, and they remained broadly perceived as advocates for democracy and human rights. This image, in turn, allowed them to use international forums to criticize the president's agenda and some of his reforms that harmed democracy. The reluctance to use radical extrainstitutional strategies also kept the opposition's domestic legitimacy intact. It allowed the anti-Uribistas to broaden their coalition in congress and keep their popular support and hindered Uribe's ability to frame the opposition-government dynamic as one between a democratic popular government against a radical undemocratic or illegal opposition. By doing so, the Colombian opposition avoided providing the president with "legitimate reasons" to remove opposition members from congress and high courts, which enabled it to use these bodies to stop Uribista antidemocratic reforms.

The coalition that opposed Uribe actively participated in the 2002 and 2006 presidential and parliamentary elections and the 2003 and 2007 regional elections, used congress and courts to obstruct and stop the president's legislation, and used protests and boycotts to draw attention to the amendments, decrease popular support for specific reforms, and boost the legitimacy of the Constitutional Court. Between 2002 and 2010, the opposition in congress used rules of procedure to obstruct the legislative debate. It strategically extended bills' transit through congress and denounced and manufactured procedural irregularities. The delays opened up windows to (a) soften otherwise radical reforms and (b) increase the public scrutiny of the bills. The procedural irregularities, in turn, facilitated judicial review by providing strong legal arguments to rule against some of these reforms. Together these strategies helped slow down the process by which the government meant to weaken other branches of government and helped the Constitutional Court stop Uribe's second reelection reform.

5.2.1. Avoiding Radical Extrainstitutional Strategies

The opposition was well aware of the importance of keeping its legitimacy domestically and abroad. To neutralize the people who criticized him or endangered his project in any way, Uribe systematically tried to discredit them. The government publicly painted opponents and critics as "antidemocratic," "anti-patriotic," or "terrorists" (Sierra 2015). It also used the security service agency (DAS) to illegally spy on opposition leaders, critical journalists, and Supreme Court justices and clerks[47] in order to find "dirt" (Coronell 2008; 2009; Morris 2010).[48] It has been proven that people close to Uribe's administration even worked with former paramilitary members to make up evidence against those who opposed the president.[49]

Uribe also employed a very successful media strategy. Especially inside the country, his smears often casted doubts on the opposition or at least diverted the public's attention away from criticisms leveled against him (Sierra 2015). Journalists called this Uribe's "teflon." His popularity survived scandals that the popularity of many other presidents would not have survived. Buying legislators to pass the first reelection; the state's police intercepting the calls and emails of justices, journalists, and opposition politicians; and extrajudicial killings by entire battalions inside the armed forces to obtain rewards that the president's security program offered for war casualties are just some examples of the many scandals he survived. Due to the security crisis and the need to "end violence," Colombians were often willing to believe that "the ends justified the means," and accepted most of what Uribe did (Borda 2012).

Under those circumstances, the opposition could not give Uribe ammunition to substantiate his attacks. When asked about their strategic choices, interviewees recognized the advantage of being inside the legislature. They all said that, although it was impossible for them to legislate, being inside congress increased their ability to be heard. According to Gustavo Triana, secretary general of the PDA, having a presence in congress

helps because the role of the parliament is to become a "loudspeaker" of what people are fighting for ... you can do ten thousand blockades in Curumaní and, if it wants, the regime can hide them. Not even inform them through the radio or the TV. Having a councilman, a deputy or a senator gives you the possibility to announce them, to make noise, to become a "loudspeaker."[50]

Opposition interviewees also agreed that opposing Uribe, even in the most moderate manner, was hard. Uribe consistently conflated opposition with

---

[47] These attacks were prompted by the Supreme Court's investigations of members of congress who had allied with paramilitary or guerrilla groups to win their seats (*parapolíticos*). By April 2010, 102 congressmen were under investigation. Two out of three were part of the government coalition (López 2010).

[48] "Confirma-DAS." *Revista Semana*, June 1, 2009; "¿Tapen, Tapen, Tapen...?" *Revista Semana*, July 13, 2009; "Las 'Chuza-DAS.'" *Revista Semana*, December 21, 2009.

[49] "Interrogantes En Caso 'Tasmania.'" *El Espectador*, March 6, 2013.

[50] Author's interview, Bogotá, November 19, 2013.

subversion.[51] According to Rodrigo Pardo, director of *Revista Cambio* during Uribe's government, criticizing the executive was like being against the nation itself.[52] The streets, broadly speaking, were not the ideal terrain to fight the president because Uribe was very popular while the opposition was not.[53] Those who publicly opposed Uribe could also end up in jail.[54] The opposition could not give the president "legitimate" reasons to remove its members from key institutions, which, like congress, were immensely valuable for them.

In order to keep its legitimacy domestically and abroad, the opposition skillfully tried to set itself aside from the polarized political landscape that Uribe wanted to create. Not only did it not use the streets to push Uribe to resign (Archila 2011), but it also distanced itself from the FARC. During Uribe's government, the number of protests increased. According to data from CINEP, between 1991 and 2001, the average number of protests a year was 429. Between August 2002 and August 2010, that number rose to 675. These mobilizations, however, did not aim to delegitimize the government. During Uribe's government, only 27 percent of the protests recorded were triggered by state decisions. Of those, 62 percent were against the national executive. These extrainstitutional strategies had moderate goals. Most of them were either related to the armed conflict (36 percent) (e.g., for or against a peace process or for a process of truth and reconciliation) or against government policies (31 percent) (e.g., agricultural, economic, fiscal, social, urban, toward displaced people). The rest were related to education; economic, social, or health issues (17 percent); government regulations (6 percent); institutional reform (4 percent); or political and civil rights (2 percent). Only two targeted the president. Both of them happened in August 2010, days before Uribe stepped down, and in celebration of the end of his government.

At the end, as Ramiro Bejarano – former joint justice for the Supreme and Constitutional courts and the Supreme Council of the Judiciary, and lawyer of CSJ justices in lawsuits introduced by the government during Uribe's presidency – says it was clear that Uribe "wasn't able to discredit the opposition, not because he stopped trying, but because he did not find elements to do so."[55]

To diminish the effect of the president's smears, the opposition also set itself apart from the FARC. The left in Colombia has a history of ambiguity with the guerrilla. Throughout most of the second half of the twentieth century, most left-wing parties refused to clearly reject the armed struggle. Even though, since

[51] Author's interview with Ernesto Samper, former President of Colombia (1994–8), Bogotá, November 15, 2013.

[52] Author's interview, Bogotá, January 14, 2014.

[53] Author's interview with César Paredes, journalist for *Revista Semana*, Bogotá, September 9, 2013.

[54] Author's interview with Germán Navas, PDA House Representative, Bogotá, November 18, 2013.

[55] Author's interview, Bogotá, November 13, 2013.

the late 1980s, it is clear that most leftist politicians have no ties with illegal groups, the PDA is often perceived as "complacent" toward guerrilla warfare.[56] Given the ill repute of the FARC domestically and abroad, it was key for the opposition[57] to go above and beyond to keep the guerrilla actions separate from what they did. In the words of Carlos Gaviria, former leader of the PDA and presidential candidate for that party in 2006:

> One of the biggest obstacles that the left has encountered is the guerrilla because when you say that you are leftist, they tie you to the armed struggle. It is very important that people get rid of the idea that every proposition of the left has to do with the use of arms.[58]

Indeed, for the most part, the opposition was strategically critical of the FARC's violent actions. Left-wing politicians sincerely opposed guerrilla warfare, but most importantly, they were vocal about this opposition. They wanted people to stop tying them to the FARC. Even if they thought that negotiation was the best way to solve the armed conflict, they were always quick to reject the guerrilla's violent methods. In June 2007, for instance, when the FARC announced the death of eleven regional deputies they had kidnapped in 2002, Gustavo Petro (PDA senator) vocally condemned the FARC and pushed the party to release a statement in which it clearly reproved the act. This gesture was recognized even by strong Uribistas like Rafael Nieto Loaiza, Uribe's vice minister of justice, who in an op-ed called for more denunciations of the FARC and their violence from the left, applauding the PDA for "unambiguously betting on democracy" (Nieto 2007).

5.2.1.1 Domestic Legitimacy

The absence of extrainstitutional strategies with radical goals (or even the appearance that they condoned anything of the sort) protected the opposition's legitimacy domestically in three ways. To begin with, it allowed the opposition to keep and, in the case of the PDA, even increase its popular support. Historically, the left has not been particularly popular in Colombia. Unlike most other Latin American countries, before 2006, leftist candidates never had a strong showing in national elections.[59] During Uribe's government, the PDA not only managed to increase its vote share in presidential elections from 6 percent in 2002 to 22 percent in 2006, and its vote share in legislative elections from approximately 2 percent in 2002 to approximately 8 percent in 2006, but also its leaders maintained and even increased their approval ratings. Luis Eduardo Garzón – presidential candidate for the left in

---

[56] "Un Fantasma Recorre El Polo..." *Revista Semana*, September 3, 2007.
[57] This is mostly the PDA. The Liberal Party did not have the same problem.
[58] "Uribe Nos Situaría En El Siglo XVIII." *Revista Semana*, April 10, 2006.
[59] The exception would be the Constitutional Assembly in 1991 where the M-19 won one-third of the seats.

2002 and PDA's candidate for Bogotá's mayorship in 2003 – had an approval rating of 23 percent before 2002. This number rose to 62 percent during the 2002 presidential elections and never went below 40 percent during Uribe's government (Gallup 2009). Something similar happened with Carlos Gaviria, a left-wing senator in 2002 and PDA's presidential candidate in 2006. His approval rating was 19 percent in 2004, went as high as 43 percent in 2006 during the presidential elections, and it never dropped below 29 percent (Gallup 2007).[60] Following a similar trend, Gustavo Petro's – senator for the PDA in 2002 and 2006, and PDA's presidential candidate in 2010 – approval rating was 15 percent in 2005, went as high as 30 percent in 2009, and never dropped below 21 percent (Gallup 2009). Petro's overall popularity at the time is not impressive, but the point remains: During Uribe's government, the former PDA Senator increased – at one point even doubled – his support. Perhaps the only outlier in the PDA is Antonio Navarro, a senator from 2002 to 2006. Navarro has a longer political trajectory than any of the politicians mentioned earlier. His approval rating before Uribe came to power was 60 percent but dropped steadily to 41 percent in 2004 and 32 percent in 2006 (Gallup 2006).

The PL had a different trend. As mentioned earlier, its popular support and vote share decreased throughout the 1990s, and the situation worsened when half of its members left to join the Uribista coalition after 2002. On April 22, roughly 22 percent of the people interviewed identified with the PL; by December 2009, this number had dropped to 14 percent (Gallup 2014). Moreover, in 2002, the PL had a 31 percent vote share in the lower and the upper house; in 2010, its vote share had shrunk to 19 percent and 15 percent, respectively.

Important members of the PL managed to keep their approval ratings somewhat intact. Piedad Córdoba's – senator for the PL in 2002 and 2006 – approval ratings, for instance, fluctuated between 25 percent and 28 percent between 2003 and 2006, but went as high as 42 percent in 2007 (Gallup 2007).[61] We cannot say the same for politicians with longer and more visible political trajectories like two-time presidential candidate (2002 and 2006) Horacio Serpa or former president César Gaviria. Their approval ratings suffered severely during Alvaro Uribe's government. César Gaviria's approval rating was 47 percent in 2002, dropped to 27 percent in 2006, and fluctuated between 27 percent and 42 percent afterward (Gallup 2007). Horacio Serpa's approval rating in 2002 was 48 percent, and afterward it fluctuated between 30 percent and 41 percent (Gallup 2006). Notwithstanding these numbers, both Serpa and Gaviria remained well-respected politicians throughout Uribe's government. They were perceived as legal, democratic, and legitimate opponents to the government.

---

[60] Unfortunately, I have no data past 2007.
[61] The data available is limited to October and December 2003, March 2004, December 2006, September and November 2004.

The anti-Uribista coalition's reluctance to use radical extrainstitutional strategies also helped to increase the opposition's coalition inside congress. Between 2002 and 2006, important and visible members of congress moved out of the government's coalition and joined the opposition. For instance, during the president's first term, Rafael Pardo – a long-standing Liberal politician and senator with Cambio Radical in 2002 – and Héctor Helí Rojas – house representative and senator for the PL between 1986–94 and 1994–2010, respectively – who had initially supported Uribe, moved out of the Uribista coalition, and led the opposition against important antidemocratic amendments like the Antiterrorist Statute and the first reelection reform.[62] Uribe also faced defections during his second term. In disagreement with the second reelection reform, Cambio Radical – one of the most "Uribista" parties until 2008 – and visible members of the PdU (named after the president) like Gina Parody and Jairo Clopatosfky joined the ranks of the anti-Uribistas.

Despite being small, these defections were important for the opposition. They reinforced the idea that those who opposed Uribe were not the "radical left." The image of Germán Vargas Lleras (CR), who had been Uribe's right hand in congress, and Gina Parody, one of Uribe's staunchest supporters, joining the opposition to fight against the second reelection referendum powerfully resonated within the country.[63] These defections also improved the opposition's ability to effectively use procedural irregularities against Uribe's amendments. When CR changed sides, for instance, they controlled the presidency of the lower house. This position was key to delay the reelection referendum debate in 2008 and 2009.

Outside congress, the opposition was also able to build a broader coalition, thanks to the absence of radical extrainstitutional strategies. For instance, former members of the 1991 Constitutional Assembly joined ranks to oppose the second reelection reform. The group Citizens' Alliance for Democracy (*Alianza Ciudadana por la Democracia*) had former Uribistas and non-Uribistas. They were only able to act together because the group agreed to fight the reform rather than the reformer. According to its leader Armando Novoa, "to say that the alliance was against Uribe meant an immediate rejection. Instead, we decided to frame our opposition in defense of institutions."[64] As I will show later, the campaign organized by the Citizens' Alliance was important to help the Constitutional Court rule against the second reelection referendum.

Although Chávez also suffered important defections during his government, these happened mostly between 1998 and 2002. As time went by and the Venezuelan opposition radicalized, it became harder for moderate Chavistas to join it. The same was not true for the opposition in Colombia. The

---

[62] Pardo left the Uribista coalition in 2005; Rojas left the Uribista coalition in 2004.
[63] "La Rebelión de Germán." *Revista Semana*, January 19, 2009.
[64] Author's interview, Bogotá, December 6, 2013.

mainstream anti-Uribista coalition refused to use (or silently endorse) radical extrainstitutional strategies to oust Uribe. By doing so, they remained viable political allies for Uribistas who might have agreed with many of the president's policies but opposed Uribe's antidemocratic reforms.

Finally, eschewing extrainstitutional strategies with radical goals also helped the opposition keep its seats in congress. For instance, in the midst of the parapolítica scandal, the attorney general used information found in guerrilla leader Raúl Reyes's computer to open investigations against eight opposition members – including five congressional representatives – for alleged ties with the FARC.[65] Three were eventually charged: Wilson Borja (PDA representative), Gloria Inés Ramírez (PDA senator), and Piedad Córdoba (PL senator). In June 2009, the Uribista inspector general, Alejandro Ordoñez, opened up a parallel disciplinary investigation against these three, as well as Jaime Caicedo (PDA council member) and Jorge Robledo (PDA senator) who were mentioned in the computers as well.[66]

The evidence against these opposition politicians was tenuous at best. The government had broken the chain of evidence with Reyes's computer,[67] the names of opposition leaders were mentioned, but there was no action attached to them,[68] and most of the documents cited were easy-to-manipulate Word files.[69] Eventually, the computer was disqualified as evidence,[70] and the processes against the opposition politicians fell apart.[71,72] Most of them kept their seats in congress and even won elections after 2010.

The one exception was Piedad Córdoba, senator for the Liberal Party and vocal opponent to Alvaro Uribe. Córdoba had worked hard to get a humanitarian agreement, an exchange of guerrilla prisoners for people who had been kidnapped or captured by the FARC. Under that framework, she was often authorized to meet with members of the guerrilla group. However, she went beyond that. Although she never openly supported violence, on various occasions she publicly endorsed the guerrilla's fight, called on people to "subvert" Uribe's government, and asked foreign nations to cut diplomatic relations with

[65] "De La 'para-Política' a La 'Farc-Política.'" *Revista Semana*, May 26, 2008.
[66] León, Juanita. "Arranca La Farcpolítica. ¿Es Equivalente a La Parapolítica?" *La Silla Vacía*, June 10, 2009.
[67] "Consejo de Estado Tumba Inhabilidad de 18 Años de Piedad Córdoba." *El Espectador*, August 9, 2016.
[68] "Corte explica fallo que declaró ilegales correos de PC de 'Raúl Reyes.'" *El Tiempo*, May 25, 2011.
[69] León, Juanita, *La Silla Vacía*, June 10, 2009.
[70] "Pruebas de Computador de 'Reyes' Son Ilícitas: Corte." *El Espectador*, May 18, 2011.
[71] "Caso de Piedad Córdoba Por Presuntos Nexos Con FARC Pasa a Fiscalía." *El Tiempo*, August 20, 2014.
[72] Five of them were either found not guilty or the CSJ did not find enough merits to continue the investigation.

Colombia.[73] The senator's open support for the guerrillas gave credit to the perception that she was closely aligned with the FARC. Even though no crime was ever proven,[74] Ordoñez was able to "legitimately" remove her from congress and disqualify her from participating in politics for eighteen years.[75]

The inspector general's decision against Córdoba provides further evidence of the importance of protecting the opposition's legitimacy. While it was announced after Uribe stepped down, Ordoñez's decision against Córdoba illustrates the vulnerability of public officers when they lose the moral "high ground." The inspector general is staunchly Uribista. Two different rulings by two different courts in 2014 and 2016 show that he had little evidence to sanction the senator. Still, he was able to remove her from congress and effectively end her political career. Borjas, Robledo, Ramírez, and Caicedo could easily show that the inspector general was launching a political witch hunt. Because Córdoba was, and still is, broadly perceived as having strong ties with the FARC, she was unable to do the same. Had Uribe been reelected in 2010, she would have been out of congress throughout his third term.

5.2.1.2 International Legitimacy

The absence of radical extrainstitutional strategies also helped the opposition keep its legitimacy abroad. Uribe tried hard to paint those who opposed him as terrorists or FARC allies. The opposition's refusal to use the streets to oust the president and their constant effort to reject guerrilla warfare undermined the president's baseless claims.

Those who opposed Uribe's iron fist policies and institutional reforms had a hard time convincing the international community that Uribe was not everything that he promised to be.[76] On paper, his security policies were democratic and respectful of human and civil rights (Borda 2012). In this context, although maintaining the opposition's legitimacy abroad did not guarantee the international community's support, it helped. It enabled unions and human rights NGOs to use these international forums to denounce Uribe's policies and tarnish his image abroad.[77]

Keeping the support of the international community, in particular, the United States, was key for Alvaro Uribe. For the Colombian president, being successful in the fight against the FARC was as important as it was for Chávez

---

[73] "Las Pruebas Del Procurador Contra Piedad Córdoba." *La Silla Vacía*, September 27, 2010.

[74] The Supreme Court did not find merit to the accusations ("Caso de Piedad Córdoba Por Presuntos Nexos Con FARC Pasa a Fiscalía." *El Tiempo*, August 20, 2014). In 2016, the Council of State removed the sanction imposed by Ordoñez, arguing that it was based on circumstantial evidence ("Consejo de Estado Tumba Inhabilidad de 18 Años de Piedad Córdoba." *El Espectador*, August 9, 2016).

[75] "Procuraduría Confirma Destitución de Piedad Córdoba." *El Espectador*, October 27, 2010.

[76] Author's interview with a member of advocacy group and human rights NGO, January 13, 2014.

[77] Author's interview with Rodrigo Pardo, Bogotá, January 14, 2014.

to reduce poverty. The international community's contributions, in particular, the United States, were key to implementing Uribe's security policies (Tickner 2007). With that in mind, unions and human rights NGOs actively lobbied foreign governments and international organizations, arguing that the government's policies threatened democracy and human and civil rights. Their objective was to obstruct or curtail the international funds disbursed to the Colombian government. Restrictions on the activities for which the money could be used and/or conditions that the government had to meet before it received the funds could force the administration to tone down criticisms against those who opposed it, promote human rights, protect unions leaders, and prosecute crimes such as extrajudicial killings, illegal wiretappings, and paramilitary's influence in the government.

Although the international community never turned against Uribe and the United States kept funding his security policies, these criticisms did not go unheard. It was hard for Uribe to enlist the support of the European Union, which distrusted his human rights record.[78] High-ranking politicians like former US Vice President Al Gore refused to appear in public with Uribe due to the parapolítica scandal and the opposition's allegations that the government had ties with paramilitary groups.[79] More seriously, US members of congress from the Democratic Party often criticized Colombia's human rights climate and called for restrictions in US aid.[80] Throughout Uribe's first term, senators Jim McGovern and Patrick Leahy tried to cut Colombia's funding and disputed the human rights certification that the Colombian government needed to receive US funds (Isacson 2006). In line with these criticisms,[81] after they won control of both houses of congress, Democrats delayed the approval of the Colombia Trade Promotion Agreement (TPA) and, more importantly, cut US military aid by 10 percent.[82]

The distrust, the restrictions, and the delays were all minor successes for the opposition. They would certainly not have stopped Uribe from eroding democracy by themselves, but they helped. They lent credibility to the anti-Uribistas complaints against the government and scratched Uribe's "teflon." The international community was important, especially toward the end when it subtly

---

[78] "La Ira Presidencial." *Revista Semana*, September 15, 2003; "Diplomáticamente Vamos de Mal En Peor ¿en Qué Estamos Fallando?" *Revista Semana*, April 21, 2008.

[79] "Uribe Se Defiende." *Revista Semana*, April 23, 2007.

[80] "Dudas Demócratas." *Revista Semana*, October 4, 2004.

[81] On October 9, 2007, the *New York Times* published an editorial where it encouraged congress to sign free trade agreements with several countries except Colombia. Uribe, they stressed, had not done enough to bring to justice the "paramilitary thugs – and their political backers – responsible for widespread human rights violations." They called, explicitly, to use the TPA as leverage to change Uribe's behavior. "Democrats talk sense" *New York Times*, October 9, 2007.

[82] "Uribe Contra El Mundo." *Revista Semana*, October 15, 2007.

signaled that it did not like Uribe's second reelection reform.[83] In 2009, when Hillary Clinton, secretary of state at the time, was asked about the reelection referendum, she refused to comment on Colombian internal affairs, but was quick to state that any institutional reform had to abide by the OAS Democratic Charter and respect checks and balances.[84] Later on, when Uribe visited US President Barack Obama in 2009, the latter emphasized that in the United States, two terms were enough.[85] It is unlikely that the United States would have changed its approach to Colombia had Uribe been reelected, but these criticisms were certainly useful in the fight against the second reelection reform.

Overall, the absence of extrainstitutional strategies with radical goals helped the opposition in Colombia. As I show earlier, despite the government's attacks and attempts to smear its reputation, the anti-Uribista coalition was able to keep its legitimacy domestically and abroad. Although it did not have the unconditional support of the people or the international community, unlike Chávez, Uribe was never able to frame the government-opposition dynamic as one between a democratic government against a radical undemocratic opposition. During the eight years he was in power, the anti-Uribista coalition was able to protect its public image, enhance its coalition, and credibly denounce human rights abuses and threats against democracy abroad.

5.2.2 How Moderate Extrainstitutional and Moderate Institutional Strategies Work

The Colombian opposition not only avoided extrainstitutional strategies with radical goals, but it also actively used institutional strategies and extrainstitutional strategies with moderate goals to fight Uribe's antidemocratic reforms in congress. Although it was very hard for those who opposed Uribe to push legislation through congress, it was clear that they "did not come [to congress] to legislate, but to prevent others from doing so."[86] Between 2002 and 2010, the opposition systematically used rules of procedure to obstruct the president's reforms. It delayed bills' transit through congress, which increased public scrutiny and helped break the coalition behind the amendments, opening up windows for friends and foes to modify, and often tame, radical reforms.

The anti-Uribista coalition also manufactured and/or denounced procedural irregularities in order to involve the court and hamper antidemocratic legislation from moving through congress. The Constitutional Court's judicial review powers are limited. It cannot rule against congressional constitutional amendments or bills to allow referendums based on their content, only based

---

[83] Interview with Rodrigo Pardo, president of RCN and former editor of magazine *Cambio*, Bogotá.

[84] "TLC o Reelcción." *Revista Semana*, June 29, 2009.

[85] "Se Murió El Referendo." *Revista Semana*, July 27, 2009.

[86] Author's interview with opposition congressman aide, Bogotá, May 14, 2015.

on irregularities that occurred during their debate. By creating and reporting procedural irregularities, the opposition "invited the court" (Botero and Gamboa 2021), giving the Constitutional Court important legal arguments to rule against Uribe's bills. Without these arguments, the court's ruling would have been much more controversial. It could have been portrayed as politically biased, hindering the court's legitimacy and, with it, its ability to protect itself against a popular president like Uribe, with the resources to ignore the courts.

Extrainstitutional strategies with moderate goals complemented the opposition's strategy inside congress. The delays in the legislature allowed the anti-Uribista coalition to decrease the support for Uribe's constitutional amendments. The opposition, in turn, capitalized on this to mobilize people into the streets to oppose the president's reforms. Not only were these extrainstitutional strategies with moderate goals important to stop some of Uribe's reforms, like the 2002 Referendum, but they also helped bolster the Constitutional Court's legitimacy, making it easier for it to rule against the president.

Below, I focus on three examples to illustrate how these causal mechanisms work: the Referendum against Bad Politics and Corruption (2002), the Antiterrorist Statue (2003), and the Reelection Referendum (2009). I chose these bills because, out of the twenty-one bills introduced by Uribe's coalition to enhance his powers and/or extend his time in office, these were the most important and visible ones.[87] Had any of them passed, as proposed by the president, they would have weakened the legislature, increased the executive's powers of decree, and/or allowed Uribe to govern for twelve years or more.

5.2.2.1 The Referendum against Bad Politics and Corruption (2002–2003)

The day he was sworn into office (August 7, 2002), Alvaro Uribe sent to congress a bill to call for a "Referendum against Bad Politics and Corruption" (*Referendo contra la Corrupción y la Politiquería*). The original version of the referendum called for a smaller unicameral legislature and mandated immediate legislative elections effectively impeaching sitting representatives. It also sought to increase the list of infractions that would allow oversight authorities to remove members of congress from office or disqualify them from participating in politics and proposed to abolish regional oversight agencies.[88] Had it passed as proposed, this bill would have seriously decreased the powers of the legislature vis-à-vis the president's, and allowed Uribe to elect a tailor-made congress, just like Chávez did in 2000.

The government's idea was to use Uribe's popularity and momentum to push the referendum bill through congress and get people to the polls during the first

---

[87] Out of the bills left, three were withdrawn, twelve were archived before the first debate (there are no records to explain why these bills never went through), two were accumulated with larger reforms (some of which I discuss in the text), and one was approved.

[88] Gaceta del Congreso 323 de 2002.

semester of 2003. Uribe was aware of the electoral advantage that his landslide victory provided and the fact that such momentum would run out fast. For his strategy to work, therefore, the referendum needed to happen soon. Otherwise, Uribe was not sure his popularity would be enough to meet the turnout requirements (25 percent of the registered voters), and there was a good chance that the referendum would not be enacted into law (Breuer 2008). Indeed, in July 2002, 76 percent of the people approved of Uribe, and 81 percent were willing to support the referendum. In January 2003, those numbers dropped to 68 percent and 46 percent, and in July 2003, they dropped even further to 64 percent and 43 percent, respectively (Bermúdez 2010, 198, 205).

Therefore, from the beginning, the referendum had all the support the government could provide. It was evident that the president was personally invested in the passage of this bill. In Colombia, the executive's support for a piece of legislation is a significant predictor of its success in congress (Cárdenas, Junguito, and Pachón 2008; Milanese 2011). Against the majorities, the resources, and the popularity of the president, there was little the opposition could do to fight the referendum.

Still, it used rules of procedure to lengthen its transit through congress, successfully delaying it (see Table 5.1). The referendum bill had three debates (see Figure 5.5).[89] On each one of them, the opposition demanded that the referendum had to be debated and voted question by question using roll call voting.[90] Before July 2009,[91] most bills could be voted on without roll call voting, except when requested by a member of congress. Politicians who opposed bills often asked to use roll call voting to stall. In this case, the opposition required roll call voting for each of the referendum's sixteen questions, as well as the amendments to each one of them. As a result, getting the referendum through congress took almost twice as much time as it would have taken otherwise. Whereas committee or plenary debates usually take one to four sessions, the referendum debates took, on average, seven sessions each.

Friends and foes of the project used this time to modify the bill, so much so that halfway through the joint committee debate, in October 2002, the president threatened to circumvent congress and collect signatures to present the referendum directly to the people.[92] When it left the legislature, the referendum no longer proposed immediate congressional elections, did not call for a unicameral legislative body, and proposed to reduce congress only by 20 percent (30 percent less than the original proposal had envisioned). Most of these changes were introduced by the president's coalition. Some of them were the

---

[89] Referendum bills usually have four debates, but Uribe introduced this bill with an urgency provision that forces the House and the Senate to have joint committee debates.
[90] Gaceta del Congreso 01 de 2003 and Gaceta del Congreso 36 de 2003.
[91] The Legislative Act No. 1 of 2009 made roll call voting mandatory starting in July 2009.
[92] "En El Nombre Del Padre." *Revista Semana*, October 14, 2002.

TABLE 5.1. *Summary of opposition moderate-institutional and extrainstitutional strategies*

	MODERATE INSTITUTIONAL STRATEGY		MODERATE EXTRAINSTITUTIONAL STRATEGY	
	Tactic	*Consequence*	*Tactic*	*Consequence*
Referendum Against Bad Politics and Corruption *(S 47/02, H 57/02)*	Legislative obstruction	Delay to modify the bill	Abstention	Stop the reform
Anti-Terrorist Statute *(H 223/03, S 15/03)*	Create/denounce procedural irregularities	Provide the Constitutional Court w/resource to rule against the bill		
Reelection Referendum *(H 138/08, S 242/09)*	Legislative obstruction	Modify reforms. Increased public scrutiny, decreasing support for the bill		
	Create/denounce procedural irregularities	Provide the Constitutional Court w/resource to rule against the bill	Demonstrations against the referendum and in support of democratic institutions	Enhance institutions' legitimacy

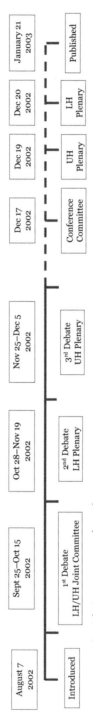

FIGURE 5.5. Legislative process referendum, 2002–3

August 7 2002	Sept 25–Oct 15 2002	Oct 28–Nov 19 2002	Nov 25–Dec 5 2002	Dec 17 2002	Dec 19 2002	Dec 20 2002	January 21 2003
Introduced	1st Debate LH/UH Joint Committee	2nd Debate LH Plenary	3rd Debate UH Plenary	Conference Committee	UH Plenary	LH Plenary	Published

outcome of negotiations early in the process.[93] Others, however, happened later as the debate dragged on and the Uribista coalition in congress became harder to control.

These modifications were essential to defeating the referendum. Not only did the bill lose the question about the impeachment of congress that promised to increase turnout (Bermúdez 2010, 205–6),[94] but without the unicameral congress provision or the threat of early elections, it no longer curtailed congress's power as much as it had before. The Constitutional Court further modified the referendum. After being reviewed by the court, it no longer had "inductive" introductory paragraphs that biased the questions, or the item that would have permitted voting on all the questions at once.

The changes introduced by congress and the CC to the referendum were critical in its failure (Bermúdez 2010, 206; Breuer 2008), but it was the opposition's extrainstitutional strategy with moderate goals that finished it off. Starting in December 2002, the left (and few members of the Liberal Party) campaigned for abstention.[95] They asked anti-Uribista voters not to show up at the polls. This campaign did not seek to delegitimize Uribe. It sought to hinder his ability to reach the threshold required for the bill to be enacted into law. The campaign was labeled "active abstention" and sold to the public as another "form of participation."[96] Its leaders even got state funds equal to the ones given to the "Yes" and "No" campaigns.[97] The opposition's obstruction in congress helped modify the bill and remove questions that would have increased turnout. With these questions, the opposition's abstention campaign would have had a harder time depressing turnout enough to prevent the reform (Breuer 2008). The opposition's strategic choices paid off. Although the electorate approved most of the referendum questions, only two of the items got the number of votes required.

The referendum's failure marked a critical step in stopping Alvaro Uribe from eroding democracy. Had the referendum passed as proposed, chances are the president would have had not only a weaker congress (vis-à-vis the executive) but also one elected mostly on his coattails. A weaker, more submissive legislature, in turn, would have made it easier for the president to co-opt courts

[93] The statement in support of the bill, in the first debate in September, called for a bicameral, albeit smaller, congress and allowed the president and congress to call for early congressional elections if both of these bodies thought it was "in the best interest of the nation."

[94] Throughout the debate, the government tried to include different articles that would increase turnout: a ban on drugs dosage for personal use and an extension of governors and mayors' term limits. The first question was declared unconstitutional by the CC; the second one was removed during the congressional debate.

[95] The opposition was divided. Most non-Uribista members of the Liberal Party led the "No" campaign.

[96] "En Sus Marcas..." *Revista Semana*, July 14, 2003.

[97] "Abstención ganó el pulso al gobierno." *El Tiempo*, February 7, 2003.

and oversight agencies,[98] and push other reforms that would have eroded democracy down the road.

5.2.2.2 The Antiterrorist Statute (2003–2004)

After the referendum debacle, the legislative debate moved to the Antiterrorist Statute. The government introduced the bill to congress on April 24, 2003, two months after the FARC bombed Bogotá's social club *El Nogal*, killing thirty-six people and injuring 165. The idea was to capitalize on this very visible attack to make permanent some presidential decree powers. More specifically, the president wanted to (a) allow members of the armed forces to work as judicial authorities aiding in the collection and analysis of evidence related to "terrorism," (b) allow raids and detentions without court orders in cases of suspected "terrorism," and (c) institute mandatory censuses in regions with frequent "terrorist" activity, without mandatory judicial review or time limits.[99] Had it been approved by the Constitutional Court, this reform would have unchecked the executive, who would have been able to suspend some civil liberties at will.

The fight against the FARC was the backbone of Uribe's government and popularity, as he was elected on a right-wing "iron fist" platform. His popularity was closely tied to his administration's performance (or perceived performance) in the war against the FARC. With that in mind, Uribe tried to increase the powers of the executive using state of emergency presidential decrees early in his first term.[100] These decrees, however, have limitations. First, they are automatically reviewed by the Constitutional Court, which can rule against them based on content or procedural irregularities, and second, they can only last up to ninety days, with the possibility of extending them up to 120 days (Constitution Article 213).

The Antiterrorist Statute bill would have circumvented both of these limitations. First, amendments to the constitution do not expire and are harder to change. Second, institutional reforms introduced via legislative acts (*actos legislativos*) are not automatically reviewed by the CC. They reach the court only when there is a lawsuit against them. Finally, whereas the CC can rule against state of emergency presidential decrees based on their content, it cannot do the same with legislative acts and referendums. It can only rule against this type of constitutional amendments based on the appropriateness of their design and congressional debate (Constitution Article 241).[101]

---

[98] Who can nominate candidates to courts and oversight agencies varies; however, which nominee gets the position is usually a decision made by congress.

[99] Gaceta del Congreso 174 de 2003.

[100] In case of a security threat, the president can declare a state of emergency. The state of emergency allows him to use presidential decrees, instead of legislation, to rule.

[101] Furthermore, to rule against a constitutional amendment, the procedural irregularities need to be irremediable. Otherwise, the bill goes back to congress to fix whatever was wrong.

Members of congress are well aware of the importance of procedure during the debate of referendum bills or legislative acts (Botero and Gamboa 2021). Those who support a reform try to avoid procedural irregularities; those who oppose it try to cause procedural irregularities and/or vocally denounce them whenever they happen. It is often the case that opposition congressmen and women denounce some procedural irregularity and ask the chair of the House or Senate to include their complaint in the official records as if they wanted to alert Constitutional Court clerks about the irregularity so that justices can use it to rule against the bill.[102] Some members of congress go even further and manufacture procedural irregularities, which is easy given that the rules of congress (Law 5 of 1992) are complicated and committee and plenary sessions are often chaotic.[103] In general, procedural irregularities are easy targets for weak oppositions, and during the Antiterrorist Statute debate, the opposition took advantage of this (see Table 5.1).

Before it was approved by congress, the Antiterrorist Statute had to go through eight legislative debates (see Figure 5.6). Security is a salient issue in Colombia, and Uribe's "iron fist" policy was popular. The government coalition had no reason to split over this reform, and the opposition was not a serious adversary. As expected, the bill went through five debates without a problem.

The bill was introduced in April 2003, and by late October, it had reached its sixth debate. On November 5, in the third session of the sixth debate, in the middle of a chaotic roll call vote for which there was no quorum, the president of the House, Alonso Acosta Osio, decided to close the session for the day, arguing that there was not enough order inside the chamber to go on.[104] María Isabel Urrutia (PDA), an anti-Uribista congresswoman, appealed the decision based on the fact that Acosta Osio had made it without formally bringing the voting to a close.[105] The president of the House put Urrutia's appeal up for a vote. The House voted in favor of the appeal, and consequently, Acosta Osio reopened the session. Immediately afterward, Joaquín José Vives (PL) claimed that reopening the session violated procedure. He argued that the House had voted, the bill had not passed, and the session was closed. Therefore, any other vote or debate from that point onward constituted a procedural irregularity. The president disregarded the claim, reminded everybody that the session was open, and – due to the chaos inside the chamber – called for a vote again the

---

[102] Author's interview with Constitutional Court clerk, Bogotá, January 17, 2014.

[103] Author's interview with member of NGO Congreso Visible, Bogotá, November 20, 2013.

[104] The presidents of the Senate and the House (or the committees) can suspend a session and schedule it for the next day whenever order inside the chamber is disturbed (Art. 77, Ley 5 de 1992).

[105] According to congressional rules of procedure, once the president of the House or Senate announces the beginning of the vote, it cannot be interrupted, unless a member of congress puts forward a complaint on how the vote is taking place (Art. 132, Ley 5 de 1992).

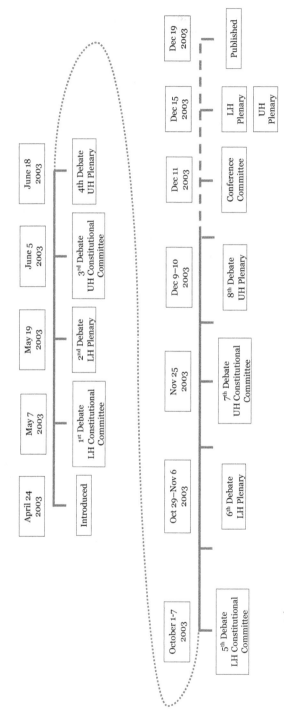

FIGURE 5.6. Legislative process antiterrorist statute, 2003

next day. This time, there was a quorum, and the bill passed.[106] Opposition congress members claimed that there had been a procedural irregularity, left a formal note of it on the record, and left the chamber in a sign of protest.[107]

Although the bill followed its regular path and was finally approved by the legislature, the opposition systematically restated the procedural irregularity during the seventh and eight debates in the Senate.[108] Members of congress from the PL and PDA repeatedly accused the president of the House of closing the session in the middle of the roll call voting to save the project. They argued that during the first roll call vote (before Acosta Osio closed the session), the bill did not have enough votes to pass; that the president of the House illegally closed the session and reopened it afterward just to allow more pro-Uribistas to vote. This argument was borrowed by different unconstitutionality lawsuits and ultimately used by the Constitutional Court to rule against the bill in August 2004.[109]

Even though the CC was essential to block the bill, it was the opposition's institutional strategy that gave the justices enough arguments to rule against it. Not only did the opposition use a chaotic situation to create a procedural irregularity, but it also noted it in the record as such. In doing so, the opposition coalition in congress provided key legal resources for the advocacy groups that presented lawsuits against the bill. Without these members of congress, it would have been hard for these groups to realize there had been a procedural irregularity. Congressional written records or videos only show bits and pieces of what happens inside these debates, and regular citizens or advocacy groups do not have the resources to attend every single debate. Unless it is duly documented and/or the relevant parties are tipped off, it is hard for those presenting the lawsuit and those judging it to notice the procedural irregularity. A member of a legal advocacy group explained to me that, "Members of the opposition in congress are important ... Advocacy groups do not have the resources to follow the debates so, most of the times, are the opposition members of congress the ones that help."[110]

In this case, the various formal notes in the record were essential for the advocacy groups and interested individuals to build lawsuits against the statute. As a leader from one of the teams that presented lawsuits against the bill said, "It is important for members of congress to be inside. They serve as a megaphone and can identify problems. They are a source of information about procedural or content irregularities. Lawsuits have succeeded because of that .... The Antiterrorist Statute had procedural irregularities. The debate

---

[106] Gaceta del Congreso 617 de 2003, 16.   [107] Gaceta del Congreso 663 de 2003, 11.
[108] Gaceta del Congreso 707 de 2003, Gaceta del Congreso 03 de 2004, and Gaceta del Congreso 04 de 2004.
[109] Corte Constitucional, Colombia, C-816-2004, M.P. Córdoba Triviño, Jaime, and Rodrigo Uprimmy Yepes, August 30, 2004.
[110] Author's interview, Bogotá, December 19, 2013.

was closed before time. Congressmen warned [us about this] they guided [us] towards that."[111]

The lawsuits against the Antiterrorist Statute criticized the bill both for its content (under the theory of the "constitution substitution"[112]) and irregularities in the process by which it was approved. Divided on whether the Constitutional Court has the authority to rule against legislative acts based on their content[113] the court ruled based on the procedural irregularities, specifically, what happened during the sixth debate – arguments rooted in content would not have been adequate to undermine these antidemocratic reforms.[114]

5.2.2.3 The Reelection Referendum (2008–2010)

After the Constitutional Court ruled against the Antiterrorist Statute, the Uribistas focused their forces on pushing through congress and the court the immediate reelection reform. Once approved, in 2005, Uribe's reelection seemed certain. Despite a historical showing by the PDA candidate, Carlos Gaviria, who placed second with a 22 percent vote share,[115] Uribe was reelected with 62 percent of the votes.

During his second term, the president introduced constitutional amendments to curtail the powers of courts and oversight agencies, maintain his majorities in congress while reducing their power, and extend his time in office beyond his second term. However, for the most part, his strategy to erode democracy changed. Rather than curtailing the powers of the courts and oversight agencies, he doubled his efforts to co-opt these institutions (Rubiano 2009a). As the first president reelected since the 1991 Constitution was approved, he had the unparalleled opportunity to intervene in the appointment of five Constitutional Court justices, six members of the disciplinary chamber of the Supreme Council of the Judiciary, all of the members of the National TV Commission, three members of the Central Bank, the General Comptroller, and the Inspector General and the Ombudsman. And while he successfully influenced some of these nominations – without a third term – he did not have enough time to influence them all.

---

[111] Author's interview, Bogotá, January 13, 2014.

[112] Some lawyers, justices, and constitutional scholars have argued that because the constitution can only be replaced via a constitutional assembly, whenever congress presents a reform that changes the pillars on which the constitution was built, it is overstepping its functions, and that can constitute a procedural irregularity in and of itself.

[113] The theory of "constitution substitution" divides the court. Some justices believe in it, others do not.

[114] Corte Constitucional, Colombia, C-816-2004, M.P. Córdoba Triviño, Jaime, and Rodrigo Uprimmy Yepes, August 30, 2004.

[115] It is the first time in Colombia's history that a leftist party placed second in a presidential election.

Uribe also targeted a different court inside the judicial branch. During his first term, he tried hard to reform the Constitutional Court; during his second term, he focused on the Supreme Court instead (Rubiano 2009a). This change was fueled by the *parapolítica* scandal. The responsibility for judging members of congress resided with the Supreme Court. It led the trials against the members of congress accused of having used the support of paramilitary groups to win their seats. As mentioned earlier, these trials affected members of the Uribista coalition the most. Close allies of the president, like Mario Uribe – the president's cousin – had to resign from their seats and are in jail today.

In an aim to protect his coalition in congress, as well as his most loyal allies, Uribe tried to (a) reform the constitution to curtail the powers of the CSJ and allow members of congress to appeal to other institution after this body had ruled against them; (b) appeal to an internal rivalry between the CC and the CSJ in order to get the former to support bills that curtailed the powers of the later (Rubiano 2009a; Ungar et al. 2010); and (c) discredit clerks and justices of the CSJ. To this last point, not only did Uribe's administration illegally intercept the phone and email of the CSJ justices, but in 2007, the president publicly disqualified a CSJ assistant justice who was leading the investigations, using the false testimony of a former member of a paramilitary group (García and Revelo 2010).

In the fallout of the parapolítica scandal, Uribe used his majorities in congress to block a series of reforms that sought to penalize parties that put forward candidates with ties with paramilitary groups. Every time a representative accused of parapolítica resigned from her seat in congress, she was replaced by a member of the same party. The reforms wanted to stop that and leave those seats empty until 2010. Because eight out of ten members of congress accused of parapolítica were Uribistas (López 2010, 51), such a reform would have effectively destroyed the president's majorities in the legislature. Although initially supportive, once this became apparent, the government sank the reforms.[116]

Besides these attempts to co-opt and reform, the most important bill put forward by the Uribista coalition during Uribe's second term was the reelection referendum bill that would have allowed the president to run for a third term. The reelection referendum was introduced to congress as a "popular initiative." It was pushed by a Reelection Committee, a group of business people, politicians, and right-wing activists[117] led by Luis Guillermo Giraldo, secretary general of the U Party at the time. Publicly, Uribe distanced himself from the project. Behind closed doors, however, he supported it (López de la Roche

---

[116] "Entierro de Quinta." *Revista Semana*, June 7, 2008.
[117] Cecilia Paz de Mosquera, Doris Angel de Villegas, Gustavo Dager Chadid, Myriam Donato de Montoya, Juan David Angel Botero, Alvaro Velasquez Cock, Hediel Saavedra Salcedo, and David Salazar Ochoa.

2014). His Minister of Interior and Justice, Fabio Valencia Cossio, worked closely with congress to pass the bill.

Similar to what happened with other pieces of legislation put forward by the government, during the reelection referendum's transit through congress, the opposition used rules of procedure to delay the bill and identify and prove legal issues with it. Although the referendum was ultimately approved, the opposition's complaints not only helped raise awareness and gather support against the initiative, but they also provided important information that the Constitutional Court later used to rule against the bill (see Table 5.1).

The referendum had serious time constraints. If Uribe was going to run for a third term, by law, he had to announce his candidacy six months before May 2010.[118] This meant that the bill had to make full transit through congress and be reviewed by the Constitutional Court with enough time to schedule the referendum before December 2009. Still, thanks to the opposition's obstruction strategies, it took the referendum a year to go through the four congressional debates required (see Figure 5.7).

By law (Art 18, Ley 134 de 1994), in order to introduce the referendum bill to congress, the Reelection Committee had to collect approximately 1,404,000 signatures – 5 percent of the electoral roll – in no more than six months (Paredes 2010). The Reelection Committee exceeded expectations, collected 5,021,873 signatures, and turned them in to the National Registrar for verification on August 11, 2008. The National Registrar certified 3,909,825 of these signatures, and the Committee submitted the referendum bill in September 2008. The expectation was that the bill would be out of the legislative body early in 2009 and the referendum would happen soon afterward. However, the bill was not approved until September 2009, roughly six months later than its supporters would have preferred.

The opposition used several stalling tactics. During the first debate (November 18, 2008)[119] in the House Committee for Constitutional Affairs, the opposition postponed the session a couple of weeks. Not only did it leak bits of weak evidence about irregularities with the funds used to pay for the signatures to support the initiative, but it also required that Luis Guillermo Giraldo, the National Registrar, and the president of the CNE appear in front of the Committee for the debate to move on.[120] All this took so long that the second debate in the Plenary of the House had to be scheduled for the last day of the legislative term (December 16, 2008). In this session, the opposition asked to do roll call voting even for the most simple procedural matters, voted

---

[118] Art. 9, Ley 996 de 2005.

[119] The appointed members of congress presented the papers for or against the bill by mid-October, and the first debate of these papers was not scheduled until a month afterward.

[120] Gaceta del Congreso 55 de 2009, 3.

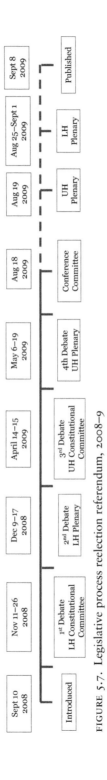

FIGURE 5.7. Legislative process reelection referendum, 2008–9

ten impediments[121] independently, and even asked for a minute of silence on behalf of a recently deceased fellow congressman.[122] If Uribe had not extended the legislative term by decree until the next day, the government coalition would not have been able to approve the project before the end of the term and would have had to wait until February 2009, putting the referendum at risk.

The referendum's transit through the Senate was faster. Together, the Committee and Plenary debates took only one month. However, the opposition was able to further delay the bill once it reached the Conference Committee, where representatives of the House and Senate had to reconcile different versions of the bill. The opposition launched a strong political and judicial battle to decide who would sit on the Conference Committee. The presidents of the House and Senate – in charge of choosing who sits in these committees – were recused pending a decision of the Ethics Committee, which took a couple of weeks to rule.[123]

In the meantime, Germán Navas, a PDA representative, introduced a malfeasance lawsuit against all eighty-six members of congress who had voted for the referendum. The lawsuit argued that they had approved a bill knowing that the signature collection process had violated funding limits. The lawsuit delayed things even more. Scared that they would be accused of malfeasance again, several Uribista congressmen and women refused to participate. In between the recusals and the lawsuit, the debate inside the Conference Committee was pushed to the next legislative term in July 2009 (Paredes 2010). It took the Conference Committee almost a month to agree on a version of the referendum, and another month for the House and Senate, where the opposition used roll call voting for every matter, including fifty impediments to approve the bill. The referendum bill was finally sanctioned by congress in September 2009.

The delays allowed the opposition to collect enough evidence to support the claim that the money used to gather the referendum signatures exceeded the legal limits. In 2008, by law, referendum campaigns could only receive up to $334,974,388 Colombian pesos in private donations.[124] According to the report the Reelection Committee gave the National Registrar, the campaign had used $2,046,328,136 COP to pay for the collection of signatures to introduce the bill. The form credited $142,870,000 COP to private donations,

---

[121] When there is a conflict of interest, members of congress can ask the floor whether they consider them unfit to participate in the debate or not.

[122] *Gaceta del Congreso* 77 de 2009.

[123] The president of the House opposed the referendum. He was recused by the head of the U Party, Luis Carlos Restrepo, who did not want him to pick people who did not support the referendum to sit in the Conference Committee. Acknowledging that the recusal would only delay matters, Restrepo withdrew his complaint, but Varón insisted on waiting for the Ethics Committee ruling.

[124] *Resolución* No. 00067 de 2008, Consejo Nacional Electoral.

but it was unclear about where the remaining $1,903,458,136 COP came from.[125] The fact that the bill's debate took so much time allowed the opposition to search for evidence to prove that the funds unaccounted for came from private donations. This meant that the Referendum Committee had violated the legal funding limits, which in turn allowed the opposition to introduce lawsuits against its members and the legislators that had supported the bill.

The requests for information as well as the lawsuits forced both the National Registrar and the CNE to produce documents publicly stating that there was money used to fund the referendum that had not been accounted for and therefore the bill did not fulfill all the requirements to go to congress. They also created a public scandal that eventually forced the head of the Committee – and secretary general of the U Party – to resign from the party and disqualified some of the Uribista members of congress from participating in the ratification of the bill (Paredes 2010). According to Germán Navas:

> I started with the pictures where you could see DMG trucks taking the papers and stuff [of the referendum material] ... I managed to divide the evidence [pertaining the funding irregularities] into doses to keep the debate alive ... During that time, we began to find the bookkeeper and the money they used, and the money they were declaring and how they were messing with the rules...[126]

The delays helped change minds and hearts as well. They gave time for serious scandals that hurt the president's image to surface. According to Germán Varón, House Representative for Cambio Radical, "despite being a minority, we managed to push forward the decision by eight months, circumstance that I think at the end helped because these eight months allowed several corruption scandals to surface and changed peoples' perception ... that, at least, showed that not everything had been that good from the side of Uribe's government."[127]

Two scandals were particularly important at this stage. A little after the debate of the referendum started, DMG, a Colombian company based in the south of the country, was accused of money laundering and leading a Ponzi scheme. As the debate moved forward, it was found that this company had aided the recollection of signatures for the referendum (Paredes 2010). The second scandal that hindered the president's public image was related to state subsidies devoted to low-income Colombian farmers. It was revealed in October 2009 that these subsidies had several irregularities, not the least of which was the fact that the Minister of Agriculture had granted some of them to large landowners who weren't supposed to receive them.

---

[125] Letter *Entrega de balance de ingresos y gastos, Comité de Promotores para la Reelección Presidencial. Registraduría Nacional del Estado Civil.* September 3, 2008.
[126] Author's interview, Bogotá, November 19, 2013.
[127] Author's interview, Bogotá, November 26, 2013.

Both the scandals and the complaints from members of congress – echoed by the press – strengthened the opposition and attracted those who, despite being Uribistas, were hesitant about the project. Partly driven by the fact that there was something "fishy" about the referendum, a group of Uribistas and non-Uribistas united against the bill. With the support of some media outlets (Semana.com, La Silla Vacía), they used creative campaigns to ask the court to rule against the project. For instance, they stood outside the Constitutional Court with lamps to "illuminate" its members to do the right thing.[128] According to a CC justice, although this show of support did not influence the justices' choice, it did make them feel more comfortable when they ruled against the bill.[129]

Finally, the opposition's obstruction tactics were instrumental in warning those in charge of judicial review about possible irregularities in the law. Every intervention against the project, noted in the congressional written records, talked about the money problems and specified how these constituted a procedural irregularity. The CC usually limits its evaluation to the bill's transit through congress. The irregularities reported in the congressional records, however, gave the court reasons to go beyond the normal review process and ask for supporting documentation of the bill before it was submitted to the legislature.[130] The court found out that the unaccounted money in the Referendum Committee's report came from loans made by a nonprofit Uribista foundation, which was receiving large amounts of money from individual donors. The donations the foundation received matched the "credits" this foundation made in favor of the Referendum Committee. In other words, the Committee was using the nonprofit to receive larger amounts of money from private donations than it was allowed to receive.[131,132]

If members of congress had not researched and noted the irregularities, it is unlikely that court staffers or members of judicial NGOs would have been able to detect this fraud.[133] Even though it is possible that the court could have ruled against the bill based on the "constitution substitution theory," or the idea that there are limits to what congress can reform, this was a controversial theory that often divided the court.[134] It was easier and safer to rule on procedural irregularities. First, the court is more likely to agree on these irregularities. Second, unlike what happens with the "constitution substitution theory," there is no question on whether the court is competent to rule against constitutional

[128] Author's interview with a member of Democracia Ciudadana December 5, 2013.
[129] Author's interview, January 20, 2014.
[130] Author's interviews with Constitutional Court clerks, Bogotá, December 10, 2012, and January 17, 2014.
[131] Author's interview with Constitutional Court clerk, Bogotá, January 24, 2014.
[132] Corte Constitucional, Colombia, C-141-10, M.P. Sierra Porto, Humberto Antonio, February 26, 2010.
[133] Authors Interview with a member of advocacy group, Bogotá, May 14, 2014.
[134] Author's interview with Germán Zafra, Constitutionalist, Bogotá, December 10, 2013.

amendments based on procedural irregularities or not. This last point is especially important when the bill is backed up by a popular president with widespread support (Gibson 2007). In other words, without the procedural irregularities, the decision would have been a lot harder to make. Under these circumstances, ruling against the referendum would have weakened the court's prestige and made it more vulnerable vis-à-vis a powerful president with the resources to ignore its decision.

The court ruled against the referendum on February 26, 2010 (only one month before the parliamentary elections, and three before the presidential elections). Although the opposition in congress had not been able to stop the project in the legislature, delaying and denouncing had proven fruitful. Not only had the court used its arguments to rule against the initiative, but also the delays had left Uribe no choice but to accept the ruling and move on. There was no time to introduce any other reform.

5.2.3 The Importance of Moderate-Institutional Strategies

The opposition's strategic choices described in Section 5.2.2 were critical to protect democracy in Colombia. Both avoiding radical extrainstitutional strategies (and staying clear of those who used them) and effectively deploying institutional and moderate extrainstitutional strategies were essential to stop Uribe's antidemocratic reforms. The former allowed the opposition to protect the few institutional resources it had. The latter enabled them to curtail, delay, modify, and provide legal arguments to help the Constitutional Court stop the president's bills. To further reinforce that point, in this section, I recount the process by which Uribe successfully changed the constitution to allow his immediate reelection.

Like the constitutional amendments discussed earlier, the first reelection reform weakened Colombia's democracy. As previously suggested, two immediate terms gave the Colombian president a disproportionate influence over court and oversight appointments, hindering the delicate structure of checks and balances put in place in 1991. Notwithstanding this threat, congress approved the bill in December 2004, and the Constitutional Court ruled in favor of it in October 2005. The amendment allowed Uribe to stay in office until 2010.

By tracing the process behind the immediate reelection reform, I leverage within-case variation to provide some preliminary evidence of the importance of not only having institutional resources but also using them effectively against presidents with hegemonic aspirations. Even though the amendment was a clear threat to democracy and the Constitutional Court was strong and independent enough to rule against it, the reform passed, potentially (at least in part), due to the ineffectiveness of the opposition.

Unlike what happened with the 2002 Referendum, the 2003 Antiterrorist Statute, and the 2008 Reelection Referendum, opposition members of congress failed to effectively obstruct the bill. They believed congress was not going to approve the reform, and even if it did, the Constitutional Court was going to rule against it because it "replaced" the constitutional framework outlined in 1991.[135] The opposition, therefore, failed to delay the project or create procedural irregularities to help the court. Without strong procedural arguments, it was harder for the CC to challenge the president. As the opposition learned early in Uribe's government, an independent and strong Constitutional Court, albeit important, was insufficient to stop the erosion of democracy.

5.2.3.1 The Immediate Reelection Reform (2004–2005)
Uribe's coalition introduced the immediate reelection reform to congress on March 16, 2004. Like the Antiterrorist Statute, the bill moved through congress very fast. Whereas debates for the 2002 Referendum took eighteen days on average, debates for this bill took only three. The bill's debate started in the Senate on April 22, 2004; it was out of congress eight months afterward (see Figure 5.8).

Although the opposition used some delaying tactics and brought forward some minor procedural irregularities, obstruction does not seem to have been the priority during the reelection reform's transit through congress. Whereas when dealing with other amendments, the opposition went above and beyond to delay the bill and/or create/denounce procedural irregularities, that is not the case of the first reelection bill. The congressional records of the bills, discussed earlier, show how the opposition identified a procedural irregularity, created a note of it on the record, and referenced it across different debates. Congressional records for the president's first reelection reform have no evidence of a similar systematic obstruction strategy. Opposition members of congress barely identified procedural irregularities, and when they did, they failed to note them in the record and/or follow up in later debates.

The reason behind the absence of such evidence is unclear. It is possible that the Uribistas were more cautious than usual in following procedural rules. The CC had ruled the Antiterrorist Statute unconstitutional for procedural irregularities in August 2004, halfway through the debate of the first reelection reform. The government was careful not to let this happen again. It is also possible that some opposition congress members, like Antonio Navarro (PDA senator), chose to hedge their bets and focus on changing the "Opposition Statute" instead of blocking the bill. The statute defined the rules under which the president was going to be allowed to run for a second term.[136] The members of congress who chose to focus on it might have believed that if the

---

[135] Interview with Hector Helí Rojas, Bogotá, November 7, 2013.
[136] The Opposition Statute was designed to guarantee that an election with the sitting president in it would be minimally fair. Among other things, it regulates the time at which the president can announce his campaign, the amount of public resources he can use, and the role of public officers under his command.

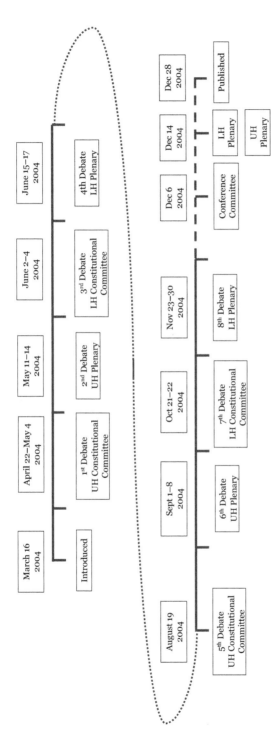

FIGURE 5.8. Legislative process reelection reform, 2004–5

opposition and the CC failed to stop the bill, it was important to have input on rules under which Uribe was going to run in 2006.

Finally, the opposition might not have prioritized obstruction because they thought the bill was not going to pass. First, together with a couple of Uribistas who disliked the reelection reform, the opposition had found the votes it needed to sink the bill in the House Committee for Constitutional Affairs. Second, even if Congress approved it, the opposition was confident the Constitutional Court was going to block the bill. Hector Helí Rojas, a senator for the Liberal Party at the time, told me he was shocked that the CC had not ruled against the first reelection reform. If there was ever a clear example of a "substitution of the constitution," the first reelection reform was it. By allowing the president to run for a second term, the law hindered the separation of powers and disabled several of the checks created in 1991 to prevent the executive from co-opting courts and oversight agencies.[137]

Both of these assumptions proved to be wrong. The day the reelection amendment was scheduled to be debated, the government used state resources to convert two opposition votes to their side. In exchange for patronage, Yidis Medina and Teodolindo Avendaño (Conservative Party) agreed to vote for the bill and miss the debate, respectively (Navas Talero 2010). This caught the opposition by surprise.[138] They were not expecting the change, nor had they prepared to give a floor fight. The reelection reform was out of committee in two days.[139] Navas Talero (PDA) sued Medina for malfeasance, and the Supreme Court eventually ruled against Congressman Avendaño, and Minister of Interior Sabas Pretel. The ruling, however, came too late, after Uribe had been reelected in 2006.

The CC reviewed four lawsuits introduced against the reform in February 2005[140] and ruled against all of them. The lawsuits focused, first and foremost, on the "constitution substitution theory." They argued that the immediate reelection reform thwarted the constitution's spirit, effectively substituting the charter. Congress, which is not enabled to substitute the constitution, had therefore overstepped its powers, effectively committing a procedural irregularity. As mentioned earlier, the "constitution substitution theory" is a debated theory. The 1991 Constitution does not have entrenchment clauses, and it is unclear which kind of reforms constitute a "constitution substitution" and

---

[137] Author's interview, November 7, 2013.   [138] Gaceta del Congreso 370 de 2004.
[139] Gaceta del Congreso 370 and 371 de 2004.
[140] Corte Constitucional, Colombia, C-1040-05, M. P. Cepeda Espinosa, Manuel José, Rodrigo Escobar Gil, Marco Gerardo Monroy Cabra, Humberto Antonio Sierra Porto, Alvaro Tafur Galvis, Clara Inés Vargas Hernández, October 19, 2005; Corte Constitucional, Colombia, C-1042-05, M. P. Cepeda Espinosa, Manuel José, October 19, 2005; Corte Constitucional, Colombia, C-1043-05, M. P. Cepeda Espinosa, Manuel José, Rodrigo Escobar Gil, Marco Gerardo Monroy Cabra, Humberto Antonio Sierra Porto, Alvaro Tafur Galvis, Clara Inés Vargas Hernández, October 19, 2005; Corte Constitucional, Colombia, C-1050-05, M. P. Cepeda Espinosa, Manuel José, October 19, 2005.

which ones do not. Accordingly, a ruling based on the "constitution substitution theory" was hard to get. Not only is this theory one on which justices rarely agreed,[141] but, because it is fiercely contested, rulings based on substitution could stand on quicksand and undermine the legitimacy of the court. During Uribe's government, the CC was systematically reluctant to use the "constitution substitution theory" to rule against the government's constitutional amendments, such as the Antiterrorist Statute and the Reelection Referendum. The case of the immediate reelection reform was no different; the CC argued that congress had not overstepped its functions when it approved the bill.[142]

Although the lawsuits also mentioned procedural irregularities, the lack of systematic evidence in congress weakened these claims. Out of the ten procedural irregularities presented, only two were backed up by Edgardo Maya, inspector general at the time, who opposed the reelection reform.[143] The first one was not backed up by the congressional record. There was no note, intervention, or systematic evidence that it had happened at all.

The second one dealt with impediments. When a member of congress feels that a bill could potentially benefit her, she can ask the chamber to "excuse" her from participating in that debate. The process to make a decision about an impediment is unclear. The law fails to explicitly state who is in charge of debating for or against impediments or the procedure by which they should be voted on. Although the opposition complained of procedural irregularities when voting on the impediments, without rules, it is impossible to support that claim. Consistent with other rulings during Uribe's government, the CC ruled that the way the impediments had been processed did not constitute a procedural irregularity.[144]

The case of the first reelection reform suggests that, without the help of members of congress, the Constitutional Court had a harder time ruling against the president. Even though it was strong, independent, and an important veto, by itself, the CC was insufficient to guarantee the survival of democracy. Uribe is one of the most popular presidents Colombia has seen in decades. As shown earlier, without the protection and active input of the opposition, it was hard for the court to rule against the executive. If the opposition had not effectively employed institutional and moderate extrainstitutional strategies, the CC

---

[141] Interview with Germán Zafra, Constitutionalist, Bogotá, December 10, 2013.

[142] Corte Constitucional, Colombia, C-1040-05, M. P. Cepeda Espinosa, Manuel José, Rodrigo Escobar Gil, Marco Gerardo Monroy Cabra, Humberto Antonio Sierra Porto, Alvaro Tafur Galvis, Clara Inés Vargas Hernández, October 19, 2005.

[143] In cases of judicial review, the CC asks the inspector general to write a recommendation.

[144] Corte Constitucional, Colombia, C-1040-05, M. P. Cepeda Espinosa, Manuel José, Rodrigo Escobar Gil, Marco Gerardo Monroy Cabra, Humberto Antonio Sierra Porto, Alvaro Tafur Galvis, Clara Inés Vargas Hernández, October 19, 2005.

would have likely found it harder to rule against some of Uribe's other antidemocratic reforms.

5.3 CONCLUSION

Despite the strength of Alvaro Uribe and the relative weakness of the opposition, unlike what happened in Venezuela, the Colombian president was not able to erode democracy. Notwithstanding his attempts to curtail the powers of the courts and extend his time in office beyond a second term, Colombia's constitutional order remained fairly strong. Uribe had to step down and give way to other presidential candidates in 2010.

Rather than focusing solely on the correlation of forces between government and opposition, what the Colombian case suggests is that we also need to pay attention to the decisions that the opposition makes. The evidence put forward in this chapter shows that even if weak, those out of power have the resources to effectively protect democracy. In contrast with the anti-Chavistas, the Colombian opposition avoided extrainstitutional strategies with radical goals and used mostly institutional strategies and extrainstitutional strategies with moderate goals to fight Uribe's attempts to increase the powers of the presidency and extend his time in office beyond a second term. These tactics allowed the opposition to keep its legitimacy domestically and abroad. Despite the government's attempts to undermine those who criticized it, most of the opposition members were able to keep their seats in congress and actively lobby against the administration abroad. In doing so, they were able to protect courts and oversight agencies from being co-opted by the executive and use them to stop Uribe's antidemocratic reforms.

The survival of democracy in Colombia was far from certain in 2002. As this chapter suggests, a strong and independent Constitutional Court, although important, was insufficient to prevent Uribe from enhancing his powers and extending his time in office. The opposition effectively employed institutional and moderate extrainstitutional strategies to delay and undermine the legislative process of Uribe's antidemocratic reforms. In doing so, it provided the CC with the arguments and the street support it required to rule against the president and keep its legitimacy intact.

Colombia's democracy is far from perfect. War-ridden, this is a country in which human rights and civil liberties are violated permanently by armed left- and right-wing groups, members of the armed forces, politicians, or a combination of all of them. However, the fact that Uribe had to step down and allow another person to become president makes this country's regime today qualitatively different from Venezuela's since 2008. Even though violations against the rule of law still happen, the fact that Uribe left office has allowed courts and oversight agencies to investigate and successfully prosecute crimes committed by members of Uribe's administration. Important members of his government have been sentenced to prison because they offered bribes in order to pass bills;[145] used the state police (DAS) to provide information to paramilitary groups;[146] spied on justices, lawyers, journalists, and opposition members;[147] and faked the demobilization of a FARC front trying to enhance the Democratic Security results.[148]

More contextually, Alvaro Uribe's successor moved far away from his political "godfather." Although Santos won the presidency on Uribe's coattails, he quickly distanced himself from the dogmatic views of his antecessor, and started a successful peace process with the FARC. In 2016, Colombia signed a peace agreement with the guerrillas, ending fifty years of armed conflict. Chances are this would not have been possible if Uribe had remained in power as he wanted to. Uribe and his followers see the FARC as a terrorist group. As such, they believe that the guerrillas should surrender their weapons unilaterally. They also believe that all guerrilla members should be jailed and be barred from participating in politics. Under those circumstances, it is very unlikely that the FARC would have negotiated with Uribe in a third or fourth term.

---

[145] Minister of Interior, Sabas Pretelt, Minister of Social Welfare, Diego Palacio, and former Secretary to the President, Alberto Velásquez.
[146] Former DAS director, Jorge Noguera.
[147] Former DAS director, Maria del Pilar Hurtado and former Secretary to the President, Bernardo Moreno.
[148] Former Peace Commissioner, Luis Carlos Restrepo.

6

Opposition Strategies Elsewhere

As I mentioned at the beginning of this book, the erosion of democracy has become pervasive. Countries in Asia, Eastern Europe, the Middle East, and Africa have seen the rise of executives with hegemonic aspirations. The threat of antisystemic populist outsiders has even spread to developed democracies in Europe and North America. In this chapter, I assess the theory outlined in the book in some of these cases. Doing so allows me to evaluate if, when, and how does the argument of this book work outside Colombia and Venezuela.

According to V-Dem (2021), since 2000, ninety-three democracies[1] have suffered declines in their level of electoral democracy. The vast majority, sixty-nine, saw a small overall decline (<0.1 in a 0–1 scale) since they last reached their highest score. All but five of them[2] remain either liberal or electoral democracies.[3] Out of that same list, ten have seen a greater decline (0.1–0.19 points) in their levels of electoral democracy. Two of them became electoral autocracies;[4] the other eight[5] are still considered electoral democracies. The last thirteen countries have experienced declines of 0.2 or more points in their level of electoral democracy. All but two – Poland and Mauritius – became closed or electoral autocracies. Bangladesh, Benin, Bolivia, Comoros, Hungary, India, Nicaragua, Serbia, Turkey, Venezuela, and Zambia moved from being electoral

---

[1] I use V-Dem's Electoral Democracy index, as well as Polity IV and Freedom House, to determine a minimum level of democracy. That is, countries that score 0.5 on V-Dem's Electoral Democracy Index upper confidence interval, 1 or 2 on Freedom House's overall score, and 6 or more on Polity IV.

[2] Papua New Guinea, Montenegro, and Lebanon moved from being electoral democracies at their highest level of democracy, to become electoral autocracies. Honduras and Kenya were classified by V-Dem's Regimes of the World index as electoral autocracies at the time they transitioned to democracy.

[3] As measured by V-Dem's the Regimes of the World index. [4] Tanzania and the Philippines.

[5] Guyana, Slovenia, Botswana, Bosnia and Herzegovina, Bulgaria, Croatia, Indonesia, and Brazil.

democracies after they transitioned to democracy, to become competitive authoritarian (in some cases, fully authoritarian) regimes.

These processes of erosion in many of these countries can be attributed to the rise of executives with hegemonic aspirations: Juan Orlando Hernández (2013–22) in Honduras, Rodrigo Duterte (2016–22) in Philippines, Rafael Correa (2007–17) in Ecuador, Donald Trump (2017–21) in the United States, Daniel Ortega (2007–present) in Nicaragua, the Serbian Progressive Party (2012–present) in Serbia, Evo Morales (2006–19) in Bolivia,[6] Recep Tayyip Erdogan (2003–present) in Turkey, Viktor Orbán (2010–present) in Hungary, and the Law and Justice Party (2015–present) in Poland. In this chapter, I analyze the development of these last four cases.

I chose these countries for three reasons. First, they all had somewhat mature democracies when they began their process of democratic erosion. Unlike other nations mentioned earlier, they all had Electoral Democracy scores over 0.6 and had been democratic for at least twenty years when a potential autocrat attained office. Like Venezuela, and to a lesser extent Colombia, these were all unlikely cases of democratic erosion. Second, they all have experienced important declines (0.10 or higher) in their level of electoral democracy. Democratic backsliding, understood as a decline in the quality of democracy (Waldner and Lust 2018a), albeit important, is not the phenomenon I am interested in, in this book. The four countries discussed in this chapter have not only seen significant drops in their level of electoral democracy, but are also broadly recognized as cases of potential or full erosion.[7]

Third, these cases are diverse (see Table 6.1). They belong to three different regions around the world, have different outcomes, and fit differently in the theory of how opposition strategic choices impact a potential autocrat's ability to erode democracy. Three of these examples conform to the argument presented in this book; one does not. In Turkey and Bolivia, the use of radical extrainstitutional and, in some instances, radical institutional strategies allowed Erdogan and Morales to successfully erode democracy. In Poland, moderate institutional and extrainstitutional strategies have, so far,[8] tamed PiS's attempts

---

[6] The V-Dem's Regimes of the World Indicator downgraded Bolivia to electoral autocracy in 2019. This change can be the outcome of two different but related events. On the one hand, the 2019 presidential elections were highly irregular. The Organization of American States deemed them as fraudulent (Organización de Estados Americanos 2019) – although it is not clear if the irregularities committed by the government where enough to change the outcome (Idrobo, Kronick, and Rodríguez 2020a). On the other hand, the opposition to Morales launched a coup that ousted him in November 2019 and put an unelected interim government in his place.

[7] The United States has experienced an important drop in its level of electoral democracy, but there is disagreement as to the extent to which democracy is in danger (Parker 2018).

[8] While the inclusion of Poland as a "failed" case is controversial, I decided to keep it in the book for two reasons. First, it is a relevant case. Second, it allows me to highlight other types of opposition institutional and moderate extrainstitutional strategies that are not present in any of the other cases.

TABLE 6.1. *Strategies, goals, and erosion across cases*

STRATEGIES AND GOALS

	Institutional		Extrainstitutional		EROSION	THEORY
	Moderate	Radical	Moderate	Radical		
MORALES (LATIN AMERICA)	✓	✓	✓	✓	Yes	Confirm
ERDOGAN (MIDDLE EAST)	✓	✓	✓	✓	Yes	Confirm
PIS (EASTERN EUROPE)	✓		✓		No	Confirm
ORBÁN (EASTERN EUROPE)	✓		✓		Yes	Deviates

to undermine democratic institutions. In Hungary, the use of moderate institutional and extrainstitutional strategies and avoidance of radical extrainstitutional strategies did not stop the erosion of democracy. Despite the opposition's best efforts, Orbán was able to co-opt congress and oversight agencies, skewing the electoral playing field to such an extent that elections in the country are no longer minimally fair.

In what follows, I outline the process by which the leaders mentioned in the previous paragraph tried or are trying to erode democracy, and the strategies used by the opposition to preserve democracy. This cross-national/regional comparison suggests that moderate institutional and extrainstitutional strategies are, in fact, better suited to protect democracy than radical extrainstitutional or – to a lesser extent – radical institutional strategies. In Bolivia and Turkey, a combination of the latter (i.e., regional violence, coups, lawsuits to ban the governing party, etc.) increased the incentives to repress while reducing the costs of doing so. These tactics gave Morales and Erdogan "legitimate" reasons to remove opposition leaders from office, prosecute and jail them, all while maintaining a democratic façade and rallying their supporters around the flag as they moved aggressively to expand their power.

Despite their influence, oppositions in these countries lost resources they had when hegemonic executives came to power, rendering them less able to prevent further antidemocratic reforms in the future. In Poland, notwithstanding serious power grabs, PiS has not been able to transform the country's democracy into a competitive authoritarian regime. Using moderate institutional and extrainstitutional strategies, the opposition has protected important resources, maintained its legitimacy domestically and abroad, delayed and tamed PiS's agenda, opened up opportunities for the European Union to reverse some of the institutional modifications introduced by the government, and even regain their Senate majority in the 2019 parliamentary election.

The following analysis also suggests, however, that institutional and extrainstitutional strategies with moderate goals are not airtight. Despite relying on moderate institutional and extrainstitutional strategies, the Hungarian opposition was unable to stop the erosion of democracy. Two factors seemed to have played against them. First, unlike what happened in any of the other countries studied in this book, Orbán had overwhelming control over the Hungarian legislative and executive branches immediately after he attained power. Two years after becoming prime minister, his party, Fidesz, expanded their control over congress, courts, and most oversight agencies. The rapid loss of their institutional presence left the opposition with fewer opportunities to fight back. Second, the Hungarian prime minister faced a weak international community. The European Union was very slow to react, and when it did, Orbán was able to rely on Russian dictator Vladimir Putin for support. Neither PiS nor Uribe had a similar "dark knight" to rely on. Hungary's case suggests we need more research to better assess the conditions under which moderate/radical institutional/extrainstitutional strategies succeed or fail. In particular, we need to further study the extent to which an international community with a normative preference for democracy and the ways in which the institutional resources available to the opposition mediate the success of these tactics.

6.1 CASES OVERVIEW

While far from identical, Bolivia, Turkey, Hungary, and Poland are similar to Colombia and Venezuela in several relevant variables. By the time Morales, Erdogan, PiS, and Orbán came to power, these countries were democratic. As shown in Table 6.2, despite some variation in their levels of democracy, they all scored above 0.5 on V-Dem's Electoral Democracy index the year these leaders were elected.

Notwithstanding differences in degree, most of these countries had party systems somewhat in flux when these politicians became heads of government. As shown in Table 6.2, for all of them, electoral volatility in congressional elections was well above 0.30. This number is slightly lower than Colombia's (2002) and Venezuela's (1998), but nevertheless high.[9] Membership in the party system was volatile as well. In all these countries, except Bolivia,[10] the year these executives with hegemonic aspirations were elected, new parties attained between 25 and 45 percent of the votes. These numbers are similar to Venezuela's, where new parties attained 42 percent of the votes in 1998, but different from Colombia's, where new parties got only 10 percent of the votes in 2002.

Like Chávez and Uribe, Erdogan and Morales gained power in the midst of state crises. Average state performance[11] between 1996 and the year they were elected was 4.72 and 4, respectively. Confidence in institutions was also relatively low, with average cumulative trust in the police, the courts, and congress scored between 2.75 and 4.41 on a scale from 0 to 10.[12] As with Colombia and Venezuela, these numbers stemmed from social, political, and/or economic crises. Hungary and Turkey faced economic downturns before the executives with hegemonic aspirations came to power. Mean economic growth per capita

---

[9] Mean lower house volatility between 1978 and 2015 in Latin America was 0.25, but 0.43 between 1990 and 2006 in Eastern Europe (Mainwaring, Gervasoni, and España-Najera 2017).

[10] In Bolivia, new parties had attained 52 percent of the votes in the previous elections. MAS, Morales's party, was largely responsible for that number.

[11] Following Handlin (2017a), state performance is measured by averaging the scores of World Governance Indicators of Rule of Law, Control of Corruption, and Government Effectiveness. The original scale was –2.5–2.5. I rescaled them to 0–10 for ease of presentation.

[12] Following Handlin (2017a), confidence in institutions is measured with the average response across questions of trust in the judiciary, the police, and congress using data from Latinobarometer (1996–2005) for Bolivia; the European Social Survey (2002–14) for Poland and Hungary; and the World Values Surveys (1990–2001) for Turkey. The data displayed in Table 6.2 shows the mean institutional confidence score for all years available up until the election of the potential autocrat.

TABLE 6.2. *Countries comparison*

	Electoral Democracy (0–1)	Lower House Volatility (0–1)	New Parties Vote Share (%)	Mean Economic Growth PC (%)	Cumulative State Performance (0–10)	Cumulative Confidence in Institutions (0–10)
Bolivia (2006)	0.76	0.31	25	1.21	4.00	2.75
Turkey (2003)	0.65	0.33	45	-0.18	4.72	4.19
Poland (2015)	0.88	0.39	23	2.94	6.17	3.91
Hungary (2010)	0.86	0.36	57	0.74	6.57	4.41
Venezuela (1999)	0.75	0.45	42	-0.45	3.49	3.18
Colombia (2002)	0.55	0.48	10	-0.77	3.99	3.57

Source:

- **Electoral Democracy:** Electoral democracy the year before the executive came to power. Data: V-Dem 2021 (Coppedge et al. 2021).
- **Lower House Volatility:** LH Volatility closest election. Data: Mainwaring (2018) for Bolivia, Colombia, and Venezuela; my own calculations using electoral data from the European Election Dataset for Turkey, Poland, and Hungary.
- **New Parties Vote Share:** Share of vote obtained by new parties in closest LH election. Data: Mainwaring (2018) for Bolivia, Colombia, and Venezuela; my own calculations using electoral data from the European Election Dataset for Turkey, Poland, and Hungary.
- **Mean Economic Growth PC:** Mean economic growth per capita five years before the executive came to power. Data: World Bank Economic Indicators.
- **Cumulative State Performance:** State performance from 1996 up until the rise of the executive. Data: my own calculations with WB Governance Indicators for Control of Corruption, Government Effectiveness and Rule of Law (rescaled 0–10).
- **Cumulative Trust in Institutions:** Trust in institutions before the rise of the executive using survey questions regarding trust in the police, the national congress, and the judicial branch. Data: my own calculations using data from Latinobarometro (1995–2018) for Colombia, Bolivia, and Venezuela; European Social Survey (2004–14) for Poland and Hungary; and the World Values Survey (1990–2001) for Turkey.

five years before Erodgan and Orbán became prime ministers was negative in Turkey and less than 1 percent in Hungary. In 2001 and 2009, Turkey and Hungary had an economic growth per capita of -7.15 percent and -6.56 percent, respectively. Although Bolivia's economy was not hurting (mean economic growth between 2000 and 2005 was positive, and growth per capita in 2004 was 2.30 percent) by the time Morales came to power, the country was in the midst of a severe political crisis. Between 2003 and 2005, massive protests had forced three Bolivian presidents out of office.

Poland is an outlier in this regard. Its economy decelerated between 2011 (4.70 percent per capita growth) and 2013 (1.19 percent per capita growth) but was bouncing back when PiS won the parliamentary elections. Growth per capita in 2014 was 3.46 percent. Unlike Bolivia, Poland was not undergoing a political crisis, nor was it in the midst of an internal conflict like Colombia or Turkey. The rest of the chapter studies the process of democratic erosion in each of these cases.

6.2 BOLIVIA

Between 1986 and 2005, Bolivia had a fairly stable, albeit exclusive, democracy. In 2005, when Evo Morales became the first indigenous president of Bolivia, the country's V-Dem's Electoral Democracy score was 0.74, well above the Latin American mean (0.70). Since then, democracy has been in decline. During his first five years in power, Morales introduced constitutional amendments to enhance his powers and extend his time in office. By 2010, he had gained two-thirds of congress, packed the courts, and co-opted oversight agencies. Since then, he used his control over state institutions to harass the opposition, decrease media freedom, use state resources to campaign, and run for a third (2015–20) and a fourth (2020–5) term.

Between 2014 and 2019, Morales's control over state institutions made it almost impossible to defeat him,[13] forcing Bolivian elections onto an increasingly uneven playing field. Democracy in Bolivia certainly did not deteriorate to the extent that Venezuela's did. Morales brought to the political arena an important segment of the population whose preferences had been ignored and was constrained by bottom-up pressures within his party (Anria 2018). By 2017 (at least), however, the Andean country had a very diminished degree of vertical accountability. Morales showed he was willing and able to overturn the popular will. In 2017, he used his control over state institutions to ignore a referendum (2016) in which 51 percent of Bolivians voted to keep the two-term limit for president and vice president, and in 2019, his administration engaged

---

[13] In 2019, the opposition was able to narrowly position itself in a situation to defeat Morales in a runoff. It did so despite the increasingly uneven playfield using electoral strategies designed to overcome the obstacles inherent to competitive authoritarian regimes (Gamboa 2020b).

in highly irregular elections[14] in order to avoid a runoff that would have threatened Morales's fourth reelection (Velasco Guachalla et al. 2021). I therefore classify Bolivia as a case of successful democratic erosion.

Like what happened with Venezuela, democracy in Bolivia did not break in a day. Morales came to power via free and fair elections in 2006. It took him five years to undermine horizontal accountability and another four to erode electoral accountability. Similar to the anti-Chavistas in Venezuela, those who opposed Morales had plenty of opportunities and institutional resources to fight back. Between 2006 and 2009, opposition parties had a third of the seats in the House, a simple majority in the Senate, a fourth of the seats in the Constitutional Assembly, and several governorships. They also had support in courts and oversight agencies.

Between 2006 and 2007, the opposition took good advantage of these resources. Using moderate institutional and extrainstitutional strategies, it was able to delay and curb Morales's project. Starting in 2008, however, regional elites began to organize protests and strikes, invade buildings, and use violence in order to push for the de facto autonomy of gas-rich provinces. These extrainstitutional strategies with radical goals hindered the opposition's legitimacy domestically and abroad. They increased the incentives and, more importantly, reduced the costs to repress. Not only was Morales able to use these events to "legitimately" remove from office and/or prosecute some regional (and eventually national) politicians, but he was also able to leverage these tactics in order to increase the vote share of his party, Movement Towards Socialism (MAS). In 2009, MAS won a simple majority in the House and two-thirds of the seats in the Senate.

During the first three years of Morales's government, the opposition was able to delay and tame some of his attempts to undermine institutions of horizontal accountability. Starting in 2010, it lost its ability to do so. Without a significant presence in congress, the opposition was unable to obstruct reforms that threatened the independence of courts and oversight agencies or limit the president's ability to reinterpret and/or modify the constitution in order to stay in office. In 2014 and 2018, the government-controlled Constitutional Court reinterpreted the constitution to allow Morales to run for a third and a fourth term. Had the opposition failed to mobilize, the electoral authorities would have also sanctioned Morales's victory in the highly irregular 2019 elections.

The erosion of democracy was not a foregone conclusion in Bolivia. The opposition started off with substantial institutional resources and, at first, used them effectively to obstruct Morales's project. Had it kept using moderate institutional and moderate extrainstitutional strategies and avoided radical

---

[14] The Organization of American States concluded that the government had engaged in fraudulent behavior (Organización de Estados Americanos 2019); however, it is not clear if the irregularities committed explain Morales's marginal victory (Idrobo, Kronick, and Rodríguez 2020a).

extrainstitutional strategies, the opposition would have likely delayed Morales's agenda, increasing the probability of stopping the erosion of democracy.

6.2.1 Moderate Institutional and Extrainstitutional Strategies

Like Hugo Chávez, Evo Morales rose to power in the midst of a state crisis. The government had become ineffective in the delivery of goods, and citizens had become disenchanted with democratic institutions (Handlin 2017a, 175–9). Although the economy began to show signs of improvement in the 1990s after a decade of negative economic growth and inflation, by the early 2000s Bolivia remained highly unequal and its political arena very exclusive. The year Morales won the presidential elections (2005), Bolivia had the second largest Gini Coefficient in the region (58.5), a cumulative average state performance of four out of ten, and the second lowest mean cumulative institutional confidence in Latin America (Handlin 2017a, 38).

In 2003, the three-party system that had governed Bolivia since 1985 – Democratic Action (ADN), Revolutionary Left Movement (MIR), and Revolutionary Nationalist Movement (MNR) – collapsed (Cyr 2017). A series of protests pushed out the sitting president and his successors[15] and forced the governing elites to call for general elections. Morales and his party came to power in 2006 after having the strongest general election performance in Bolivia's democratic history (Cyr 2017, 176). The indigenous leader had a vote share of 54 percent – twice the vote share he received in 2002 (21 percent) – and MAS won seventy-two seats in the House (55 percent) and twelve seats in the Senate (44 percent) – more than twice the seats it had won three years earlier.

The opposition against Evo Morales was originally composed of two largely disjointed factions of national and regional political elites. Between 2006 and 2009, it had 44 percent (fifty-eight) of the seats in the House,[16] 55 percent of the seats in the Senate,[17] and six out of nine governorships (*prefecturas*).[18] Initially, these resources helped the opposition tame and slow down Morales's attempts to undermine democratic institutions. Using moderate institutional and extrainstitutional strategies, the opposition leveraged them to protect its legitimacy and remain in office, while curbing reforms enacted in the Constitutional Assembly and, to a certain extent, protecting the independence of the Supreme and Constitutional Courts.

---

[15] Gonzalo "Goni" Sanchez de Lozada (2002–3) was replaced by Carlos Mesa (2003–5), and Eduardo Rodríguez (2005–6).
[16] *Poder Democrático y Social* (Podemos) had forty-three seats (33 percent), *Frente de Unidad Nacional* (UN) had eight (6 percent), and MIR had seven (5 percent).
[17] Podemos had thirteen seats (48 percent); UN and MNR had one (3 percent) each.
[18] Beni, Pando, La Paz, Cochabamba, and Tarija.

6.2.1.1 *The Constitutional Assembly*

Evo Morales's first attempt to concentrate power was a constitutional assembly (AC). Unlike what happened in Venezuela, however, the Bolivian opposition was able to effectively use its numbers in congress to influence the body's rules. With this moderate institutional strategy, the anti-Morales coalition guaranteed election rules that did not automatically favor the incumbent, required a two-thirds majority for all decisions, and limited the power of the AC vis-à-vis congress (Postero 2010). The opposition was also able to guarantee that the new constitution would recognize the autonomy of any region that voted for it in referendums scheduled for July 2006 (Centellas 2011). Albeit imperfect, these rules limited Morales's ability to write a tailor-made constitution.

The elections for the Constitutional Assembly took place in July 2006, alongside the autonomy referendums. Even though the results favored MAS – which won 137 seats out of 255 (54 percent) – the opposition won a sizable representation in this body. Opposition parties won eighty-seven (34 percent) seats,[19] enough to block major decisions if they worked together (Deheza 2008).

The Constitutional Assembly began deliberating in August 2006. In September, MAS tried to bypass the rules agreed upon by congress. It voted to change the rules of debate, authorize simple majorities to approve all decisions except the final text, and declared the AC to be foundational (i.e., not subject to the previous constitution or the institutions set by it). The government also disregarded its promise to grant political, administrative, and financial autonomy (in particular, control over gas taxes) to the provinces that had voted in favor of regional autonomy (i.e., Santa Cruz, Beni, Tarija, and Pando) in the July referendum (Centellas 2011).

Attempts to bypass the rules and agreements made in congress unleashed a political firestorm. To oppose these power grabs, the opposition used a mix of moderate extrainstitutional and institutional strategies. First, it submitted a complaint to Bolivia's Supreme Court and refused to continue debating until the court ruled on it. Later, in October, when the government refused to abide by the high court's ruling, upholding preexisting rules and declaring the AC to be "derived" (i.e., subject to the previous constitution and subject to the rules that congress had designed), the opposition organized street demonstrations, conducted hunger strikes, and boycotted the Constitutional Assembly (Deheza 2008).

Together, these tactics paid off. In February 2007, after Morales found himself unable to credibly delegitimize the opposition, Masistas and anti-Masistas agreed that the constitution articles would be approved by a qualified majority in commission and ratified by the plenary of the AC; that the final text

---

[19] Social and Democratic Power (Podemos) sixty seats (24 percent), National Unity (UN) eight seats (3 percent), and the different MRN factions eighteen seats (7 percent).

would be submitted to a referendum; and that disputed articles would have to be approved by a special committee or by public vote in the aforementioned referendum. Unfortunately, this settlement did not dissolve the tensions inside the Constitutional Assembly. The AC's deadline was August 2007. A couple of months before that date, the government and the opposition were not even close to submitting a draft of the constitution. The opposition had successfully used the two-thirds majority requirement to stall the debate.

The situation reached a new climax in March when the anti-Morales coalition proposed to move the legislative and executive offices to Sucre (an opposition stronghold) rather than keep them in La Paz (a government stronghold) (Azcui 2007). In order to enhance their positions inside the Constitutional Assembly, both sides mobilized supporters to protest for or against the proposal. The looming August deadline and the increasingly heated situation in the streets led congress to broker another agreement. The legislative body extended the deadline for the constitutional draft to December 2007. In exchange for the extra time, the opposition agreed that a simple majority of voters, rather than a majority in each state, would be enough to approve the new constitution, and MAS agreed to hold a two-stage referendum: the first one to decide over questions the Assembly was unable to resolve, the second to ratify the constitution.

Despite this settlement, both sides kept their supporters in the streets. Mobilizations in Sucre (where the AC was holding its meetings), coupled with an opposition boycott to the AC, brought the constitution-making process to a halt. To break the stalemate, in October 2007, a multi-partisan coalition drafted another agreement. In it, MAS gave up several of its most radical proposals like the creation of a fourth government branch (*Poder Social Plurinacional*) with powers over the other branches, the transfer of natural resources' administration to autonomous indigenous territories, and the restructuring of congress. It suggested, instead, to create four different types of autonomies: regional, departmental, municipal, and indigenous. The *media luna* prefects believed the latter would undercut their authority and control over important mineral resources (Deheza 2008; Eaton 2007) and pressured opposition assembly members to reject the agreement (Mayorga 2009).

At this point, the opposition's use of moderate institutional and extrainstitutional strategies had held up and substantially curbed Morales's constitutional project. Fearing more delays, in November 2007 – almost two years after Morales became president – the government moved the AC meetings to a military facility, where, without any opposition delegates, MAS approved a constitutional draft. In order to sanction the details, which required a two-thirds majority, Morales's supporters surrounded the congressional building and prevented opposition senators and representatives from coming onto the premises. Alone, MAS congress members passed a bill allowing the AC to move its location outside Sucre (to Oruro). Once out of the opposition's stronghold, MAS delegates were able to prevent opposition AC delegates from participating and approved the details of the constitutional draft in one session, with 164 out of 255 members present (Deheza 2008).[20] The proposed constitutional text included reforms that decreased the checks on the executive and increased his time in office. It established that Supreme and Constitutional Court justices would be popularly elected, changed electoral laws in a manner that favored the ruling party, and allowed for one (effectively two) presidential reelections (Uggla 2009).[21]

The opposition's reaction to this power grab was twofold. While regional politicians reacted with radical extrainstitutional strategies such as violent separatist protests, national politicians kept using institutional strategies to delay the approval of the constitutional draft. The rules stipulated that in order to enact the constitution, Bolivian citizens had to approve it via a referendum sanctioned by congress. The opposition used its majority in the Senate to delay the ratification of the referendum law, and when the government tried to bypass it and unilaterally call for a referendum (February 2008), the opposition used the National Electoral Court (CNE) to stop the measure. The tribunal ruled against the president's referendum a month later (Uggla 2009).

The CNE ruling brought the constitutional debate back to square one. In order to disentangle the situation, stop another constitutional referendum, and regain the visibility it had lost, in May 2008, the opposition in the Senate approved a recall referendum against the president and all but one of the sitting prefects.

The vote took place in August 2008. Following the theory outlined in this book, this radical institutional strategy increased both the costs and the incentives to repress. Although it kept the opposition resources intact, it radicalized the government. Morales was ratified and remained in office; only the prefects of La Paz and Cochabamba (neither of which was involved in the autonomy movement) were revoked. The referendum strengthened both the president and the *media luna* prefects, all of whom increased their vote share vis-à-vis 2005 (Uggla 2010).

Leveraging this display of popular support, on August 28, the government tried to unilaterally schedule another referendum to ratify its constitutional draft. As was expected, opposition factions rejected the measure. Four days later, the CNE backed them, establishing that a referendum to ratify the constitution could only be called by the legislature, where the opposition still had significant numbers. The strategy paid off. Unable to delegitimize national politicians and remove them from office without severely damaging his democratic façade, Morales had no choice but to negotiate the constitutional draft approved in 2007. As a result of these negotiations, the opposition was able to

[20] They reinterpreted the rules to approve the text with two-thirds of the votes of the delegates present, rather than two-thirds of the total number of delegates.
[21] The draft established that presidential terms before the constitution was approved would not count, allowing Morales to govern for three terms.

strengthen regional autonomy and get the government coalition to count Morales's 2006–10 term as his first one, thus allowing one, not two, reelections afterward. The opposition was also able to keep the size of the House of Representatives (130 members instead of the 121 proposed by MAS) and guarantee that seventy of its members would be elected in plurinominal rather than uninominal districts (as the government suggested initially).[22]

Although it was unable to backtrack the establishment of popular elections for the supreme, constitutional, and agricultural courts or the Council of the Judiciary – which would reinforce the regime's majoritarian tendencies and reduce the checks on the executive – the opposition was able to change the CNE's appointment process. The 2007 draft stipulated that indigenous communities and farmers would directly elect this body's members. The new draft allowed these groups to nominate candidates but gave congress the last word over the final appointments. Finally, the opposition was able to keep the requirement of a qualified majority in the legislature to reform the constitution (Romero Bonifaz 2009). Congress reached an agreement over the constitutional text in October 2008 and called for a referendum to ratify the charter in January 2009. Almost two years after its original deadline, an overwhelming majority of voters approved the constitution.

Using moderate institutional and extrainstitutional strategies, the opposition delayed the erosion of democracy in Bolivia. Endowed with important veto powers in the legislature and relying on somewhat independent courts, opposition leaders at the national level used moderate institutional and extrainstitutional strategies to protect their legitimacy and curtail the ability of the government to unilaterally approve a tailor-made constitution. In doing so, not only were they able to delay the government's agenda and but also shape the new constitution.

6.2.1.2 *Protecting the Courts*[23]

The anti-Morales coalition also used institutional strategies to delay and prevent the co-optation of high courts and oversight agencies. As soon as he became president, Morales tried to co-opt and curtail the power of the Supreme Tribunal of Justice (TSJ)[24] and the Constitutional Plurinational

---

[22] Under these rules, 54 percent of the house members would be elected via proportional representation within departments, instead of in single-member districts prone to manipulation by the government.

[23] This section was written using Pérez-Liñán and Castagnola's (2011) excellent analysis of fall of the Supreme and Constitutional Courts in Bolivia.

[24] Before 2009, the Supreme Court in Bolivia was called Bolivian Supreme Court of Justice. After 2009, it changed its name to Supreme Tribunal of Justice. For clarity, I use the latter name throughout.

Tribunal (TCP).[25] Unable to upend all the rules that governed the judiciary, he used impeachment and harassment campaigns to pressure unfriendly justices to resign. The opposition played a key role in delaying this particular power grab.

During Morales's first year in power, Chief Justice Rodríguez Veltzé (TSJ) was charged with treason, Justice Rocha Orozco (TSJ) gave up his seat in response to a 32 percent cut in the justices' salaries, and Justice Ruiz Pérez (TSJ) stepped down as a result of political harassment by the executive. Between 2007 and 2008, Justices Rosario Canedo and Beatriz Sandoval (TSJ) were accused of malfeasance for stopping an arrest warrant against Luis Alberto Valle (La Paz former governor), and Justices Morales Baptista and Irusta (TSJ) were impeached for ruling in favor of Leopoldo Fernández (Pando's former prefect). The government also initiated impeachment procedures against Chief Justice Eddy Fernández (TSJ) for allegedly delaying Sánchez de Losada's corruption trial and against the TCP justices for disqualifying the interim Supreme Justices that the government had appointed using powers of decree during the legislative recess in 2006 (Castagnola and Pérez-Liñán 2011).

The fact that the opposition had an important presence in congress substantially delayed and tamed the government's ability to co-opt the courts. The anti-Morales coalition was unable to stop all the resignations and impeachments but was able to use its majority in the Senate to stop Morales's attempts to negatively decide over the indictments and obstruct the election of government loyal replacements. For instance, in 2006, the Senate acquitted TCP magistrates who had been accused of receiving bribes and, a year later, reinstated them in their positions. The upper house was also able to reverse Canedo's impeachment after the government-controlled House of Representatives had ruled against her.

Unfortunately, without a majority in either chamber of congress, the opposition could stall but not prevent the impeachment procedures or the naming of new justices.[26] With several of their members either gone or suspended, between May and November 2009, the TSJ and TCP had lost the quorum they needed to work (Castagnola and Pérez-Liñán 2011). Eventually, the government was able to dismantle and co-opt the court. Thanks to the opposition, however, the process took five years instead of two. It was only after the 2010 election, when the opposition no longer had a significant presence in congress, that Morales was able to fill in the courts' vacant seats with loyalists.

---

[25] Before 2009, the Constitutional Court was called Bolivian Constitutional Tribunal. It changed its name to Plurinational Constitutional Tribunal in 2009. For clarity, I use the latter name throughout.
[26] Neither government nor opposition had the two-thirds required to elect Supreme or Constitutional Court justices.

6.2.2 Extrainstitutional Strategies with Radical Goals

Whereas the Bolivian national elites resorted to institutional strategies to fight Morales, regional elites in Tarija, Pando, Beni, and Santa Cruz resorted to radical extrainstitutional strategies to do the same. The latter backfired. They increased Morales's incentives and decreased his costs to repress. Not only did they threaten Morales's presidency, but also they limited the opposition's ability to present itself as democratic, either domestically or abroad, giving the executive enough cover to push for more aggressive antidemocratic reforms after removing prosecuting, or jailing opposition officeholders.

In December 2007, the prefects of these provinces unilaterally released autonomy statutes and called for referendums to ratify them between May and June 2008. The statutes greatly increased the powers of regional authorities, in particular regarding natural resources and tax revenues. These four regions are the wealthiest provinces in the country. Santa Cruz alone occupies a third of the territory and is home to Bolivia's most productive activities (Eaton 2007; Romero 2007a). The autonomy statutes, which fell short of calling for independence (Romero 2007b), would have effectively defunded Morales's government (Uggla 2009; Farthing and Kohl 2014, 44–50). In response to this radical extrainstitutional strategy, Morales pushed for a speedy ratification of the constitutional draft approved in December 2007, which would have undermined the autonomy statues.

In an attempt to diffuse the situation, in March 2008, the CNE decided against both the constitutional and the regional referendums (Uggla 2009). Ignoring the ruling, however, the prefects kept protesters in the streets and moved forward with the vote (Postero 2010). The demonstrations soon turned violent. In May, for example, students surrounded the city stadium in Sucre, to prevent Morales from addressing his supporters. Using stones, firecrackers, and dynamite, they attacked the police who were trying to secure the area. In the process, they captured, kicked, punched, and racially insulted eighteen of Morales's supporters. They marched them to the town square, made them strip to the waist, kneel, and burn their pro-Morales clothing. They made it very easy for the government to frame the protests as the unmeasured reaction of a white elite, unwilling to give up its privileges and wealth (Gustafson 2010).[27]

The 2008 recall referendum further fueled this turmoil. Strengthened by the ballot box and enraged by Morales's second attempt to ratify the 2007 constitutional draft, the prefects relaunched their offense to press for full autonomy. In late August, the governors of Tarija, Pando, Beni, and Santa Cruz stepped up the street demonstrations. The protesters physically attacked government supporters and members of the police, took over roads and airports, and occupied

---

[27] Opposition protesters were not alone in the use of violence, yet – likely because of their viciousness and racial undertones – their actions are highlighted in 2009's international reports such as Human Rights Watch's and Amnesty International's.

state institutions. Rather than admonishing against the violence, shortly afterward, the prefects announced that the institutions controlled by their supporters would be transferred to departmental authorities, following the autonomy statutes. It was the equivalent of a regional coup (Uggla 2009).

In a savvy move, Morales refused to repress the demonstrations. Despite attacks against state institutions, the government kept the police and the military in their barracks. Instead, MAS called its supporters to mobilize against the protests. The regional authorities took the bait. On September 11, 2008, people tied to Leopoldo Fernández, Pando's prefect, fired against government supporters traveling to a pro-government rally in El Porvenir. Although most of Morales's supporters escaped, some were dragged out of ambulances, kicked and beaten, grabbed as they were fleeing, and whipped with barbed wire and/or detained and beaten while questioned. Nineteen people were killed (Ledebur and Walsh 2008; Gustafson 2010).

This radical extrainstitutional strategy undercut the regional opposition's legitimacy. The violent attacks against Morales's supporters – in particular, those in Pando – increased the incentives and decreased the costs to remove opposition members from office and allowed Morales to rally around the flag in support for more aggressive reforms. The El Porvenir massacre also eliminated the opposition's democratic legitimacy domestically and abroad. Inside the country, outraged indigenous groups and other social movements mobilized in defense of the government. Internationally, Human Rights Watch[28] and Amnesty International[29] condemned the opposition. In response to the massacre, UNASUR also issued a declaration condemning the events and warning that the organization was not going to tolerate actions that compromised Bolivia's territorial integrity (Ledebur and Walsh 2008).

The violence in the *media luna* provinces ended the opposition's ability to present itself as a victim in the fight for democracy. After the massacre in El Porvenir, Morales declared a state of siege and arrested Fernández, as well as other civil leaders charged with crimes related to the violence. Down the road, the events in Pando would also give the potential autocrat leeway to remove high court justices and members of the opposition.[30]

The move also hurt the opposition at the ballot box. In 2009, Morales was not only able to rally around the flag and increase his support in government strongholds, but also – with a friendly interim governor put in place after Fernández's arrest – he was able to move and register "masista" voters in

---

[28] Human Rights Watch. 2009. *World Report 2009 (Events of 2008)*. New York, NY: Human Rights Watch. www.hrw.org/world-report-2009.

[29] Amnesty International. 2009. *Amnesty International Report 2009 – Bolivia*. Amnesty International. www.refworld.org/docid/4a1fadfc55.html.

[30] In 2008, Supreme Court Justices Morales Baptista and Irusta approved Fernández's request to move his trial from La Paz (government stronghold) to Sucre (opposition stronghold). In response, MAS initiated impeachment procedures against them.

Pando. Using a resettlement program to distribute land (*Plan Nacional de Distribución de Tierras y Asentamientos Humanos*), the government moved 1,300 families from La Paz and Chapare to Pando (Buitrago 2010). The enactment of this plan just before the elections was criticized by the Carter Center (2009, 9).[31] Between 2005 and 2009, the number of registered voters in this province increased by 60 percent (almost twice the mean national increase).[32] Although it is impossible to know the affiliation of these new voters, in 2009, Pando – where the opposition had won all four Senate seats in 2005 – lost half of its senators to MAS, enough to lose a qualified majority in the upper house.

Overall, the extrainstitutional strategies with radical goals used by the opposition prefects paved the way for Morales to erode democracy. The calls for autonomy, coupled with the anti-government violence during 2008, increased the incentives and reduced the costs to repress. They hurt the opposition's legitimacy abroad. UNASUR signed a declaration condemning their actions and warning they would not recognize "...any situation that implies an attempted civil coup, the rupture of the constitutional order, or endangers Bolivia's territorial integrity."[33] Rather than a movement that sought to protect democracy, they were seen as a strident association willing to break Bolivia's territorial integrity in order to halt Morales's agenda.

Threatened, the president not only had the incentives but also the opportunity to remove opposition leaders from office and push for more power grabs. In 2009, he not only rallied around the flag but also increased the number of voters in battleground states. These moves, together with the traditional parties' inability to form a cohesive block, hindered the opposition's ability to win the general elections. Not only did Morales win the presidential elections with a vote share of 64.2 percent (11 percent higher than his vote share in 2005), but also his party obtained eighty-eight seats in the House (68 percent) and twenty-six in the Senate (72 percent). With a super majority in both chambers, the president was able to circumvent the two-thirds requirement to change the constitution, elect six of seven members of the CNE – which the opposition had successfully blocked for four years – and finish the pending impeachments of Supreme Tribunal of Justice and Constitutional Plurinational Tribunal justices.

---

[31] Using a resettlement program to distribute land (*Plan Nacional de Distribución de Tierras y Asentamientos Humanos*), Morales's government moved 1,300 families from La Paz and Chapare to Pando (Buitrago 2010). The enactment of this plan just before the elections was criticized by the Carter Center (2009, 9).

[32] Between 2005 and 2009, the number of registered voters increased across the country from 3,671,153 to 4,970,461 (a 26 percent increase).

[33] Comisión para el Esclarecimiento de los Hechos de Pando. "Informe de La Comisión de UNASUR Sobre Los Sucesos de Pando." UNASUR, November 2008.

6.2.3 Summary

The process of erosion in Bolivia resembles the one in Venezuela. The opposition started off strong with a simple majority in the Senate, a third of the seats in the lower house, support inside courts and oversight agencies and control of significant regional offices. Using institutional and extrainstitutional strategies with moderate goals, between 2006 and 2007, it was able to use these resources to significantly influence the constitution-writing process and obstruct the co-optation of courts and oversight agencies. When it switched to radical extrainstitutional strategies in 2008, however, the opposition jeopardized these resources and eventually lost them all. It gave the president a golden opportunity to remove opposition leaders from key offices and rally around the flag in the 2009 general elections.

Although it is possible that Morales would have found other ways to increase his hold over congress, courts, and oversight agencies, the opposition's strategic choices made it undeniably easier. Had it avoided extrainstitutional strategies with radical goals, the anti-Morales coalition would have been better able to protect the institutional and noninstitutional resources it had and used them to delay – even prevent – more aggressive power grabs. Once it lost the regional leverage and its seats in the Senate, Morales's moved swiftly to erode democracy. Without meaningful opposition, between 2010 and 2015, Morales increased his hold over the judiciary. In 2010, MAS approved a series of laws that allowed the president to name interim TSJ and TCP justices, as well as members of the judiciary, to fill the vacancies created by its own smear campaigns (Castagnola and Pérez-Liñán 2011), transferred the authority to conduct judicial review to Congress (Mayorga 2017), and allowed MAS to unilaterally nominate partisan candidates for the Supreme and Constitutional tribunals, the Agro-Environmental Court, and the Judicial Council. Controlled by the government, in 2014, the TCP circumvented the agreements reached in 2008 and allowed Morales to run for a third term.

The laws introduced between 2010 and 2015 also curtailed the power of regional authorities and put opposition politicians in a vulnerable position. They enabled the government to suspend sitting governors and mayors facing criminal charges and prosecute (former) elected officials. Former presidents Gonzálo Sánchez de Lozada and Jorge Quiroga were charged with corruption for approving hydrocarbon contracts "against national interests" (Freedom House 2013), and several sitting politicians were removed from office, prosecuted, jailed, or exiled. In 2016, there were seventy-five politically motivated judicial cases (Freedom House 2017a).[34] Fear of prosecution significantly affected opposition leaders' ability to effectively fight the president.

---

[34] Senator Roger Pinto Molina faced criminal charges after denouncing corruption in the government. Opposition leader Luis Ayllón was sentenced to two years in prison accused of embezzlement for his alleged loss of a camera (Freedom House 2016). Assemblywoman Hilda Saavedra

The government also used its control over state institutions to curb freedom of expression. Using a series of vague laws that penalize reporting that "condones" racism or discrimination (Freedom House 2011) and stipulate the media's obligation to contribute to the moral, ethical, and civil values of the nation's cultures (Freedom House 2012), the government harassed opposition media outlets and journalists. Following Venezuela's example, Morales also enlarged the network of state-owned media outlets both by buying outlets and by denying broadcasting licenses to the opposition (Freedom House 2011, 2012, 2016).

Whether Bolivia remained democratic or not in 2019, when Morales was forced out of office, is debated. Some scholars (Lehoucq 2008; Levitsky and Loxton 2013a; Weyland 2013; Velasco Guachalla et al. 2021) suggest it had crossed the threshold into a competitive authoritarian regime; others (Anria 2016; Cameron 2018; Cleary and Öztürk 2020) suggest that, notwithstanding its defects, the regime still had enough vertical accountability to remain in the democratic camp. I side with the former. Since 2014, the Bolivian electoral playing field was significantly skewed. Uneven access to resources, uneven access to the media, and – more importantly – manipulation of electoral laws made it almost impossible to defeat Morales and his party. Morales's lawsuit in 2017 to invalidate the results of a referendum in which a majority of the people had voted against the possibility of indefinite reelections and the numerous irregularities in the elections that followed only underscore this point. Vertical accountability can hardly be effective when rules, regulations, and even electoral results change always in favor of the incumbent.

6.3 TURKEY

Between 1985 and 2013, Turkey was a democracy. In 2002, when Recep Tayyip Erdogan's party, the Justice and Development Party (AKP), won the parliamentary elections, Turkey's V-Dem Electoral Democracy score was (0.67), far above the MENA mean (0.42) and close to the Latin American (0.70) and above the Eastern European (0.63) means. Since then, Turkey has transitioned into an authoritarian regime. Between 2003 and 2014, Erdogan consolidated his control over the executive, the legislative, and the judicial branch. Ever since, he has used them to curb freedom of expression, harass the opposition, manipulate electoral laws, and extend his time in office almost indefinitely.

Democracy in Turkey did not break in one day. It took Erdogan more than ten years to erode horizontal and vertical accountability. Similar to the anti-Chavista and anti-Morales coalitions, the opposition to the AKP had several opportunities and resources to fight against the prime minister's power grabs.

was accused of conspiring to commit a crime and obstruction of the electoral process after she led a vigil outside a regional Electoral Tribunal (Freedom House 2016).

Despite its parliamentary weakness (it won only 32 percent of the seats in 2002), the opposition controlled the presidency, the military, the bureaucracy, and – to a lesser extent – the judiciary and the police.[35]

Using radical institutional and extrainstitutional strategies, however, it lost them all. Together, a coup threat in 2007 and an attempt to use the courts to ban AKP in 2008 threatened the survival of the government and gave Erdogan a "legitimate" excuse to repress. Between 2007 and 2011, the prime minister gained a hold over the presidency, purged the armed forces, and increased his influence over high courts and oversight agencies with the approval of the international community.

He strengthened that hold in 2014 after opposition-controlled bureaucrats launched a series of corruption investigations that endangered Erdogan's rule. This radical institutional strategy failed to legitimate repression, but radicalized the prime minister, who furthered his control over the judiciary and the police, leaving the opposition very few resources – mainly some support in Turkey's Constitutional Court. The opposition lost this as well. In 2016, a failed coup gave the Turkish head of state enough cover to prosecute members of the opposition and push for a referendum that changed Turkey from a parliamentary to a hyper-presidential system. Endowed with unprecedented powers, Erdogan will have the ability to rule unchecked until 2023, potentially 2028.[36]

Like Bolivia or Venezuela, the erosion of Turkish democracy was not a foregone conclusion. Erdogan faced a particularly strong opposition in the early 2000s with substantial resources to fight back. Had it used mostly moderate institutional and extrainstitutional strategies and abstained from using radical institutional and extrainstitutional strategies, the latter might have been better able to protect these resources. Erdogan might not have felt the need to co-opt courts and oversight agencies or – as shown by the 2013 nonviolent protests launched at Gezi Park – he might have had to do it at the expense of his democratic façade. It is impossible to know if this would have been enough to save democracy in Turkey. Oppositions face particularly hard trade-offs when opposing a potential autocrat. A different set of strategies, however, would have given the opposition a better shot to survive.

6.3.1 Radical Institutional and Extrainstitutional Strategies

Recep Tayyip Erdogan became prime minister in 2003[37] in the midst of crisis. Turkey had been unstable politically and economically since its transition to

---

[35] Although secularist "Kemalist" elites have traditionally controlled the courts and the police; the Gülen movement had made inroads in these bodies (Jenkins 2009).

[36] Erdogan won the 2018 election. His term ends in 2023, but the Constitution allows him to run for one immediate reelection.

[37] Although the AKP attained power in November 2002, at the time Erdogan was still banned from office.

democracy in 1983. The armed forces had kept tight control over the country. In the name of stability and secularism, they often exerted undue influence over civilian governments, hindering Turkey's ability to consolidate its nascent democracy. Turkey also suffered from a long-standing armed conflict between the Turkish government and the Kurdish Workers Party (PKK) in southeast Turkey (Updegraff 2012) that continued to disrupt politics in the country. Moreover, Turkey had a struggling economy. Between 1980 and 2001, it saw three major economic crises with a -7.36 growth per capita in 2001.

The economic and political instability during the 1990s discredited the (more) traditional Turkish parties. Understanding that shift, in 2002, the AKP downplayed its Islamic tradition, and presented itself as a "socially conservative center-right party that supported state reform, anti-corruption measures, democratization to empower society vis-a-vis the state, ... European Union membership ... [and] social justice" (Keyman and Gumuscu 2014, 33). It became a fresh alternative to both the ultra-secularist traditional elite and the radical Islamist parties. With the support of conservatives, globalists,[38] market-oriented business owners, and minorities like the Kurds (Müftüler-Baç and Keyman 2012; Keyman and Gumuscu 2014, 33), the AKP was able to win 363 seats (out of 550) in that year's parliamentary elections,[39] enough to form a unitary government.

The opposition to the AKP was initially led by the traditional "Kemalist" elites,[40] organized mostly in the Republican People's Party (CHP) as well as other minor parties like the Nationalist Movement Party (MHP).[41] In 2013, the Islamic Gülen movement – traditionally opposed to the "Kemalist" elites – turned against AKP as well.[42] It was followed by the Kurdish parties, Peace and Democracy Party (BDP) and the People's Democratic Party (HDP) in 2014–15.[43]

The opposition coalition described earlier had decades-long rivalries. The divergent goals they stood for (radical-secularism, Kurdish independence, and an Islam-driven government) and Turkey's long history of violence and authoritarianism had created deep grudges among them. Consequently, the Turkish opposition worked a little like a hydra with each faction acting unilaterally almost always. The nature of the opposition resulted in a diverse set of

---

[38] People in favor of joining the European Union.
[39] Although AKP only received 34 percent of the vote, most other parties lost their seats because they could not reach the 10 percent voting threshold required to seat their candidates.
[40] That is, people who subscribe to a radical view of secularism that opposes any manifestation of religion in the public sphere.
[41] Since 2017, MHP has been part of the government coalition.
[42] AKP's relationship with the Gülen movement is ambiguous. Between 2002 and 2013, they worked in tandem. Since 2013, however, Erdogan and the Gülenists have been at war with each other (Özbudun 2015).
[43] Initially, the AKP established a conciliatory discourse toward the "Kurdish question." That tone changed in 2013, when the peace talks broke down.

strategies. Between 2002 and 2016, it used a mixed bag of tactics to oppose the regime, including radical institutional and extrainstitutional actions like a coup threat (2007), litigation to ban the governing party (2008), a criminal investigation against Erdogan in (2013–14), and a military coup (2016).

6.3.1.1 The Coup Threat

When Erdogan became prime minister, Turkey still lived under a constitution written by the dictatorship and had a recent history of undue military influence over politics (Somer 2016). The AKP's first constitutional reforms in the early 2000s sought to reduce these authoritarian legacies. They did not significantly threaten the opposition resources and were overall considered as a step forward for Turkey's democracy (Öniş 2016). Four years after Erdogan came to power, those who opposed him still had a hold over the presidency, as well as influence over the military, the bureaucracy, and – to a lesser extent – the judiciary and the police.

The presidency was a particularly powerful veto in Turkey's parliamentary system. President Ahmet Necdet Sezer (2000–7), a staunch secularist, had the power to make or oversee high-level bureaucratic and judicial appointments. Between 2002 and 2007, the president used these powers to block hundreds of AKP's appointments (Migdalovitz 2007; Jenkins 2009).

When Sezer's term came to an end, in 2007, AKP had enough votes in parliament to choose his successor.[44] On April 25, Erdogan nominated Abdullah Gül – AKP cofounder, former prime minister (2002–3), and former minister of foreign affairs. To oppose the appointment, the CHP used moderate and radical institutional strategies. It boycotted the vote in parliament and filed a lawsuit in the Constitutional Court, arguing that the first-round presidential election was void because it was made without the two-thirds quorum required by law.[45] Although initially moderate, this tactic – which, ultimately, sought to undermine the prime minister – morphed into a radical institutional strategy. In a clear example of *constitutional hardball*, CHP did not propose an alternative candidate for the presidency, and its leader asked opposition parties to boycott the first round of elections before Erdogan nominated Gül. The opposition knew that, ultimately, failure to elect a president would trigger early parliamentary elections and give them the opportunity to replace the prime minister.

The military doubled down. Immediately after the opposition introduced the lawsuit, the Office of the Chief of the General Staff (commander of the armed

---

[44] Turkish presidents were elected either with two-thirds of the votes in the first or second of two consecutive debates, or if nobody was elected with a simple majority in a third or fourth debate. AKP's simple majority in the legislature was enough to elect a candidate of their choice in three rounds.

[45] The constitution does not stipulate a required quorum for presidential appointments. Traditionally, the quorum required to pass legislation in the Turkish parliament had been 184 MPs, not the 367 MPs the CHP argued.

forces) published a statement on its website that read, "it must not be forgotten that the Turkish Armed Forces do take sides in this debate . . . and are sure and certain defenders of secularism . . . [T]hey will make their position and stance perfectly clear as needs be. Let nobody have any doubt about this."[46] The message was understood domestically and abroad as a coup threat (Taşpınar 2007). Four days after the military issued the statement, the Constitutional Court (AYM) voided Gül's election and established 367 MPs as the legal quorum, making it impossible for the AKP to unilaterally appoint its candidate.[47]

These strategies increased the incentives and reduced the costs to repress. The lawsuit combined with the coup threat created a severe menace to Erdogan's government. In 1997, the armed forces and the judiciary had used a similar strategy to ban the Welfare Party and force the prime minister, Necemettin Erbakan (1996–7), to resign. These tactics were thus seen as unreasonable, hurting the opposition's legitimacy inside and outside Turkey. Erdogan had restated his commitment to secularism and democracy and so had his presidential nominee. In contrast, although CHP claimed they wanted a consensus candidate, it rejected Erdogan's nominee a priori and never proposed an alternative aspirant. It was easy to frame this strategy as an attempt to force a democratically elected prime minister out of power. When Erdogan's Minister of Justice described the Chief of General Staff's statement as inconceivable in a democracy (Migdalovitz 2007), he was backed up by the EU enlargement commissioner, Olli Rehn, who stated that this presidential election was a "test" of the military's democratic commitment (Smith and Temko 2007).

Taking advantage of that discourse, Erdogan rallied the public against the opposition, claiming they were blocking the legitimate election of a president (Turan 2015, 135). Blaming the armed forces for unduly pressuring the Constitutional Court (Migdalovitz 2007), the prime minister called for early general elections in July 2007, and won by a landslide (47 percent vote share). Although the governing party lost some seats,[48] the mandate it gained with that vote share guaranteed Gül's appointment as president in August of the same year.

The 2007 landslide also encouraged Erdogan to push for more aggressive reforms (Jenkins 2009). As a consequence of the dispute over the presidential election, the prime minister introduced to parliament a referendum proposing constitutional amendments to elect the president via popular vote, reduce the presidential term to four years and allow one reelection, and set the parliamentary quorum at 184. Weakened, Sezer's and the CHP's moderate institutional

---

[46] Cited in Migdalovitz (2007, 4).   [47] The AKP only had 353 seats.
[48] Several other parties made the 10 percent vote-share threshold. Therefore, AKP was not able to pick up as many of their seats as it did in 2002.

strategies[49] failed to block the referendum, which took place in October 2007 (Migdalovitz 2007). Tapping into June's electoral victory, Erdogan was able to mobilize 68 percent of all registered voters and win the referendum with a 69 percent vote share. Just like that, the opposition had lost one of the most important vetoes it controlled.

The coup threat weakened the armed forces as well. In 2007 and 2009, government prosecutors launched two far-reaching investigations ("Ergenekon" and "Sledgehammer") against the so-called deep state (clandestine units with links to Turkish security forces). Both cases became mechanisms to prosecute representatives of the secular opposition (Jenkins 2009; Rodrik 2014). The trials dragged out until 2012 and 2013 with waves of detentions, indictments, and arrests that included opposition politicians, journalists, and members of the armed forces. Together, these two investigations led to the arrest of one-tenth of the Turkish Armed Forces (as of 2010),[50] the trial of more than 200 active and retired military officers,[51] and the mass resignation of Turkey's General, Army, Navy, and Air Chiefs of General Staff in 2011.[52] The government was quick to fill in all the vacancies with loyalists.

The investigations were plagued with violations of due process, yet few openly criticized them (Rodrik 2014). The recent history of the Turkish Armed Forces, as well as their behavior during the 2007 crisis, gave the government enough "legitimacy" to move forward. Throughout the 2000s, the formal and informal interference of the military in politics had become unacceptable. Even secularists who opposed Gül's appointment rejected the idea of a military coup (Gürsoy 2012). When "Ergenekon" and "Sledgehammer" started, journalists, politicians, and academics had conflicting opinions about the investigations. Many thought these could enhance Turkey's democracy (Park 2008; Bardakçi 2013). While noting the irregularities, for instance, the European Union qualified them as an opportunity to investigate criminal activities against democracy (Commission of the European Communities 2009, 2010, 2011).

6.3.1.2 AKP's Ban Threat

Despite losing the presidency and jeopardizing the military, after October 2007, the opposition still enjoyed the benefits of a somewhat independent (or even "Kemalist" leaning) establishment (i.e., courts, bureaucracy, police force, etc.). Unfortunately, in 2008, it introduced a lawsuit to ban AKP, a radical

---

[49] The outgoing president vetoed the amendments in May 2007, but parliament approved them again in June. Together with CHP, he also petitioned the Constitutional Court to void the referendum, arguing procedural irregularities. The court, however, ruled against them in July.

[50] Tuysuz, Gul, and Sabrina Tavernise. "Turkey's Top Military Leaders Resign." *The New York Times*, July 29, 2011.

[51] Tuysuz, Gul. "Trial Begins for Nearly 200 Suspected of Plotting to Overthrow Turkish Government." *Washington Post*, December 17, 2010.

[52] "Turkey's Military Chiefs Resign." *BBC News*, July 29, 2011.

institutional strategy that jeopardized these resources by increasing Erdogan's incentives to repress.

On February 2008, AKP tried to lift Turkey's headscarf ban. In a clear attempt to end AKP's reign, the Chief Prosecutor of the Supreme Court of Appeals – with the support of CHP – asked the Constitutional Court to outlaw AKP for undermining the principle of secularism protected by the constitution.[53] The court decided not to close the party, but it cut its financial aid in half.[54]

Although the radical institutional strategy did not significantly hurt the opposition's legitimacy, it increased the incentives to repress. Threatened at his core, Erdogan targeted the judiciary. In 2010, he launched a second referendum to amend the constitution in order pack the courts. The proposition made it harder to outlaw political parties, increased the size of the High Council of Judges and Prosecutors (HSYK)[55] (from seven to twenty-two) and the Constitutional Court (eleven to seventeen), and allowed judicial review for personnel decisions made by the Higher Military Council[56] (Lancaster 2014).

Notwithstanding controversial, the fact that the opposition had tried to use the courts to end Erdogan's term lend legitimacy to the referendum that was seen as beneficial for Turkish democracy. It was approved in September 2010, with a turnout of 73 percent and a vote share of 59 percent and described in the EU 2011 Accession Report as a "step in the right direction" (89). The articles passed as a consequence of the vote also received positive comments from the European Commission for Democracy through Law (Venice Commission) (Özbudun 2015).

6.3.1.3 The Corruption Investigation

By 2011, mostly under the disguise of democracy, the government had chipped away important vetoes on the executive – the presidency and the military – and significantly weakened the judiciary. Despite increasing concern for a steep decline in freedom of expression,[57] Turkey was still considered democratic. In

---

[53] The 1982 Constitution stipulated that the Constitutional Court had the authority to close political parties that threatened the principles of "democratic and secular Republic" (Art. 68).

[54] "Turkey's Court Decides Not to Close AKP, Urges Unity and Compromise." *Hürriyet*, June 30, 2008.

[55] This organization deals with the admission of judges and public prosecutors into the profession, appointments, transfers, temporary powers, and promotions within the judiciary, imposition of disciplinary penalties, as well as removals from office. The president appoints five of its seven members from nominees by the High Court of Appeals and the Council of State (Art. 159, Constitution 1982).

[56] The referendum allowed both president and parliament to elect CC justices, removed the articles that protected the 1980 coup leaders from prosecution, extended collective bargaining rights to state employees, banned positive discrimination against women, and created an ombudsman.

[57] Using an old antiterrorist law that allows the government to punish terrorists, their supporters or anyone who expresses separatists sentiments (Updegraff 2012), the government harassed journalists, politicians, activists, and academics who espoused opinions against the government, in particular, those allied with or supportive of Kurdish autonomy. They jailed several Kurdish

2011 and 2012, Polity IV gave it a whopping nine (out of ten) on its democracy scale, Freedom House rated it as "Partly Free," and V-Dem scored it 0.55 and 0.54 (in a 0–1 scale) in its Electoral Democracy index. A series of nonviolent protests in the spring of 2013 – discussed in more detail later – poked holes in that perception. Strengthened by these demonstrations, in December 2013, police raids revealed that there was an ongoing investigation for corruption involving politicians, businessmen, and bureaucrats close to Erdogan. The investigation was triggered by members of the Gülenist Movement inside the police and the prosecutor's office and was seen by many[58] as the outcome of a rift between this movement and AKP.[59] It echoed smear tactics used by Erdogan's and Gülen's movements in the past to push the military out of politics.[60]

This radical institutional strategy increased the incentives to repress. Threatened by this very personal affront, Erdogan initiated a whole new set of power grabs. To decrease the influence of the Gülenists and thwart the investigation, the government changed the judicial police rules, forcing those in charge of the ongoing investigation to inform the corresponding administrative authorities that they were being investigated. The measure guaranteed that the government would learn about any investigation and replace the police officers involved with loyalists (Özbudun 2015).

When the Supreme Council of Judges and Public Prosecutors (HSYK) protested these changes, AKP introduced a bill to strengthen the role of the minister of justice inside this institution (Law No. 6524). Empowered by his new authority, in the spring of 2014, the latter substituted two anti-government board members with loyalists in order to replace the judges and prosecutors involved in the corruption investigations with pro-government officers, and started a large-scale purge of suspected pro-Gülen justices, prosecutors, and officers (Özbudun 2015). Although the opposition sued the bill and the Constitutional Court annulled nineteen of its thirty-five provisions, the decision did not reverse the changes.

politicians and activists accusing them of belonging to the PKK or its affiliate, the People's Confederation of Kurdistan (KCK). According to Updegraff (2012), by 2012 more than 3,000 Kurdish nationalists, including five MPs, were detained awaiting trial.

[58] Uras, Umut. "Turkish Probe Marks AKP-Gulen Power Struggle." *Al Jazeera*, December 24, 2013.

[59] The Gülenists and Erdogan started off as allies. However, after 2010 the relationship had begun to deteriorate. In 2011, alleged Gülenist police officers wiretapped Erdogan's office and home. The government, in return, cut the Gülenists from their main source of revenue, closing their private preparatory classes in 2012. Then a prosecutor with alleged Gülenist ties revealed that the National Intelligence Organization had been recruiting agents from within the Kurdistan Communities Union (KCK) who had carried out acts of violence against Turkish officials. Erdogan responded in kind, closing the Gülenist "prep-schools" in order to cripple the movement's financial and human resources (Jenkins 2009).

[60] Arango, Tim. "Raids and Graft Inquiry in Turkey Are Seen by Some as Muslim Cleric's Plot." *The New York Times*, December 18, 2013.

In October of that same year, Turkey's judges and juries voted for ten new HSYK seats. Erdogan, elected president of Turkey in August 2014 once his term as prime minister expired, supported a pro-government group called Platform for Unity in the Judiciary. This group won all ten seats, securing the simple majority they needed to control the council.[61] In December 2014, the institution suspended the four public prosecutors behind the December 2013 corruption investigations.

6.3.1.4 *The Military Coup*

The 2007, 2008, and 2014 power grabs significantly weakened Turkey's democracy, but it was not entirely dead. In 2012, Polity had downgraded its score to 3, but Freedom House still qualified the country as "Partly Free," and its V-Dem's Electoral score remained above 0.5 (0.54). Erdogan controlled the presidency, the legislature, and several important organizations inside the judiciary (like the HYSK), but was not yet fully unchecked. For starters, Erdogan had not been able to fully co-opt the Constitutional Court. Endowed with great powers, the latter was able to check the government. Throughout 2014 and 2015, it reversed the 2014 HYSK bill, overturned a government Twitter and YouTube ban, ruled against a bill that expanded the government's authority to block internet content (Freedom House 2015),[62] and decided against violations of due process, such as unduly long detentions (Özbudun 2015).

The opposition had also grown its presence in congress. The Gezi Park nonviolent protests in 2013, the rupture with the Güelenists throughout 2014, and talks about a potential constitutional reform to shift Turkey from a parliamentary to a presidential system had diminished AKP's popularity. Since 2002, the governing party had been steadily losing seats, from 363 in 2002 to 317 in November 2015.

In other words, in 2016, the opposition still had some resources left. The final blow to Turkey's already dying democracy was the 2016 failed military coup. On July 15, the Turkish Air Force and Army tried to overthrow the government, but Erdogan – who like Chávez had a well-mobilized base of support (Laebens 2020; Baykan, Gürsoy, and Ostiguy 2021) – was able to activate enough supporters to stop the coup (Esen and Gumuscu 2017). On July 16, he had regained control over the government.

Although the evidence suggests that most pro-coup forces were Gülenist with little or no support from other opposition factions (Yavuz and Koç

---

[61] The Plenary of the HSYK is composed by the Minister of Justice, the Undersecretary, four members appointed by the president, seven appointed by judiciary institutions, ten directly elected by judges and prosecutors. All the members appointed by the judiciary stood against the government; all other HSYK members supported the government.

[62] The bill defined various and very broad matters in which the government could intervene: matters concerning the protection of life, private property, national security, public order, crime, and public health. It has ruled against the government on matters of due process as well.

2016), Erdogan seized the opportunity to crack down on all opposition members regardless of whether they had supported the putsch or not. The coup was, in his words, a "gift from God" (Esen and Gumuscu 2017, 69). Right after the coup, the government announced a three-month state of emergency that allowed the president to purge over 10,000 members of the armed forces and dismiss, detain, or arrest over 150,000 people, including opposition legislators, soldiers, police officers, and judicial officials.[63] Erdogan also used the state of emergency to close 184 media outlets and approximately 375 NGOs.[64] The Turkish leader was particularly harsh with HDP legislators. Accused of links with either the PKK or the Gülenist movement, between September and November, seventy-three HDP mayors were removed from their posts and twelve HDP deputies were arrested. By the end of the year, 2,700 local HDP politicians had been jailed (Freedom House 2017b).

The coup also allowed Erodgan to rally around the flag in favor of a referendum to significantly enhance his powers and increase his time in office. Presidents in Turkey were endowed with immense powers (e.g., the appointment of Chief of General Staff, Chief of Public Prosecutors, several members of the Supreme Council of Judges and Public Prosecutors, and all members of the Constitutional Court) but had to resign their party membership. Changing Turkey from a parliamentary to a presidential system allowed Erdogan to keep this office's vast powers and his party leadership.

The referendum entered to parliament in October 2016. The reforms it proposed made the president head of government and state, endowed him with authority to issue, largely unregulated, decrees with force of law[65] and declare timeless states of emergency in the event of internal or external war, and empowered him to finish co-opting the judiciary.[66] The amendments reduced the Supreme Council of Judges and Public Prosecutors and the Constitutional Court to thirteen and fifteen members, respectively, all of them appointed by the government[67] with very few requirements.[68]

---

[63] Including three members of the Supreme Electoral Council.

[64] Allen, Kate. "Turkey's Huge Crackdown Is Destroying Civil Society." *The Guardian*, January 30, 2018.

[65] While Article 104 of the Constitution stated that presidential decrees could not alter fundamental or individual rights or duties, all other areas of law are fair game (Venice Commission 2017).

[66] European Commission for Democracy through Law (Venice Commission). Opinion No. 875/2017. *Unofficial Translation of the Amendments of the Constitution*. Strasbourg, February 6, 2017.

[67] Four of the HYSK members would be appointed by the president, seven would be appointed by the AKP-controlled congress, and two would be appointed by Erdogan's handpicked Minister of Justice and his undersecretary. Twelve of the CC justices would be appointed by the president (from nominees selected by various courts); the other three would be appointed by the AKP-controlled congress.

[68] Whereas in the past the president had to appoint the Chairperson to the State Supervisory Council, the Commander in Chief, and the Chief of the General Staff from groups chosen by other institutions or meeting certain qualifications, after the amendment he no longer had those

The reforms proposed also curtailed congress's powers and extended the executive's time in office. They curbed the legislature's ability to investigate and impeach the president (Makovsky 2017) and allowed the president to rule for two periods of five years. Erdogan's first term under these amendments would not start until the general elections of 2019.

Erdogan had floated the idea of changing the system of government from a parliamentary to a presidential system, as early as 2015. At the time, it had lukewarm support.[69] The putsch changed that. AKP managed to enlist the support of the MHP[70] to get the required three-fifths of the votes to pass the referendum bill on January 21, 2017 (barely twenty-two days after it was introduced). The vote was scheduled for April 16, 2017. The campaign was neither free nor fair (Coban 2017; Hintz and Dunham 2017). Amid criticism over the elections and accusations of fraud, the government won the referendum with 51 percent of the votes.

The coup was the final blow to Turkey's moribund democracy. By 2015, Erdogan's regime still had a tattered but intact democratic façade. Despite mounting criticism against Erdogan, the coup was still seen as unwarranted domestically and abroad. Like what happened in Venezuela, it gave the head of state the information and the excuse he needed to purge opponents and dissenters, as well as the popularity boost he required to pass a constitutional amendment that transformed Turkey's parliamentary system into a hyperpresidential one with very few checks on the executive. Since then, Turkey has become a competitive authoritarian regime. Although there are elections and the opposition is allowed to compete, they do so on very uneven footing.

6.3.2 Moderate Institutional and Extrainstitutional Strategies

As shown earlier, radical institutional and extrainstitutional strategies helped Erdogan erode democracy. They increased the incentives and decreased the costs to repress. In the following paragraphs, I discuss two instances in which the Turkish opposition resorted to moderate institutional and extrainstitutional strategies: the Gezi Park protests in 2013 and the 2015 elections. In line with the theory outlined in Chapter 2, these tactics failed to increase the incentives or decrease the costs to repress. Alongside the strategies discussed earlier, these tactics were insufficient to stop the erosion of democracy, but helped poke holes in Erdogan's democratic façade and protected the resources the opposition had.

---

limitations (Makovsky 2017). European Commission for Democracy through Law (Venice Commission). Opinion No. 875/2017.

[69] Beauchamp, Zack. "A Guide to This Week's Shocking Election in Turkey – and What Happens Next." *Vox*, June 9, 2015.

[70] Support for the referendum split the MHP in two. The faction led by the party's leader, Devlet Bahçeli, supported Erdogan. The splinter faction, Good Party (*Her Iyi Parti*), led by Meral Aksener, opposed the referendum (Hintz and Dunham 2017).

6.3.2.1 The Gezi Park Protests

As mentioned earlier, despite his power grabs against the presidency, the military, and the courts, by 2011, Erdogan had been able to keep up democratic appearances. Notwithstanding concern for declines in freedom of expression, Turkey was still considered democratic and on track to become a member of the European Union. Using moderate extrainstitutional strategies, the opposition damaged that image.

In 2013, a small group of environmentalists gathered at Gezi Park to peacefully protest plans to replace the park with a shopping mall. The government refused to negotiate and dispersed the protesters violently instead. The abusive and unmeasured response sparked three months of mostly peaceful, nationwide demonstrations. The police responded with violence to those as well. In three months, 8,000 people were injured, five people died, and approximately 5,653 people were detained in relation to the protests.[71]

Although they were not thought as such, the Gezi Park protests were useful to make visible the increasing discontent with Erdogan's authoritarian practices[72] and gnaw away at his democratic façade. The protesters used the streets to peacefully advocate for moderate goals. They were not related, organized, or driven by the already tainted armed forces nor were they trying to remove Erdogan and the AKP from office; they were just trying to protect a park.

The unmeasured reaction of the government had severe consequences for its legitimacy domestically and abroad. Inside the country, this moderate extrainstitutional strategy ended the alliance between independent, non-partisan, liberal democrats and religious conservatives that had helped pass the 2010 referendum (Özbudun 2014) and revealed differences between the prime minister and the president, when Gül called for moderation stressing that "democracy is not just about elections" (Simsek 2013). The rupture of this alliance could help explain, to a certain extent, AKP's electoral losses in June 2015.

Internationally, the way the government handled the protests invited criticism from a formerly very cautious, silent, and even praising international community. The United Nations Secretary-General called on the authorities to end the violence, Amnesty International and Human Rights Watch published very negative reports,[73] the United States called for an investigation for excessive use of force,[74] and the European Parliament drafted a resolution

---

[71] Sinclair-Webb, Emma. "Dispatches: One Year after Turkey's Gezi Protests, Activists on Trial." *Human Rights Watch*, June 11, 2014; "Gezi Park: Brutal Denial of the Right to Peaceful Assembly in Turkey." *Amnesty International*, October 2, 2013.

[72] *Amnesty International*. October 2, 2013.

[73] Sinclair-Webb, Emma. "Dispatches: One Year after Turkey's Gezi Protests, Activists on Trial." *Human Rights Watch*, June 11, 2014; Gezi Park. "Brutal Denial of the Right to Peaceful Assembly in Turkey." *Amnesty International*, October 2, 2013.

[74] McCarthy, Tom and Matthew Weaver. "US on Turkey Protests: 'Vast Majority of the Protesters Have Been Peaceful' – As It Happened." *The Guardian*, June 3, 2013.

condemning the abuses and urging the Turkish authorities to respect human rights.[75] It was the first time the international community strongly condemned the Turkish leader.

6.3.2.2 Electioneering in 2015

The second moderate tactic used by the opposition was electioneering. Unlike what happened in Venezuela (until 2006), the opposition kept fighting the government at the voting booth. By 2011, it had chipped away nearly 10 percent of the parliamentary seats AKP had won in 2002. When the 2015 June parliamentary elections came around, AKP's support had significantly declined. The Gezi Park protests in 2013, the rift with the Güelenists throughout 2014, and talks about a potential constitutional reform to shift from a parliamentary to a presidential system had diminished the governing party's popularity. Riding the wave, and giving salience to a new cleavage the CHP, MHP, and HDP, together, won 292 seats (out of 550) (Selçuk and Hekimci 2020).

The 2015 June victory was an important triumph for the opposition. The governing party still had the largest seat share (AKP's 47 percent versus CHP's 24 percent, MHP's 15 percent, and HDP's 15 percent) but did not get enough votes to form a government majority to pass the constitutional amendment Erdogan wanted to enact. The opposition, in the meantime, increased its seat share by 12 percent (vis-à-vis 2007), enough to build a coalition government.

Unfortunately, the victory did not last long. The opposition parties had gained their seats leveraging constituencies with very different programmatic interests, which hindered their ability to form a coalition government. While HDP's core constituency was conservative Kurds disenchanted with the government-PKK peace process, MHP's core constituency was Turkish nationalists who opposed PKK's requests for autonomy. With Erdogan pulling strings to delay coalition talks in hopes of forcing a new election, the HDP and the MHP became essential to form a government. Although the CHP had the potential to sit in between the MHP and the DHP, neither of these two parties was willing to meet each other halfway (Öniş 2016). Devlet Bahçeli (HDP) refused to move toward the center in regard to the Kurdish question, and the HDP was unable to disassociate itself from an increasingly violent PKK. After forty-five days, the official deadline to form a government, President Erdogan called for general elections. His party won 317 seats, recovering the simple majority it had lost.

The June 2015 election was a lost opportunity, but an opportunity nonetheless. Using this moderate institutional strategy, the opposition decreased the incentives and increased the costs to repress. Unlike what happened with the coup threat in 2007, the attempt to ban AKP in 2008, the corruption investigations in 2013 and the 2016 coup, this tactic lowered the stakes for Erdogan, and limited his ability to remove opposition leaders from office, prosecute or

---

[75] European Parliament Resolution No. EU P7_TA (2013) 0277, September 12, 2013.

jail them. Had the opposition taken advantage of these seats in parliament, it might have been able to delay or even stop the government's power grabs.

6.3.3 Summary

Like Venezuela and Bolivia, the erosion of democracy in Turkey did not happen in one day. It took Erdogan fourteen years to erode horizontal and electoral accountability. When the AKP came to power, the opposition had several institutional resources at its disposal: allies in the presidency and the armed forces, and influence over the judiciary and the state bureaucracy. Using radical institutional and extrainstitutional strategies, however, it lost them all. The attempt to ban AKP via the Constitutional Court in 2008, the corruption investigation in 2013, the coup threat in 2007, and the failed coup in 2016 increased the incentives to repress and, in some cases, gave Erdogan the legitimacy he needed to co-opt courts and oversight agencies, purge the armed forces, and remove from office, prosecute, or jail opponents while keeping a democratic façade.

Had the opposition avoided radical extrainstitutional strategies – especially at the beginning of the process of erosion – it would have likely protected its institutional resources. Allies in the presidency, the armed forces, the judiciary, and the state bureaucracy would have helped delay, or perhaps even stop, some of Erdogan's more aggressive antidemocratic reforms. The opposition could have also been able to gain, and even leverage, international support earlier in the process. Up until 2007, Erdogan was able to protect its democratic façade. His power grabs were mostly seen as reforms to eliminate the military's undue influence over civilian governments (Turan 2015, 216). It would have been easier for the opposition to oppose Erdogan alongside influential actors like the European Union, if their actions had not reinforced the idea that Turkey's secularists were keen on keeping authoritarian legacies in Turkey.

In 2016, Turkey began a process of deepening authoritarianism. The 2017 referendum was neither free nor fair. Things have only gotten worse since then. In 2018, Erdogan moved up the 2019 general elections in order to capitalize on the successes of the war against the Kurds in Syria and preempt a potential economic downturn (Eissenstat 2018). Not only did he win the presidency with a 52 percent vote share, but AKP and MHP (now allies) won 344 out of the 600 parliamentary seats. Moreover, the 2018 elections were plagued with irregularities. The government kept in place the 2016 state of emergency, enjoyed a sizable advantage in resources and media coverage, and – for the first time since Erdogan came to power – engaged in extensive electoral fraud (Aydogan 2018). Notwithstanding these irregularities, Erdogan was sworn into office in July of that same year. He will likely stay in office until at least 2023.

6.4 POLAND

Since 1991, Poland has enjoyed a high-level democracy. Between 1991 and 2014, it was one of the top twenty-five democracies in the world, with a 0.88 average V-Dem Electoral Democracy score. Since then, democracy in the country has declined. Its electoral democracy score has dropped 0.26 points, reaching its lowest level (0.63) since 1990 in 2020.

The steep decline in Polish democracy can be attributed in large part to the rise to power of the Law and Justice Party (PiS), an anti-system conservative organization led by Jarosław Kaczyński. Since 2015, when it won the presidency and a plurality of the seats in the House (*Sejm*) and Senate, PiS has introduced a series of institutional reforms aimed to curtail the power of or co-opt courts and oversight agencies, and undermine freedom of expression.

Despite its resolve to dismantle the checks on the executive and significant popular support, so far, PiS has been unable to erode democracy. Unlike what happened in Venezuela, Bolivia, or Turkey, those who oppose PiS have avoided radical extrainstitutional strategies and used moderate institutional and extrainstitutional strategies instead. Although Poland's democracy is still in danger of becoming competitive authoritarian, so far these tactics have paid off. When Kaczyński's party came to power, the Polish opposition had two-fifths of the seats in the Sejm and a third of the seats in the Senate, support inside courts and oversight agencies, and the ability to mobilize millions of Poles to the streets. Employing litigation and nonviolent demonstrations, the opposition has been able to protect and even expand some of these resources. It has delayed PiS agenda, tamed some of the party's most radical proposals, and leveraged institutions inside the European Union to reverse some of the government's undemocratic reforms. Although PiS was able to co-opt the Constitutional Court in 2016 and the National Council of the Judiciary (KRS) in 2017, its attempts to significantly curtail freedom of expression (2016–17) and pack the Supreme Court (SN) have fallen short.

While it is unclear whether Poland will successfully avoid an erosion of democracy or not, using nonviolent demonstrations in conjunction with domestic and international litigation, the opposition has bought precious time. Elections in Poland are still free and fair. The opposition tactics have protected and enhanced its legitimacy inside and outside the country. They have given opposition leaders a chance to compete in the 2019 parliamentary elections and regain their majority in the Senate that, despite being weaker than the Sejm, can be used to further delay the co-optation of other state institutions.[76]

---

[76] "5 Takeaways from the Polish Election." *POLITICO*, October 14, 2019. www.politico.eu/article/poland-pis-tougher-times-despite-winning-election/.

6.4.1 Moderate Institutional and Extrainstitutional Strategies in Defense of the Judiciary

PiS came to power in 2015, after defeating the center-right party Civil Platform (PO) that had governed the country since 2007. Notwithstanding strong institutions and positive economic achievements,[77] the population had become disenchanted with the ruling elites. Government exhaustion, brand dilution, infighting and allegations of corruption, and cronyism against PO had weakened the government coalition (Szczerbiak 2017). Despite relatively high[78] scores in the mean state performance (6.17 on a 0–10 scale), Poland's confidence in institutions in 2014 was 3.91 on a 0–10 scale; lower than Turkey's (5.72) and close to Venezuela's (3.18), which had a mean state performance of 4.72 and 3.49 between 1996–2002 and 1996–8, respectively.

PiS was quick to capitalize on that discontent. Toning down its antiestablishment rhetoric and giving visibility to figures less polarizing than Jarosław Kaczyński, it was able to attract centrist support. In May 2014, PO pulled ahead of PiS in the European Parliament election by a very slim margin (32.1 percent compared to 31.8 percent);[79] in May 2015, its candidate lost the presidential elections to the PiS candidate, Andrzej Duda, who received 51 percent of the votes; and two months later, the incumbent party lost its majority in the Sejm with a vote share of 24 percent (vis-à-vis PiS's vote share of 37.6 percent). By November 2015, PiS controlled the Sejm (51 percent of the seats), the Senate (61 percent of the seats), and the presidency.

The survival of democracy is far from guaranteed in Poland. Kaczyński is a potential autocrat, and PiS is a radical conservative party with authoritarian undertones (Norris and Inglehart 2019a, 236). Under his leadership, the ruling coalition has been willing to undermine democratic institutions in order to advance its policy agenda (Slomczynski and Shabad 2012; Przybylski 2018). Since it came to power in November 2015, PiS has introduced institutional reforms that seek to co-opt the Constitutional Tribunal (TK)(2015–16), the KRS (2017–18), the SN (2017–18), the Ordinary Courts (2017), and the National Electoral Commission (2017) (Tworzecki 2019). It has also introduced laws that undermine freedom of expression. Between 2015 and 2018, the party has approved reforms that allowed the government to bypass the national media oversight council and name partisan national media oversight officers, introduce rules that limit journalists' access to the parliament building, and used the government-controlled media authorities to harass independent media outlets (Applebaum 2017; Chapman 2017). Latching on the COVID-19 pandemic, they have furthered some of these provisions.

---

[77] Despite some deceleration, Poland's economic growth was 3.9 percent in 2015. The country's Gini Coefficient was 0.31, and the unemployment was 7.5 percent (ILO estimate).

[78] Poland scored in the top 77th percentile for mean state performance between 1996 and 2015.

[79] In 2009, PO had a vote share of 44 percent – seventeen points higher than PiS's (27.40 percent).

Notwithstanding being weak, the opposition has not been helpless when facing these attacks. Between PO, Modern, and the Polish Peasant Party (PSL), it started off with 40 percent of the seats in the Sejm and 35 percent of the seats in the Senate, enough to block constitutional amendments; access to independent courts and oversight agencies; and important mobilization resources. Poland has a vibrant civil society. Notwithstanding being independent from PO, Modern, and the PSL, for the past three years, several NGOs have campaigned and mobilized thousands of Poles in support for democracy (Cienski and Harper 2016; Grzymala-Busse 2016).

Like the anti-Uribista coalition in Colombia, the Polish opposition has taken good care of these resources. They have used institutional and extrainstitutional strategies with the explicit intent of curbing antidemocratic reforms, rather than removing PiS from office outside of elections. These strategies have paid off. Between 2016 and 2018, the government was able to co-opt the TK (2015–16) and the KRS (2017), but unable to pack the SN or suppress private media accountability (2018). Not only did domestic litigation and street protests protect the opposition's democratic credentials, but they delayed PiS's power grabs enough to allow the opposition to raise awareness among Western allies, leverage institutions inside the European Union, and tame PiS attempts to co-opt Poland's highest court and sideline independent media outlets.

6.4.1.1 *The Constitutional Tribunal*

Immediately after attaining power, PiS moved to curb the authority of and co-opt the Constitutional Tribunal. The judicial branch in Poland has three main bodies: the Supreme Court (SN), the Constitutional Tribunal (TK), and the National Council of the Judiciary (KRS). The second one is in charge of assessing the constitutionality of legislation and legal norms applied by lower courts. PiS introduced a series of reforms in order to co-opt it.

Before Civic Platform left office in October 2015, it elected five candidates to replace some of its retiring members in an attempt to block PiS from nominating the new justices. President Duda (sworn in, in August) refused to swear in any of the justices. Instead, as soon as it took office in November, PiS approved the Act of Constitutional Tribunal, a reform that shortened and terminated the tenures of the court's president and vice president (by March 2016) and nullified the election of the new justices (Szuleka, Wolny, and Szwed 2016). Covered by this amendment, the PiS government appointed and swore in new five justices on December 2, 2015.

The opposition reaction to this power grab was two-pronged. On the one hand, it used moderate institutional strategies. Opposition MPs, the Commissioner for Human Rights, the other branches of the judiciary, and the head of the SN submitted motions to the TK asking it to revise PiS's amendments based on procedural irregularities. On December 3 and 9, the TK ruled against the provisions that limited and cut short the tenures of the court's president and vice president and Duda's refusal to swear in the justices appointed in October and declared three of the five justices appointed in December illegitimate (Szuleka, Wolny, and Szwed 2016). Although the president refused to replace the judges he had sworn in, the court's chief justice, Andrezj Rzepliński, sidelined them from any deliberation.

Blocked by the high court, on December 15, PiS introduced a second amendment requiring the TK to rule with a quorum of thirteen judges (full bench) and a two-thirds qualified majority (Szuleka, Wolny, and Szwed 2016).[80] The changes were meant to force Rzepliński to include the three "illegitimate justices" in the deliberations and give more weight to their votes. Opposition MPs, the SN, the Commissioner for Human Rights, and the KRS introduced motions to review the constitutionality of this bill as well. They were supported by civil society organizations like the Polish Bar Council, National Council of Attorneys, the Helsinki Foundation for Human Rights, and the Stefan Batory Foundation. Once again, the court ruled in their favor (Szuleka, Wolny, and Szwed 2016).

On the other hand, the opposition used moderate extrainstitutional strategies. In support of the TK, civil society groups organized peaceful demonstrations against the power grab. A group of citizens, for example, created the Committee for the Defense of Democracy (KOD). With the explicit intent, not to "overturn the legally elected authorities of the country" but rather defend democracy (Cienski and Harper 2016), the committee mobilized thousands of Poles to the streets. On December 12, 50,000 people gathered to protest PiS attempts to pack the TK. Other demonstrations followed on December 19 and 28 (Karolewski 2016).

In line with the theory outlined in this book, these strategies decreased the incentives and increased the costs to repress. Not only did they delay PiS agenda, but also they gave salience to the power grab. On January 13, the European Commission announced a formal investigation into violations of the rule of law in Poland,[81] specifically PiS's attacks to the TK and a media law that allowed the government to fire all executives of public media broadcasters and replace them with loyalists (Foy 2015). The announcement marked the first step to trigger the European Union Rule of Law Framework,[82] which could potentially end with Poland losing its voting rights inside the European Union.

Although the opposition strategies did not stop PiS from co-opting the TK, they helped delay the process one year. In the spotlight, the Polish government was belligerent, but cautious not to cross the bright lines of democracy. It refused to recognize, abide by, or even publish the court's rulings but did not

---

[80] Later versions of the bill introduced three- and six-month deadlines for organizing a hearing and did not foresee any time between the promulgation of a law and the time it took effect.
[81] European Commission Press Release. "Rule of Law in Poland: Commission Starts Dialogue." January 13, 2016.
[82] European Commission Press Release. "European Commission Presents a Framework to Safeguard the Rule of Law in the European Union." March 11, 2014.

do anything to enforce its amendments either. Instead, it kept trying to reform the TK from parliament.[83] It was not until December 2016, when Rzepliński's term expired, that PiS was finally able to replace the court's president, move aside its vice president, and seat the three "illegitimate judges" chosen in December 2015.

6.4.1.2 *The Supreme Court*

Controlling the TK was the first step in a larger takeover. In 2017, the government targeted the Supreme Court (SN) and the National Council of the Judiciary (KRS). The former is the highest court in Poland; it functions as the highest appellate court. It is in charge of determining the validity of nationwide referenda and parliamentary elections, and serves as gatekeeper in the disbursement of state funding for political campaigns (Nalepa 2017a). The latter is an independent body, in charge of appointments and disciplinary actions against members of the judiciary (Nalepa, Vanberg, and Chiopris 2018).

To co-opt them, in January, PiS introduced three bills: the *Draft Act on Ordinary Courts* to enhance the powers of the minister of justice and general prosecutor[84] to appoint or dismiss presidents and deputy presidents of lower courts, as well as to promote or discipline lower court judges; the *Draft Act on the National Council of the Judiciary* to terminate the mandates of the sitting KRS justices and allow the PiS-controlled parliament to elect twenty-one out of twenty-five of its replacements; and the *Draft Act on the Supreme Court* to give the minister of justice and general prosecutor control over the status, retirement, and disciplinary proceedings of the SN justices. This last amendment also introduced the compulsory retirement of sitting justices (except those excused by President Duda), regrouped the four existing chambers of the high court into two chambers, and created a disciplinary chamber in charge of all disciplinary matters pertaining members of the judiciary.[85] Together, these bills would have not only ended the independence of the judiciary but also increased the government's control over electoral processes (Kisilowski 2017; Nalepa 2017a).

The reforms ignited a strong opposition. Once again, the strategy was two-pronged. Initially, the opposition used moderate institutional strategies. In

---

[83] In April 2016, PiS MPs introduced another set of amendments. The latter forced the TK's president to assign cases to the "illegitimate justices," gave the president control over justices' term limits, granted the president and the Prosecutor General (both PiS loyalists) competence to decide when the TK should consider a case as a full bench, and force the court to consider cases in the sequence in which they were filed unless the Polish president motioned otherwise (Szuleka, Wolny, and Szwed 2016).

[84] Before PiS came to power, these were two separate offices. In a move similar to Uribe's merge of the Ministry of Interior and Ministry of Justice (2002), in 2015, PiS merged these two offices.

[85] See OSCE-ODIHR Opinion No. JUD/POL/313/2017.

parliament, opposition MPs tried to slow down the bills' transit in congress (Lyman 2017).[86] Outside of parliament, in February 2017, the KRS asked the European Office for Democratic Institutions and Human Rights (OSCE-ODIHR) to review the Draft Act on the National Council of the Judiciary (KRS). The request leaned on the Rule of Law Framework procedure the European Union had opened a year earlier. In May, the OSCE-ODIHR found that the amendments raised serious concerns regarding the separation of powers and the independence of the judiciary,[87] and in July, the European Commission wrote to the Polish government expressing concerns about the legislative proposals.[88] The OSCE-ODIHR request was followed by an open letter by the SN president, Małgorzata Gersdorf, asking their fellow judges to "fight for every inch of justice"[89] and a broadcast of the TK's justices[90] dissenting opinions regarding the court's decision on the constitutionality of the existing KRS statute (Sadurski 2018).

Notwithstanding being useful to give visibility to the issue and inform the Rule of Law Infringement Proceedings, these efforts did not stop the bills. In July 15, the Senate approved the draft laws on the KRS and the Ordinary Courts. Seven days later, it approved the draft law on the SN. At this point, the opposition resorted to extrainstitutional strategies with moderate goals. For nine days, thousands of Poles rallied all over the country demanding that President Duda veto the reforms (Koper and Kelly 2017). The largest of these protests (Warsaw) had 50,000 people. Demonstrators had a clear message: They were not there to replace the government, but rather to support the constitution and the judiciary (Bilewicz 2017).

The pressure worked. Unable to delegitimize the opposition inside or outside the country and concerned about PiS's democratic façade, on July 24 and 25, the president signed into law the Ordinary Courts bill but vetoed the other two. This was a marginal yet important victory for the Polish opposition because their strategies tamed the reforms. In September 2017, Duda reintroduced the SN and the KRS's bills with amendments. Notwithstanding being minimal, the changes proposed gave the opposition some space to influence the election of the new council members or, at the very least, delay it.[91] The new bills also softened the provisions regarding the SN. Rather than summarily retiring all its justices, the new bill lowered the retirement age to sixty-five years, effectively

---

[86] What strategies they used, or to what extent were these successful requires a full analysis using archival research in Poland's parliament.

[87] See OSCE-ODIHR. Opinion No. JUD-POL/305/2017-Final[AIC/YM]. Warsaw, May 5, 2017.

[88] See Commission Recommendation No. (EU) 1520/2017. July 26, 2017.

[89] Cited in Davies, Christian. "Polish Judges Urged to 'fight Every Inch' for Their Independence." *The Guardian*, February 26, 2017.

[90] Those appointed before November 2015.

[91] The original bill stipulated that the new KRS members would be elected by simple majority in the Sejm; the new bill stipulated they would be elected by three-fifths or, if that failed, a simple majority in a second round (see Venice Commission, Opinion No. 904/2017).

terminating thirty-four out of eighty-seven of them (Nalepa 2017b), allowing parliament to choose their successors.[92]

Perhaps more importantly, the opposition tactics delayed the power grab. Even though the president's amendments did little to reduce the politization of the judiciary (Pacula 2017), by pushing Duda to veto the original bills, the anti-PiS coalition was able to stall the process significantly. It took two months before the president introduced the new reforms, and then another three before parliament approved them. Had the bills been signed into law in July, the changes would have likely entered into force in September (when the Law of Ordinary Courts took effect).[93] Instead, the new Act of the Supreme Court and the KRS were not ratified until December 2017 and did not take effect until February 2018.

The extra time allowed the European Union's Rule of Law Infringement process to run its course. Because of its severity,[94] there is a lengthy process before the European Union can trigger Article 7 of the Lisbon Treaty.[95] The process can take years, allowing executives with hegemonic aspirations to buy time. Unfortunately, like any other international organization, the European Union is walking a thin line. If it rushes its actions, it gives credence to criticisms for meddling in a country's internal affairs. If it moves too slowly, it allows potential autocrats to push forward reforms past a point of no return. The delays in Poland eased this dilemma. They allowed the European Commission to trigger all the steps required, including mandated deadlines and dialogue with Polish authorities, in order to begin to activate Article 7 in December 2017,[96] before the government implemented changes to the KRS and the SN. In other words, although the European Union's process to prevent democratic

---

[92] The new bill also changed the provisions regarding the structure of the Supreme Court. These changes, however, were mostly cosmetic. The September reform gave up on the idea of converting four chambers into two. Instead, it kept the disciplinary chamber proposed initially and added an extraordinary appeals chamber with active participation of "lay members" (nonlawyers) appointed by the legislature. Together, these chambers were designed to take on disciplinary cases of judges in other chambers, deal with cases with particularly lengthy procedures, review any judgment issued by other chambers, and examine "politically sensitive cases" such as electoral disputes, elections, or referendums (see Venice Commission, Opinion No. 904/2017. December 11, 2017).

[93] European Commission. 2017. Commission Recommendation of 20.12.2017 Regarding the rule of law in Poland. C(2017) 9050. Brussels, December 20, 2017.

[94] Article 7 allows members to sanction countries for violating any of the EU pillar values (listed in Article 2 of the TEU). They could even suspend the country's voting rights.

[95] It has three stages, Commission Assessment, Commission Recommendation, and Commission Follow-Up, that include intensive dialogue between the country under investigation and the European Commission (see "European Commission presents a framework to safeguard rule of law in the European Union." Press Release European Commission, Strasbourg, March 11, 2014).

[96] Another lengthy process that includes preventive measures and sanction mechanisms.

erosion in Poland was lengthy and cumbersome, by delaying the amendments the opposition was able to buy some time.

Although PiS still pushed the amendments through, it did so at a high reputational cost. Throughout 2018, Poland was in the spotlight. In December, when Duda approved the new reforms, the European Commission issued a new recommendation[97] and activated Article 7.[98] In July, when Duda tried to forcibly retire several SN justices in compliance with the disputed law, the European Union opened a second process for Infringement to the Rule of Law[99] and referred Poland to the European Court of Justice (September 2018).[100] With the support of the international community, the opposition took to the streets. International media outlets published pieces depicting Justice Małgorzata Gersdorf defying the government's mandatory retirement with the support of thousands of protesters.

Together, these developments highlighted the plight for democracy in Poland just in time for the October 2018 local elections, delivering a bittersweet victory to the governing party (Szczerbiak 2018). PiS had a vote share of 34 percent: a 7 percent increase compared to 2014, but a 3 percent decrease compared to 2015. The party also won a plurality of the seats in nine out of sixteen assemblies. Individually, no opposition could match it. The closest was Civic Platform, which had a vote share of 27 percent and won a simple majority of the seats only in seven assemblies. Together, however, PO, the Polish People's Party, and the Democratic Left Alliance received a healthy 45 percent vote share and held the majority of the seats in nine out of the sixteen regional assemblies. They also won the mayorships of all major cities.

The elections were perceived more or less as a defeat for PiS, which was polling at 40 percent (Berendt and Santora 2018). A month later, in compliance with an order issued by the European Court of Justice in October,[101] the government had to reinstate and stop all procedures to replace the SN justices it had forcibly retired. On December 17, the president formalized the reinstatements.

---

[97] See European Commission Recommendation No. 9050/2017. December 20, 2017.

[98] "Rule of Law: European Commission Acts to Defend Judicial Independence in Poland." Press Release European Commission, Strasbourg, December 20, 2017.

[99] In July 2017 and 2018, the European Commission opened a second process against Poland for Infringement to the Rule of Law in relation to the Act of Ordinary Courts and the changes to the Supreme Court ("European Commission launches infringement against Poland over measures affecting the judiciary." European Commission Press Release, Brussels, July 29, 2017, and "Rule of Law: European Commission launches infringement procedure to protect the independence of the Polish Supreme Court." European Commission Press Release, Brussels, July 2018).

[100] "Rule of Law: European Commission refers Poland to the European Court of Justice to protect the independence of the Polish Supreme Court." European Commission Press Release, Brussels, September 24, 2018.

[101] See CJEU Press Release No. 159/2018.

In other words, when the government tried to overhaul the judiciary in 2017, the opposition fought back using moderate institutional and extrainstitutional strategies. Although the latter were insufficient to stop most of the government's amendments, they delayed and tamed the process. The delays, in turn, allowed the European Union to advance legal procedures to protect the rule of law in Poland, gave salience to the issue during an important electoral process, and aided in the protection of the SN.

6.4.2 Moderate Institutional and Extrainstitutional Strategies in Defense of Civil Liberties

The judiciary has not been PiS's only target. Since it came to power, it has also introduced laws and used government-controlled agencies to undermine civil liberties. It has submitted reforms to co-opt media oversight agencies (2015–16), limit journalists' access to parliament (2016), and imposed unwarranted fines on the largest opposition media outlet (2018). The government has also introduced legislation to limit citizen's ability to gather in public spaces (2017) and punish with jail time anybody who states that Poland was complicit in the Holocaust (2018). Against these aggressive attempts to undermine freedom of expression, the opposition has successfully deployed moderate institutional and extrainstitutional strategies.

6.4.2.1 *PiS Attacks on the Media*

In December 2015, shortly after PiS came to power, it introduced transitional provisions that allowed the government to temporarily replace public TV and radio broadcast boards and managers, for up to six months. The "Small Media Law," as this provision was called, was meant to serve as a placeholder while the governing coalition drafted a larger bill that would overhaul media oversight agencies and guidelines in Poland (Chapman 2017). Behind the shadow of the TK crisis, the government quickly signed the bill (January 2016).[102]

In tandem with the tactics used to stop the attacks against the high court, the opposition used moderate institutional and extrainstitutional tactics to oppose this power grab. The European Union's formal rule of law investigation, announced in January 2016, was meant to look into the government's attempts to undermine the independence of the judiciary as well as the freedom of the press.[103] The Committee for the Defense of Democracy's protests in support for democracy organized in December 2015 and January 2016 called on the government to stop its attacks against courts and media oversight agencies (Chapman 2017).

---

[102] "Polish Government to Control State Media." *BBC*, January 7, 2016.
[103] European Commission Press Release. "Rule of Law in Poland: Commission Starts Dialogue." January 13, 2016.

The result of these strategies was mixed. Facing criticism inside and outside the country, the government did not follow through with the more permanent media legislation. The latter contained vague provisions that mandated public media outlets to spread the views of the ruling coalition and encouraged them to broadcast content that, among other things, preserved "national traditions, patriotic, and human values," contributed to "fulfilling the spiritual needs of listeners and viewers," and respected "the Christian value system" (Chapman 2017). PiS did, however, set up a government-controlled[104] National Media Council that sidelined the National Broadcasting Council (*Krajowa Rada Raiofonii i Telewizji*), the body traditionally in charge of overseeing public media outlets. In this sense, while the opposition's strategic choices did tame the government's antidemocratic reform, they did not tame it enough. Throughout 2016, more than 200 journalists in public media outlets either resigned or were laid off. The lack of independent journalists combined with the self-censorship of journalists who remained turned these outlets into government mouthpieces (Chapman 2017).

The opposition was more successful at stopping later attempts to hinder freedom of the press. In December 2016, PiS announced that it would restrict journalists' access to parliament's building. A particular mix of institutional and extrainstitutional strategies with moderate goals ensued. Journalists gathered outside the Sejm in protest, and media outlets included a chyron reminding viewers that they would not be able to see congressional clips starting on January 2017. Leveraging their position inside the Sejm, opposition MPs doubled down by showing up to the budget vote with notes that read "Free media in the Sejm" (Nalepa 2016)[105] and organizing a sit-in that blocked the main parliamentary chamber for almost a month. Opposition leaders also organized demonstrations in front of parliament to support the MPs. Together, these strategies forced PiS to backtrack the regulations that restricted media access to the Sejm (Berendt 2017).

International pressure, brought about, in part, thanks to the opposition's legitimacy and its ability to enlist international support, has further protected freedom of the press in Poland. In July 2017, the PiS-controlled tax authorities charged back taxes to TVN, the largest private channel in the country. Later that year, in December, the government fined the same outlet for its coverage of the 2016 parliament protests.[106] The fines came amid rising pressure from the European Union regarding the reforms to the judiciary. The government had just appointed a new prime minister (Mateusz Morawiecki) in an attempt to soften its image abroad (Santora 2018). The United States doubled down. TVN

---

[104] Three of its five members were close to PiS.
[105] Similar signs were used by opposition congress members in Colombia throughout the debates on the reelection referendum.
[106] "Poland slaps $415,000 fine on TVN24 over coverage of protests in parliament." *Reuters*, Warsaw, December 11, 2017.

is owned by an American company. When Poland's government fined it, the State Department issued a strong statement criticizing the decision.[107] The pressure worked. On January 10, days after the European Commission had invoked Article 7(1) of the Treaty on the European Union, the government annulled the fine.[108]

The opposition success in protecting freedom of the press has been marginal but meaningful. While public media outlets have become government mouthpieces, and the ruling coalition keeps harassing independent media outlets (Mong 2019), private newspapers, radio stations, and newspapers remain open and independent; and opposition candidates can use these media outlets to campaign.

6.4.2.2 *PiS Attack to Freedom of Assembly*

In November 2016, PiS introduced a bill that limited public gatherings in an attempt to curtail people's ability to protest. The bill established that when asking for permits, "cyclical demonstrations" (e.g., rallies organized repeatedly on the same date and place) and gatherings organized by state or religious organizations would receive priority over other meetings.

The opposition fought the changes using moderate institutional and extra-institutional strategies. NGOs sent petitions to the Sejm, requesting that they reconsider the bill[109] and when parliament approved the amendment, together with the OSCE-ODHIR and the Supreme Court, they submitted documents asking Duda to veto the bill.[110] These petitions were backed up by thousands of Poles who mobilized in order to protest the reform (Lyman and Berendt 2016).

The pressure had a small, but by no means insignificant, effect. In line with the theory outlined in this book, the opposition's strategic choices not only increased the costs to remove opposition members from office but also delayed and tamed the reform. On December 13, parliament removed the provisions that would have given priority to state- or church-sponsored public gatherings. Duda refused to sign the bill and sent it to the TK, instead. Although it was unlikely that the latter – by now packed with PiS loyalists – was going to rule against the amendment, the president's move delayed the reform by three

---

[107] U.S. State Department. "Poland: National Broadcasting Council's Fine on TVN24." Washington DC, December 12, 2017.

[108] "Poland annuls 1.5 min zloty fine on TVN24 over coverage of protests in parliament." *Reuters*, January 10, 2018.

[109] See "Opinion by the Helsinki Foundation for Human Rights." No. 2180/2016/MLP/BGM. Warsaw, November 29, 2016.

[110] See "European Human Rights Officials Voice Serious Concerns over Changes to Polish Laws on Freedom of Assembly | OSCE." December 5, 2016. "Statement of Non-Government Organisations Regarding Amendments to the Law on Assemblies." December 6, 2016.

months and set a precedent. It was the first time Duda refused to immediately approve a PiS bill.[111]

Although the amendments to the Law on Assemblies, heightened surveillance laws, and government harassment have curtailed the ability of the opposition to demonstrate, they have not stopped it. Between November 2015 and 2017, Poland had eighteen protests: three in 2015, nine in 2016, and six in 2017. Between January and March of 2018, Poles used street demonstrations once a month. Although the number of protests declined between 2016 and 2017, after PiS came to power, Poland has had on average more than eight protests a year, four times the number of protests per year between 2010 and 2014.[112]

6.4.3 Summary

Despite its strength and willingness, the Law and Justice Party in Poland has not been able to erode democracy. Notwithstanding its attempts to co-opt the judiciary, undermine civil liberties, and skew free and fair elections, Kaczyński's party has not hindered the electoral playing field to such an extent that it is impossible to defeat the incumbents. Unlike what happened in Venezuela, Bolivia, or Turkey, the Polish opposition has avoided radical institutional and extrainstitutional strategies and used moderate institutional and extrainstitutional strategies instead. These tactics have, so far, paid off. Not only has the Polish opposition been able to keep its legitimacy inside and, more importantly, outside the country, but by combining litigation, electioneering, and nonviolent demonstrations, it has tamed, delayed, and even stopped some of the most radical reforms introduced by PiS.

Although it is unclear whether PiS will successfully erode democracy or not, the opposition's strategic choices have, so far, protected its legitimacy and bought it time. Six years into its government, PiS has not been able to erode democracy. Unlike what happened with Chávez, Morales, or Erdogan, international prodemocratic support to those who stand against PiS has not wavered. The European Union has fought every one of the Polish government's power grabs. While the mechanisms are slow, the opposition strategic choices have given the organization time to work while Poland is still democratic, before the government has too much control over government institutions or abandons its democratic façade. Thanks to these tactics, five years after PiS attained power, the opposition has a real opportunity to stop the erosion of democracy in Poland. Despite attempts to the contrary – notwithstanding irregularities – elections in the country remain free and fair. And the opposition has stepped up its mobilization efforts. In 2019, it was able to win a simple

---

[111] "Polish President Sends Freedom of Assembly Bill to Constitutional Court." *Reuters*, December 29, 2016.

[112] Calculations using data from Clark and Reagan's Mass Mobilization Data Project V3, 2019.

majority in the Senate, and in 2020, it lost the presidency by a very slim margin. Although PiS remains in power and could certainly try to undermine democratic institutions even further, using moderate institutional and extrainstitutional strategies, the opposition has been able to open up the set of possible outcomes.

6.5 HUNGARY

Between 1990 and 2010, Hungary had a fairly stable democracy. It was in the first group of Eastern European countries to join the European Union (2004) and one of the first former-communist countries to join NATO (1999). In 2010, when Viktor Orbán became prime minister, Hungary's V-Dem Electoral Democracy score was 0.81, well above the Latin American (0.68) and Eastern European (0.64) means. Since then, Hungary has become a competitive authoritarian regime. In 2010, Orbán's party, Federation of Young Democrats-Hungarian Civic Alliance (*Fiatal Demokraták Szövetsége-Magyar Polgári Szövetség – Fidesz*), won a qualified majority of seats in parliament, enough to unilaterally change the constitution. During his first year in government, the prime minister introduced institutional reforms that severely curtailed the powers of the Constitutional Court and allowed him to co-opt oversight agencies. He used his hold over all three branches of government to introduce and quickly approve a new constitution that further decreased the checks on the executive and changed the electoral law to his advantage. Since 2013, Orbán has used his newfound authority to curb freedom of expression, harass the opposition, and skew the electoral playing field to such an extent that it has become almost impossible to defeat his party.

Like what happened in Colombia and Poland, the opposition in Hungary used moderate institutional and extrainstitutional strategies against Fidesz's efforts to erode democracy. Unlike what happened in these two countries, however, these tactics failed to prevent or significantly slow down the erosion of democracy. Although international litigation, electioneering, and street protests did, at times, limit or delay some of Orbán's power grabs, draw international attention to democratic backsliding in Hungary, and energize the opposition, their effect was marginal and, ultimately, negligible. Two important factors could explain this outcome: lack of time and the absence of meaningful international constraints.

The Hungarian case is, in this sense, a great opportunity to explore the reach of some of the scope conditions of the argument. The theory outlined in Chapter 2 and explored throughout the rest of this book is contingent on four factors: The country is democratic, the executive has no normative preference for democracy, the erosion of democracy happens over time (giving the opposition ample opportunities to fight back), and the head of government wishes to appease domestic and international audiences with a normative preference for democracy. The last two were largely absent in Hungary.

While democracy in Hungary did not break in a day, it did break down at a much faster pace than its counterparts. It took Orbán only two years to secure almost full control over all three branches of government and three years to transform Hungary's democracy into a competitive authoritarian regime; the entire process took Chávez six. The speed of erosion in Hungary is the outcome of both Orbán's immediate institutional strength and his ability to push for aggressive antidemocratic reforms without fear of reprisal.

The erosion of democracy is slightly easier (yet not predetermined) in parliamentary regimes. Unlike what happens in presidential regimes, where divided government is a possibility, prime ministers with authoritarian tendencies start off with a hold over the legislative and the executive branch (Weyland 2020). This kind of control helps potential autocrats undermine democracy (Pérez-Liñán, Schmidt, and Vairo 2019), particularly when they have enough seats in parliament to curb the authority of courts and oversight agencies as well. In this sense, Orbán had to jump through fewer hoops than any of his counterparts. However, he would not have introduced very aggressive antidemocratic reforms – or at least would not have done so from day one – if he had had incentives to keep a democratic façade. He did not. Unlike what happened in the other countries analyzed in this book, Hungary had less international pressure to preserve the appearances of democracy. The European Union failed to exert effective pressure to curb Orbán's behavior. Backsliding in Hungary caught them by surprise. Unlike what happened in Poland, they were very slow to react (Bozóki and Hegedűs 2018). More importantly, unlike Colombia or even Poland, Orbán could more easily eschew the endorsement of prodemocratic European nations. Orbán relied on the support of Vladimir Putin's (2000–present) Russia (Buzogány 2017). Unlike the Law and Justice Party, Fidesz moderated its anti-Russia discourse before 2010 and, once in office, moved closer to Putin (Buzogány 2017). Russia's endorsement might have emboldened the prime minister to push for more overtly authoritarian reforms than other hegemonic executives.

6.5.1 Fidesz's Power Grab Blitz

Like Erdogan and Chávez, Orbán came to power in the midst of crisis. Between 2007 and 2009, Hungary's GDP growth per capita went from 0.4 percent to −6.5 percent. The economic downturn, coupled with corruption scandals, discredited the left-wing coalition that had governed Hungary since 2002. State performance declined precipitously 0.87 in 2002 to 0.63 in 2009, and trust in institutions went from five in 2002 to 3.6 in 2009. Fidesz quickly picked up the support the incumbents had lost (Batory 2016b). Together with the Christian Democratic People's Party (*Kereszténydemokrata Néppárt – KDNP*), in 2010, Orbán's supporters won 263 out of the 386 (68 percent) seats in parliament.

Fidesz's electoral landslide gave its leader, Viktor Orbán, the votes he needed to unilaterally reform the constitution. Within a year, he packed the Constitutional Court (MA), the National Electoral Commission (*NVI*), and the National Media and Infocommunications Authority (*NMHH*), and approved a new constitution that entered into force on January 2012. The latter further curtailed the powers of the judiciary and modified electoral rules, severely skewing the playing field. In 2013, the ruling party introduced a new set of constitutional reforms. The *Fourth Amendment*, as these changes were known, eliminated any vestige of power left in courts and oversight agencies. In 2014, elections in Hungary were already highly irregular. Using and abusing state resources and electoral regulations, Fidesz won 66 percent of the seats with 53 percent of the vote. The situation became more acute in 2018. Intensifying previous tactics, Fidesz kept 66 percent of the seats with 49 percent of the vote.

6.5.1.1 Co-Opting the Constitutional Court
Similar to the Colombian high courts, the Hungarian Constitutional Court was the strongest check on the executive (Kovacs and Toth 2011). Not only did it have extensive judicial review powers, but also it was highly respected among Hungarians (Scheppele, von Bogdandy, and Sonnevend 2015). Orbán's first move aimed to bring this body under his control.

In July and September 2010, Fidesz introduced and unilaterally approved two constitutional reforms that changed the composition of the Constitutional Court (MA). The first changed the justices' nomination procedure.[113] The second increased the number of MA justices from elven to fifteen. Between 2010 and 2011, the party was able to choose seven MA justices. Although judges appointed before 2010 still held a simple majority of the seats, the change moved the court to the right and closer to Fidesz. Before 2010, the MA had four left-leaning justices, one swing justice, and four right-leaning justices. By 2011, the court had three left-leaning justices, one centrist justice, and eleven right-wing justices. Seven of the eleven right-wing justices were elected by Fidesz (Szente 2016).

6.5.1.2 Co-Opting Oversight Agencies
In addition to his rapid consolidation of power over the courts, Orbán co-opted oversight organizations as well in his first years in power. Two months after attaining power, Fidesz terminated the mandate of the National Election Commission (NVI) members and filled five of its ten seats with loyalists. The changes guaranteed the government a simple majority in this body (Bánkuti,

---

[113] Originally, MA justices were elected by two-thirds of parliament from nominees selected with the approval of a simple majority of all parliamentary parties. The reform removed this last requirement. Since then, MA justices have been nominated by a parliamentary committee that mirrors the composition of the legislative (Szente 2016).

Halmai, and Scheppele 2015),[114] and with that the ability to manipulate future elections and hinder the opposition's ability to challenge the prime minister's reforms via referendum (Bozóki 2015).

Orbán also sought to take control over media outlets. Between June and November 2010, his party introduced a series of bills – the "media law package" – to replace the National Media and Infocommunications Authority (NMHH) with a five-member loyalist-stacked Media Council, with the power to levy fines on media outlets for, among other things, failing to have "balanced" news coverage (Haraszti 2011; Bánkuti, Halmai, and Scheppele 2015).

6.5.1.3 *The Fundamental Law*

Parallel to these power grabs, Fidesz started the process of writing a new constitution. In June 2010, Orbán established a council to elaborate a draft and a parliamentary committee to develop the regulatory framework of the Fundamental Law. Although nominally representative, the opposition did not have significant power inside this new committee.

The constitution-writing process, like Orbán's other consolidations of power, moved rapidly. In December 2010, the parliamentary committee announced the new constitution principles. Three months later, a parliamentary resolution gave MPs a week to come up with draft constitutions. The legislature had a month to debate them.[115] In a party line vote, the new constitution was finally approved on April 25, 2011, and went into effect on January 1, 2012.

The *Fundamental Law* eroded democracy even further. Not only did it curtail to a greater extent the powers of the Constitutional Court and tilted the electoral playing field but did so using instruments such as organic laws which required qualified majorities to be changed. Even if Fidesz lost power, it would have been hard for the opposition to restore the independence of democratic institutions (Bozóki and Hegedűs 2018).

The new constitution limited the ability to use the Constitutional Court as an effective tool against the erosion of democracy. Whereas in the past, anyone could challenge a law's constitutionality (*actio popularis*), after 2012, only individuals who had been concretely affected by the application of a law could file petitions after going through ordinary courts (Bánkuti, Halmai, and Scheppele 2015; Scheppele, von Bogdandy, and Sonnevend 2015).[116] The measure not only limited the opposition's ability to access the court but also delayed any action it could have taken against Fidesz's power grabs.

---

[114] The other five seats were distributed among the other parties (one per party).

[115] The opposition presented a draft as well, but it never received a serious hearing (Bánkuti, Halmai, and Scheppele 2015, 41).

[116] The only way around that requirement was to gather the support of 25 percent of MPs.

The new constitution also manipulated Hungary's electoral rules to Fidesz's advantage. Before 2012, the country's electoral law distributed 386 seats in a two-round system for single-member constituencies, which assigned remainders to the losing party (thus increasing proportionality). The Fundamental Law changed that. It cut the parliamentary seats from 386 to 199, abolished the two-round system, and replaced it with a plurality system for 106 seats and a nationwide proportional system for the remaining ninety-three (Bojar 2016). The new constitution also modified the electoral boundaries, gerrymandering districts in Fidesz's favor (Batory 2016c). As a consequence of these changes, the disproportionality index in Hungary went from 5.1 in 2010, to 10.1 in 2014 (Bojar 2016).

6.5.1.4 The Fourth Amendment

Alongside the Fundamental Law, Fidesz also approved a series of Transitional Provisions in December 2011. Although these were meant to clarify and smooth out the transition between the old and the new constitutions, they were used to, among other things, harass the opposition and co-opt and curtail the power of courts and oversight agencies. They, for example, decreased the power of several offices inside the judiciary (Article 11.3). They created a National Judicial Office (Orzágos Bírósági Hivatal) with the authority to appoint, promote, or demote judges; begin disciplinary procedures; select the court leaders; and move cases across courts. They also terminated the position of the Commissioner for Data Protection as soon as January 2012 and mandated the immediate retirement of judges who were at or had passed the newly approved retirement age (Article 12). By lowering the retirement age (from seventy to sixty-two) and making it retroactive, the institutional reform terminated the period of approximately 10 percent of the members of the judiciary.

As I will show later, the Constitutional Court used some of the power it had left to annul some of these provisions in December 2012. In response to the challenge, three months later, Fidesz introduced a new set of reforms that nullified all MA rulings delivered prior the Fundamental Law, limited the ability of the MA to rule against reforms that conflicted with the constitutional principles, and prohibited the MA from evaluating constitutional amendments on substantive grounds (Novoszádek 2013; Scheppele, von Bogdandy, and Sonnevend 2015). The changes not only backtracked important rulings that protected freedom of the press and the independence of the courts but also limited the ability of the MA to use precedent to curb some of Orbán's power grabs (Novoszádek 2013).

6.5.2 Moderate Institutional and Extrainstitutional Strategies

Fidesz's adversaries were split in two disjointed groups. The first group was composed by the Hungarian Socialist Party (*MSZP*) and Politics Can be Different (*LMP*) as well as civil society groups concerned with the fate of

Hungarian democracy. The second group was composed of the far-right-wing party Jobbik (*Jobbik Magyaroszágért Mozgalom*), which opposed the government out of policy differences. These organizations have not worked together. Although Jobbik has tried to move to the center, its stances remain untenable for MSZP, LMP, other small parties, and most prodemocracy civil society groups (Schultheis 2018).

Against Fidesz's fast-paced power grabs, the opposition used moderate institutional and extrainstitutional strategies: uploading, litigating, and electioneering, as well as peaceful demonstrations. Although the tactics delayed, curtailed, and reversed some of Fidesz's antidemocratic reforms, their effect was limited. The delays were too short, the changes to the bills marginal, and the reversals temporary. The pace of democratic erosion in Hungary as well as the lack of international leverage in Hungary could explain their failure.

6.5.2.1 Moderate Institutional Strategies

UPLOADING. The rapid pace of Orbán's reforms surprised the opposition. Aware of disadvantage in the domestic sphere, it "uploaded" issues pertaining the rule of law to the European Union where it had better chances of outvoting the government (Batory 2014). The actions taken against the "media law package" and the Fundamental Law are prime examples of that strategy.

The media law package unleashed criticism outside the country.[117] Sensing a friendly environment, the Hungarian opposition influenced and provided information to party federations and the European Parliament, in hopes of getting the European Union to intervene (Batory 2014). The strategy worked. On December 23, Neelie Kroes, the European Union's Media Commission Vice President, raised questions about the legality of the media package. She was reinforced by José Manuel Barroso, president of the European Commission, who raised the issue in a meeting with Orbán on January 2011 (Castle 2011). In January 2011, the Social and Democrats Group called on the Committee on Civil Liberties to analyze the media law so that the European Parliament could consider launching Article 7 proceedings against Hungary. The request was followed with a resolution, in March, condemning the Hungarian government.

The tactic was partially successful. In response to the criticisms, Hungary agreed to change the bill. The modifications were, however, underwhelming. The inadequate changes exempted media firms legally established and authorized in other member states from complying with the requirements of having "balanced coverage," eased authorization and registration of media outlets,

---

[117] "OSCE Media Freedom Representative Calls on Hungarian Government to Halt Media Legislation Package, Start Public Consultations." OSCE Press Release. June 24, 2010; "Hungarian Media Legislation Severely Contradicts International Standards of Media Freedom, Say OSCE Media Freedom Representative." OSCE Press Release. September 7, 2010; "Hungarian Media Law Further Endangers Media Freedom, Says OSCE Media Freedom Representative." OSCE Press Release. December 21, 2010.

and specified the prohibition of media content that may "not cause offense,"[118] but failed to address more fundamental threats to the rule of law. After all, Orbán need only make minimal changes[119] to get the Commission to close the infringements (Batory 2016b). The composition of the newly formed Media Council, staffed by Fidesz loyalists and ultimately in charge of overseeing media outlets in the country, remained intact.

Another good example of "uploading" is the debate of the Fundamental Law. The opposition uploaded its fight against the new constitution to the European Union. It brought it to the attention of the Venice Commission and, more importantly, the European Parliament. Both bodies criticized the Fundamental Law and the process by which it had been approved.[120] When Fidesz failed to address any of the concerns expressed by the EP, the European Commission opened infringement proceedings against the country.[121]

Once again, the limited framework[122] for the infringement allowed Orbán to creatively comply (Batory 2016b) and hindered the impact of this moderate institutional strategy. The prime minister acquiesced to the Commission's request to eliminate a provision that allowed the minister of finance to attend the meetings,[123] but let the other complaints run their course. The process went all the way to the European Court of Justice (ECJ). By the time the ECJ ruled against Hungary,[124] the laws in question had taken effect. Orbán agreed to backtrack them, but he refused to reappoint the data protection commissioner or the judges who had already been replaced.

DOMESTIC LITIGATION. The opposition used domestic litigation to fight Orbán's power grabs as well. In March 2012, Hungary's Ombudsman Máté Szabó asked the Constitutional Court to examine the Transitional Provision Act of the Fundamental Law. Using the powers of review that it had left, the

---

[118] European Commission Press Release. "Media: Commission Vice-President Kroes Welcomes Amendments to Hungarian Media Law."

[119] Circumscribed to the very narrow purview of the EU's Audiovisual Media Services Directive.

[120] Venice Commission. "Opinion on the New Constitution of Hungary. Strasbourg: Venice Commission – Council of Europe," June 20, 2011; "Revised Hungarian Constitution." P7_TA(2011) 0315, July 5, 2011.

[121] "European Commission Launches Accelerated Infringement Proceedings against Hungary over the Independence of Its Central Bank and Data Protection Authorities as well as over Measures Affecting the Judiciary." European Commission Press Release. January 17, 2017.

[122] The Transitional Provisions Act which threatened: (a) the Central Bank's independence, (b) called for the replacement of the Hungarian data protection commissioner before the end of his term, and (c) lowered the age of compulsory retirement in the judiciary, resulting in the removal of 10 percent of the judges (Batory 2016b).

[123] In 2013, when the Central Bank governor's term expired, he appointed said minister to replace him.

[124] "Court of Justice rules Hungarian forced early retirement of judges incompatible with EU law." European Commission Memo, November 6, 2012; "Court of Justice upholds independence of data protection authorities in case against Hungary." European Commission Memo, April 8, 2014.

MA ruled in favor of the ombudsman. It annulled provisions pertaining to the crimes committed during the communist regime and those responsible for them, voided the provision that allowed parliament to decide which were "recognized" churches and which were not, and nullified the provision that allowed the National Judicial Office president to transfer cases from one court to another.

Emboldened by these rulings, the MA also announced that it would follow earlier decisions in future rulings. In 2012, it used precedent to strike down several reforms, including a law that restricted political campaigning to public media and overturned a law that criminalized homelessness. These successes were, nevertheless, short-lived. In March 2013, Fidesz introduced the "Fourth Amendment," reversing all MA rulings and some of the concessions Hungary had made due to pressure from the European Council and hindering the MA's ability to revise future constitutional amendments or use precedent in their rulings (Novoszádek 2013).

ELECTIONEERING. The anti-Fidesz opposition challenged the government in elections as well, and between 2014 and 2017, it seemed to be making headway. Energized by a series of protests that took place in 2012, in 2014 several opposition parties ran for office. Unfortunately, the electoral system created in 2012 played against them. Divided between a set of small parties on the left (MSZP, LMP, and others) and one growing party on the right, *Movement for a Better Hungary* (Jobbik), the opposition did not win enough seats to outweigh the disproportionality of the electoral system. Fidesz attained 133 seats (67 percent) with 52 percent of the vote, keeping its two-thirds majority by one seat.

In 2015, there were three special elections, two of them to replace Fidesz MPs. Thanks to strategic voting by Jobbik (far right) and MSZP (left) voters, the former won one of them (April 2015), and an independent candidate won the other one (February 2015) (Bojar 2017). The extent to which this is a victory for democracy is debatable. On the one hand, by losing these two seats, Orbán lost the two-thirds majority he needed to further reform the constitution. On the other hand, Jobbik has a history of xenophobia, racism, and a weak commitment to democracy.[125]

Not having a two-thirds majority was costly for Fidesz. In October 2016, the government organized a referendum to reject the quota of refugees assigned by the European Union. Very much like the Colombian opposition, MSZP and other left-wing parties campaigned to boycott it (Gessler 2017),[126] preventing the government from reaching the turnout required to approve the bill (50 percent). Days later, Fidesz tried to turn around the results by introducing a

---

[125] "Hungary's Jobbik Party Tries to Sound Less Extreme." *The Economist*. November 15, 2017.
[126] Jobbik strongly supports anti-immigration legislation. Although they campaigned alongside Fidesz, they criticized the government for even calling a referendum, and asked Orbán to resign if it failed (Gessler 2017).

constitutional amendment that vaguely limited the scope of the European Union's influence in Hungarian politics. Having lost the two-thirds majority, however, it was forced to negotiate with Jobbik to approve it.[127] Unable to reach an agreement, Orbán eventually had to drop the reform (Gessler 2017).

Up until 2018, using institutional strategies, the opposition had been able to keep and increase its seats in parliament, diminish the ruling party's MPs, and stop antidemocratic reforms – all despite its electoral weaknesses. Unfortunately, these wins did not last. Although MSZP leaders were secretly considering a "technical" electoral alliance with Jobbik, the agreement remained untenable (Simon 2018). Divided and hampered by gerrymandering, the opposition lost the 2018 parliamentary elections. Although Fidesz's vote share decreased (49 percent), it was able to keep 133 seats (67 percent) (Krekó and Enyedi 2018), enough to push any reform it desires.

6.5.2.2 Moderate Extrainstitutional Strategies

While anti-Fidesz politicians sought our domestic and international mechanisms to stop the erosion of democracy, prodemocratic activists resorted to street demonstrations to challenge or even reverse some of the government's power grabs. In December 2010, the day after the media law was approved, Péter Juhasz, communication expert and civil activist, created a Facebook page, *One Million For the Freedom of the Press* (Milla), calling for demonstrations against the bill (Petócz 2015). A year later, in October 2011, members of law enforcement and chemical workers unions and a Milla splinter group (*One Million for Democracy-Civic Association*) founded the Hungarian *Solidarity Movement* (Boris and Vári 2015). Between 2011 and 2012, Milla and Solidarity organized dozens of demonstrations against the media law and the new constitution. Together, they mobilized thousands of Hungarians across the country (Bozóki 2015).

The demonstrations were partially successful, but ultimately insufficient. They drew domestic and international attention to the process of democratic erosion in Hungary, created opportunities for the opposition to regroup, and forced the government to backtrack some minor laws, but failed to significantly slow down the process of democratic erosion in Hungary.

Pressure from the streets helped the opposition upload issues like the "media law package" and the Fundamental Law to the European Union and fostered a space for politicians to coalesce before the 2014 elections. Fidesz's landslide in 2010 and the sweeping pace of its authoritarian reforms had left the opposition parties in disarray. Milla and Solidarity reenergized the anti-Fidesz coalition (Boris and Vári 2015; Petócz 2015). On October 2012, their leaders created an umbrella organization called Together 2014, and they invited other opposition

---

[127] Jobbik wanted the government to end the residency bonds, which granted non-Hungarians permanent residency and eventually citizenship if they invested a certain amount of money (or more) in the country.

parties to forge a united electoral front for 2014 (Bozóki 2015). There were several attempts to collaborate with MSZP and LMP. Unfortunately, internal divisions, the overall sense of anti-politics, and parties' inability to renovate their cadres, as well as Fidesz's non-programmatic campaign tactics hindered the 2014 electoral alliance (Bozóki 2015; Mares and Young 2018).

Civil society pressure also helped stop reforms that threatened freedom of speech. In October 2014, a student movement gathered under the slogan *One Hundred Thousand against the Internet Tax* launched a massive protest against Orbán's attempts to tax the use of the Internet. Approximately a hundred thousand people gathered in Budapest, and tens of thousands gathered in other Hungarian cities. It was the largest demonstration since Fidesz came to power (Ferrari 2019). After two days, the government backed down from the proposed internet tax.[128]

Despite this, street demonstrations proved insufficient to stop the erosion of democracy in Hungary. As shown earlier, notwithstanding public outcry and EU pressure, the basic and most dangerous tenets of the "media law package" and the Fundamental Law remained in place. Despite the nest built by civil society movement, opposition parties failed to unite for the 2014 elections and outweigh the electoral disproportionality. Although Internet remained untouched, media authorities are still in the hands of Fidesz, and have found other ways to curb freedom of expression (Repucci 2019).

6.5.3 Why Did Moderate Institutional and Extrainstitutional Strategies Fail?

All in all, although the moderate institutional and extrainstitutional strategies discussed earlier contained and delayed the prime minister's attempts to erode democracy, they were ultimately ineffective in stopping the erosion of democracy. As shown in Chapter 2, in order for opposition strategies to work the way I say they do, the country must be democratic when the potential autocrat comes to power, the executive must have authoritarian tendencies, domestic and international audiences must have a normative preference for democracy that incentivizes leaders to keep a democratic façade, and democracy must erode over time leaving the opposition institutional and noninstitutional resources to fight back. The last two conditions seem to have failed in Hungary.

6.5.3.1 *The Pace and Resources of Democratic Erosion*
Unlike other oppositions studied in this book, the anti-Fidesz coalition very quickly ran out of institutional resources to fight the government. Hungary's

---

[128] "Hungary Scraps Controversial Web Tax." *BBC News*, October 31, 2014.

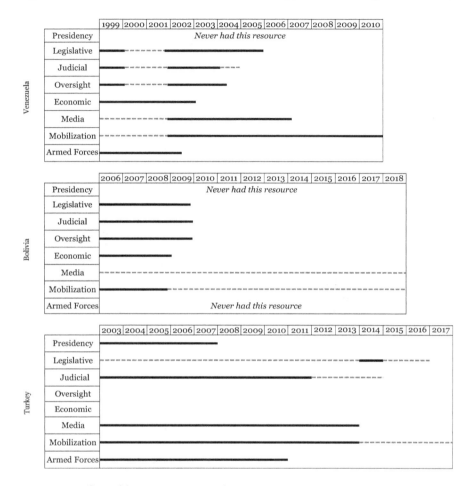

FIGURE 6.1. Opposition resources over time

parliamentary system coupled with Orbán's electoral landslide allowed him to lead a power grab blitz between May 2010 and February 2013 that, akin to a traditional coup, kneecapped any institution the opposition could have weaponized against the incumbent, including elections. As illustrated in Figure 6.1, Fidesz's power grabs happened faster than any of the other power grabs studied in this book. Three years after Orbán came to office, the Hungarian opposition had lost access to courts, electoral authorities, and media oversight agencies. In comparison, three years into Chávez's government (January 2002), the Venezuelan opposition had access to and significant influence over courts and congress, the armed forces, the oil company, and the country's most important media outlets.

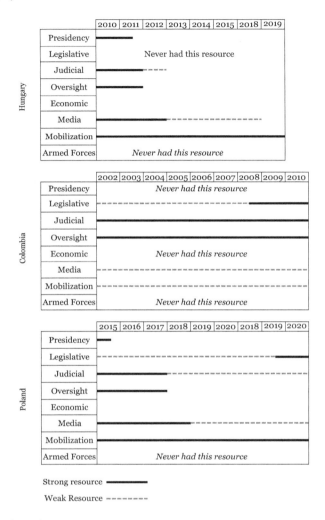

FIGURE 6.1. *(cont.)*

It is hard to fight the erosion of democracy when your resources are depleted this fast. Moderate institutional and extrainstitutional strategies are not useful (or even available) in traditional democratic breakdowns because these democratic reversals happen rapidly. The opposition does not have the resources or the opportunities to fight back. In this sense, Hungary did not see a traditional democratic breakdown. Rather, Orbán's overwhelming initial set of resources, and the speed in which he deployed them to co-opt the rest, crippled the opposition's ability to effectively fight the rapid erosion of democracy.

6.5.3.2 Absence of International Constraints
This lack of resources was further compounded by an international order that
hindered the opposition's ability to leverage the potential autocrat's international legitimacy constraints in its favor. Chávez, Morales, Erdogan, Uribe,
and PiS took care to keep a democratic façade. The opposition's moderate
institutional and extrainstitutional strategies catered to these leaders' need to
maintain national and international democratic legitimacy. Without a "legitimate reason," any attempt to fully override democratic institutions would risk
that façade. By using moderate institutional and extrainstitutional strategies,
the opposition deprived the potential autocrat of that excuse, in hopes that the
autocrat would choose to slow down the erosion of democracy rather than
risking losing his democratic façade. That logic did not seem to work with
Orbán. Of all the leaders discussed in this book, Orbán is the only one who has
openly declared he wants to turn Hungary into an "illiberal democracy."
    Two reasons could explain that disdain: the European Union's lack of
enforcing mechanisms and, more importantly, the support of Vladimir Putin.
Democratic erosion in Hungary caught the European Union by surprise. At the
time Orbán came to office, the only option available to prevent the erosion of
democracy in a member country was to invoke Article 7 of the Treaty of the
European Union (TEU), which grants the European Council the authority to
recommend the suspension of a member if there is a serious breach of the
European Union's values (Article 2-TEU).
    When Orbán began eroding democracy, even starting the process to invoke
Article 7 required votes its proponents did not have. Article 7 of the TEU is a
two-step process. The first step requires a two-thirds majority in the European
Parliament and the support of four-fifths of the European Council. As part of
the European People's Party, Fidesz had a hold of 30 percent of the seats in the
EP, which refused to vote in favor of any initiative to open Article 7 infringement procedures. The leeway Hungary enjoyed stands in contrast with the
pressure put on Poland. By the time PiS began eroding democracy, the
European Union had approved the Rule of Law Framework (2014). The latter
has allowed the European Commission to exert a more effective, even if not
entirely impactful, pressure on Kaczyński and his party, whose coalition
(European Conservatives and Reformists) held (until 2019) less than 10 percent
of the seats in the European Parliament.
    Since he came to office, Orbán also benefited from Vladimir Putin's support.
Although initially "anti-Russian," Orbán softened his discourse toward the
neighbor country shortly before the election. Unlike Poland, Hungary depends
on Russia for its energy supply. Both that dependence and the economic crisis
that preceded the rise of Fidesz called for a more pragmatic approach with
Putin. Building on that relationship and facing mounting criticism from the
West, Orbán has moved closer to his powerful neighbor (Buzogány 2017).
Since 2010, Fidesz has eschewed its "atlanticists" foreign policy experts and
replaced them with pro-Russian diplomats and increased its visits to Russia and

Central Asia. The stronger relationship has been fed by "their desire to quench their own international legitimacy deficit through mutual recognition." (Magyar, Bálint 2016 cited in Buzogány 2017, 1317). Unlike PiS – who cannot shun its "anti-Russian" stance and depends on the European Union for legitimacy and support – Orbán is less concerned with EU criticism. He does not care if he loses his democratic façade, and thus, does not need to wait for the opposition to give him "legitimate" excuses in order to advance antidemocratic reforms.

6.5.4 Summary

Like the Colombian and Polish oppositions, the anti-Fidesz coalition used moderate institutional and extrainstitutional strategies to fight Viktor Orbán's power grabs. Unlike the Venezuela, Bolivia, or Turkey, however, it was unable to stop the erosion of democracy in Hungary. The effect of uploading, litigation, electioneering, and peaceful demonstrations was marginal and, ultimately, insufficient.

Two factors could explain this outcome. On the one hand, the Hungarian opposition did not have enough time to fight back. In three years, Orbán had taken full control over courts, congress, and oversight agencies. Akin to what happens with traditional democratic breakdowns, very quickly, the opposition was left without resources to fight back. On the other hand, unlike other cases in this book, international audiences with a normative preference for democracy had less leverage over the Hungarian prime minister. Although the European Union criticized Fidesz's power grabs, it did not have adequate tools to fight them. Orbán was able to "creatively comply" to the few requests they made. Second, and not entirely unrelated, Orbán has the support of a powerful "black knight." Unlike Chávez, Morales, Erdogan, Uribe, or PiS, he does not need to keep a democratic façade because he relies on Russia for international support.

6.6 CONCLUSION

The cases reviewed in this chapter suggest that the theory outlined in this book works outside Colombia and Venezuela. In Poland, moderate institutional and extrainstitutional strategies have, so far, helped protect the country's democracy. They have shielded the opposition's legitimacy domestically and abroad, slowed down PiS power grabs, and even helped reverse significant antidemocratic reforms. At their best, these strategies can help stop the erosion of democracy; at their worst, they can protect the opposition's institutional resources long enough to open the set of possible outcomes. Poland is certainly not out of the woods, but thanks to these strategies, the anti-PiS still has a shot to stop the erosion of democracy.

In Bolivia and Turkey, on the contrary, radical extrainstitutional (and even institutional) strategies helped executives with hegemonic aspirations erode democracy. They delegitimized the opposition and gave Morales and Erdogan an opportunity to remove opposition leaders from office, prosecute, or jail them without losing their democratic façade. Both Morales and Erodgan faced fairly strong oppositions. They had plenty of institutional and noninstitutional resources. However, by using radical extrainstitutional strategies, they squandered them all. Not only did these tactics delegitimize the opposition domestically and abroad, but also they increased the executive's support, and with that, his leverage to push for more aggressive antidemocratic reforms.

This last chapter also shows that the theory put forward in Chapter 2 is not watertight. Although the Hungarian opposition used moderate institutional and extrainstitutional strategies, it was unable to stop the erosion of democracy. The case of Fidesz and Viktor Orbán allows us to explore some of the scope conditions that could potentially affect the theory of the book. The resources time grants and international leverage are important conditions for opposition strategies to work the way I claim they do. Orbán was able to erode democracy despite the opposition strategic choices because he did so quickly and without concern for his democratic façade.

7

Conclusion

The erosion of democracy has become globally pervasive. New and old democracies around the world are now led by executives willing to undermine democratic institutions in order to achieve their policy goals. The booming literature on democratic backsliding has, for the most part, focused on the factors that drive these executives with hegemonic aspirations to power (Handlin 2017b; Norris and Inglehart 2019b) or the resources they have available to successfully undermine democratic institutions (Corrales 2018b; Levitsky and Ziblatt 2018b; Ginsburg and Huq 2019b; Weyland and Madrid 2019b). The underlying assumption of these theories is that popular and economically solvent heads of government in institutionally weak countries are almost always going to erode democracy, while their less popular and economically solvent counterparts in institutionally strong countries are almost always going to fail.

Opposition at the Margins challenges that assumption. Moving the focus away from correlation of forces between incumbent and opposition, I develop a novel theory of democratic erosion that highlights the latter's tactical choices. I do that, first, by defining the erosion of democracy as a type of democratic breakdown that happens over time. The process of erosion, I contend, can be thought of in two stages. The first one focuses on the factors that bring potential autocrats to power, the second one focuses on the mechanisms that allow some executives, but not others, to successfully undermine democracy.

Albeit interrelated, the circumstances that bring executives with hegemonic aspirations to power are not the same that allow them to transform their democracies into competitive authoritarian regimes. As I showed in Chapter 3, whereas weak states with governance problems, inchoate party systems, and – to a lesser extent – poor economic performance increase the likelihood of electing leaders willing to circumvent democracy in Latin America, they cannot fully explain the variation between the ones that successfully erode democracy and the ones that fail. In order to better understand that process, I have focused on the role of the opposition. The fact that the erosion of democracy happens over time provides the opposition ample opportunities to respond. The strategies used by oppositions and the goals they use them for are key to understanding why some executives are able to erode democracy while others are not. I depart from the assumption that most executives with hegemonic aspirations face domestic and international audiences with a normative preference for democracy, and thus need to maintain a democratic façade. Small immediate payoffs, notwithstanding, moderate institutional strategies are better suited to stop the erosion of democracy than radical ones. When successful, moderate tactics and goals hinder these incumbents' ability to remove opposition members from office, prosecute or jail them without losing their democratic façade. They enhance the opposition's ability to keep its seats in congress, prevent the co-optation of state institutions, and use these resources to delay or stop more aggressive antidemocratic reforms. When failed, moderate tactics allow the erosion of democracy to continue unhindered, but the opposition lives to fight another day.

On the contrary, radical extrainstitutional strategies are less well suited to protect democracy. If they fail (and they often do), this set of tactics and goals provides executives with "legitimate" reasons to remove opposition members from courts, congress, and oversight agencies without losing their democratic façade. Potential autocrats can further use these strategies as an excuse to gather enough support to push for more aggressive reforms that, out of office, the opposition can hardly stop. If these tactics and goals succeed, they could potentially stop the erosion of democracy immediately, but at the cost of breaking democracy altogether, further polarizing society, and/or martyrizing the potential autocrat to such an extent that she could stage a comeback. Moderate extrainstitutional strategies and radical institutional strategies can go either way. In some situations, they might help prevent the erosion of democracy. In others, they can risk accelerating it.

I assess this theory in Chapters 4 and 5 using comparative historical analysis with a case of successful erosion – Hugo Chávez in Venezuela – and a case of failed erosion – Alvaro Uribe in Colombia. Despite different ideologies, these presidents were alike in many ways. They both came to power in contexts of crisis, after decades of democratic stability, and they both tried to dismantle the checks on the executive and extend their time in office beyond a second term. Chávez and Uribe were similarly populistic and polarizing. They both portrayed themselves as sole bearers of the state, addressed private and local issues in a personalistic manner, and depicted those who criticized them as enemies of the state. In order to achieve their policy goals, these presidents were equally willing to erode democracy. Chávez's government manipulated electoral rules, threatened and forced justices and public servants to resign, and harassed journalists and opposition members. Uribe's government bought legislators; used the state apparatus to spy on justices, journalists, and politicians; made up evidence to falsely convict people who testified against Uribista officials; and facilitated information to paramilitary groups.

As I show in Chapter 4, the erosion of democracy was not fait accompli in Venezuela. It took Chávez nine years to transform this country's democracy into a competitive authoritarian regime. During most of that time, the opposition was fairly strong. They had important institutional and noninstitutional resources to fight the government: a meaningful presence in congress, some influence over courts and oversight agencies, control over the oil company, significant support inside the armed forces, and the ability to mobilize millions of Venezuelans to the streets. However, using extrainstitutional strategies with radical goals, they squandered them all.

The evidence displayed in Chapter 4 shows how the 2002 coup, the 2002–3 strike, and the 2005 electoral boycott, reduced the opposition's ability to portray Chávez's attempts to remove its members from key institutions as "illegitimate" or "undemocratic," and allowed the president to purge and fully control the military and PDVSA, and get a 100 percent Chavista congress. The latter, I further show, replaced the Supreme Tribunal of Justice and the Electoral Council and sped up Chávez's legislative agenda. After 2005, the government was not only able to pass more laws, but also it was able to do so almost six times faster than it did before.

Albeit flawed, moderate institutional strategies would have likely been less detrimental. As I show in this same chapter, between 2000 and 2005, the Venezuelan opposition coalition in congress was able to use rules of procedure to significantly delay the government's agenda. Had it remained in congress between 2006 and 2010, chances are it would have been able to do the same during Chávez's second term. Interviewees suggest that had the opposition avoided the "insurrectional" route, they might have even defeated Chávez in the 2006 elections.

Like the Venezuelan president, Alvaro Uribe introduced several reforms that sought to enhance his powers and extend his time in office. As shown in Chapter 5, unlike the Venezuelan case, the opposition Uribe faced was not particularly strong. It had some presence in congress, some friendly newspapers and online media outlets, and some ability to mobilize people to the streets. Unlike its Venezuelan counterpart, however, it had little or no access to TV or radio outlets, no support inside the armed forces, and its mobilizations were not as visible or massive as those organized by the anti-Chavistas. Although Colombia had a strong and independent Constitutional Court and it played a critical role in stopping Uribe, this is insufficient to explain the survival of democracy in Colombia. Not only did Uribe threaten to close, co-opt, and curtail the powers of the high tribunals, but, as I show, without input from congress, it would have been harder for the CC to rule against the president.

Unlike what happened in Venezuela, however, the opposition in Colombia refrained from using radical extrainstitutional strategies and used moderate institutional and extrainstitutional strategies to stop specific reforms. As shown in Chapter 5, the absence of extrainstitutional tactics with radical goals helped protect the opposition's legitimacy domestically and abroad and slowed down Uribe's co-optation of state institutions. The effective use of moderate institutional and extrainstitutional tactics complemented these efforts and helped the Constitutional Court rule against Uribe's reforms. In congress, the opposition used rules of procedure to delay the debates, allow for changes in important bills, and create and/or report procedural irregularities that helped the CC rule against Uribista institutional reforms. Outside of congress, the opposition used the streets to show support for the Court. As shown with the first reelection reform, without its active and coordinated effort, it would have been harder for the CC to rule against Uribista bills that would have harmed democracy.

While relevant, neither the variables that brought these leaders to power nor the resources they had available throughout their presidencies could have predicted the erosion of democracy in Venezuela or the survival of democracy in Colombia. As Chapter 3 shows, weak states with governance problems, weakly institutionalized party systems and – to a lesser extent – economic crisis have a significant effect in the election of executives with hegemonic aspirations. While important, these variables, however, cannot guarantee that, once in office, these presidents will successfully erode democracy.

This is not surprising, given that most of these factors vary throughout an executive's term in office. Good economic performance, but in particular popularity, polarization, and unstable institutions, can certainly help presidents undermine democracy. They are not, however, sufficient to explain why some leaders successfully erode democracy while others fail. As shown in the Venezuelan and Colombian cases, the opposition's strategic choices can affect if or when these factors are available to the executive, and/or the extent she can use them successfully.

Chapter 6 assesses my theory in Bolivia with Evo Morales, Turkey with Recep Tayyip Erdogan, Poland with the Law and Justice Party, and Hungary with Viktor Orbán. The cross-regional comparison suggests that the argument is generalizable, and opposition strategies and goals can work the way I claim they do outside Colombia and Venezuela. In Bolivia and Turkey, radical extrainstitutional strategies (e.g., regional violence, coups, lawsuits to ban the government party, etc.) gave the incumbents "legitimate" reasons to crack down on the opposition while keeping a democratic façade. In Poland, on the contrary, moderate institutional and extrainstitutional strategies have so far proven helpful to delay the erosion of democracy. Despite PiS's open disregard for liberal democracy, the government has not been able to hinder horizontal accountability to such an extent that it would hurt electoral accountability as well. Using parliament and demonstrations in support of courts and oversight agencies, the Polish opposition has bought itself time to fight more aggressive antidemocratic reforms.

Chapter 6 also highlights some of the scope conditions of the theory. Although it used moderate institutional and extrainstitutional strategies, the Hungarian opposition was unable to stop the erosion of democracy. Two factors seemed to have been key in this outcome. The fact that Orbán had an initial overwhelming control over the legislative and executive branches, and the fact that he faced weak international pressure countered by a "black knight" (Russia). Together, these variables allowed him to speed up the process of erosion limiting the resources and time available for the opposition to fight back.

7.1 THEORETICAL IMPLICATIONS

The theory outlined in this book has important theoretical implications. First, it explicitly introduces time into the study of democratic erosion. Most democracies today suffer a gradual, rather than a sudden, death (Bermeo 2016b). Although scholars have increasingly recognized the particularities of slow democratic erosion (Dresden and Howard 2016b; Waldner and Lust 2018b; Ginsburg and Huq 2019b), with few exceptions (Gamboa 2017; Cleary and Öztürk 2020) the literature has not fully engaged with the implications of the pace in which democracy dies. Up until recently, most analyses of this phenomena focused on the factors that brought these types of authoritarian leaders to power but paid little attention to what happened afterward (Carreras 2012b; Mainwaring 2012b; Diamond 2015b; Haggard 2016b; Svolik 2015a).

However, because the erosion of democracy happens over time, to understand why some democracies erode but others do not, we need to analyze not only what brings executives with hegemonic aspirations to power but also what happens after they become heads of government. By providing a more nuanced understanding of the erosion of democracy, I join recent trends in the literature (2017b; Levitsky and Ziblatt 2018b; Weyland and Madrid 2019b) and analyze the factors that bring hegemonic presidents to power, independently from the factors that help or hinder their ability to erode democracy.

The implications of that distinction are twofold. First, I contribute to the literature on the variables that make democratic regimes vulnerable to erosion. I provide a clear operationalization of which democratically elected executives are likely to be hegemonic based on their willingness to circumvent democracy. Furthermore, I test the conditions that allow these leaders to win elections. Using a combination of existing and original data, I measure incumbents' readiness to erode democracy, regardless of whether they succeed or fail in doing so and assess the conditions that brought them to power.

Second, understanding the erosion of democracy as a process rather than a one-shot game allows me to move the attention away from the president to the opposition. As of today, the erosion of democracy has been studied mostly through the lens of the executive. Almost all analyses of democratic backsliding have focused on the incumbent's strategic choices (Balderacchi 2017b), ex-anti popularity (Levitsky and Loxton 2013b; Corrales 2018b; Weyland and Madrid 2019a), access to economic (Hawkins 2010b; Mazzuca 2013b) or institutional resources (Handlin 2017b; Weyland and Madrid 2019a), and/or the strength of the institutional framework he is in (Weyland and Madrid 2019a; Ginsburg and Huq 2019b; Weyland 2020). These analyses have often dismissed the role of those who oppose the president, with the underlying assumption that only weak hegemonic presidents in strong institutional contexts fail.

By closely looking at the process of erosion, this book turns that conclusion on its head. Because it happens over time, unlike classic democratic breakdowns, the erosion of democracy grants the opposition two important tools: institutional resources and time. The executive's strength is not determined ex ante. What she can and cannot do is contingent on the process of erosion itself. Rather than focusing on the correlation of forces, therefore, I highlight the mechanisms that help or hinder, the government's ability to protect, increase, and effectively use these resources. In particular, how the opposition's strategic choices can (fail to) leverage the executive's need to protect his democratic credentials, to enhance or diminish his capacity to crack down on the opposition and advance more aggressive antidemocratic reforms.

In other words, leaders with hegemonic aspirations are neither all powerful and resourceful, nor hopelessly feeble and weak. As shown by the Colombian and the Polish cases, despite being popular and having control of congress, potential autocrats can fail or struggle to erode democracy. As shown by Venezuela, Turkey, or Bolivia, despite being less popular and/or having access to little institutional resources, hegemonic executives can successfully erode democracy. Democratic institutions, after all, cannot survive by themselves. Congress, courts, and oversight agencies need the support of citizens and political elites to remain alive. Without their endorsement, even strong institutions can be delegitimized to a point that allows an executive with hegemonic aspirations to dismantle or co-opt them, but with their support, even weak institutions can withstand the attacks of hyper-ambitious heads of government trying to delegitimize them to uncheck the executive.

Future research should focus on the conditions that allow either of these outcomes. As suggested by the Hungarian case, the theory put forward by this book is not airtight. To the extent that institutional or moderate extrainstitutional strategies are more normally desirable than radical extrainstitutional strategies (which could end democracy in the country anyway), we should further our understanding of these strategies and better assess the circumstances that incentivize oppositions to use them and do so effectively.

This last point is fundamental to advance this research. Why do some oppositions use radical extrainstitutional strategies while others do not is an important question, and deserves more attention than the one I can give it in this book. In line with more recent research on opposition strategic choices to fight the erosion of democracy (McCoy and Somer 2021) or outright authoritarian regimes (Selçuk and Hekimci 2020; Jiménez 2021; Ong 2021), new research on this topic should address the motivations (i.e., strategic or psychological) that oppositions have to pick different tactics and goals.

7.2 POLICY IMPLICATIONS

Paying attention to the opposition has important policy contributions as well. The rise of executives with hegemonic aspirations is hard to prevent. First, the processes that bring these leaders to power happen over a long span of time. It is hard to notice or foresee these processes' consequences before it is too late. Moreover, even if we were able notice them, it is improbable that we could do anything to stop them or avoid their consequences. Economic development and growth, state capacity, and institutional strength are factors that change slowly; it is unlikely that we can do something to improve a country's performance on these variables in time to stop the rise of a potential autocrat.

Ultimately, the dictates of democracy suggest that, unless they do something illegal, polarizing, populist, and antisystemic leaders with radical agendas are entitled to run for office, and as long as they don't cheat, they are allowed to win. By the time we notice that leaders willing to undermine democracy are headed to power, the only effective solution would be to use undemocratic means to prevent them from attaining office (Capoccia 2007). That solution is far from ideal and could hurt democracy just as much as allowing the potential autocrat to become head of government.

If we move away from the assumption that the erosion of democracy depends upon the correlation of forces between government and opposition, and pay attention to the strategies the latter uses, there is, however, some hope. We might not be able to avoid the rise of potential autocrats, but we can learn and train oppositions to fight these executives and develop international tools appropriate to help them protect democracy.

This does not mean that democratic oppositions have an easy road ahead. The election of a potential autocrat poses a significant threat to democracy. Oppositions who want to prevent the erosion of democracy face a Sophie's choice. They have difficult alternatives and, as with most political phenomena, no guarantee of success. This book does not mean to underestimate that difficulty, nor does it claim to have a silver bullet to protect countries against the erosion of democracy. Rather it seeks to call attention to the role of the opposition, an actor often dismissed as hopeless in the face of a strong potential autocrat. By shedding light on some of the mechanisms by which the opposition's strategic choices and goals can help or hinder democracy, not only do I hope to help those already fighting to protect democracy, but I also hope to spark more research on the conditions that allow or prevent these strategies and goals to work, as well as other potential combinations of tactics and objectives that could work.

7.3 STRATEGIES AGAINST THE EROSION OF
DEMOCRACY TODAY

The choices oppositions face are more complicated today than they were when Chávez or Uribe came to power. The opposition's ability to use strategies and goals to protect democracy from executives with hegemonic aspirations in the way I describe here depends on the regime preferences of domestic and international audiences. For the most part, hegemonic heads of government have sought to protect their democratic façade because citizens, foreign powers, and international organizations have had a normative preference for democracy. Potential autocrats fear that overt attacks against democratic institutions could trigger an adverse response domestically or abroad, and therefore choose to wait until they have "legitimate" reasons to crack down on the opposition or introduce aggressive antidemocratic reforms. It is the potential autocrat's desire to protect her democratic credentials that gives the opposition the leverage I describe in the book.

Unfortunately, it is unclear if oppositions facing the threat of erosion can rely on these audiences' normative preference for democracy. As I write these conclusions, antisystemic populistic leaders have attained power in the United States and the United Kingdom and have come very close in the Netherlands, Germany, and France. Democracies that we had written off as stable are (or have been) in danger of backsliding. Even if they do not erode, the fact that this type of leaders has or could become heads of government is concerning for the future of democracy elsewhere in the world. Not only do these leaders diminish the international support for democratic regimes, but the fact that democracy is no longer an important item in their foreign agenda allows authoritarian powers to enhance their influence and potentially shift domestic audiences' regime preferences as well.

Donald Trump's disregard for democracy inside and outside the United States, for example, emboldened like-minded would-be autocrats across the world. Without sanctions or even the threat of sanctions, ideologically aligned hegemonic heads of government like Nayib Bukele (2019–present) in El Salvador were able to push antidemocratic legislation or constitutional amendments without fear of reprisal. Trump's – and in consequence, the United States' – lack of normative preference for democracy implied that these and other potential autocrats no longer needed "legitimate" reasons to remove opposition leaders from office, prosecute or jail them. They could crack down on the opposition unafraid of international sanctions, hindering the opposition's ability to leverage moderate institutional strategies to protect the institutional resources it has and buy time.

The rise of populistic antisystemic leaders in Europe and the United States has also led to the retreat of the Western powers from the international stage (Diamond 2019; Johns, Pelc, and Wellhausen 2019). The lack of interest of the United States in democracy promotion has opened up spaces for authoritarian powers like China and Russia to increase their influence in Eastern Europe, the Middle East, and Latin America (Walker et al. 2017). These countries are either actively promoting authoritarianism or endorsing executives with hegemonic aspirations regardless of their attacks against democracy (Diamond 2019; Gvosdev 2019).

Some of these potential autocrats are no longer in office. Yet the consequences of their governments remain. Democracy, as a normatively desirable form of government, has lost ground. Even in well-developed democracies, support for democracy has decreased (Foa and Mounk 2016; Diamond 2019). In increasingly polarized environment, domestic audiences have weakened their normative preference for democracy, proven willing stand by politicians who push for antidemocratic provisions as long as they are co-partisan (Graham and Svolik 2020). This kind of disregard for democratic institutions embolden potential autocrats and their allies to overtly attack democratic institutions diminishing the time and resources available to those who oppose them.

This gives all the more reason to focus on opposition tactics and goals. The fact that the erosion of democracy is not fait-au-complete when the potential autocrat comes to power is good news. Future research should analyze how this changing environment can help or hinder the tactics oppositions have at hand; to what extent different sets of strategies and goals can help water down or fuel other factors that contribute to the erosion of democracy (like polarization), and the conditions that would allow oppositions to use them successfully to stop this current wave of autocratization.

Appendix A

Qualitative Methodology

In order to assess the mechanisms that allow some presidents but not others to erode democracy, I use comparative historical analysis, comparing a case of erosion, Hugo Chávez in Venezuela, and a case of near-erosion, Alvaro Uribe in Colombia. I use process tracing with data collected during twelve months of fieldwork in Colombia during the fall of 2013 and Venezuela during the spring-summer of 2014. During this fieldwork, I conducted interviews with politicians, academics, justices, clerks, members of NGOs, pollsters, and journalists and conducted archival research in newspapers and congress.

INTERVIEWS

I conducted a total of eighty-eight interviews, fifty-two in Venezuela and thirty-six in Colombia. All but two of the interviews were semi-structured.[1] I chose my interviewees based on (a) specific characteristics deemed relevant for my analysis (i.e., purposive sample) and (b) recommendations from other interviewees (i.e., snowball sampling). I did so, following the advice of the literature. Qualitative researchers argue that non-probability samples are better for process tracing when the purpose of the interviews is to develop causal explanations rather than drawing generalizations from a small sample to a larger group of people (Kapiszewski, McLean, and Read 2015, 212; Lynch 2013; Tansey 2007).

The interviewees were politicians, journalists, academics, activists, justices, clerks, pollsters, or members of advocacy groups who had a strong knowledge of, or had participated in, national politics between 1998 and 2013 in Venezuela, and 2002 and 2010 in Colombia. The purposive sample was

---

[1] I prepared questions in advance but allowed the interview to deviate from the questionnaire when needed.

initially built using information found in secondary sources. However – as is common in this type of research (Kapiszewski, MacLean, and Read 2015, 213) – I was eventually able to improve that list with information gathered as I spent more time in the field.

In Venezuela, I interviewed:

- seventeen politicians (ten in office, seven out of office)
- two former members of the Constitutional Assembly
- two members of the electoral opposition NGO *Súmate*
- a former member of the business association *Fedecámaras*
- a member of the Supreme Tribunal of Justice (TSJ)
- a former member of the Supreme Tribunal of Justice (TSJ)
- a former member of the National Electoral Council (CNE)
- a political operative (opposition)
- a member of the Carter Center
- two pollsters (*Datanálisis* and *Consultores 21*)
- three journalists (*Tal Cual, Globovisión, El Universal*)
- fifteen academics (*Universidad de Oriente, Centro de Estudios del Desarrollo, Universidad Central de Venezuela, Universidad Centro Andrés Bello, Instituto de Estudios Superiores de Administración*)

In Colombia, I interviewed:

- ten politicians (eight in office, two out of office)
- five Constitutional Court clerks (one serving as justice when interviewed)
- three legislative staffers
- three academics (*Universidad de los Andes, Universidad Javeriana, Universidad Nacional de Colombia*)
- three member of anti-reelection civil society group (*Alianza Ciudadana por la Democracia*)
- five members of human rights and advocacy groups (*Comisión Colombiana de Juristas, DeJusticia*)
- a member of an NGO that monitors Congress (*Congreso Visible*)
- four journalists (*Revista Semana, El Tiempo, RCN*)
- one retired member of the armed forces.

My work focused on assessing the role of the opposition in the erosion of democracy. Accordingly, I interviewed mostly members of the opposition to Hugo Chávez and Alvaro Uribe. However, to the extent possible,[2] I interviewed

---

[2] In Venezuela, in February 2014, some sectors of the opposition started a three-months-long anti-government protest. In such a heated anti-government environment, my research was seen with suspicion, and my requests for interviews with government officials were broadly declined. In Colombia, the problems were twofold. First, due to the "parapolítica" and other corruption scandals, many Uribista politicians are currently serving time in prison. Second, at the time in which I conducted my fieldwork (fall of 2013), the Uribista faction was building a political party (Centro Democrático) to participate in the parliamentary and presidential elections of 2014.

supporters of these presidents as well. In Venezuela, eight of my interviewees supported the government at the time of the interview and three had supported the government in the past. In Colombia, eight of my interviewees supported the government at the time of the interview and two had supported it in the past.

Following IRB protocol, all of my interviewees were informed about who I was, what my research was about, which institution I was affiliated with, and the objective of the interview. They were all informed that the participation in the interview was voluntary and that they could stop it at any point in time. All of my interviewees gave me verbal consent; however, not all of them authorized me to cite them and/or give their names. In order to protect my subjects, I use the citations of all the interviewees who authorized me to do so, but I name only those who gave me explicit permission to do so. For the citations in which I did not get explicit permission to use the interviewee's name, I provide basic information to inform the reader about the interviewee's role and how his/her testimony fits in the argument being made.[3]

ARCHIVAL RESEARCH

Newspaper

I conducted newspaper and congressional archival research in Colombia and Venezuela. In Colombia, I researched the archival records of *Revista Semana* (2002–10), a very serious long-standing political magazine that comes out every week. In Venezuela, I researched of ten years of *El Nacional*'s archives (1998–2010), a long-standing newspaper that comes out every day.

When doing newspaper archival research, it is hard to find a "neutral" media outlet. *Revista Semana* and *El Nacional* are not exceptions. *Semana* had an anti-Uribista slant, while *El Nacional* had an even stronger anti-Chavista slant. I chose them despite their bias for two reasons. First, they provided comprehensive information about the opposition. Chavista or Uribista media outlets are more likely to disregard opposition news than anti-Chavista or anti-Uribista media outlets. Second, they allowed me to do comprehensive archival research in a brief time frame. Newspaper archival research using microfilm or print copies is very time-consuming. In Venezuela, I was able to use *El Nacional*'s electronic database, which speeded up my research.[4] In Colombia – where written media outlets do not have publicly available electronic databases and is hard to do narrow searches using online

There were two or three requests that were not declined, but it was impossible to find a time to meet within those six months.

[3] Given the hostile environment that human rights NGOs and advocacy groups face in Colombia, I cite DeJusticia and CCJ interviewees, broadly as "members of advocacy groups."

[4] Other newspapers were available in print at the National Library. However, they were incomplete. Newspapers like *Ultimas Noticias* or *El Universal* had missing issues in key dates such as April 11–13, 2002.

databases – *Semana* allowed me to do less intensive archival research. Rather than going through eight years of daily issues in a major newspaper, I went through eight years of weekly issues. Given the high quality of this magazine, I am confident that little information was lost.

Congress

I conducted archival research in congress for both countries as well. In Colombia, *Congreso Visible* compiled and made available a comprehensive list of constitutional reforms introduced during Alvaro Uribe's government. Using that list, and information I collected on members of congress's support for the government, I was able to identify sixteen constitutional reforms introduced by the government, in which it sought to increase the legislative and nonlegislative powers of the president and/or extend Uribe's time in office. Using information available online (www.congresovisible.org, www.senado.gov.co, www.camara .gov.co), I was then able to identify which congressional records (*Gacetas del Congreso*) contained the debates and trace the arguments put forward by supporters and detractors throughout. Most of these records were available online (http://svrpubindc.imprenta.gov.co/senado/).

Congressional archival research was more difficult in Venezuela. The Congressional Diaries of the Constitutional Assembly and the Legislative Commission (*Diarios de Debates*) were public and available at the National Assembly Library. Collecting these was a fairly easy task. Unfortunately, starting in 2001, the National Assembly stopped publishing the Congressional Diaries. Although they exist as PDFs at the National Assembly Archive, accessing them when I was doing fieldwork was an impossible task. Unless you were part of the government,[5] you needed to request permission to the National Assembly Secretary to access the files. In order to get that permission, the National Assembly Secretary required documents that I was unable to provide. A couple of National Assembly functionaries tried to give me access to the Congressional Diaries. They were told, however, that it was "dangerous" for them to ask for these files.

Although the National Assembly Archive did not give me full access to the Congressional Diaries, it did give me a list of all the bills that were introduced to the National Assembly between 2000 and 2010. With this list, I was able to go to the Legislative Information Office (*Dirección de Información Legislativa* [*DIL*]), which has the files of all bills approved[6] since 2000. Luckily, these files included copies of the debates. At this office, I was able to photograph and review the debates of fifteen bills (post-1999 referendum bills and organic laws).

[5] In the spring of 2014, the Chavista party (PSUV) controlled the National Assembly. That changed in 2016, when the opposition won a majority of the seats.
[6] This office does not have files of bills that were not approved by the National Assembly. Therefore, I was not able to review the debates of non-sanctioned bills.

Appendix B

The Rise of Presidents with Hegemonic Aspirations

I identify presidents with hegemonic aspirations using a combination of existing and new data. I measured preferences for democracy using Mainwaring and Pérez-Liñán's (2013) dataset and an original database on presidents' attempts to introduce institutional reforms in order to increase their powers and/or extend their time in office, regardless of whether these reforms were successful or not.

The database for the dependent variable includes 134 presidents across eighteen Latin American countries between 1978 and 2019. Countries enter the sample either in 1978 or the year the first democratically elected president came to power. They exit the sample the year the last democratically elected president came to power. See Table B.1 for details.

Mainwaring and Pérez-Liñán (2013) coded governments' normative preference for democracy between 1945 and 2010. With the help of research assistants, I used their coding rules to update that information to 2019, adding thirty presidents to the list (see Table B.2). Mainwaring and Pérez-Liñán (2013) score actors' regime preferences for democracy as strong (1), inconsistent (0.5), or absent (0). I qualified presidents who scored 0 in this measurement as potential autocrats. Twenty-two democratically elected presidents fit this criterion.

I complement Mainwaring and Pérez-Liñán's updated dataset with an original database on presidents' attempts to introduce institutional reforms in order to increase their powers and/or extend their time in office. I gave country experts – political scientists, lawyers, historians, and justices – a list of democratically elected presidents from 1978 to 2013 and asked them to assess whether these leaders had introduced reforms that increased the powers of

Appendices

TABLE B.1. *Presidents by country*

Country	Years Included	No. Presidents
Argentina	1983–2015	7
Bolivia	1982–2006	9
Brazil	1990–2019	7
Chile	1990–2018	7
Colombia	1978–2018	9
Costa Rica	1978–2018	11
Dominican Republic	1978–2012	7
Ecuador[1]	1979–2007	11
El Salvador	1994–2019	6
Guatemala	1986–2016	9
Honduras	1982–2014	9
Mexico	2000–2018	4
Nicaragua	1990–2007	4
Panamá	1994–2019	6
Paraguay	1993–2018	8
Perú	1980–2018	8
Uruguay	1985–2015	7
Venezuela	1979–1999	5

the executive (vis-à-vis courts and congress)[2] and/or increase the president's time in office. The survey also contained follow-up questions, asking the respondents to provide details on the constitutional amendments they said presidents introduced.

---

[1] Ecuador has eleven observations because in several instances, the sitting president was replaced by his vice president. Jaime Roldós (1979–81) died in office and was replaced by Osvaldo Hurtado (1981–4); Jamil Mahuad (1998–2000) was impeached by congress and replaced by his vice president Gustavo Noboa (2000–2); Lucio Gutiérrez was impeached by congress and replaced by his vice president Alfredo Palacios (2005–7). Abdalá Bucaram was also impeached; his successor, Fabián Alarcón, does not appear in the dataset because it is unclear whether he attained power democratically or not.

[2] I used Negretto's (2013) list of characteristics that increase the legislative and nonlegislative powers of the executive.

TABLE B.2. *Presidents added to Mainwaring and Pérez-Liñán database*

Country	Name	Term
Argentina	Mauricio Macri	2015–19
Brazil	Dilma Rousseff	2011–16
	Michel Temer	2016–18
	Jair Bolsonaro	2019–present
Chile	Sebastián Piñera	2010–14
		2018–22
	Michelle Bachelett	2014–18
Costa Rica	Laura Chinchilla	2010–14
	Luis Guillermo Solis	2014–18
Colombia	Juan Manuel Santos	2010–18
	Iván Duque	2018–22
El Salvador	Salvador Sanchez Ceren	2014–19
	Nayib Bukele	2019–present
Guatemala	Otto Pérez Molina	2012–15
	Alejandro Maldonado	2015–16
	Jimmy Morales	2016–19
Honduras	Porfirio Lobo Sosa	2010–14
	Juan Orlando Hernandez	2014–22
Mexico	Enrique Peña Nieto	2012–18
	Andrés Manuel López Obrador	2018–present
Panama	Juan Carlos Varela	2014–19
	Laurentino Cortizo	2019–present
Paraguay	Federico Franco	2012–13
	Horacio Cartes	2013–18
	Mario Abdo Benitez	2018—present
Peru	Ollanta Humala	2011–16
	Pedro Pablo Kuczynski	2016–18
	Martín Vizcarra	2018–20
Dominican Republic	Danilo Medina	2012–20
Uruguay	José Mujica	2010–15
	Tabaré Vásquez	2015–20

I used the experts' surveys as a first step to assess whether presidents had manipulated electoral norms to enhance their powers and stay in office. In cases where the information was unclear, I used the follow-up questions to search for secondary literature that could help clarify or confirm the scores they gave. I also followed up with some of the experts via email in order to get more detailed information and used student research assistants to double-check my final coding and update the information up to 2016. Below, I summarize the overall distribution of amendments attempts.

Out of the 134 presidents in the sample, thirty-six (27 percent), introduced at least one amendment that sought to augment the powers of the executive and twenty-four (18 percent) proposed at least one reform that sought to extend the president's time in office. Of those, eleven (8 percent of the sample)[3] introduced one or more amendments to enhance their powers and one or more amendments to increase their time in office.[4] Seven (6 percent) of them introduced one or more amendments in order to strengthen the powers of the executive and lengthen their time in office beyond a *second* term. Five of them coincide with the twenty-two potential autocrats identified using Mainwaring and Pérez-Liñán's data for president's behavior during government. I added the other two – Alvaro Uribe and Carlos Ménem – to the list.

I further complement this information by assessing a president's normative preference for democracy before she attains power. Whenever possible, I used Mainwaring and Pérez-Liñán's (2013) coding. Many Latin American presidents were relevant actors before they became presidents and have regime preference scores before their presidential term. Others, however, appear for the first time once they become heads of government. I scored the latter executives using information obtained either on Mainwaring and Pérez-Liñán's coder reports and/or primary and secondary sources. Presidents who scored zero in their pre-government normative preference for democracy were qualified as potential autocrats. Fifteen out of the twenty-two presidents classified as potential autocrats based on their normative preference for democracy while in government showed absence of a normative preference for democracy before they attained power as well. The new measurement added only one president to the list: Ollanta Humala (Peru, 2011–16).

MEASURING PERCEPTIONS OF THE ECONOMY

I measure economic perceptions using Latinobarómetro survey data. Since 1995, Latinobarómetro has conducted public opinion surveys across

---

[3] Raúl Alfonsín, Carlos Menem, Evo Morales, Alvaro Uribe, Sixto Durán, Rafael Correa, Manuel Zelaya, Daniel Ortega, Hugo Chávez.

[4] Two of them, Alberto Fujimori and Jorge Serrano Elías, outright closed congress and the courts.

most countries in Latin America.[5] The surveys ask respondents to describe their country's economic situation on a scale from 1 to 5, where 1 is "Very good" and 5 is "Very bad."[6] I inverted the scale to make it more intuitive and created country-year averages. I use the election year average to make a preliminary assessment of the impact that mean economic perceptions have on the likelihood of electing a potential autocrat.

Latinobarómetro has a wealth of data and is the most time-comprehensive public opinion dataset available for Latin America. Unfortunately, it is far from perfect. It does not have data for most presidents elected before 1996 or presidents elected in 1999, 2012, or 2014. It is only available for sixty-four presidents.

MEASURING STATE CRISIS

Following Handlin's (2017) operationalization of state crisis, I measure the first one using the Worldwide Governance Indicators (compiled by the World Bank since 1996, and available in V-Dem's dataset), and the second one using Latinobarómetro (1995–2018) questions regarding trust on institutions. The WGI has six governance indicators. Following Handlin (2017a, 271–5), I create a state-performance index averaging three of these indicators—control of corruption, government effectiveness, and rule of law – in a –2.5–2.5 scale. I use the average state performance in election year for the analysis. While imperfect (Apaza 2009), the WGI indicators have not only been widely used to assess state performance, but also they are available for most years since 1996 and are highly correlated (0.88) with Hanson and Sigman's state capacity indicator.

Latinobarómetro has several questions regarding trust in institutions. Following Handlin's operationalization as well, I use three of these questions – confidence in congress, courts, and the police – to build a trust in institutions index. The questions ask how much confidence respondents have on each of these institutions, and measures the response on a 1–4 scale, where 1 is "A lot of confidence" and 4 is "No confidence."[7] I inverted the scale for each variable and, following Handlin's formula (2017a, 271–5), averaged them together to create an individual "trust in institutions" index. I then averaged that index for each country-year. I use mean trust on institutions on election year in the analysis.

---

[5] The survey has been conducted every year except 1999, 2012, and 2014. Argentina, Brazil, Chile, México, Paraguay, Peru, and Venezuela have been surveyed since 1995. Dominican Republic has been surveyed since 2004. All other countries have been surveyed since 1996.

[6] The question is, *In general, how would you describe the present economic situation of the country?* This question was asked every year, for which there is data available.

[7] Question: *How much trust/confidence do you have in each of the following groups/institutions [Police, National Congress/Parliament, Judicial Branch]?* 1 "A Lot," 2 "Some," 3 "Little," 4 "No."

Appendices

MEASURING EROSION OF DEMOCRACY

TABLE B.3. *Indicator for democratic erosion*

NELDA Variables	V-Dem Variables
In the run-up to the election, were there allegations of media bias in favor of the incumbent? *(nelda16)*	In this national election, was there evidence of other intentional irregularities by incumbent and/or opposition parties, and/or vote fraud? *(v2elirreg)*
Is there evidence that the government harassed the opposition? *(nelda15)*	Taking all aspects of the preelection period, election day, and the postelection process into account, would you consider this national election to be free and fair? *(v2elfrfair)*
Were opposition leaders prevented from running? *(nelda13)*	In this national election, were opposition candidates/parties/ campaign workers subjected to repression, intimidation, violence, or harassment by the government, the ruling party, or their agents? *(v2elintim)*
Did some opposition leaders boycott the election? *(nelda14)*	Does the government directly or indirectly attempt to censor the print or broadcast media? *(v2mcenefm)*
Before elections, were there significant concerns that elections will not be free and fair? *(nelda11)*	Is there self-censorship among journalists when reporting on issues that the government considers politically sensitive? *(v2meslfcen)*
	How restrictive are the barriers to forming a party? *(v2psbars)*

Appendix C

Experts Survey

SURVEY DETAILS

I sent out seventy surveys. Fifty-nine (84 percent) of the country experts opened the survey, but only forty-two (57 percent) of them finished it. The response rate was 57 percent, which gave most countries two to three coders. Dominican Republic, El Salvador, Nicaragua, Paraguay, and Uruguay have a single coder. For Colombia, I did not use country experts. I coded the country myself using congressional records.

SURVEY TEXT

1. Please select the country about which you will answer the questions
   a. Argentina
   b. Bolivia
   c. Brasil
   d. Chile
   e. Colombia
   f. Costa Rica
   g. Ecuador
   h. El Salvador
   i. Guatemala
   j. Honduras
   k. Mexico
   l. Nicaragua
   m. Panama
   n. Paraguay
   o. Peru
   p. Uruguay

q. Venezuela

r. República Dominicana

2. For all [COUNTRY] presidents since [1978 OR YEAR OF FIRST DEMOCRATIC ELECTION], please select below which introduced a constitutional reform in order to enhance the powers of the presidency and/or extend his/her time in office.

Your answer should reflect the constitutional reforms and/or referendum that the president, members of his cabinet or members of his legislative coalition introduced to congress, the courts or the people (regardless of whether they were approved or not). It should not reflect constitutional reforms that the president, members of his cabinet, or members of his legislative coalition said they would do but never formalized.

If no president since 1990 has ever introduced a constitutional reform in order to enhance the powers of the presidency or extend his/her time in office, please select the boxes for the line that says "No president" at the end of the list.

	Enhance Powers of the Presidency	Increase the President's Term in Office
[PRESIDENT NAME AND TERM] (1)		
[PRESIDENT NAME AND TERM] (2)		
[PRESIDENT NAME AND TERM] (2)		
NO PRESIDENT		

3. The next questions ask for details about the answers previously provided. For each president you selected, there is a list of types of reforms. To the extent you can remember, please select the type(s) of reform(s) each president introduced and as many details as you can recall about these reforms. Any information you can provide will be very useful.

4. Please select the type(s) of reforms that [PRESIDENT NAME], members in his cabinet or his coalition in congress, introduced between [PRESIDENT TERM]. Whenever possible, please write any detail you can remember about the reform(s) (i.e., date, characteristics, title, number, etc.).

	Select All that Apply	Provide Details
Reforms that increase the presidential term and/or allow for immediate reelection		
Reforms that increase the president's ability to appoint or dismiss cabinet members without congress or the court's oversight		
Reforms that increase political or administrative centralization		
Reforms that increase the president's emergency powers		
Reforms that increase the president's control over the budget		
Reforms that create areas of exclusive legislation for the president		
Reforms that increase the decree powers of the president		
Reforms that increase the obstacles to override a presidential veto		
Reforms that increase the president's control over legislative meetings		
Reforms that decrease congress or court's ability to question or censure executive branch officials		
Reforms that decrease the congress ability to impeach the president		
Reforms that decrease the autonomy of the legislative		
Reforms that increase the president's power to call for referendums		
Reforms that increase the president's control over the appointment of court magistrates or members of oversight agencies		
Reforms that decrease judicial review		
Other (please specify in the space provided for details)		

Appendix D

Other Analyses Stage 1

DIFFERENCES IN MEANS AND DISTRIBUTION ACROSS
POTENTIAL AUTOCRATS

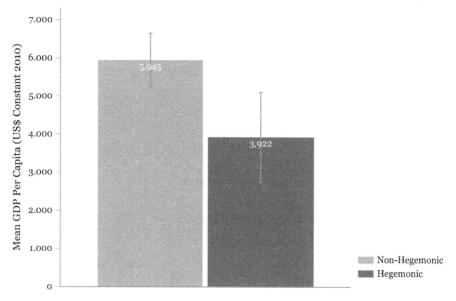

Source: World Bank Economic Indicators

FIGURE D.1. Mean GDP per capita by potential autocrats

TABLE D.1. *Potential autocrats above/below Latin American mean GDP PC*

	Below LA Average	Above LA Average	Total
Nonhegemonic	59	47	106
Hegemonic	21	4	25
Total	80	51	131

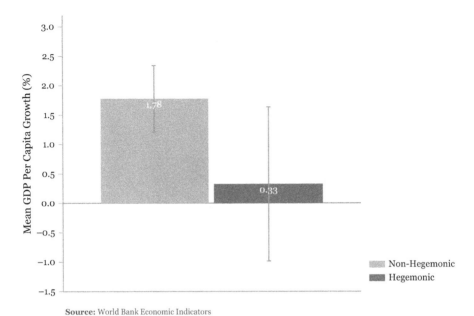

Source: World Bank Economic Indicators

FIGURE D.2. Mean GDP per capita growth by potential autocrats

TABLE D.2. *Potential autocrats above/below Latin American mean GDP PC growth*

	Below LA Average	Above LA Average	Total
Nonhegemonic	46	60	106
Hegemonic	16	9	25
Total	62	69	131

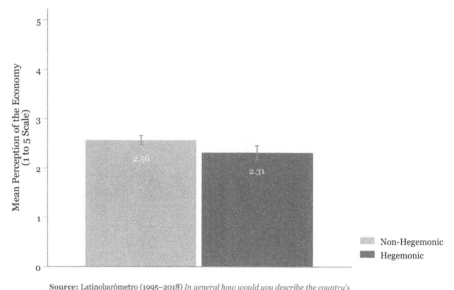

Source: Latinobarómetro (1995–2018) *In general how would you describe the country's present economic situation? Would you say it is 1 'Very Good', 2 'Good', 3 'About Average' 4 'Bad' or 5 'Very Bad' (reversed)*

FIGURE D.3. Mean perception of the economy by potential autocrats

TABLE D.3. *Potential autocrats above/below Latin American mean perception of the economy*

	Below LA Average	Above LA Average	Total
Nonhegemonic	23	28	51
Hegemonic	10	3	13
Total	33	31	64

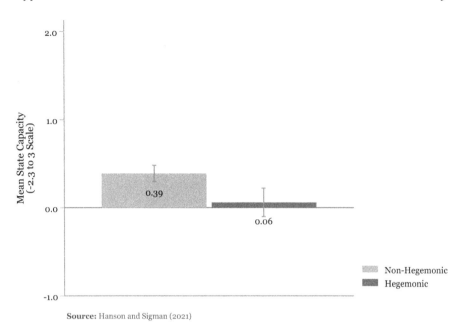

Source: Hanson and Sigman (2021)

FIGURE D.4. Mean state capacity by potential autocrats

TABLE D.4. *Potential autocrats above/below Latin American mean state capacity*

	Below LA Average	Above LA Average	Total
Nonhegemonic	51	50	101
Hegemonic	19	4	23
Total	70	54	124

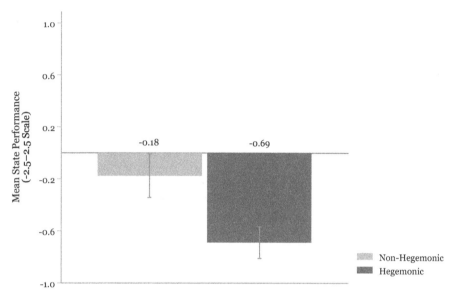

Source: Author's index using World Bank Governance Indicators for Control of Corruption, Government Effectiveness and Rule of Law

FIGURE D.5. Mean state performance by potential autocrats

TABLE D.5. *Potential autocrats above/below Latin American mean state performance*

	Below LA Average	Above LA Average	Total
Nonhegemonic	30	25	55
Hegemonic	14	0	14
Total	44	25	69

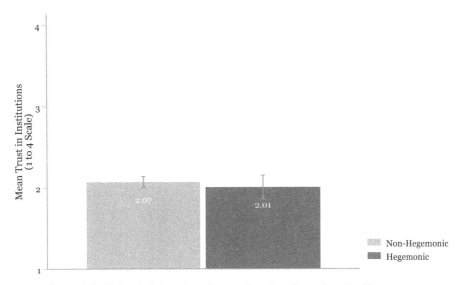

Source: Author's index using Latinobarómetro (1995–2018) questions: *How much trust/confidence do you have in each of the following groups/institutions [Police, National, Congress/Parliament, Judicial Branch]? 1 'A lot' 2 'Some', 3 'Little', 4 'None' (reversed)*

FIGURE D.6. Mean trust in institutions by potential autocrats

TABLE D.6. *Potential autocrats above/below Latin American mean trust in institutions*

	Below LA Average	Above LA Average	Total
Nonhegemonic	24	27	51
Hegemonic	8	5	13
Total	32	32	64

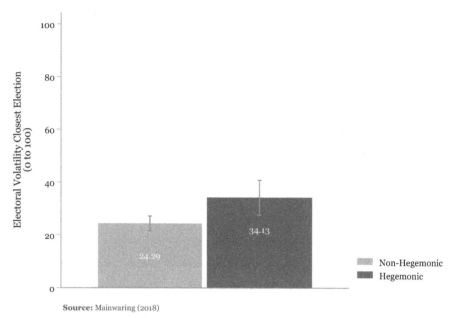

Source: Mainwaring (2018)

FIGURE D.7. Mean LH volatility by potential autocrats

TABLE D.7. *Potential autocrats above/below Latin American mean LH volatility*

	Below LA Average	Above LA Average	Total
Nonhegemonic	61	36	97
Hegemonic	8	16	24
Total	69	52	121

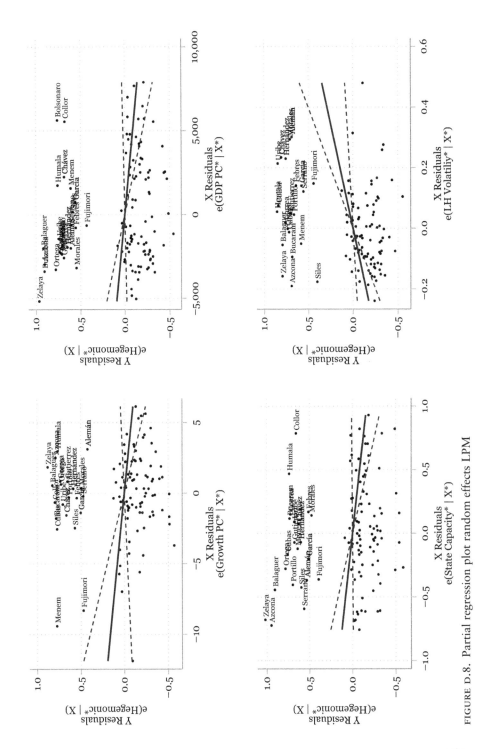

FIGURE D.8. Partial regression plot random effects LPM

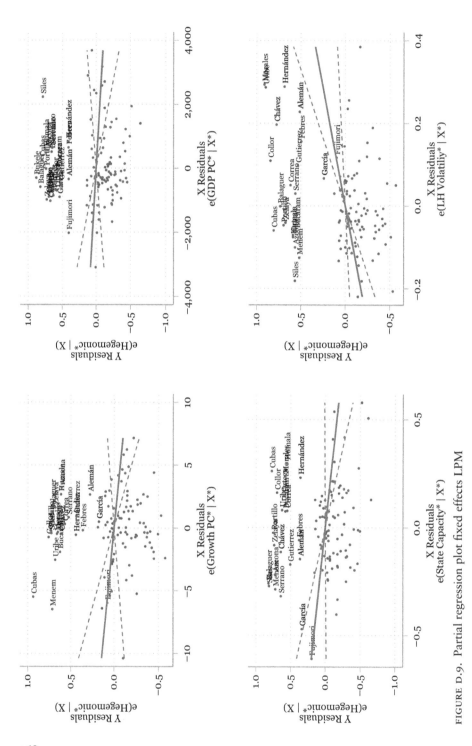

FIGURE D.9. Partial regression plot fixed effects LPM

TABLE D.8. *Potential autocrats scores for election year independent variables*

Name	GDP PC (US$ Const)	GDP PC Growth (%)	Perceptions of the Economy (1–5)	State Capacity (–2.3 to 3)	State Performance (–2.5 to 2.5)	Trust Institutions (1–5)	LH Volatility (1–100)	Inter-Branch Crises (0–1)	Constitutional Changes (0–1)	Combined Index (–1.5 to 1.5)
Carlos Menem	6,497	–8.54		0.08			17.63	0.25	0.00	–0.31
Hernan Siles Zuazo	1,649	–3.45		–0.75			21.69			–1.17
Evo Morales	1,700	2.57	2.41	0.32	–0.73	1.88	65.14	0.29	0.17	–0.53
Fernando Collor de M.	8,390	1.37		0.89			35.62	0.09	0.50	0.16
Jair Bolsonaro	11,131	0.99	2.14		–0.37	2.12	28.92	0.09	0.85	–0.14
Alvaro Uribe	4,914	0.95	2.21	0.30	–0.46	2.05	47.75	0.18	0.54	–0.40
Leon Febres	3,615	0.09		0.12			47.45	0.00	0.60	–0.48
Abdala Bucaram	3,826	–0.42	2.52	0.37	–0.54	2.17	23.01	0.64	0.47	–0.33
Lucio Gutierrez	3,827	2.28	2.34	0.23	–0.81	1.67	38.21	0.61	0.52	–0.72
Rafael Correa	4,372	2.67	2.65	0.50	–0.93	1.62	33.99	0.82	0.44	–0.61
Nayib Bukele	3,581	2.11			–0.59		11.63	0.00	0.28	0.21
Jorge Serrano Elias	2,162	0.32		–0.53			45.30	0.00	0.25	–0.53
Alfonso A. Portillo	2,500	1.42		–0.07			36.03	0.38	0.15	–0.40
Roberto Suazo	1,523	–4.21		–0.32						–1.46
Jose Azcona del Hoyo	1,497	2.51		–0.33			4.21	1.00	0.67	–0.87
Jose Manuel Zelaya	1,779	3.55	2.36	0.09	–0.75	2.35	6.11	0.05	0.74	–0.03

(continued)

TABLE D.8. (*continued*)

Name	GDP PC	GDP PC Growth	Perceptions of the Economy	State Capacity	State Performance	Trust Institutions	LH Volatility	Inter-Branch Crises	Constitutional Changes	Combined Index
Juan O. Hernandez	2,001	0.95	2.12	0.13	-0.95	1.70	44.19	0.03	0.66	-0.76
Arnoldo Aleman	1,152	4.34	1.93	-0.20	-0.55	2.52	61.53	0.50	0.33	-0.58
Daniel Ortega	1,447	2.73	2.21	0.16	-0.77	1.98	29.80	0.50	0.31	-0.49
Raul Cubas	3,862	-2.08	2.01	0.19	-1.09	2.20	18.60	0.33	0.17	-0.40
Alan Garcia	3,265	-0.28		-0.21			49.80		0.00	-0.52
Alberto Fujimori	2,650	-6.95		-0.39			50.95	0.00	0.10	-0.82
Ollanta Humala	5,360	5.47	2.87	0.74	-0.32	1.90	37.84	0.00	0.16	0.36
Joaquin Balaguer	2,625	1.44		-0.20			18.72	0.00	0.00	0.12
Hugo Chavez	12,726	-1.65	2.28	0.26	-0.80	1.93	44.95	0.14	0.08	-0.14

TABLE D.9. *Potential autocrats' scores for independent variables during president's term*

Name	Mean GDP PC	Mean GDP PC Growth	Mean Fuel Exports	Mean Approval	Mean Polarization	Combined Index	Combined Index w/weak institutions
	(US$ Const)	(%)	(%)	(%)	(−3.5 to 3.5)	(−1.2 to 1.3)	(−1.2 to 9.5)
Carlos Menem	7,711	2.69	10.55	41.10	−0.01	0.17	−0.25
Hernan Siles Zuazo	1,396	−3.94	52.27		0.29	−0.29	−0.29
Evo Morales	1,989	3.35	48.00	50.75	0.91	0.56	0.20
Fernando Collor de M.	7,913	−2.42	1.72	31.03	1.42	−0.25	−0.04
Jair Bolsonaro	11,203	0.65	13.45	35.99	2.99	0.63	0.95
Alvaro Uribe	5,744	3.24	42.43	64.54	0.79	0.93	0.84
Leon Febres	3,672	0.75	48.35	39.92	−0.14	0.09	0.31
Abdala Bucaram	3,932	1.67	25.84	51.66	0.29	0.25	0.29
Lucio Gutierrez	3,989	3.70	49.41	47.00	0.47	0.58	0.57
Rafael Correa	4,787	2.80	57.14	68.73	1.45	1.15	0.91
Nayib Bukele	3,581	2.11	3.37		0.78	0.01	−0.09
Jorge Serrano Elias	2,205	1.52		54.73	1.60	0.40	0.13
Alfonso A. Portillo	2,547	0.71	6.68	31.12	−0.75	−0.60	−0.64
Roberto Suazo	1,455	−0.37	0.55		−2.04	−0.98	−0.98

(continued)

TABLE D.9. (*continued*)

Name	Mean GDP PC	Mean GDP PC Growth	Mean Fuel Exports	Mean Approval	Mean Polarization	Combined Index	Combined Index w/weak institutions
Jose Azcona del Hoyo	1,561	1.10	0.14	43.45	-2.16	-0.69	-0.18
Jose Manuel Zelaya	1,902	1.36	3.97	44.19	-1.29	-0.46	0.06
Juan O. Hernandez	2,095	2.13	0.22	46.60	-0.08	-0.19	0.17
Arnoldo Aleman	1,249	2.66	1.19	37.02	0.31	-0.29	-0.24
Daniel Ortega	1,645	2.77	0.63	53.65	0.33	0.03	-0.03
Raul Cubas	3,730	-3.42	0.15	41.28	-1.31	-0.83	-0.80
Alan Garcia	3,211	-3.66	12.86	35.42	0.13	-0.64	-0.83
Alberto Fujimori	2,622	-1.15	6.10	40.68	0.36	-0.40	-0.56
Ollanta Humala	5,987	3.17	10.08	21.66	-0.13	-0.24	-0.38
Joaquin Balaguer	2,959	2.57	0.01		1.11	0.05	-0.41
Hugo Chavez	12,857	1.32	86.59	47.22	1.30	1.35	0.66

Appendix E

Presidents Approval in Colombia and Venezuela

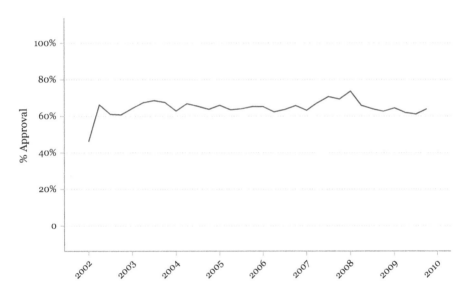

Source: Executive Approval Project 2.0 (Carlin et.al. 2019)

FIGURE E.I. Alvaro Uribe's approval rating (quarterly)

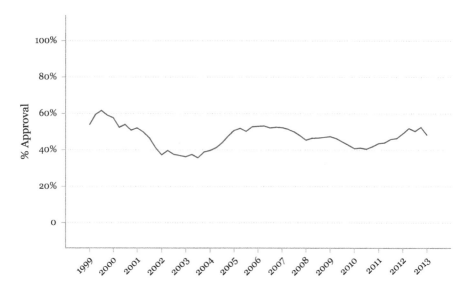

Source: Executive Approval Project 2.0 (Carlin et.al. 2019)

FIGURE E.2. Hugo Chávez's approval rating (quarterly)

References

Abi-Hassan, Sahar. 2019. "Populism in Venezuela: The Role of the Opposition." In *The Ideational Approach to Populism*, edited by Kirk A. Hawkins, Ryan E. Carlin, Levente Littvay, and Cristóbal Rovira Rovira Kaltwasser, 311–25. New York: Routledge.

Alarcón, Benigno, Ángel E. Álvarez, and Manuel Hidalgo. 2016. "Can Democracy Win in Venezuela?" *Journal of Democracy* 27 (2): 20–34. https://doi.org/10.1353/jod .2016.0030.

Albarracín, Juan, Laura Gamboa, and Scott Mainwaring. 2018. "Deinstitutionalization without Collapse: Colombia Party System." In *Latin America Party Systems: Institutionalization, Decay and Collapse*, edited by Scott Mainwaring, 227–54. New York: Cambridge University Press.

Aldrich, John H. 1995. *Why Parties? The Origin and Transformation of Politicalparties in America*. Chicago: The University of Chicago Press.

Alegrett, Raúl. 2003. "Evolución y Tendencias de Las Reformas Agrarias En América Latina." 2003/2. Reforma Agraria Colonización y Cooperativas. Food and Agriculture Organization. www.fao.org/docrep/006/j0415t/j0415tob.htm#fn29.

Alesina, Alberto, Arnaud Devleeschauwer, William Esterly, Sergio Kurlat, and Romain Wacziarg. 2003. "Fractionalization." *Journal of Economic Growth* 8 (2): 155–94.

Andersen, David, Jørgen Møller, Lasse Lykke Rørbæk, and Svend-Erik Skaaning. 2014. "State Capacity and Political Regime Stability." *Democratization* 21 (7): 1305–25.

Anria, Santiago. 2016. "More Inclusion, Less Liberalism in Bolivia." *Journal of Democracy* 27 (3): 99–108. https://doi.org/10.1353/jod.2016.0037.

——— 2018. *When Movements Become Parties: The Bolivian MAS in Comparative Perspective*. Cambridge Studies in Comparative Politics. New York: Cambridge University Press.

Apaza, Carmen R. 2009. "Measuring Governance and Corruption through the Worldwide Governance Indicators: Critiques, Responses, and Ongoing Scholarly Discussion." *PS: Political Science and Politics* 42 (1): 139–43.

Applebaum, Anne. 2017. "The Polish Government Is Cracking Down on Private Media – In the Name of Combating 'Fake News.'" *Washington Post*, December

11, 2017, sec. Global Opinions. www.washingtonpost.com/news/global-opinions/
wp/2017/12/11/the-polish-government-is-cracking-down-on-private-media-in-the-
name-of-combating-fake-news/.

Arceneaux, Craig, and David Pion-Berlin. 2007. "Issues, Threats, and Institutions:
Explaining OAS Responses to Democratic Dilemmas in Latin America." *Latin
American Politics and Society* 49 (2): 1–31.

Archila, Mauricio. 2011. "Latin American Social Movements at the Start of the Twenty-
First Century: A Colombian Case Study." *Labor: Studies in Working-Class History
of the Americas* 8 (1): 57–74.

Aydogan, Abdullah. 2018. "Why the Results of Turkey's Election Are Surprising."
Monkey Cage – Washington Post (blog), July 31, 2018. www.washingtonpost
.com/news/monkey-cage/wp/2018/07/31/why-the-results-of-turkeys-election-are-
surprising/?utm_term=.bbd5758643e7.

Azcui, Mabel. 2007. "La 'guerra' entre Sucre y La Paz enciende Bolivia." *El País*, July
23, 2007, sec. Internacional. https://elpais.com/diario/2007/07/23/internacional/
1185141611_850215.html.

Balderacchi, Claudio. 2017. "Political Leadership and the Construction of Competitive
Authoritarian Regimes in Latin America: Implications and Prospects for
Democracy." *Democratization* 25 (3): 504–23.

Bánkuti, Miklós, Gábor Halmai, and Kim Lane Scheppele. 2015. "Hungary's Illiberal
Turn: Disabling the Constitution." In *The Hungarian Patient: Social Opposition to
an Illiberal Democracy*, edited by Peter Krasztev and Jon Van Til, 1–33. Budapest:
Central European University Press.

Bardakçi, Mehmet. 2013. "Coup Plots and the Transformation of Civil–Military
Relations in Turkey under AKP Rule." *Turkish Studies* 14 (3): 411–28. https://doi
.org/10.1080/14683849.2013.831256.

Bartels, Larry M. 1986. "Issue Voting under Uncertainty: An Empirical Test." *American
Journal of Political Science* 30 (4): 709–28.

Basabe Serrano, Santiago, and John Polga Hecimovich. 2013. "Legislative Coalitions
and Judicial Turnover under Political Uncertainty: The Case of Ecuador." *Political
Research Quarterly* 66 (1): 154–66.

Batory, Agnes. 2014. "Uploading as Political Strategy: The European Parliament and the
Hungarian Media Law Debate." *East European Politics* 30 (2): 230–45.

2016a. "Defying the Commission: Creative Compliance and Respect for the Rule of Law
in the EU." *Public Administration* (3): 685. https://doi.org/10.1111/padm.12254.

2016b. "Populists in Government? Hungary's 'System of National Cooperation.'"
Democratization 23 (2): 283–303.

Baykan, Toygar Sinan, Yaprak Gürsoy, and Pierre Ostiguy. 2021. "Anti-Populist Coups
d'état in the Twenty-First Century: Reasons, Dynamics and Consequences." *Third
World Quarterly* 42 (4): 793–811. https://doi.org/10.1080/01436597.2020
.1871329.

Bejarano, Ramiro, Iván Cepeda, Daniel Coronell, Vladimir Florez, Adam Isacson,
Alfredo Molano, Hollman Morris, Germán Navas Talero, et al. 2010. "La
Justicia Sitiada." In *Las Perlas Uribistas*, 11–24. Bogotá: Debate.

Bennett, Andrew. 2010. "Process Tracing and Causal Inference." In *Rethinking Social
Inquiry: Diverse Tools, Shared Standards*, edited by Henry E. Brady and David
Collier, 207–19. Lanham, MD: Rowman & Littlefield.

Bennett, Andrew, and Jeffrey T. Checkel. 2015. "Process Tracing: From Philosophical Roots to Best Practices." In *Process Tracing: From Metaphor to Analytic Tool*, edited by Andrew Bennett and Jeffrey T. Checkel, 3–38. Cambridge: Cambridge University Press.

Berendt, Joanna. 2017. "Opposition Party in Poland Ends Monthlong Occupation of Parliament." *The New York Times*, January 12, 2017. www.nytimes.com/2017/01/12/world/europe/poland-parliament-protest-opposition.html?login=email&auth=login-email.

Berendt, Joanna, and Marc Santora. 2018. "In Poland Elections, Populists Fail to Sway Moderates, Exit Polls Suggest." *The New York Times*, October 22, 2018, sec. World. www.nytimes.com/2018/10/21/world/europe/poland-elections-2018-populists.html.

Berinsky, Adam J., and Jeffrey B Lewis. 2007. "An Estimate of Risk Aversion in the US Electorate." *Quarterly Journal of Political Science* 2 (2): 139–54.

Berman, Sheri. 1998. *The Social Democratic Moment: Ideas and Politics in the Making of Interwar Europe*. Cambridge, MA: Harvard University Press.

Bermeo, Nancy. 1997. "Myths of Moderation: Confrontation and Conflict during Democratic Transitions." *Comparative Politics* 29 (3): 305.

———. 2016. "On Democratic Backsliding." *Journal of Democracy* 27 (1): 5–19. https://doi.org/10.1353/jod.2016.0012.

Bermúdez, Jaime. 2010. *La Audacia Del Poder: Momentos Claves Del Primer Gobierno de Uribe Contados Por Uno de Sus Protagonistas*. Bogotá: Planeta.

Bernhard, Michael, Allen Hicken, Christopher Reenock, and Staffan I. Lindberg. 2015. "Institutional Subsystems and the Survival of Democracy: Do Political and Civil Society Matter?" Varieties of Democracy Working Papers. www.v-dem.net/media/filer_public/62/8e/628e4e08-ffb4-45ee-84c5-a25032d1b0dc/v-dem_working_paper_2015_4.pdf.

Bilewicz, Michał. 2017. "Poland's Ruling Party Tried a Judicial Power Grab and Then Saw It Backfire. Here Is Why." *Monkey Cage – Washington Post* (blog), July 31, 2017. www.washingtonpost.com/news/monkey-cage/wp/2017/07/31/polands-ruling-party-tried-a-judicial-power-grab-and-then-saw-it-backfire-heres-why/?utm_term=.faedffa1f1a0.

Bojar, Abel. 2016. "Fidesz and Electoral Reform: How to Safeguard Hungarian Democracy." *Europpblog* (blog), March 21, 2016. http://blogs.lse.ac.uk/europpblog/2016/03/21/fidesz-and-electoral-reform-how-to-safeguard-hungarian-democracy/.

———. 2017. "Hungary in 2017: Could the Left and Far-Right Unite to Keep Orban out of Power?" *EUROPP* (blog), January 10, 2017. http://blogs.lse.ac.uk/europpblog/2017/01/10/hungary-2017-left-and-far-right-unite-to-keep-orban-out/.

Booth, John A., and Mitchell A. Seligson. 2009. *The Legitimacy Puzzle in Latin America: Political Support and Democracy in Eight Nations*. New York: Cambridge University Press.

Borda, Sandra. 2012. "La Administración de Alvaro Uribe y Su Política Exterior En Materia de Derechos Humanos: De La Negación a La Contención Estratégica." *Análisis Político* 25 (75): 111–37.

Boris, János, and Gyóry Vári. 2015. "The Road of the Hungarian Solidarity Movement." In *The Hungarian Patient: Social Opposition to an Illiberal*

Democracy, edited by Peter Krasztev and Jon Van Til, 181–205. Budapest: Central European University Press.

Botero Marino, Catalina, and Juan Fernando Jaramillo. 2006. "El Conflicto de Las Altas Cortes Colombianas En Torno a La Tutela Contra Sentencias." *Foro Constitucional Iberoamericano*, no. 12: 42–81.

Botero, Sandra, and Laura Gamboa. 2021. "Corte al Congreso: Poder Judicial y Trámite Legislativo En Colombia." *Latin American Research Review* 56 (3): 592–606. http://doi.org/10.25222/larr.757.

Bozóki, András. 2015. "Broken Democracy, Predatory State, and Nationalist Populism." In *The Hungarian Patient: Social Opposition to an Illiberal Democracy*, edited by Peter Krasztev and Jon Van Til, 1–33. Budapest: Central European University Press.

Bozóki, András, and Dániel Hegedűs. 2018. "An Externally Constrained Hybrid Regime: Hungary in the European Union." *Democratization* 25 (7): 1173–89. https://doi.org/10.1080/13510347.2018.1455664.

Breuer, Anita. 2008. "Policymaking by Referendum in Presidential Systems: Evidence from the Bolivian and Colombian Cases." *Latin American Politics and Society* 50 (4): 59–89.

Brewer Carías, Allan-Randolph. 2008. *Historia Constitucional de Venezuela*. Vol. 2. Caracas: Editorial Alfa.

Brewer-Carías, Allan Randolph. 2000. "El Desequilibrio Entre Soberanía Popular y Supremacía Constitucional y La Salida Constituyente En Venezuela En 1999." *Revista Anuario Iberoamericano de Justicia Constitucional* 3: 31–56.

2010. *Dismantling Democracy in Venezuela: The Chávez Authoritarian Experiment*. New York: Cambridge University Press.

Brinks, Daniel, and Michael Coppedge. 2006. "Diffusion Is No Illusion: Neighbor Emulation in the Third Wave of Democracy." *Comparative Political Studies* 39 (4): 463–89. https://doi.org/10.1177/0010414005276666.

Brinks, Daniel M., Steven Levitsky, and María Victoria Murillo. 2020. "The Political Origins of Institutional Weakness." In *The Politics of Institutional Weakness in Latin America*, edited by Daniel M. Brinks, Steven Levitsky, and María Victoria Murillo, 1–40. Cambridge: Cambridge University Press. https://doi.org/10.1017/9781108776608.

Brownlee, Jason. 2007. *Authoritarianism in An Age of Democratization*. New York: Cambridge University Press.

Brownlee, Jason, Tarek Masoud, and Andrew Reynolds. 2013. "Why the Modest Harvest?" *Journal of Democracy* 24 (4): 29–44.

Buitrago, Miguel. 2010. "Bolivia: How Absolute Is Morales' Power?" GIGA Focus International Edition. Hamburg: GIGA German Institute of Global and Area Studies – Leibniz-Institut für Globale und Regionale Studien. https://nbn-resolving.org/urn:nbn:de:0168-ssoar-274291.

Bunce, Valerie, and Sharon L Wolchik. 2011. *Defeating Authoritarian Leaders in Postcommunist Countries*. Cambridge: Cambridge University Press.

Buzogány, Aron. 2017. "Illiberal Democracy in Hungary: Authoritarian Diffusion or Domestic Causation?" *Democratization* 24 (7): 1307–25. https://doi.org/10.1080/13510347.2017.1328676.

Cameron, Maxwell A. 2018. "Making Sense of Competitive Authoritarianism: Lessons from the Andes." *Latin American Politics & Society* 60 (2): 1–22. https://doi.org/10.1017/lap.2018.3.

Capoccia, Giovanni. 2007. *Defending Democracy: Reactions to Extremism in Interwar Europe*. Baltimore, MD: John Hopkins University Press.

Cárdenas, Mauricio, Roberto Junguito, and Mónica Pachón. 2008. "Political Institutions and Policy Outcomes in Colombia: The Effects of the 1991 Constitution." In *Policymaking in Latin America: How Politics Shapes Policies*, edited by Pablo T. Spiller, Ernesto Stein, Mariano Tommasi, and Carlos Scartascini, 199–242. Washington, DC: Inter-American Development Bank; David Rockefeller Center for Latin American Studies.

Carey, John M. 2003. "The Reelection Debate in Latin America." *Latin American Politics and Society* 45 (1): 119–33.

Carlin, Ryan E., Jonathan Hartlyn, Timothy Hellwig, Gregory J. Love, Cecilia Martinez-Gallardo, and Matthew M. Singer. 2019. "Executive Approval Database 2.0." www.executiveapproval.org.

Carlin, Ryan E., Gregory J. Love, and Cecilia Martínez-Gallardo. 2015. "Cushioning the Fall: Scandals, Economic Conditions, and Executive Approval." *Political Behavior* 37 (1): 109–30. https://doi.org/10.1007/s11109-014-9267-3.

Carlin, Ryan E., and Matthew M. Singer. 2011. "Support for Polyarchy in the Americas." *Comparative Political Studies* 44 (11): 1500–26. https://doi.org/10 .1177/0010414011407471.

Carreras, Miguel. 2012. "The Rise of Outsiders in Latin America, 1980–2010: An Institutionalist Perspective." *Comparative Political Studies* 45 (12): 1451–82.

Carrillo, Silvio. 2017. "America's Blind Eye to Honduras's Tyrant." *The New York Times*, December 19, 2017, sec. Opinion. www.nytimes.com/2017/12/19/opinion/ america-honduras-hernandez-trump.html.

Carroll, Royce, and Monica Pachón. 2016. "The Unrealized Potential of Presidential Coalitions in Colombia." In *Legislative Institutions and Lawmaking in Latin America*, edited by Eduardo Alemán and George Tsebelis, 122–47. Oxford: Oxford University Press.

Carter Center. 2005. "Observing the Venezuela Presidential Recall Referendum: Comprehensive Report." *Carter Center*. www.cartercenter.org/documents/2020.pdf.

——— 2009. "Misión de Observación Del Proceso de Empadronamiento En Bolivia 2009 – Informe Final." Altanta, GA: The Carter Center.

Castagnola, Andrea, and Aníbal Pérez-Liñán. 2011. "Bolivia: The Rise (and Fall) of Judicial Review." In *Courts in Latin America*, edited by Gretchen Helmke and Julio Ríos Figueroa, 278–305. New York: Cambridge University Press.

Castle, Stephen. 2011. "Hungarian Leader Takes on Foreign Critics." *The New York Times*, January 6, 2011, sec. Europe. www.nytimes.com/2011/01/07/world/europe/ 07iht-hungary07.html.

Centellas, Miguel. 2011. "*Countries at the Crossroads 2011: Bolivia*." Countries at the Crossroads. Washington, DC: Freedom House. https://freedomhouse.org/report/ countries-crossroads/countries-crossroads-2011.

Centro de Nacional de Memoria Historica. n.d. "¡Basta Ya! Colombia: Memorias de Guerra y Dignidad." ¡Basta Ya! Colombia: Memorias de Guerra y Dignidad. Accessed February 8, 2016. www.centrodememoriahistorica.gov.co/micrositios/ informeGeneral/descargas.html.

Chapman, Annabelle. 2017. "Pluralism Under Attack: The Assault on Press Freedom in Poland." *Special Report*. Washington, DC: Freedom House. https://freedomhouse .org/report/special-reports/assault-press-freedom-poland.

Cheibub, José Antônio. 2007. *Presidentialism, Parliamentarism, and Democracy.* *Cambridge Studies in Comparative Politics.* New York: Cambridge University Press.

Chenoweth, Erica. 2020. "The Future of Nonviolent Resistance." *Journal of Democracy* 31 (3): 69–84. https://doi.org/10.1353/jod.2020.0046.

Cienski, Jan, and Jo Harper. 2016. "Hipster behind Poland's Anti-Government Resistance." *Politico,* April 19, 2016. "Today they walk under the red-and-white banner, but they despise Poland," Kaczyński, the leader of PiS, said in a recent speech. He's also accused Kijowski's movement, called the Committee for the Defense of Democracy (KOD), of acting on behalf of "foreign forces" which want Poland to be "something like a colony."

Cingolani, Luciana. 2013. *"The State of State Capacity: A Review of Concepts,* Evidence and Measures." UNU-MERIT.

Cleary, Matthew R., and Aykut Öztürk. 2020. "When Does Backsliding Lead to Breakdown? Uncertainty and Opposition Strategies in Democracies at Risk." *Perspectives on Politics,* 20 (1): 205–21. https://doi.org/10.1017/S1537592720003667.

Coban, Mustafa. 2017. "How Erdoğan Subjected Turkey to a Year of Cynical Doublespeak." *The Conversation* (blog), December 21, 2017. http://theconversation.com/how-erdogan-subjected-turkey-to-a-year-of-cynical-double speak-89112.

Commission of the European Communities. 2009. "Turkey 2009 Progress Report." SEC(2009) 1334, Brussels. www.europarl.europa.eu/cmsdata/61457/att_20091125ATT65266-3799513575359405127.pdf.

———. 2010. "Turkey 2010 Progress Report." SEC(2010) 1327, Brussels. https://ec.europa.eu/neighbourhood-enlargement/sites/near/files/pdf/key_documents/2010/package/tr_rapport_2010_en.pdf.

———. 2011. "Turkey 2011 Progress Report." SEC(2011) 1201, Brussels. https://ec.europa.eu/neighbourhood-enlargement/sites/near/files/pdf/key_documents/2011/package/tr_rapport_2011_en.pdf.

Coppedge, Michael. 2005. "Explaining Democratic Deterioration in Venezuela through Nested Inference." In *The Third Wave of Democratization in Latin America: Advances and Setbacks,* edited by Frances Hagopian and Scott Mainwaring, 289–316. New York: Cambridge University Press.

———. 2012. *Democratization and Research Methods.* New York: Cambridge University Press.

Coppedge, Michael, John Gerring, Carl Henrik Knutsen, Staffan I. Lindberg, Jan Teorell, David Altman, Michael Bernhard, et al. 2021. *V-Dem Dataset V11.1.* Varieties of Democracy (V-Dem) Project. www.v-dem.net/en/data/data/v-dem-dataset-v111/.

Cornell, Agnes, and Victor Lapuente. 2014. "Meritocratic Administration and Democratic Stability." *Democratization* 21 (7): 1286–304.

Coronell, Daniel. 2008. "Inteligencia Superior." *Revista Semana,* October 27, 2008.

———. 2009. "Aló Presidente." *Revista Semana,* March 2, 2009.

Corrales, Javier. 2011. "Why Polarize? Advantages and Disadvantages of Rational-Choice Analysis of Government–Opposition Relation Sunder Hugo Chávez." In *The Revolution in Venezuela: Social and Political Change Under Chávez,* edited by

Thomas Ponniah and Jonathan Eastwood, 67–95. Cambridge, MA: Harvard University Press.

2015. "Autocratic Legalism in Venezuela." *Journal of Democracy* 26 (2): 37–51.

2016. "Can Anyone Stop the President? Power Asymmetries and Term Limits in Latin America, 1984–2016." *Latin American Politics and Society* 58 (2): 3–25.

2018. *Fixing Democracy: Why Constitutional Change Often Fails to Enhance Democracy in Latin America*. Oxford, New York: Oxford University Press.

Corrales, Javier, and Michael Penfold-Becerra. 2011. *Dragon in the Tropics: Hugo Chávez and the Political Economy of Revolution in Venezuela. 1st Edition. A Brookings Latin America Initiative Book*. Washington, DC: Brookings Institution Press.

2015. *Dragon in the Tropics: The Legacy of Hugo Chávez*. 2nd Edition. Brookings Latin America Initiative Book. Washington, DC: The Brookings Institution.

Cunningham, Kathleen Gallagher. 2013. "Understanding Strategic Choice: The Determinants of Civil War and Nonviolent Campaign in Self-Determination Disputes." *Journal of Peace Research* 50 (3): 291–304.

Cyr, Jennifer. 2017. *The Fates of Political Parties: Institutional Crisis, Continuity, and Change in Latin America*. New York: Cambridge University Press.

Da Corte, María Lilibeth. 2005. "Chávez Exigió Enterrar 'La Famos Lista' Del Diputado Luis Tascón." *El Universal*, April 16, 2005. http://www.eluniversal.com/2005/04/16/pol_art_16186B2.

Daguerre, Anne. 2011. "Antipoverty Programmes in Venezuela." *Journal of Social Policy* 40 (October): 835–52.

Datanálisis. 2013. "*Encuesta Nacional Ómnibus*." Caracas.

Davenport, Christian. 2007. "State Repression and Political Order." *Annual Review of Political Science* 10: 1–23.

Deheza, Grace Ivana. 2008. "Bolivia: Is the Formation of a New State Possible? The Constituent Assembly and the Departmental Autonomies." *Revista de Ciencia Política (Santiago)* 28 (1): 61–79.

Diamond, Larry. 2008. "The Democratic Rollback: The Resurgence of the Predatory State." *Foreign Affairs* 87 (2): 36–48. https://doi.org/10.2307/20032579.

2015. "Facing up to the Democratic Recession." *Journal of Democracy* 26 (1): 141–55.

2019. *Ill Winds: Saving Democracy from Russian Rage, Chinese Ambition, and American Complacency*. New York: Penguin Press.

Döring, Herbert. 1995. "Time as a Scarce Resource: Goverment Control of the Agenda." In *Parliaments and Majority Rule in Western Europe*. Mannheim: Mannheim Centre for European Social Research.

Dresden, Jennifer Raymond, and Marc Morjé Howard. 2016. "Authoritarian Backsliding and the Concentration of Political Power." *Democratization* 23 (7): 1122–43. https://doi.org/10.1080/13510347.2015.1045884.

Dugas, John. 2003. "The Emergence of Neopopulism in Colombia? The Case of Álvaro Uribe." *Third World Quarterly* 24 (6): 1117–36.

Eaton, Kent. 2007. "Backlash in Bolivia: Regional Autonomy as a Reaction against Indigenous Mobilization." *Politics & Society* 35 (1): 71–102. https://doi.org/10.1177/0032329206297145.

Echandía Castilla, Camilo, and Eduardo Bechara Gómez. 2006. "Conducta de La Guerrilla Durante El Gobierno Uribe Vélez: De Las Lógicas de Control Territorial a Las Lógicas de Control Estratégico." *Análisis Político* 19 (57): 31–54.

Edwards, Barry, Michael Crespin, Ryan D. Williamson, and Maxwell Palmer. 2017. "Institutional Control of Redistricting and the Geography of Representation." *The Journal of Politics* 79 (2): 722–26. https://doi.org/10.1086/690633.

Eissenstat, Howard. 2018. "Turkey's President Will Win the Country?S Snap Elections. Here's Why They Still Matter." *Monkey Cage – Washington Post* (blog), April 20, 2018. www .washingtonpost.com/news/monkey-cage/wp/2018/04/20/turkeys-president-will-win-the-countrys-snap-elections-heres-why-they-still-matter/?utm_term=.2e179de90a10.

Elkins, Zachary, and Tom Ginsburg. 2021. "Characteristics of National Constitutions, Version 3.0." Comparative Constitution Project.

Ellner, Steve. 2004. "Hugo Chávez y Alberto Fujimori: Análisis Comparativo de Dos Variantes de Populismo." *Revista Venezolana de Economía y Ciencias Sociales* 10 (1): 13–37.

Erdmann, Gero. 2011. "Decline of Democracy: Loss of Quality, Hybridisation and Breakdown of Democracy." In *Regression of Democracy? Zeitschrift Für Vergleichende Politikwissenschaft Comparative Governance and Politics*, edited by Gero Erdmann and Marianne Kneuer, 21–58. Wiesbaden: VS Verlag für Sozialwissenschaften. http://dx.doi.org/10.1007/978-3-531-93302-3_2.

Esen, Berk, and Sebnem Gumuscu. 2017. "Turkey: How the Coup Failed." *Journal of Democracy* 28 (1): 59–73. https://doi.org/10.1353/jod.2017.0006.

EU Election Expert Mission. 2019. "Bolivia 2019 (Final Report): General Elections 20 October 2019."

European Union Election Observation Mission. 2006. "*Final Report: Presidential Elections Venezuela 2006*." Caracas: European Union.

Farthing, Linda C., and Benjamin H. Kohl. 2014. *Evo's Bolivia: Continuity and Change.* Austin, TX: University of Texas Press.

Febres Cordero, Maria M., and Bernardo Márquez. 2006. "A Statistical Approach to Assess Referendum Results: The Venezuelan Recall Referendum 2004." *International Statistical Review/Revue Internationale de Statistique* 74 (3): 379–89.

Ferrari, Elisabetta. 2019. "'Free Country, Free Internet': The Symbolic Power of Technology in the Hungarian Internet Tax Protests." *Media, Culture & Society* 41 (1): 70–85. https://doi.org/10.1177/0163443718799394.

Fish, M. Steven. 2005. *Democracy Derailed in Russia: The Failure of Open Politics. Cambridge Studies in Comparative Politics.* New York: Cambridge University Press.

Fish, M. Steven, and Robin S Brooks. 2004. "Does Diversity Hurt Democracy?" *Journal of Democracy* 15 (1): 154–66.

Fish, Steven. 2001. "The Dynamics of Democratic Erosion." In *Postcommunism and the Theory of Democracy*, edited by Richard Anderson, M. Steven Fish, Stephen Hanson, and Philip Roeder, 54–95. Princeton, NJ: Princeton University Press.

Foa, Roberto Stefan, and Yascha Mounk. 2016. "The Democratic Disconnect." *Journal of Democracy* 27 (3): 5–17. https://doi.org/10.1353/jod.2016.0049.

Fortin, Jessica. 2011. "Is There a Necessary Condition for Democracy? The Role of State Capacity in Postcommunist Countries." *Comparative Political Studies* 45 (7): 903–30.

Foy, Henry. 2015. "Poland's New Governmetn Cracks down on State Media." *Financial Times*, December 29, 2015. www.ft.com/content/729e39d0-ae31-11e5-993b-c425a3d2b65a.

Freedom House. 2011. "Freedom in the World: Bolivia." Freedom in the World. Freedom House. https://freedomhouse.org/report/freedom-world/2011/bolivia.

2012. "Freedom in the World: Bolivia." Freedom in the World. Freedom House. https://freedomhouse.org/report/freedom-world/2012/bolivia.

2013. "Freedom in the World: Bolivia." Freedom in the World. Freedom House. https://freedomhouse.org/report/freedom-world/2013/bolivia.

2015. "Freedom in the World." Freedom House. https://freedomhouse.org/report/freedom-world/2015/turkey.

2016. "Freedom in the World: Bolivia." Freedom in the World. Freedom House. https://freedomhouse.org/report/freedom-world/2016/bolivia.

2017a. "Freedom in the World: Bolivia." Freedom in the World. https://freedomhouse.org/report/freedom-world/2017/bolivia.

2017b. "Freedom in the World: Turkey." Freedom in the World. Freedom House. https://freedomhouse.org/report/freedom-world/2017/turkey.

Gallup. 2006. "La Encuesta de Los Medios." Bogotá.

2007. "Encuesta Gallup Bimestral." Bogotá.

2009. "Encuesta Gallup Bimestral." Bogotá.

2014. "Encuesta Gallup Colombia." Bogotá.

Gamboa, Laura. 2017. "Opposition at the Margins: Strategies against the Erosion of Democracy in Colombia and Venezuela." *Comparative Politics* 49 (4): 457–77.

2020a. "Parties and Regime Change in Latin America." In *Oxford Encyclopedia of Latin American Politics*. Oxford: Oxford University Press. DOI: 10.1093/acrefore/9780190228637.013.1671.

2020b. "What Should the Opposition Do in Authoritarian Regimes? Here Are Lessons from Bolivia." *Mischiefs of Faction* (blog), February 21, 2020. www.mischiefsoffaction.com/post/what-should-the-opposition-do-in-authoritarian-regimes-here-are-lessons-from-bolivia.

García, Mauricio, and Javier Revelo. 2010. "Procesos de Captura y Resistencia En La Rama Judicial." In *Y Refundaron La Patria: De Cómo Mafiosos y Políticos Reconfiguraron El Estado Colombiano*, edited by Claudia López, 457–500. Bogotá: Debate.

García, Mauricio, and Javier Eduardo Revelo. 2009. "La Concentración Del Poder En Colombia." In *Mayorías Sin Democracia: Desequilibrio de Poderes y Estado de Derecho En Colombia, 2002–2009*, edited by Mauricio García and Javier Eduardo Revelo, 328–71. Colección Dejusticia. Bogotá: Dejusticia.

García-Guadilla, María Pilar. 2018. "The Incorporation of Popular Sectors and Social Movements in Venezuelan Twenty-First-Century Socialism." In *Reshaping the Political Arena in Latin America*, edited by Eduardo Silva and Federico Rossi, 60–77. Pittsburgh, PA: University of Pittsburgh Press. https://upittpress.org/books/9780822965121/.

Gartner, Scott, and Patrick Regan. 1996. "Threat and Repression: The Non-Linear Relationship between Government and Opposition Violence." *Journal of Peace Research* 33 (3): 273–87.

Geddes, Barbara. 1999. "What Do We Know about Democratization after Twenty Years?" *Annual Review of Political Science* 2 (1): 115–44.

Gélineau, François, and Matthew M. Singer. 2015. "The Economy and Incumbent Support in Latin America." In *The Latin American Voter: Pursuing Representation and Accountability in Challenging Contexts*, edited by Ryan E. Carlin, Matthew M. Singer, and Elizabeth J. Zechmeister, 1–27. Ann Arbor, MI: University of Michigan Press. www.press.umich.edu/8402589/latin_american_voter.

George, Alexander, and Andrew Bennett. 2005. *Case Studies and Theory Development in the Social Sciences*. Cambridge, MA: MIT Press.

Gerring, John. 2008. "Case Selection for Case Study Analysis: Qualitatie and Quantitative Techniques." In *The Oxford Handbook of Political Methodology*, edited by Janet M. Box-Steffensmeier, Henry E. Brady, and David Collier, 661–79. The Oxford Handbooks of Political Science. Oxford: Oxford University Press.

Gerschewski, Johannes. 2021a. "Erosion or Decay? Conceptualizing Causes and Mechanisms of Democratic Regression." *Democratization* 28 (1): 43–62. https://doi.org/10.1080/13510347.2020.1826935.

2021b. "Explanations of Institutional Change: Reflecting on a 'Missing Diagonal.'" *American Political Science Review* 115 (1): 218–33. https://doi.org/10.1017/S0003055420000751.

Gervasoni, Carlos. 2018. *Hybrid Regimes within Democracies: Fiscal Federalism and Subnational Rentier States*. New York: Cambridge University Press.

Gessler, Theresa. 2017. "The 2016 Referendum in Hungary." *East European Quarterly* 45 (1–2): 85–97.

Gibson, James L. 2007. "The Legitimacy of the U.S. Supreme Court in a Polarized Polity." *Journal of Empirical Legal Studies* 4 (3): 507–38.

Ginsburg, Tom, and Aziz Huq. 2018. "Democracy's Near Misses." *Journal of Democracy* 29 (4): 16–30. https://doi.org/10.1353/jod.2018.0059.

Ginsburg, Tom, and Aziz Z. Huq. 2019. *How to Save a Constitutional Democracy*. Chicago, IL: The University of Chicago Press. www.press.uchicago.edu/ucp/books/book/chicago/H/bo28381225.html.

Goertz, Gary. 2017. *Multimethod Research, Causal Mechanisms, and Case Studies*. Princeton, NJ: Princeton University Press. http://proxy.library.nd.edu/login?url=http://search.ebscohost.com/login.aspx?direct=true&scope=site&db=nlebk&db=nlabk&AN=1510360.

Goertz, Gary, and James Mahoney. 2012. *A Tale of Two Cultures: Qualitative and Quantitative Research in the Social Sciences*. Princeton, NJ: Princeton University Press.

González, María Fernanda. 2013. *Hugo Chávez y Alvaro Uribe: La Fuerza de Las Palabras. Dos Discursos Para Gobernar*. Bogotá: Instituto Caro y Cuervo.

Graham, Matthew H., and Milan W. Svolik. 2020. "Democracy in America? Partisanship, Polarization, and the Robustness of Support for Democracy in the United States." *American Political Science Review* 114 (2): 392–409. https://doi.org/10.1017/S0003055420000052.

Greene, Kenneth F. 2011. "Campaign Persuasion and Nascent Partisanship in Mexico's New Democracy." *American Journal of Political Science* 55 (2): 398–416.

Grzymala-Busse, Anna. 2016. "Why Would Poland Make Its Already Strict Abortion Law Draconian?" *Monkey Cage – Washington Post* (blog), April 18, 2016. www.washingtonpost.com/news/monkey-cage/wp/2018/07/10/poland-may-be-forcibly-retiring-dozens-of-supreme-court-justices/.

Gürsoy, Yaprak. 2012. "The Changing Role of the Military in Turkish Politics: Democratization through Coup Plots?" *Democratization* 19 (4): 735–60. https://doi.org/10.1080/13510347.2011.623352.

Gustafson, Bret. 2010. "When States Act Like Movements: Dismantling Local Power and Seating Sovereignty in Post-Neoliberal Bolivia." *Latin American Perspectives* 37 (4): 48–66.

Gutiérrez Sanín, Francisco. 2007. *Lo Que El Viento Se Llevó?: Los Partidos Políticos y La Democracia En Colombia 1958-2002*. Bogotá: Grupo Editorial Norma.

Gvosdev, Nikolas K. 2019. "Is Russia Sabotaging Democracy in the West?" *Orbis* 63 (3): 321–33. https://doi.org/10.1016/j.orbis.2019.05.010.

Haggard, Stephan. 2016. *Dictators and Democrats: Masses, Elites, and Regime Change*. Princeton++: Princeton University Press.

Haggard, Stephan, and Robert Kaufman. 2021. *Backsliding*. Cambridge: Cambridge University Press.

Hale, Henry E. 2011. "The Myth of Mass Russian Support for Autocracy: The Public Opinion Foundations of a Hybrid Regime." *Europe-Asia Studies* 63 (8): 1357–75.

Handlin, Samuel. 2017. *State Crisis in Fragile Democracies: Polarization and Political Regimes in South America*. New York: Cambridge University Press.

2017b. "Observing Incumbent Abuses: Improving Measures of Electoral and Competitive Authoritarianism with New Data." *Democratization* 24 (1): 41–60. https://doi.org/10.1080/13510347.2016.1149814.

2018. "The Logic of Polarizing Populism: State Crises and Polarization in South America." *American Behavioral Scientist* 62 (1): 75–91. https://doi.org/10.1177/0002764218756922.

Hanson, Jonathan K., and Rachel Sigman. 2021. "Leviathan's Latent Dimensions: Measuring State Capacity for Comparative Political Research." *The Journal of Politics*, May. https://doi.org/10.1086/715066.

Haraszti, Miklós. 2011. "Hungary's Media Law Package." *IWM* (blog), February 11, 2011. www.iwm.at/transit-online/hungarys-media-law-package/.

Hausmann, Ricardo, and Roberto Rigobon. 2011. "In Search of the Black Swan: Analysis of the Statistical Evidence of Electoral Fraud in Venezuela." *Statistical Science* 26 (4): 543–63.

Hawkins, Kirk A. 2010. *Venezuela's Chavismo and Populism in Comparative Perspective*. New York: Cambridge University Press.

2010b. "Who Mobilizes? Participatory Democracy in Chávez's Bolivarian Revolution." *Latin American Politics and Society* 52 (3): 31–66.

Hawkins, Kirk A., Rosario Aguilar, Erin Jenne, Bojana Kockijan, Jan Rovira Katlwasser, and Bruno Castanho Silva. 2019. "Global Populism Database: Populism Dataset for Leaders 1.0." https://populism.byu.edu.

Hawkins, Kirk A., and Bruno Castanho Silva. 2019. "Textual Analysis: Big Data Approaches." In *The Ideational Approach to Populism*, edited by Kirk A. Hawkins, Ryan E. Carlin, Levente Littvay, and Cristóbal Rovira Kaltwasser, 27–59. Abingdon, Oxon: Routledge.

Helmke, Gretchen. 2003. "Checks and Balances by Other Means: Strategic Defection and Argentina's Supreme Court in the 1990s." *Comparative Politics* 35 (2): 213–30. https://doi.org/10.2307/4150152.

2017. *Institutions on the Edge: The Origins and Consequences of Inter-Branch Crises in Latin America*. Illustrated edition. New York: Cambridge University Press.

2020. "Presidential Crises in Latin America." In *The Politics of Institutional Weakness in Latin America*, edited by Daniel M. Brinks, Steven Levitsky, and María Victoria Murillo, 98–118. Cambridge: Cambridge University Press. https://doi.org/10.1017/9781108776608.

Hendrix, Cullen S. 2010. "Measuring State Capacity: Theoretical and Empirical Implications for the Study of Civil Conflict." *Journal of Peace Research* 47 (3): 273–85.

Hidalgo, Manuel. 2009. "Hugo Chávez's 'Petro-Socialism.'" *Journal of Democracy* 20 (2): 78–92.

Hill, Thomas M. 2018. "What Trump's Budget Would Mean for the State Department —Snap Judgments." *Brookings* (blog), February 13, 2018. www.brookings.edu/blog/fixgov/2018/02/13/what-trumps-budget-would-mean-for-the-state-department-snap-judgments/.

Hintz, Lisel, and Melina Dunham. 2017. "Turkey's President Erdogan Has Gone to Extremes to Win Sunday's Referendum. Here's Why." *Monkey Cage – Washington Post* (blog), April 14, 2017. www.washingtonpost.com/news/monkey-cage/wp/2017/04/14/turkish-president-erdogan-resorted-to-unusual-tactics-before-sundays-referendum-vote-heres-why/.

Hiroi, Taeko, and Lucio Renno. 2014. "Dimensions of Legislative Conflict: Coalitions, Obstructionism, and Lawmaking in Multiparty Presidential Regimes." *Legislative Studies Quarterly* 39 (3): 357–86.

Hsieh, Chang-Tai, Edward Miguel, Daniel Ortega, and Francisco Rodriguez. 2009. "The Price of Political Opposition: Evidence from Venezuela's Maisanta." *Center for International and Development Economics Research*, April.

Hyde, Susan D., and Nikolay Marinov. 2015. "National Elections Across Democracy and Autocracy 4.0."

Idrobo, Nicolás, Dorothy Kronick, and Francisco Rodríguez. 2020a. "Do Shifts in Late-Counted Votes Signal Fraud? Evidence from Bolivia." *SSRN Scholarly Paper ID 3621475*. Rochester, NY: Social Science Research Network. https://papers.ssrn.com/abstract=3621475.

Inter-American Commission of Human Rights. 2018. "Gross Human Rights Violations in the Context of Social Protests in Nicaragua." OEA/Ser.L/V/II Doc. 86. Organization of American States. www.oas.org/en/iachr/reports/pdfs/Nicaragua2018-en.pdf.

Isacson, Adam. 2006. "In Harmony, for the Moment." *Center for International Policy* (blog), June 11, 2006. www.ciponline.org/research/entry/in-harmony-for-the-moment.

Jacoby, William G. 2000. "Loess: A Nonparametric, Graphical Tool for Depicting Relationships between Variables." *Electoral Studies* 19 (4): 577–613.

Jenkins, Gareth H. 2009. *Between Fact and Fantasy: Turkey's Ergenekon Investigation*. Silk Road Paper. Central Asia-Caucusus Institute and Silk Road Studies Program.

Jensen, Carsten, and Svend-Erik Skaaning. 2012. "Modernization, Ethnic Fractionalization, and Democracy." *Democratization* 19 (6): 1117–37.

Jiménez, Maryhen. 2021. "Contesting Autocracy: Repression and Opposition Coordination in Venezuela." *Political Studies*, May, 00323217211999975. https://doi.org/10.1177/00323217211999975.

Jiménez, Raúl. 2011. "Forensic Analysis of the Venezuelan Recall Referendum." *Statistical Science* 26 (4): 564–83.

Johns, Leslie, Krzysztof J. Pelc, and Rachel L. Wellhausen. 2019. "How a Retreat from Global Economic Governance May Empower Business Interests." *The Journal of Politics* 81 (2): 731–38. https://doi.org/10.1086/702231.

Karolewski, Ireneusz Paweł. 2016. "Protest and Participation in Post-Transformation Poland: The Case of the Committee for the Defense of Democracy (KOD)." *Communist and Post-Communist Studies, Special issue: Citizen Participation in Post-Communist Region after the EU Enlargement,* 49 (3): 255–67. https://doi.org/10.1016/j.postcomstud.2016.06.003.

Keyman, Emin Fuat, and Sebnem Gumuscu. 2014. *Democracy, Identity and Foreign Policy in Turkey: Hegemony tThrough Transformation.* Houndmills: Palgrave Macmillan.

Kiewiet de Jonge, Chad P. 2013. "Political Learning and Democratic Commitment in New Democracies." Notre Dame, IN: University of Notre Dame.

Kisilowski, Maciej. 2017. "Poland's Point of No Return." *POLITICO,* July 14, 2017. awww.politico.eu/article/pis-polands-point-of-no-return/.

Koper, Anna, and Lidia Kelly. 2017. "Protests in Poland Condemn Controversial Judicial Reforms." *Reuters,* July 16, 2017. www.reuters.com/article/us-poland-politics-protests-idUSKBN1A10S3.

Kovacs, Krista, and Gabor Attila Toth. 2011. "Hungary's Constitutional Transformation." *European Constitutional Law Review* 7: 183–203.

Krekó, Péter, and Zsolt Enyedi. 2018. "Explaining Eastern Europe: Orbán's Laboratory of Illiberalism." *Journal of Democracy* 29 (3): 39–51. https://doi.org/10.1353/jod.2018.0043.

Kuntz, Philipp, and Mark R. Thompson. 2009. "More than Just the Final Straw: Stolen Elections as Revolutionary Triggers." *Comparative Politics* 41 (3): 253–72.

Laebens, Melis G. 2020. "*Incumbents against Democracy: Leaders, Ruling Parties and Gradual Executive Takeover.*" New Haven: Yale University.

Lagos, Marta. 2001. "Between Stability and Crisis in Latin America." *Journal of Democracy* 12 (1): 137–45. https://doi.org/10.1353/jod.2001.0009.

Lancaster, Caroline. 2014. "The Iron Law of Erdogan: The Decay from Intra-Party Democracy to Personalistic Rule." *Third World Quarterly* 35 (9): 1672–90. https://doi.org/10.1080/01436597.2014.970866.

Landau, David. 2013. "Abusive Constitutionalism." *U.C. Davis Law Review* 47: 189.

Landau, David, Rosalind Dixon, and Yaniv Roznai. 2019. "From an Unconstitutional Constitutional Amendment to an Unconstitutional Constitution? Lessons from Honduras." *Global Constitutionalism* 8 (1): 40–70. https://doi.org/10.1017/S2045381718000151.

Latinobarometer. 1998. "Data Bank." Corporación Latinobarómetro. www.latinobarometro.org.

— 2001. "Data Bank." Corporación Latinobarómetro. www.latinobarometro.org.

Ledebur, Kathryn, and John Walsh. 2008. "Bolivia's Recall Referendum." WOLA and AIN.

Lehoucq, Fabrice. 2008. "Bolivia's Constitutional Breakdown." *Journal of Democracy* 19 (4): 110–24.

Levitsky, Steven. 2000. "The 'Normalization' of Argentine Politics." *Journal of Democracy* 11 (2): 56–69.

2011. "Peru's 2011 Elections: A Surprising Left Turn." *Journal of Democracy* 22 (4): 84–94.

2018. "Democratic Survival and Weakness." *Journal of Democracy* 29 (4): 102–13. https://doi.org/10.1353/jod.2018.0066.

Levitsky, Steven, and James Loxton. 2013a. "Populism and Competitive Authoritarianism in the Andes." *Democratization* 20 (1): 107–36.

Levitsky, Steven, and Lucan Way. 2010. *Competitive Authoritarianism: Hybrid Regimes after the Cold War*. New York: Cambridge University Press.

Levitsky, Steven, and Daniel Ziblatt. 2018. *How Democracies Die*. New York: Crown Publishing.

Lindberg, Staffan, ed. 2009. *Democratization by Elections*. Baltimore, MD: Johns Hopkins University Press.

Linz, Juan J. 1978. *The Breakdown of Democratic Regimes: Crisis, Breakdown, and Reequilibration*. Baltimore, MD: Johns Hopkins University Press.

Linz, Juan J., and Alfred C. Stepan. 1996. *Problems of Democratic Transition and Consolidation: Southern Europe, South America, and Post-Communist Europe*. Baltimore, MD: Johns Hopkins University Press.

López, Claudia. 2010. "'La Refundación de La Patria', De La Teoría a La Evidencia." In *Y Refundaron La Patria: De Cómo Mafiosos y Políticos Reconfiguraron El Estado Colombiano*, edited by Claudia López, 29–68. Bogotá: Debate.

López de la Roche, Fabio. 2014. *Las Ficciones Del Poder: Patriotismo, Medios de Comunicación y Reorientación Afectiva de Los Colombianos Bajo Uribe Vélez (2002–2010)*. Biblioteca IEPRI 25 Años. Bogotá: Debate.

López Maya, Margarita. 2007. "Venezuela Después Del Golpe: La Segunda Insurgencia." In *Chávez: Una Revolución Sin Libreto*, edited by Medófilo Medina, Margarita López Maya, and Luis E. Lander, 147–204. Bogotá: Ediciones Aurora.

Lührmann, Anna, and Staffan I. Lindberg. 2019. "A Third Wave of Autocratization Is Here: What Is New about It?" *Democratization* 26 (7): 1095–1113. https://doi.org/10.1080/13510347.2019.1582029.

Lupu, Noam, Virginia Oliveros, and Luis Schiumerini. 2019. "Toward a Theory of Campaigns and Voters in Developing Democracies." In *Campaigns and Voters in Developing Democracies: Argentina in Comparative Perspective*, edited by Noam Lupu, Virginia Oliveros, and Luis Schiumerini, 1–27. Ann Arbor, MI: University of Michigan Press.

Lyman, Rick. 2017. "The Polish Parliament Reshapes Courts, Drawing Criticism." *The New York Times*, December 9, 2017, sec. World. www.nytimes.com/2017/12/08/world/europe/poland-laws-courts.html.

Lyman, Rick, and Joanna Berendt. 2016. "Protests Erupt in Poland over New Law on Public Gatherings." *The New York Times*, December 13, 2016, sec. World. www.nytimes.com/2016/12/13/world/europe/poland-protests.html.

Lynch, Julia F. 2013. "Aligning Sampling Strategies with Analytic Goals." In *Interview Research in Political Science*, edited by Layna Mosley. Ithaca, NY: Cornell University Press.

Machado, Juan Carlos. 2008. "Ecuador: …hasta Que Se Fueron Todos." *Revista de Ciencia Política (Santiago)* 28 (1): 189–215.

Madrid, Raúl L. 2008. "The Rise of Ethnopopulism in Latin America." *World Politics* 60 (03): 475–508.

Maeda, Ko. 2010. "Two Modes of Democratic Breakdown: A Competing Risks Analysis of Democratic Durability." *The Journal of Politics* 72 (4): 1129–43. https://doi.org/10.1017/S0022381610000575.

Magdaleno, John. 2014. "Análisis de Las Protestas Iniciadas En Febrero 2014." 4. *Informe Político*. Venezuela: Polity CA.

Magyar, Bálint. 2016. *Post-Communist Mafia State*. Budapest: Central European University Press.

Mahoney, James. 2003. "Strategies of Causal Assessment in Comparative Historical Analysis." In *Comparative Historical Analysis in the Social Sciences*, edited by James Mahoney and Dietrich Rueschemeyer, 337–68. New York: Cambridge University Press.

Mahoney, James, and Kathleen Thelen, eds. 2015. "Comparative-Historical Analysis in Contemporary Political Science." In *Advances in Comparative-Historical Analysis*, 3–37. New York: Cambridge University Press.

Mainwaring, Scott. 2006. "State Deficiencies, Party Competition, and Confidence in Democratic Representation in the Andes." In *The Crisis of Democratic Representation in the Andes*, edited by Scott Mainwaring, Ana María Bejarano, and Eduardo Pizarro Leongómez, 295–346. Stanford, CA: Stanford University Press.

2012a. "From Representative Democracy to Participatory Competitive Authoritarianism: Hugo Chávez and Venezuelan Politics." *Perspectives on Politics* 10 (04): 955–67.

2018a. "Party System Institutionalization, Predictability, and Democracy." In *Latin America Party Systems: Institutionalization, Decay and Collapse*, edited by Scott Mainwaring, 71–101. New York: Cambridge University Press.

2018b. "Party System Stability and Volatility in Latin America." In *Latin America Party Systems: Institutionalization, Decay and Collapse*, edited by Scott Mainwaring. New York: Cambridge University Press.

Mainwaring, Scott, Ana María Bejarano and Eduardo Pizarro Leóngomez. "The Crisis of Democratic Representation in the Andes: An Overview." In Crisis of Democratic Representation in the Andes, edited by Scott Mainwaring, Ana María Bejarano, and Eduardo Pizarro Leóngomez, 1–46. Stanford, CA: Stanford University Press.

Mainwaring, Scott, Fernando Bizarro, and Ana Petrova. 2018. "Party System Institutionalization, Decay and Collapse." In *Latin America Party Systems: Institutionalization, Decay and Collapse*, edited by Scott Mainwaring, 17–33. New York: Cambridge University Press.

Mainwaring, Scott, Carlos Gervasoni, and Annabella España-Najera. 2017. "Extra- and within-System Electoral Volatility." *Party Politics* 23 (6): 623–35. https://doi.org/10.1177/1354068815625229.

Mainwaring, Scott, and Aníbal Pérez-Liñán. 2013. *Democracies and Dictatorships in Latin America: Emergence, Survival and Fall*. New York: Cambridge University Press.

Mainwaring, Scott, and Timothy Scully. 1995. "Introduction: Party Systems in Latin America." In *Building Democratic Institutions: Party Systems in LatinAmerica*, edited by Scott Mainwaring and Timothy R. Scully, 1–33. Stanford, CA: Stanford University Press.

Makovsky, Alan. 2017. "Erdoğan's Proposal for an Empowered Presidency." Center for American Progress. www.americanprogress.org/issues/security/reports/2017/03/22/428908/erdogans-proposal-empowered-presidency/.

Malkin, Elisabeth. 2017. "La desconfianza prevalece en las elecciones de Honduras." *The New York Times*, November 25, 2017, sec. América Latina. www.nytimes.com/es/2017/11/25/honduras-juan-orlando-hernandez-manuel-zelaya-reeleccion/.

Mares, Isabela, and Lauren E. Young. 2018. "The Core Voter's Curse: Clientelistic Threats and Promises in Hungarian Elections." *Comparative Political Studies* 51 (11): 1441–71. https://doi.org/10.1177/0010414018758754.

Martínez Meucci, Miguel Angel. 2012. *Apaciguamiento: El Referéndum Revocatorio y La Consolidación de La Revolución Bolivariana*. Colección Hogueras 58. Caracas: Editorial Alfa.

Masoud, Tarek. 2014. "Egyptian Democracy: Smothered in the Cradle, or Stillborn." *Brown Journal of World Affairs* 20: 3.

Mayka, Lindsay R. 2016. "Colombia's Surprising Resilience." *Journal of Democracy* 27 (3): 139–47. https://doi.org/10.1353/jod.2016.0050.

Mayorca, Javier Ignacio. 2002. "Se Profundizó La Crisis de Liderazgo En La Fuerza Armada." *El Nacional*, September 11, 2002, sec. Política.

Mayorga, René Antonio. 2009. "El Proyecto Político Del MAS: ¿hacia La Construcción de Un Gobierno Mayoritario?" In *¿Autoritarismo o Democracia?: Hugo Chávez y Evo Morales*, edited by Julio Aibar Gaete and Daniel Vázquez, 171–218. México, D.F.: FLACSO México.

——— 2011. "Populismo Radical y Desmontaje de La Democracia: El Camino Hacia La Dictadura Plebiscitaria." Notre Dame, IN.

——— 2017. "Populismo Autoritario y Transición Regresiva: La Dictadura Plebiscitaria En La Región Andina." *Revista Latinoamericana de Política Comparada* 12 (January): 39–69.

Mazzuca, Sebastián. 2013. "Natural Resources Boom and Institutional Curses in the New Political Economy of South America." In *Constructing Democratic Governance in Latin America*, edited by Jorge I. Domínguez and Michael Shifter, Fourth edition, 102–27. Inter-American Dialogue Book. Baltimore, MD: The John Hopkins University Press.

McAdam, Doug. 1999. *Political Process and The Development of Black Insurgency, 1930–1970*. 2nd Edition. Chicago, IL: University of Chicago Press.

McAdam, Doug, and Sidney Tarrow. 2000. "Nonviolence as Contentious Interaction." *PS: Political Science and Politics* 33 (2): 149–54.

McClintock, Cynthia. 2006. "A 'Left Turn' in Latin America? An Unlikely Comeback in Peru." *Journal of Democracy* 17 (4): 95–109.

McCoy, Jennifer, and Francisco Diez. 2011. *International Mediation in Venezuela*. Washington, DC: United States Institute of Peace.

McCoy, Jennifer, Tahmina Rahman, and Murat Somer. 2018. "Polarization and the Global Crisis of Democracy: Common Patterns, Dynamics, and Pernicious Consequences for Democratic Polities." *American Behavioral Scientist* 62 (1): 16–42. https://doi.org/10.1177/0002764218759576.

McCoy, Jennifer, and Murat Somer. 2019. "Toward a Theory of Pernicious Polarization and How It Harms Democracies: Comparative Evidence and Possible Remedies."

The Annals of the American Academy of Political and Social Science 681 (1): 234–71. https://doi.org/10.1177/0002716218818782.

2021. "Overcoming Polarization." *Journal of Democracy* 32 (1): 6–21. https://doi .org/10.1353/jod.2021.0012.

Medina, Medófilo, and Margarita López Maya. 2003. *Venezuela: Confrontación Social y Polarización Política*. Bogotá: Ediciones Aurora.

Metcalf, Lee Kendall. 2000. "Measuring Presidential Power." *Comparative Political Studies* 33 (5): 660–85.

Meyerrose, Anna M. 2020. "The Unintended Consequences of Democracy Promotion: International Organizations and Democratic Backsliding." *Comparative Political Studies* 53 (10–11): 1547–81. https://doi.org/10.1177/0010414019897689.

Migdalovitz, Carol. 2007. "Turkey's 2007 Elections: Crisis of Identity and Power." *CRS-RL34039*. Washington, DC: Library of Congress Washington DC Congressional Research Service. http://www.dtic.mil/docs/citations/ADA469078.

Milanese, Juan Pablo. 2011. "Participación Éxito y Prioridad: Un Análisis Macro de Los Equilibrios En Las Relaciones Entre Los Poderes Ejecutivo y Legislativo En Colombia 2002–2006." *CS En Ciencias Sociales*, no. 8 (July): 111–45.

Møller, Jørgen, and Svend-Erik Skaaning. 2011. "Stateness First?" *Democratization* 18 (1): 1–24.

Mong, Attila. 2019. "Gagging Orders, Legal Action, and Communist Era Laws Used to Try to 'choke' Polish Press." *Committee to Protect Journalists* (blog), January 10, 2019. https://cpj.org/blog/2019/01/gagging-orders-legal-action-and-communist-era-laws.php.

Morgan, Jana. 2011. *Bankrupt Representation and Party System Collapse*. University Park, PA: Pennsylvania State University Press.

Morgenstern, Scott, Juan Javier Negri, and Aníbal Pérez-Liñán. 2008. "Parliamentary Opposition in Non-Parliamentary Regimes: Latin America." *The Journal of Legislative Studies* 14 (1–2): 160–89. https://doi.org/10.1080/13572330801921166.

Morgenstern, Scott, and Elizabeth Zechmeister. 2001. "Better the Devil You Know Than the Saint You Don't? Risk Propensity and Vote Choice in Mexico." *The Journal of Politics* 63 (1): 93–119.

Morris, Hollman. 2010. "El DAS Una Cacería Criminal." In *Las Perlas Uribistas*, 155–84. Bogotá: Debate.

Mounk, Yascha. 2018. *The People vs. Democracy: Why Our Freedom Is in Danger and How to Save It*. Cambridge, MA; London, England: Harvard University Press.

Müftüler-Baç, Meltem, and E. Fuat Keyman. 2012. "The Era of Dominant-Party Politics." *Journal of Democracy* 23 (1): 85–99. https://doi.org/10.1353/jod.2012 .0000.

Nalepa, Monika. 2016. "Why Are There Protests in Poland? Here Are the Five Things You Need to Know." *Monkey Cage – Washington Post* (blog), December 19, 2016. www.washingtonpost.com/news/monkey-cage/wp/2016/12/19/why-are-there-pro tests-in-poland-here-are-the-five-things-you-need-to-know/?utm_term= .62e609aba466.

2017a. "The Attack on Poland's Judicial Independence Goes Deeper Than You May Think. Here Are 5 Things to Know." *Monkey Cage – Washington Post* (blog), July 23, 2017. www.washingtonpost.com/news/monkey-cage/wp/2017/07/23/the-attack-on-polands-judicial-independence-goes-deeper-than-you-think-here-are-5-things-to-know/.

2017b. "Poland's in Crisis Again. Here's What You Should Know about the Far Right's Latest Power-Grab." *Monkey Cage – Washington Post* (blog), November 28, 2017. www.washingtonpost.com/news/monkey-cage/wp/2017/11/28/polands-in-crisis-again-here-are-3-things-you-need-to-know-about-the-law-and-justice-partys-attempt-to-take-over-the-courts/.

Nalepa, Monika, Georg Vanberg, and Caterina Chiopris. 2018. "Authoritarian Backsliding." www.monikanalepa.com/uploads/6/6/3/1/66318923/auth_back_chicago.pdf.

Navas Talero, Germ\'{a}n. 2010. "Democracia o Demos Gracias." In *Las Perlas Uribistas*, 81–93. Bogotá: Debate.

Negretto, Gabriel. 2013. *Making Constitutions: Presidents, Parties, and Institutional Choice in Latin America*. New York: Cambridge University Press.

Nelson, Brian A. 2009. *The Silence and the Scorpion: The Coup against Chávez and the Making of Modern Venezuela*. New York: Nation Books.

Nieto, Rafael. 2007. "Con Petro." *Revista Semana*, September 17, 2007.

Norris, Pippa, and Ronald Inglehart, eds. 2019a. *Cultural Backlash: Trump, Brexit, and Authoritarian Populism*. New York: Cambridge University Press.

North, Douglass Cecil. 1990. *Institutions, Institutional Change and Economic Performance. Political Economy of Institutions and Decisions*. New York: Cambridge University Press.

Novoszádek, Nóra. 2013. "Some Factual Notes on the Fourth Amendment to Hungary's Fundamental Law." *Heinrich Böll Foundation* (blog), April 2, 2013. www.boell.de/en/2013/04/02/some-factual-notes-fourth-amendment-hungarys-fundamental-law.

O'Donnell, Guillermo. 1994. "Delegative Democracy." *Journal of Democracy* 5 (1): 55–69.

2007. "Democratic Theory and Comparative Politics." In *Dissonances Democratic Critiques of Democracy*, 1–48. Notre Dame, IN: University of Notre Dame Press.

O'Donnell, Guillermo, and Philippe Schmitter. 1986. *Transitions from Authoritarian Rule*. Baltimore, MD: Johns Hopkins University Press.

Ong, Elvin. 2021. "What Are We Voting for? Opposition Alliance Joint Campaigns in Electoral Autocracies." *Party Politics*, July, 13540688211032368. https://doi.org/10.1177/13540688211032367.

Öniş, Ziya. 2016. "Turkey's Two Elections: The AKP Comes Back." *Journal of Democracy* 27 (2): 141–54. https://doi.org/10.1353/jod.2016.0021.

Organización de Estados Americanos. 2019. "Análisis de Integridad Electoral: Elecciones Generales Del Estado Plurinacional de Bolivia." www.oas.org/es/sap/deco/informe-bolivia-2019/0.1%20Informe%20Final%20-%20Analisis%20de%20Integridad%20Electoral%20Bolivia%202019%20(OSG).pdf.

Ortega Hegg, Manuel. 2007. "Nicaragua 2006: El Regreso Del FSLN al Poder." *Revista de Ciencia Política (Santiago)* 27: 205–19.

Ortiz Ayala, Alejandra, and Miguel García Sánchez. 2014. "Porque Te Quiero Te Apoyo: Estilo de Gobierno y Aprobación Presidencial En América Latina." *Revista de Ciencia Política (Santiago)* 34 (2): 373–98. https://doi.org/10.4067/S0718-090X2014000200002.

Özbudun, Ergun. 2014. "AKP at the Crossroads: Erdoğan's Majoritarian Drift." *South European Society and Politics* 19 (2): 155–67. https://doi.org/10.1080/13608746.2014.920571.

2015. "Turkey's Judiciary and the Drift toward Competitive Authoritarianism." *The International Spectator* 50 (2): 42–55. https://doi.org/10.1080/03932729.2015 .1020651.

Pachano, Simón. 2006. "Outsiders and Neopupulism: The Road to Plebiscitary Democracy." In *The Crisis of Democratic Representation in the Andes*, edited by Scott Mainwaring, Ana María Bejarano, and Eduardo Pizarro Leongómez, 100–31. Stanford, CA: Stanford University Press.

Pacula, Paulina. 2017. "Polish President Disappoints EU on Judicial Reform." *EUObserver*, September 26, 2017. https://euobserver.com/justice/139148.

Paredes, César. 2010. "*Referendo Reeleccionista: El Estado de Derecho Prevaleció Sobre El 'Estado de Opinión.'*" Medellín: Universidad de Antioquia.

Park, Bill. 2008. "Turkey's Deep State." *The RUSI Journal* 153 (5): 54–9. https://doi .org/10.1080/03071840802521937.

Parker, Christopher S. 2018. "A Discussion of Steven Levitsky and Daniel Ziblatt's How Democracies Die." *Perspectives on Politics* 16 (4): 1099–100. https://doi.org/10 .1017/S153759271800289X.

Penfold, Michael, Javier Corrales, and Gonzalo Hernández. 2014. "Los Invencibles: La Reelección Presidencial y Los Cambios Constitucionales En América Latina." *Revista de Ciencia Política (Santiago)* 34 (3): 537–59.

Pérez-Baltodano, Andrés. 2010. "Nicaragua: The Consolidation of the Rule by Law and the Weakening of the Rule of Law." *Revista de Ciencia Política (Santiago)* 30 (2): 397–418.

Pérez-Liñán, Aníbal. 2007. *Presidential Impeachment and the New Political Instability in Latin America. Cambridge Studies in Comparative Politics*. New York: Cambridge University Press.

Pérez-Liñán, Aníbal, and Scott Mainwaring. 2013. "Regime Legacies and Levels of Democracy: Evidence from Latin America." *Comparative Politics* 45 (4): 379–97.

Pérez-Liñán, Aníbal, Nicolás Schmidt, and Daniela Vairo. 2019. "Presidential Hegemony and Democratic Backsliding in Latin America, 1925–2016." *Democratization* 26 (4): 606–25. https://doi.org/10.1080/13510347.2019 .1566321.

Pericchi, Luis, and David Torres. 2011. "Quick Anomaly Detection by the Newcomb— Benford Law, with Applications to Electoral Processes Data from the USA, Puerto Rico and Venezuela." *Statistical Science* 26 (4): 502–16.

Petkoff, Teodoro. 2011. *El Chavismo al Banquillo: Pasado, Presente y Futuro de Un Proyecto Político*. Bogotá: Planeta Colombiana.

Petócz, György. 2015. "Milla: A Suspended Experiment." In *The Hungarian Patient: Social Opposition to an Illiberal Democracy*, edited by Peter Krasztev and Jon Van Til, 207–29. Budapest: Central European University Press.

Pevehouse, Jon. 2002. "Democracy from the Outside-In? International Organizations and Democratization." *International Organization* 56 (03): 515–49.

Pizarro Leongómez, Eduardo. 2006. "Giants with Feet of Clay: Political Parties in Colombia." In *The Crisis of Democratic Representation in the Andes*, edited by Scott Mainwaring, Ana María Bejarano, and Eduardo Pizarro Leongómez, 78–99. Stanford, CA: Stanford University Press.

Postero, Nancy. 2010. "The Struggle to Create a Radical Democracy in Bolivia." *Latin American Research Review* 45: 59–78.

Prado, Raquel, and Bruno Sansó. 2011. "The 2004 Venezuelan Presidential Recall Referendum: Discrepancies between Two Exit Polls and Official Results." *Statistical Science* 26 (4): 517–27.

Przeworski, Adam, Michael Alvarez, José Antonio Cheibub, and Fernando Limongi. 2000. *Democracy and Development: Political Institutions and Well-Being in the World, 1950–1990. Cambridge Studies in the Theory of Democracy*. Cambridge: Cambridge University Press.

Przeworski, Adam, and José María Maravall, eds. 2003. *Democracy and the Rule of Law. Cambridge Studies in Comparative Politics*. New York: Cambridge University Press.

Przybylski, Wojciech. 2018. "Can Poland's Backsliding Be Stopped?" *Journal of Democracy* 29 (3): 52–64. https://doi.org/10.1353/jod.2018.0044.

Quinche Ramírez, Manuel Fernando. 2010. "La Seguridad Jurídica Frente a Sentencias Definitivas. Tutela Contra Sentencias." *Revista de Estudios Socio-Jurídicos* 12 (1): 99–126.

Repucci, Sarah. June 2019. "Media Freedom: A Downward Spiral." Freedom and the Media 2019. Freedom House. https://freedomhouse.org/report/freedom-and-media/2019/media-freedom-downward-spiral.

Repucci, Sarah, and Amy Slipowitz. 2021. *"Freedom in the World 2021: Democracy under Siege."* Freedom in the World. Freedom House.

Revelo, Javier Eduardo. 2009. "El Consejo Superior de La Judicatura: Entre La Eliminación y La Cooptación." In *Mayorías Sin Democracia: Desequilibrio de Poderes y Estado de Derecho En Colombia, 2002–2009*, edited by Mauricio García and Javier Eduardo Revelo, 249–80. Colección Dejusticia. Bogotá: Dejusticia.

Rhodes-Purdy, Matthew. 2017. *Regime Support Beyond the Balance Sheet*. New York: Cambridge University Press.

Roberts, Kenneth M. 2019. "Parties, Populism, and Democratic Decay: A Comparative Perspective on Political Polarization in the United States." In *When Democracy Trumps Populism: European and Latin American Lessons for the United States*, edited by Kurt Weyland and Raúl Madrid, 154–86. Cambridge; New York: Cambridge University Press.

Rodríguez, Cecilia Graciela. 2019. "Elections under Suspicion. Analysis of the General Elections in Honduras 2017." *Estudios Políticos*, no. 54 (April): 203–32. https://doi.org/10.17533/udea.espo.n54a11.

Rodríguez-Raga, Juan Carlos. 2011. "Strategic Deference in the Colombian Constitutional Court." In *Courts in Latin America*, edited by Gretchen Helmke and Julio Ríos Figueroa, 81–98. New York: Cambridge University Press.

Rodrik, Dani. 2014. "The Plot against the Generals." http://drodrik.scholar.harvard.edu/files/dani-rodrik/files/plot-against-the-generals.pdf.

Rogin, Josh. 2017. "State Department Considers Scrubbing Democracy Promotion from Its Mission." *Washington Post*, August 1, 2017, sec. Josh Rogin Opinion Opinion A column or article in the Opinions section (in print, this is known as the Editorial Pages). www.washingtonpost.com/news/josh-rogin/wp/2017/08/01/state-department-considers-scrubbing-democracy-promotion-from-its-mission/.

Romero Bonifaz, Carlos. 2009. "Bolivia: De La Confrontación al Pacto Político." In *Del Conflicto al Diálogo: Memorias Del Acuerdo Constitucional*, edited by Carlos

Romero Bonifaz, Carlos Böhrt Irahola, and Raúl Peñaranda, 9–48. La Paz: FBDM-FES-ILDIS.

Romero, Simon. 2007a. "Bolivia on Alert over States' Autonomy Push." *The New York Times*, December 14, 2007, sec. Americas. www.nytimes.com/2007/12/14/world/americas/14iht-bolivia.4.8751747.html.

2007b. "Protesters in Bolivia Seek More Autonomy." *The New York Times*, December 16, 2007, sec. Americas. www.nytimes.com/2007/12/16/world/amer icas/16bolivia.html.

Ross, Michael L. 2001. "Does Oil Hinder Democracy?" *World Politics* 53 (3): 325–61.

Rubiano, Sebastián. 2009a. "La Corte Constitucional: Entre La Independencia Judicial y La Captura Politica." In *Mayorías Sin Democracia: Desequilibrio de Poderes y Estado de Derecho En Colombia, 2002–2009*, edited by Mauricio García and Javier Eduardo Revelo. Colección Dejusticia. Bogotá: Dejusticia.

2009b. "La Independencia Del Banco de La República y La Reelección Presidencial." In *Mayorías Sin Democracia: Desequilibrio de Poderes y Estado de Derecho En Colombia, 2002–2009*, edited by Mauricio García and Javier Eduardo Revelo, 206–43. Colección Dejusticia. Bogotá: Dejusticia.

Ruhl, J Mark. 2010. "Honduras Unravels." *Journal of Democracy* 21 (2): 93–107.

Sadurski, Wojciech. 2018. "How Democracy Dies (in Poland): A Case Study of Anti-Constitutional Populist Backsliding." SSRN Scholarly Paper ID 3103491. Rochester, NY: Social Science Research Network. https://papers.ssrn.com/abstract=3103491.

Sanchez Urribarri, Raul A. 2011. "Courts between Democracy and Hybrid Authoritarianism: Evidence from the Venezuelan Supreme Court." *Law & Social Inquiry* 36 (4): 854–84.

Savoia, Antonio, and Kunal Sen. 2015. "Measurement, Evolution, Determinants, and Consequences of State Capacity: A Review of Recent Research." *Journal of Economic Surveys* 29 (3): 441–58.

Schedler, Andreas. 1998. "What Is Democratic Consolidation?" *Journal of Democracy* 9 (2): 91–107. https://doi.org/10.1353/jod.1998.0030.

2013. *The Politics of Uncertainty: Sustaining and Subverting Electoral Authoritarianism*. Oxford: Oxford University Press.

Schenoni, Luis L., and Scott Mainwaring. 2019. "US Hegemony and Regime Change in Latin America." *Democratization* 26 (2): 269–87. https://doi.org/10.1080/13510347.2018.1516754.

Scheppele, Kim Lane, Armin von Bogdandy, and Pál Sonnevend. 2015. "Understanding Hungary's Constitutional Revolution." In *Constitutional Crisis in the European Constitutional Area*, 124–37. Nomos Verlagsgesellschaft.

Schlipphak, Bernd, and Oliver Treib. 2017. "Playing the Blame Game on Brussels: The Domestic Political Effects of EU Interventions against Democratic Backsliding." *Journal of European Public Policy* 24 (3): 352–65. https://doi.org/10.1080/13501763.2016.1229359.

Schultheis, Emily. 2018. "How Hungary's Far-Right Extremists Became Warm and Fuzzy." *Foreign Policy* (blog), April 6, 2018. https://foreignpolicy.com/2018/04/06/how-hungarys-far-right-extremists-became-warm-and-fuzzy/.

Seawright, Jason. 2012. *Party-System Collapse: The Roots of Crisis in Peru and Venezuela*. Stanford, CA: Stanford University Press.

Seawright, Jason, and John Gerring. 2008. "Case Selection Techniques in Case Study Research: A Menu of Qualitative and Quantitative Options." *Political Research Quarterly* 61 (2): 294–308.

Selçuk, Orçun, and Dilara Hekimci. 2020. "The Rise of the Democracy – Authoritarianism Cleavage and Opposition Coordination in Turkey (2014–2019)." *Democratization* 27 (8): 1496–514. https://doi.org/10.1080/13510347.2020.1803841.

Shugart, Matthew Soberg, and John M Carey. 1992. *Presidents and Assemblies: Constitutional Design and Electoral Dynamics*. New York: Cambridge University Press.

Sierra, Luz Maria. 2015. "Alvaro Uribe: Un Presidente de Teflón. La Estrategia de Opinión Pública Que Lo Hizo Inmune a Las Crisis." In *De Uribe, Santos y Otras Especies Políticas: Comunicación de Gobierno En Colombia, Argentina y Brasil*, edited by Omar Rincón and Catalina Uribe, 65–100. Bogotá: Universidad de los Andes.

Sikkink, Kathryn. 1991. *Ideas and Institutions: Developmentalism in Brazil and Argentina. Cornell Studies in Political Economy*. Ithaca, NY: Cornell University Press.

Simon, Zoltan. 2018. "Hungarian Opposition Negotiations Falter in Boost to Orban." *Bloomberg*, March 20, 2018. www.bloomberg.com/news/articles/2018-03-20/high way-huddle-fails-to-unite-hungarian-opposition-against-orban.

Simsek, Ayhan. 2013. "Turkey: Two Roads to Power." *Deutch Welles*, May 7, 2013. http://www.dw.com/en/turkey-two-roads-to-power/a-16931307.

Sing, Ming. 2010. "Explaining Democratic Survival Globally (1946–2002)." *The Journal of Politics* 72 (2): 438–55. https://doi.org/10.1017/S0022381609990892.

Singer, Matthew M. 2011. "Who Says 'It's the Economy'? Cross-National and Cross-Individual Variation in the Salience of Economic Performance." *Comparative Political Studies* 44 (3): 284–312. https://doi.org/10.1177/0010414010384371.

Slomczynski, Kazimierz, and Goldie Shabad. 2012. "Perceptions of Political Party Corruption and Voting Behaviour in Poland." *Party Politics* 18 (6): 897–917. https://doi.org/10.1177/1354068810393266.

Smith, Helena, and Ned Temko. 2007. "Turkey Faces Military Crisis." *The Guardian*, April 28, 2007, sec. World News. www.theguardian.com/world/2007/apr/29/turkey.eu.

Snyder, Edward C. 1994. "Dirty Legal War: Human Rights and the Rule of Law in Chile 1973–1995." *Tulsa Journal of Comparative & International Law* 2: 253.

Soifer, Hillel David. 2012. "Measuring State Capacity in Contemporary Latin America." *Revita de Ciencia Politica* 32 (3): 585–98.

Somer, Murat. 2016. "Understanding Turkey's Democratic Breakdown: Old vs. New and Indigenous vs. Global Authoritarianism." *Southeast European and Black Sea Studies* 16 (4): 481–503. https://doi.org/10.1080/14683857.2016.1246548.

Somer, Murat, and Jennifer McCoy. 2018. "Déjà vu? Polarization and Endangered Democracies in the 21st Century." *American Behavioral Scientist* 62 (1): 3–15. https://doi.org/10.1177/0002764218760371.

Stephan, Maria J., and Erica Chenoweth. 2008. "Why Civil Resistance Works: The Strategic Logic of Nonviolent Conflict." *International Security* 33 (1): 7–44.

Stoner-Weiss, Kathryn. 2010. "Comparing Oranges and Apples: The Internal and External Dimensions of Russia's Turn Away from Democracy." In *Democracy and Authoritarianism in the Postcommunist World*, edited by Valerie Bunce, Michael McFaul, and Kathryn Stoner-Weiss, 253–73. New York: Cambridge University Press.

Svolik, Milan W. 2008. "Authoritarian Reversals and Democratic Consolidation." *The American Political Science Review* 102 (2): 153–68.

2015. "Which Democracies Will Last? Coups, Incumbent Takeovers, and the Dynamic of Democratic Consolidation." *British Journal of Political Science* 45 (04): 715–38.

Szczerbiak, Aleks. 2017. "An Anti-Establishment Backlash That Shook up the Party System? The October 2015 Polish Parliamentary Election." *European Politics and Society* 18 (4): 404–27. https://doi.org/10.1080/23745118.2016.1256027.

2018. "Who Really Won Poland's Local Elections?" London School of Economics and Political Science. *EUROPP* (blog), November 5, 2018. https://blogs.lse.ac.uk/europpblog/2018/11/05/who-really-won-polands-local-elections/.

Szente, Zoltán. 2016. "The Political Orientation of the Members of the Hungarian Constitutional Court between 2010 and 2014." *Constitutional Studies* 1 (1): 123–49.

Szuleka, Małgorzata, Marcin Wolny, and Marcin Szwed. 2016. "*The Constitutional Crisis in Poland 2015–2016.*" Warsaw: Helsinki Foundation for Human Rights. www.hfhr.pl/wp-content/uploads/2016/09/HFHR_The-constitutional-crisis-in-Poland-2015-2016.pdf.

Tanaka, Martín. 2011. "Peru's 2011 Elections: A Vote for Moderate Change." *Journal of Democracy* 22 (4): 75–83. https://doi.org/10.1353/jod.2011.0061.

Tanaka, Martín, and Carlos Meléndez. 2014. "The Future of Perú's Brokered Democracy." In *Clientelism, Social Policy, and the Quality of Democracy*, edited by Diego Abente Brun and Larry Jay Diamond, 65–87. Baltimore, MD: Johns Hopkins University Press.

Tansey, Oisín. October 2007. "Process Tracing and Elite Interviewing: A Case for Non-Probability Sampling." *PS: Political Science & Politics*, no. 04: 765–72.

Tarrow, Sidney. 2010. "Bridging the Quantitative–Qualitative Divide." In *Rethinking Social Inquiry: Diverse Tools, Shared Standards*, edited by Henry E. Brady and David Collier, 101–22. Rowman & Littlefield.

Taşpınar, Ömer. 2007. "The Old Turks' Revolt: When Radical Secularism Endangers Democracy." *Brookings* (blog), November 1, 2007. www.brookings.edu/articles/the-old-turks-revolt-when-radical-secularism-endangers-democracy/.

Taylor, Jonathan. 2005. "Too Many Ties? An Empirical Analysis of the Venezuelan Recall Referendum." http://esdata.info/pdf/Taylor-Ties.pdf.

The Economist. 2017. "America's Foreign Policy: Embrace Thugs, Dictators and Strongmen," June 3, 2017. www.economist.com/news/international/21722834-past-presidents-believed-american-power-should-be-used-force-good.

Tickner, Arlene B. 2007. "Intervención Por Invitación." *Colombia Internacional*, no. 65 (June): 90–111.

Torre, Carlos de la. 2013. "Technocratic Populism in Ecuador." *Journal of Democracy* 24 (3): 33–46.

2017. "Hugo Chávez and the Diffusion of Bolivarianism." *Democratization* 24 (7): 1271–88. https://doi.org/10.1080/13510347.2017.1307825.

Torre, Carlos de la, and Andrés Ortiz Lemos. 2016. "Populist Polarization and The Slow Death of Democracy in Ecuador." *Democratization* 23 (2): 221–41.

Torre, Cristina de la. 2005. *Alvaro Uribe o El Neopopulismo En Colombia*. Carreta Política. Medellín, Colombia: La Carreta.

Trejo, Guillermo. 2014. "The Ballot and the Street: An Electoral Theory of Social Protest in Autocracies." *Perspectives on Politics* 12 (02): 332–52.

Turam, Berna. 2012. "Are Rights and Liberties Safe?" *Journal of Democracy* 23 (1): 109–18. https://doi.org/10.1353/jod.2012.0007.

Turan, Ilter. 2015. *Turkey's Difficult Journey to Democracy: Two Steps Forward, One Step Back*. Oxford: Oxford University Press.

Tworzecki, Hubert. 2019. "Poland: A Case of Top-Down Polarization." *The Annals of the American Academy of Political and Social Science* 681 (1): 97–119. https://doi.org/10.1177/0002716218809322.

Uggla, Annika Mokvist. 2010. "Bolivia: A Year of Consolidation." *Revista de Ciencia Política (Santiago)* 30 (2): 191–211.

Uggla, Fredrik. 2009. "Bolivia: Un Año de Vivir Peligrosamente." *Revista de Ciencia Política (Santiago)* 29 (2): 247–73.

Ungar, Elisabeth, Juan Felipe Cardona, Mauricio García Villegas, Javier Revelo Revolledo, and Rodrigo Uprimy Yepes. 2010. "Confluencia de Los Poderes Legislativo y Ejecutivo En La Reconfiguración Del Estado." In *Y Refundaron La Patria: De Cómo Mafiosos y Políticos Reconfiguraron El Estado Colombiano*, edited by Claudia López. Bogotá: Debate.

Updegraff, Ragan. 2012. "The Kurdish Question." *Journal of Democracy* 23 (1): 119–28. https://doi.org/10.1353/jod.2012.0010.

Uribe, Alvaro. 2002. "Manifiesto Democrático – 100 Puntos Álvaro Uribe Vélez." www.mineducacion.gov.co/1621/articles-85269_archivo_pdf.pdf.

Velasco Guachalla, V. Ximena, Calla Hummel, Sam Handlin, and Amy Erica Smith. 2021. "Latin America Erupts: When Does Competitive Authoritarianism Take Root?" *Journal of Democracy* 32 (3): 63–77. https://doi.org/10.1353/jod.2021.0034.

Waldner, David, and Ellen Lust. 2018. "Unwelcome Change: Coming to Terms with Democratic Backsliding." *Annual Review of Political Science* 21 (1): 93–113. https://doi.org/10.1146/annurev-polisci-050517-114628.

Walker, Christopher, Jessica Ludwig, Juan Pablo Cardenal, Jacek Kucharczyk, Grigorij Meseznikov, and Gabriela Pleschova. 2017. "Sharp Power: Rising Authoritarian Influence." National Endowment for Democracy. www.ned.org/sharp-power-rising-authoritarian-influence-forum-report/.

Wasow, Omar. 2020. "Agenda Seeding: How 1960s Black Protests Moved Elites, Public Opinion and Voting." *American Political Science Review* 114 (3): 638–59. https://doi.org/10.1017/S000305542000009X.

Weyland, Kurt. 2013. "The Threat from the Populist Left." *Journal of Democracy* 24 (3): 18–32.

2017. "Populism: A Political-Strategic Approach." In *Oxford Handbook of Populism*, edited by Cristóbal Rovira Kaltwasser, Paul Taggart, Paulina Ochoa

Espejo, and Pierre Ostiguy, 48–72. Oxford: Oxford University Press. https://doi .org/10.1093/oxfordhb/9780198803560.013.2.

2020. "Populism's Threat to Democracy: Comparative Lessons for the United States." *Perspectives on Politics* 18 (2): 389–406. https://doi.org/10.1017/S1537592719003955.

Weyland, Kurt, and Raúl Madrid. 2019a. "Introduction: Donald Trump's Populism." In *When Democracy Trumps Populism: European and Latin American Lessons for the United States*, edited by Kurt Weyland and Raúl Madrid, 1–34. Cambridge: Cambridge University Press.

Weyland, Kurt, and Raúl Madrid, eds. 2019b. *When Democracy Trumps Populism: European and Latin American Lessons for the United States.* Cambridge: Cambridge University Press.

Weyland, Kurt, Raúl Madrid, and Wendy Hunter. 2010a. "The Policies and Performance of the Contestatory and Moderate Left." In *Leftist Governments in Latin America: Successes and Shortcomings*, edited by Kurt Weyland, Raúl Madrid, and Wendy Hunter. New York: Cambridge University Press.

2010b. *Leftist Governments in Latin America.* New York: Cambridge University Press.

Wills Otero, Laura. 2014. "Colombia: Analyzing the Strategies for Political Action of Alvaro Uribe's Government, 2002–10." In *The Resilience of the Latin American Right*, edited by Juan Pablo Luna and Cristóbal Rovira Kaltwasser, 194–215. Baltimore, MD: Johns Hopkins University Press.

Yavuz, M. Hakan, and Rasim Koç. 2016. "The Turkish Coup Attempt: The Gülen Movement vs. the State." *Middle East Policy* 23 (4): 136–48. https://doi.org/10 .1111/mepo.12239.

Zechmeister, Elizabeth J., and Daniel Zizumbo-Colunga. 2013. "The Varying Political Toll of Concerns about Corruption in Good Versus Bad Economic Times." *Comparative Political Studies* 46 (10): 1190–218. https://doi.org/10.1177/ 0010414012472468.

Index

Printed in the USA
CPSIA information can be obtained
at www.ICGtesting.com
LVHW041916060923
757378LV00002B/101

9 781009 164078